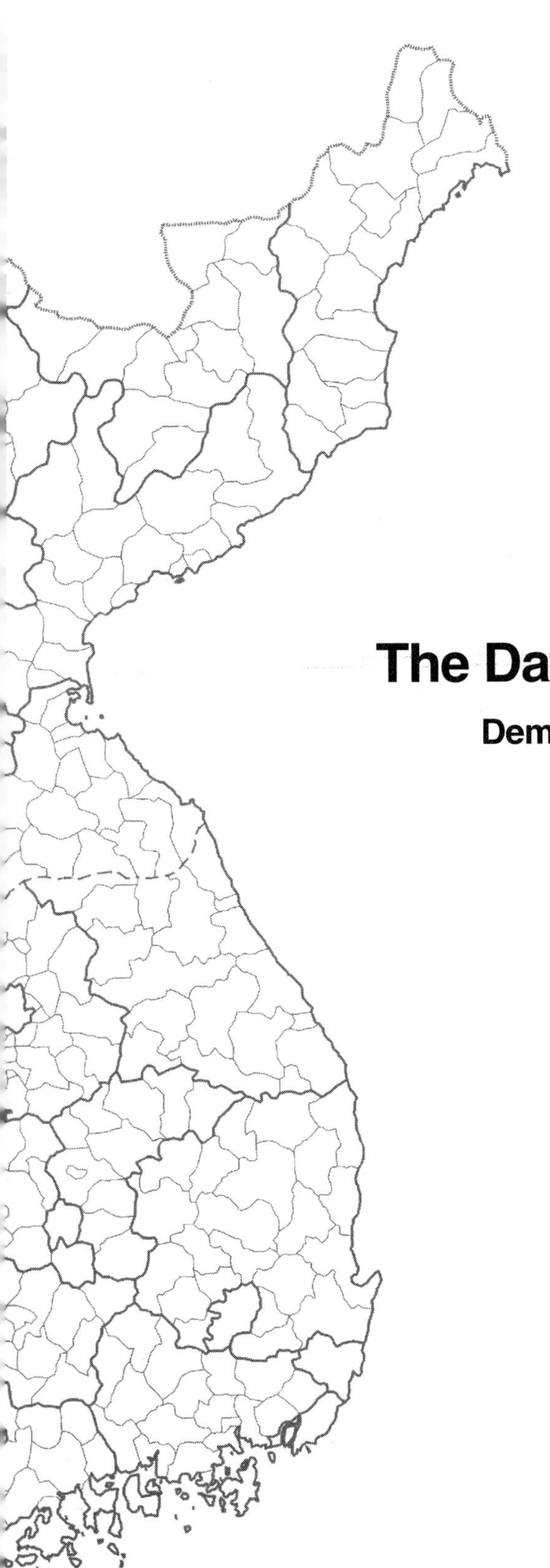

The Data Atlas of South Korea:

Demography, Society, Economic Activity

Daniel J. Schwekendiek

JIMOONDANG

Jimoondang
85 Gwanginsa-gil, Paju-si, Gyeonggi-do, 413-756, Korea
82 Donhwamun-ro, Jongno-gu, Seoul, 110-360, Korea
Phone: 82-2-743-3096 E-mail: edit@jimoon.co.kr
82-2-743-3192~3 E-mail: sale@jimoon.co.kr
Fax: 82-2-743-0227, 82-2-742-4657
Homepage: www.jimoon.co.kr

The National Library of Korea Cataloging-in-Publication (CIP)
The Data Atlas of South Korea: Demography, Society, Economic Activity / By Daniel J. Schwekendiek
Paju, Seoul and Edison: Jimoondang, 2014
ISBN 978-89-6297-161-3 93310 330.911-KDC5 301.09519-DDC21 CIP2014007335

Printed in Korea

Acknowledgements

This research is supported by the National Research Foundation of Korea (NRF-2007-361-AL0014). Many thanks to Andrew Brennfoerder for proofreading the manuscript. Needless to say, all possible remaining errors are my sole responsibility. Finally and most importantly, I am grateful to my wife, Jeong-Eun, for her patience and support she has given me over the years.

Foreword

Containing numerous maps representing the population of South Korea, "The Data Atlas of South Korea" complements my previous book titled "The Data Atlas of North Korea" published by the Institute for Peace and Unification Studies at Seoul National University (IPUS-SNU). The current work assesses the demographic, social, and economic states of the southern half of the Korean peninsula by drawing upon the most recent census (2010) of the South Korean population. Although the focus of the book is on South Korea, it occasionally utilizes corresponding census data from North Korea (reference year of 2008) in order to offer some comparative demographic perspectives of a unified peninsula. As such, the data atlas serves as a useful and unique reference book for readers interested in both South Korea and Korean reunification.

In a practical sense, both Koreas resort to four administrative divisions: national level data, province level data (urban 'teukbyeolsi' or 'gwankyeoksi' in South Korea as well as urban 'chikalsi' in North Korea as opposed to rural 'do'), county level data (urban 'si' and rural 'gun'), and district level data (urban 'dong' and rural 'ri'). All data maps depicting solely the South Korean population are at the county ('gun' or 'si') level due to data availability reasons in the South Korean census report, whereas most maps covering the entire Korean peninsula are limited to the province level due to limited data presentation issues in the North Korean census report. In all, there are 225 maps, including 161 maps depicting South Korea at the county level, 56 maps covering the entire Korean peninsula at the province level, and eight maps assessing the entire Korean peninsula at the county level.

Korean names of administrative divisions were transcribed into English using the Revised Romanization (RR) system, which has been endorsed by the government of the Republic of Korea. All ages are given according to conventional Western age, which might differ by up to two years from Korean age classifications due to the inclusion of gestational age as well as application of the lunar calendar (instead of individual birthdays) when calculating age.

The Republic of Korea (ROK) is hereafter referred to as 'South Korea' and the Democratic People's Republic of Korea (DPRK) as 'North Korea'. Although most provinces within the two Koreas have unique names, both Koreas contain Gangwon Provinces due to the division of the Korean peninsula following Japanese colonization (1910-1945) and establishment of the Demilitarized Zone (DMZ) after the Korean War (1950-1953). For clarification, the two Gangwon Provinces are labeled as 'Gangwon (ROK)' in South Korea and 'Gangwon (DPRK)' in the North. Also note that some counties in the North and South bear alternative names. For instance, 'Chilgok County' in South Korea's North Chungcheong Province is also known as 'Waegwon County', whereas 'Gyongheung County' located in North Korea's North Hamgyeong Province is sometimes referred to as 'Saebyeol County'. For additional explanation, the Appendix lists all provinces and counties, including their alternative names. All data maps are for illustrative purposes only. None of the maps shown herein reflect a position held by myself regarding the legal status of any country or territory or the delimitation of any frontier. All views expressed herein are solely my own and do not necessarily constitute the policy of the publisher.

After assessing the South Korean census, comparisons with the North were made wherever possible—sometimes after making adjustments or widening the age group (see notes below the maps). When there were no North Korean data plotted on the map, corresponding data could unfortunately not be retrieved.

Variables plotted on the data maps are commonly broken into five classes ('very high', 'high', 'average', 'low', 'very low'). As a follow up to my previous work, "The Data Atlas of North Korea" (SNU-IPUS 2009), I also opted to use 'equivalent' cut-offs. Equivalence implies that a roughly even number of administrative units (i.e. counties or provinces) are distributed to a given variable. For instance, breaking 26 provinces into five classes yields five observations per class (except for the middle class, which is automatically allocated six observations), thereby allowing the reader to easily interpret the mapped variable as a percentile distribution. Advantages of this method are that the relative positions of the counties are emphasized as well as that all five classes are roughly balanced in number. A drawback of the equivalent method is that the cut-offs of a given variable are often uneven, as the variable is 'forced' into five categories. For illustration, the variable "number of persons (6 years of older) with no formal education" is broken into the following five equivalent classes: 'very low' (below 47,731.0 persons), 'low' (47,731.0 to below 77,846.4 persons), 'average' (77,846.4 to below 103,262.1 persons), 'high' (103,262.1 to below 147,514.7 persons), and 'very high' (147,514.7 persons or higher), with each class represented by five provinces (except for the middle one represented by six provinces, as discussed above). These cut-offs are more difficult to grasp compared to 'smooth' cut-offs of 'below 40,000 persons', '40,000 to below 80,000 persons', etc. For the sake of completeness, I explain the exact cut-off points in the footnote below the respective data map.

In my previous work, "The Data Atlas of North Korea", I consistently showed all variables plotted on maps in terms of total numbers (e.g. number of males in each county) as well as proportions (e.g. percentage of males in the population of each county). Here, I opted to show only a limited number of data maps illustrating the same variable as a percentage while primarily focusing on total numbers (i.e. number of persons in most maps). My reason for doing this was to keep the number of pages reasonably low. Note that all percentage distributions in the book refer to the share in the respective county (and not to the share in the nation), unless otherwise stated.

This work is primarily a reference book—not a textbook or research monograph. As such, I hope it will provide assistance to teachers, scholars, students, policy makers, and journalists who are interested in assessing the state of the population of Republic of Korea and, occasionally, the South in comparison with the Northern half of the Korean peninsula.

Daniel J. Schwekendiek
Sungkyunkwan University

Contents

Overview of Maps

1. Administrative Divisions

Map 1.1 The Korean peninsula

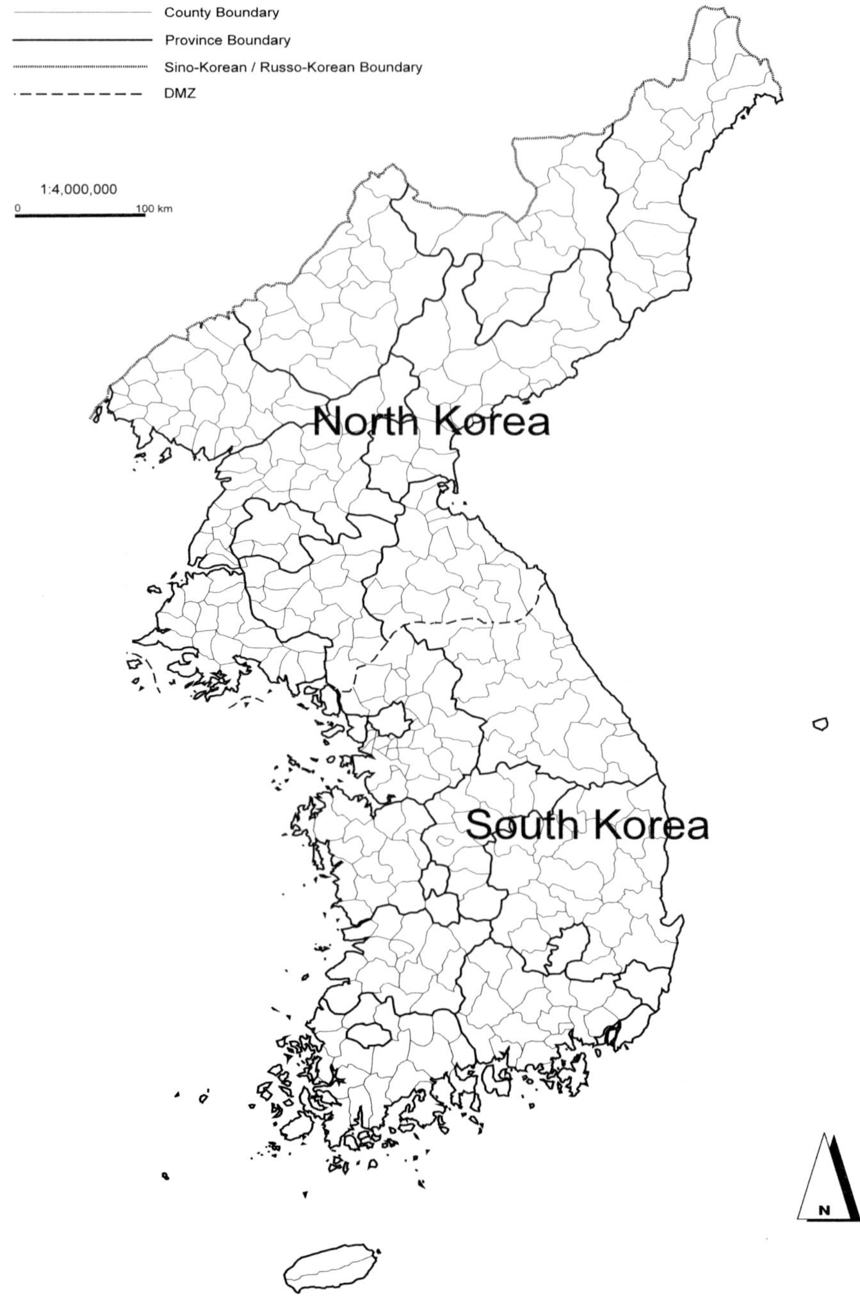

Notes: DMZ = Demilitarized Zone.

Map 1.2 Provinces of the Korean peninsula

Notes: All provinces were transcribed from Korean into English according to the RR system.

Map 1.3 Counties of the Korean peninsula

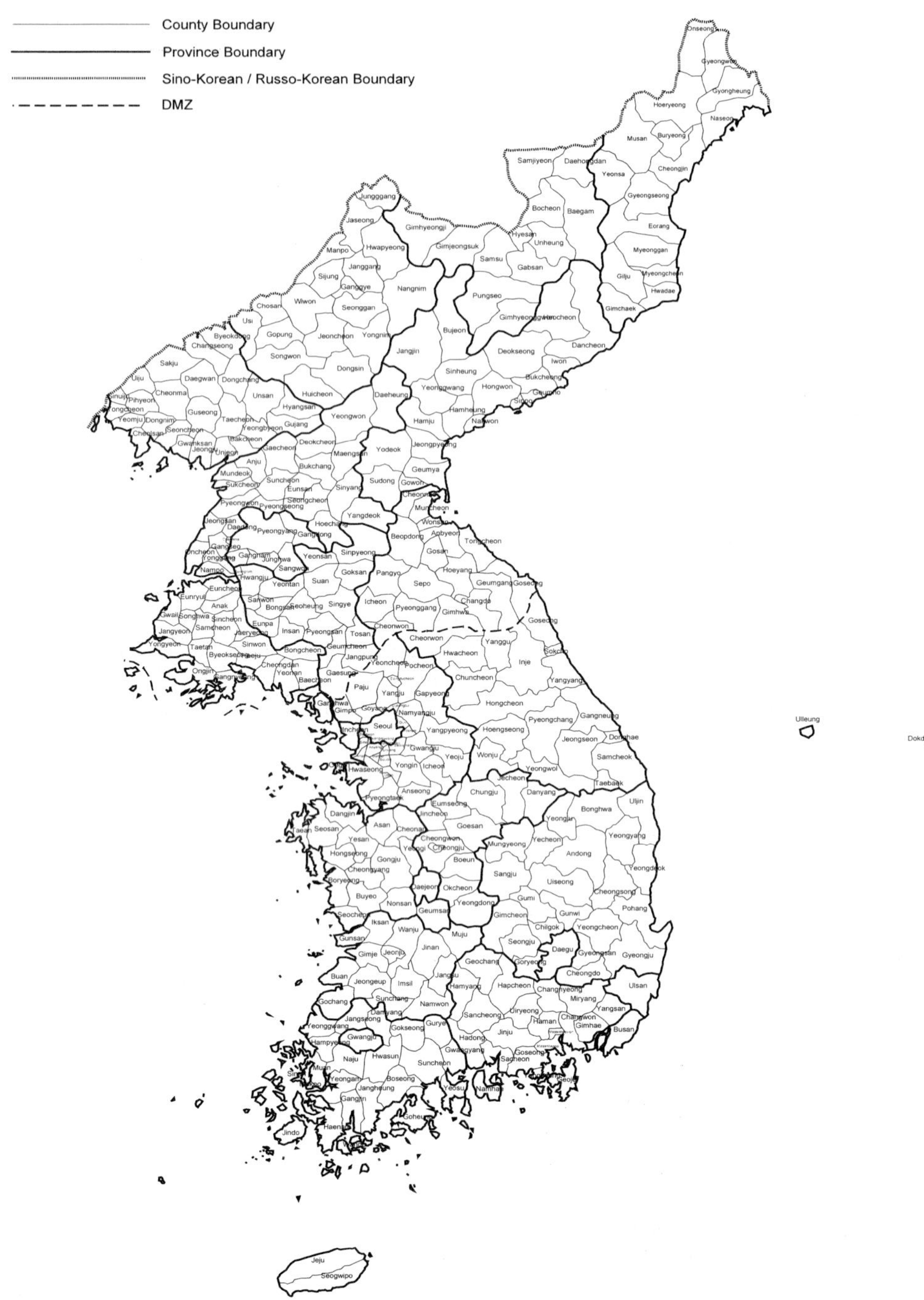

Notes: All counties were transcribed from Korean into English according to the RR system. The island of Dokdo located in the far east of the Korean peninsula is not a county per se but has a special status.

2. Basic Population

Map 2.1 Total population of the Korean peninsula

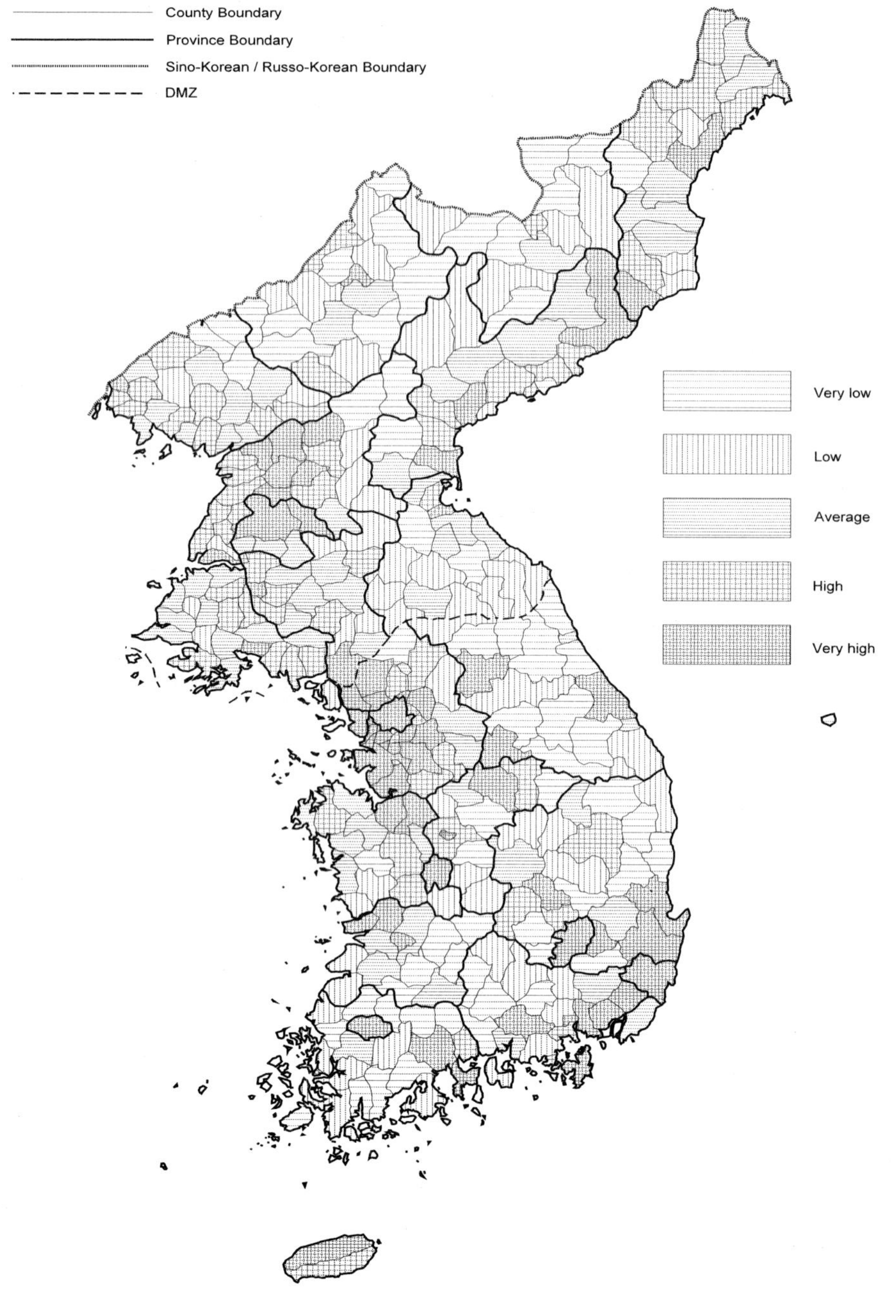

Notes: Unit = persons. Cut-offs = below 42986.2, 42986.2 to below 69095.7, 69095.7 to below 110380.5, 110380.5 to below 198831.4, 198831.4 or above.

Map 2.2 Total population of South Korea

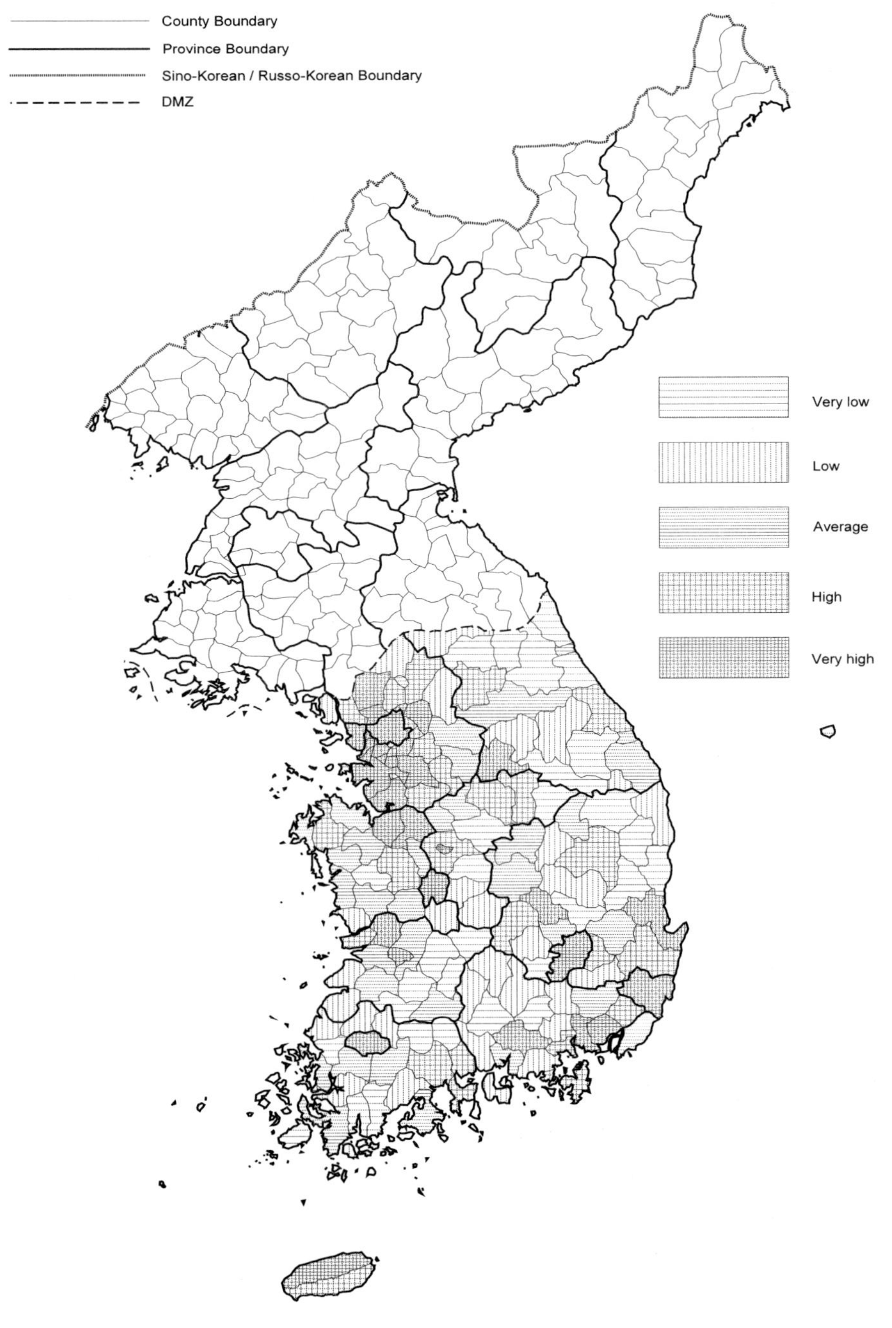

Notes: Unit = persons. Cut-offs = below 36557.3, 36557.3 to below 60906.1, 60906.1 to below 121859.9, 121859.9 to below 277527.7, 277527.7 or above.

Map 2.3 Male population of the Korean peninsula

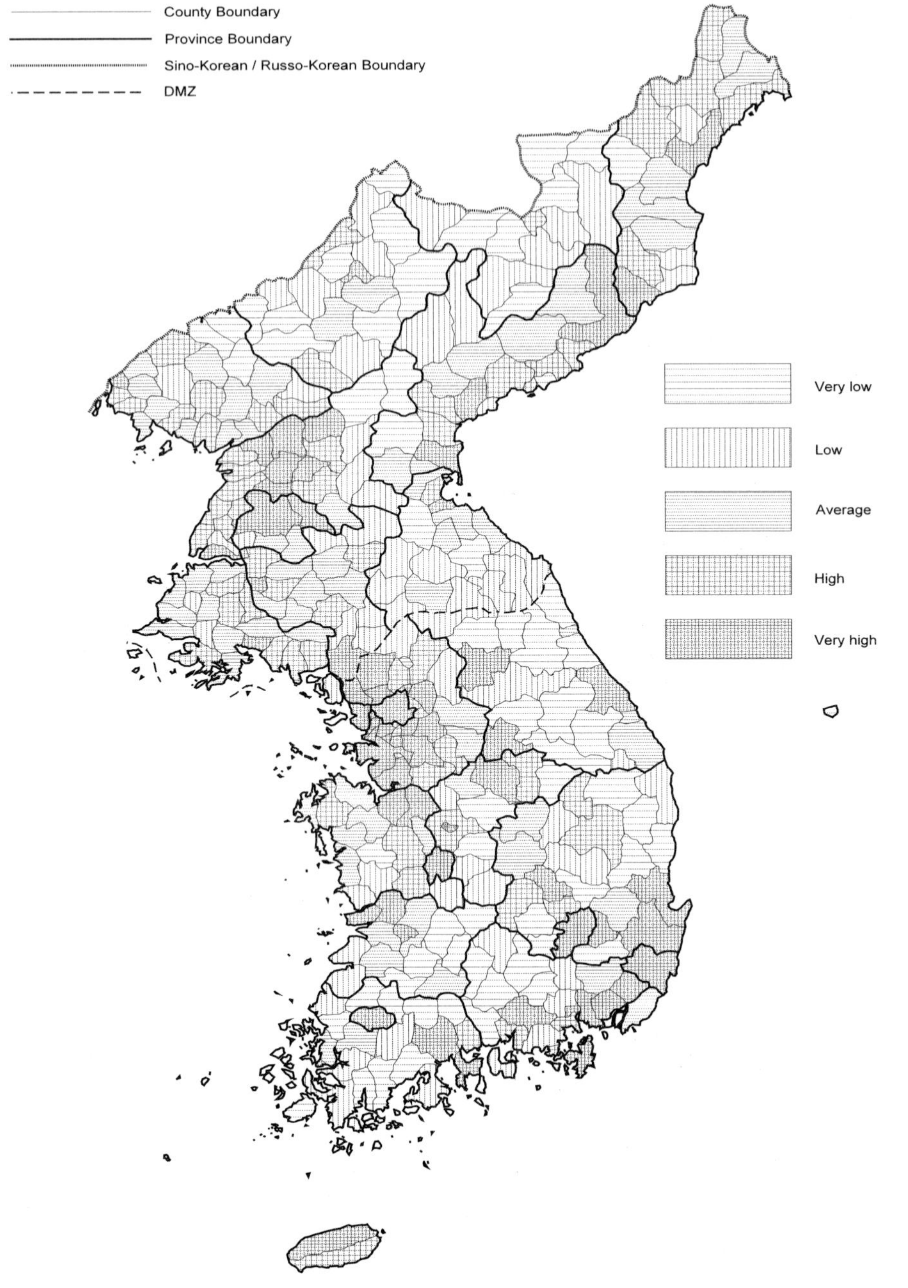

Notes: Unit = persons. Cut-offs = below 20271.2, 20271.2 to below 33283.5, 33283.5 to below 53084.5, 53084.5 to below 97155.3, 97155.3 or above.

Map 2.4 Male population of South Korea

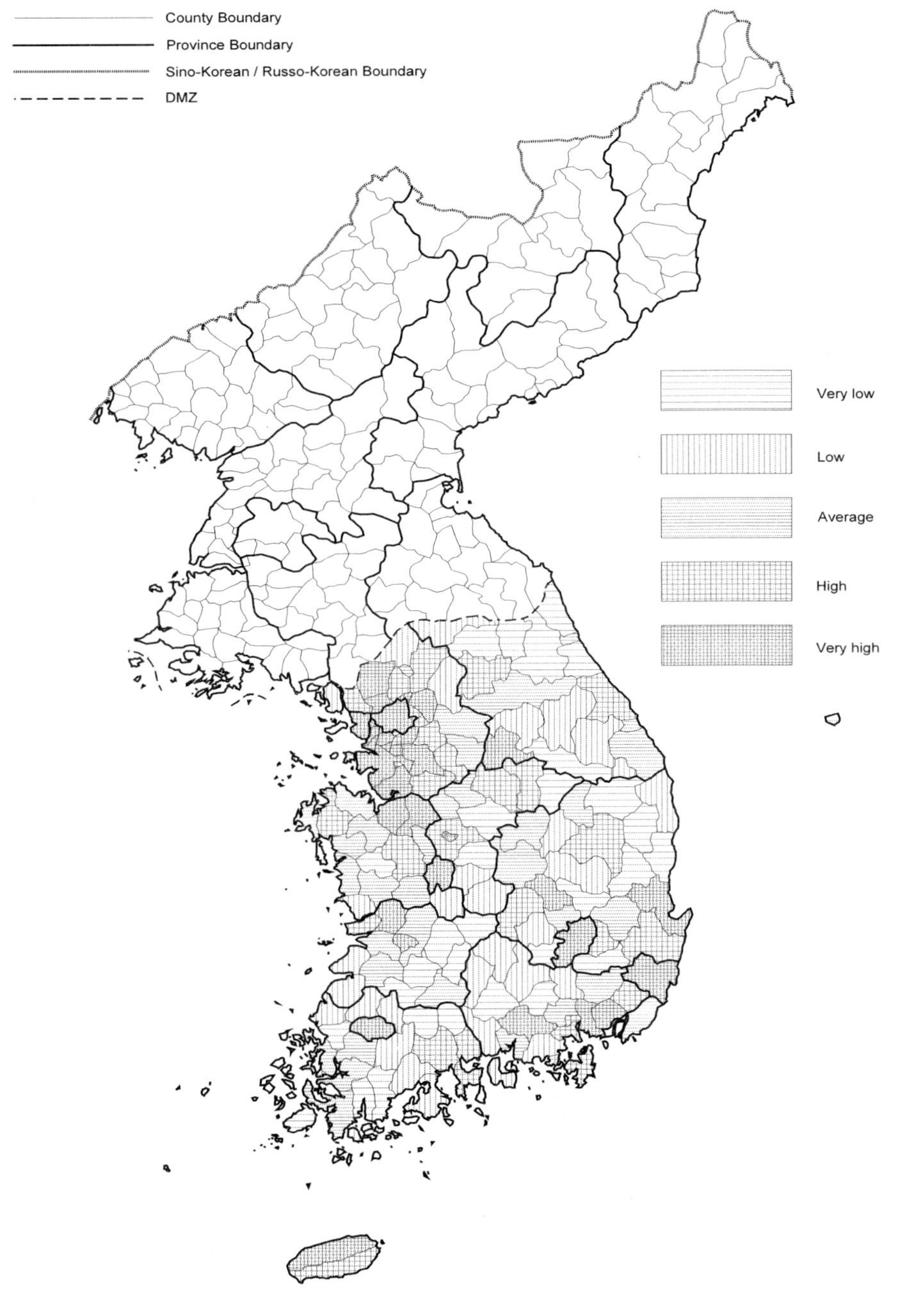

Notes: Unit = persons. Cut-offs = below 17665.7, 17665.7 to below 29561.9, 29561.9 to below 59637.3, 59637.3 to below 137623.1, 137623.1 or above.

Map 2.5 Female population of the Korean peninsula

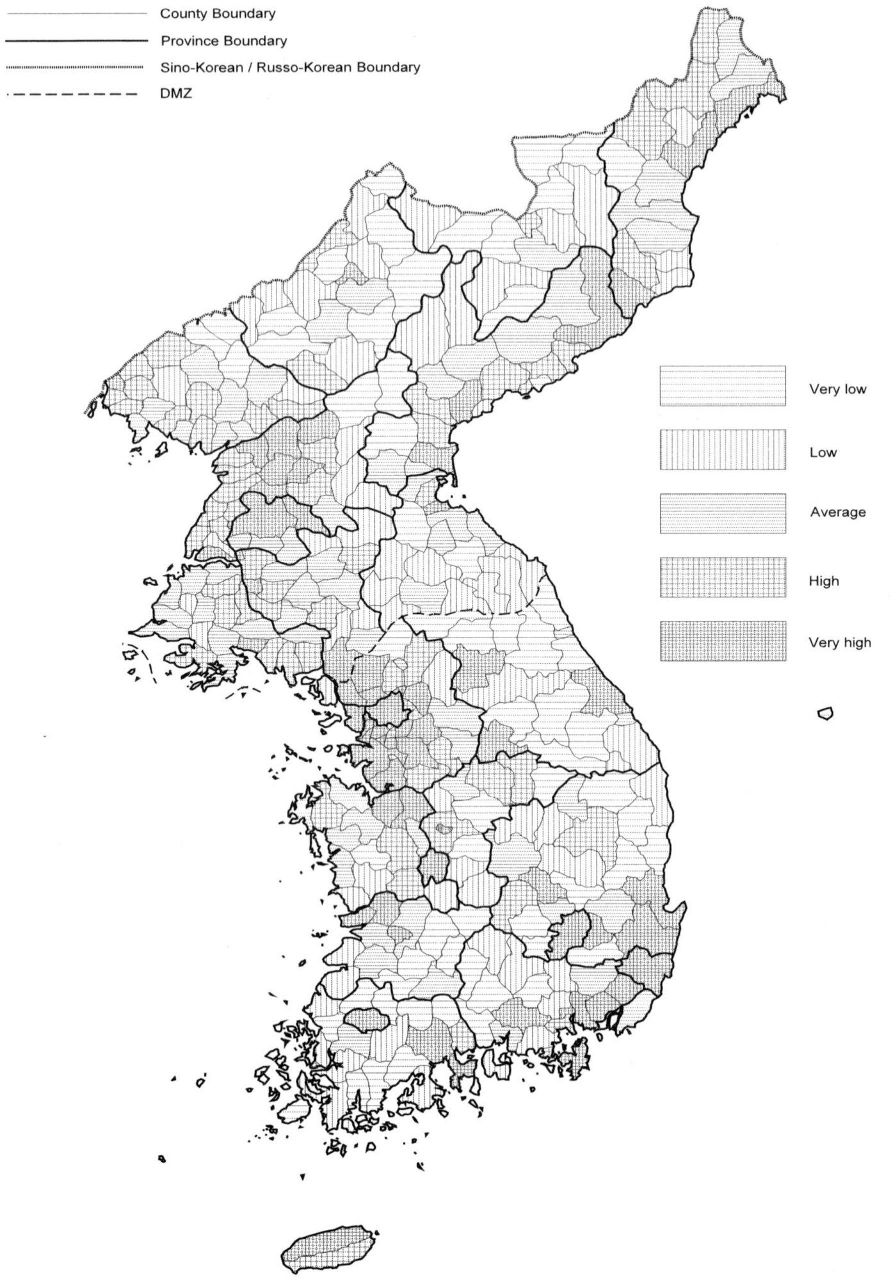

Notes: Unit = persons. Cut-offs = below 22663.8, 22663.8 to below 36103.7, 36103.7 to below 57372.4, 57372.4 to below 103509.4, 103509.4 or above.

Map 2.6 Female population of South Korea

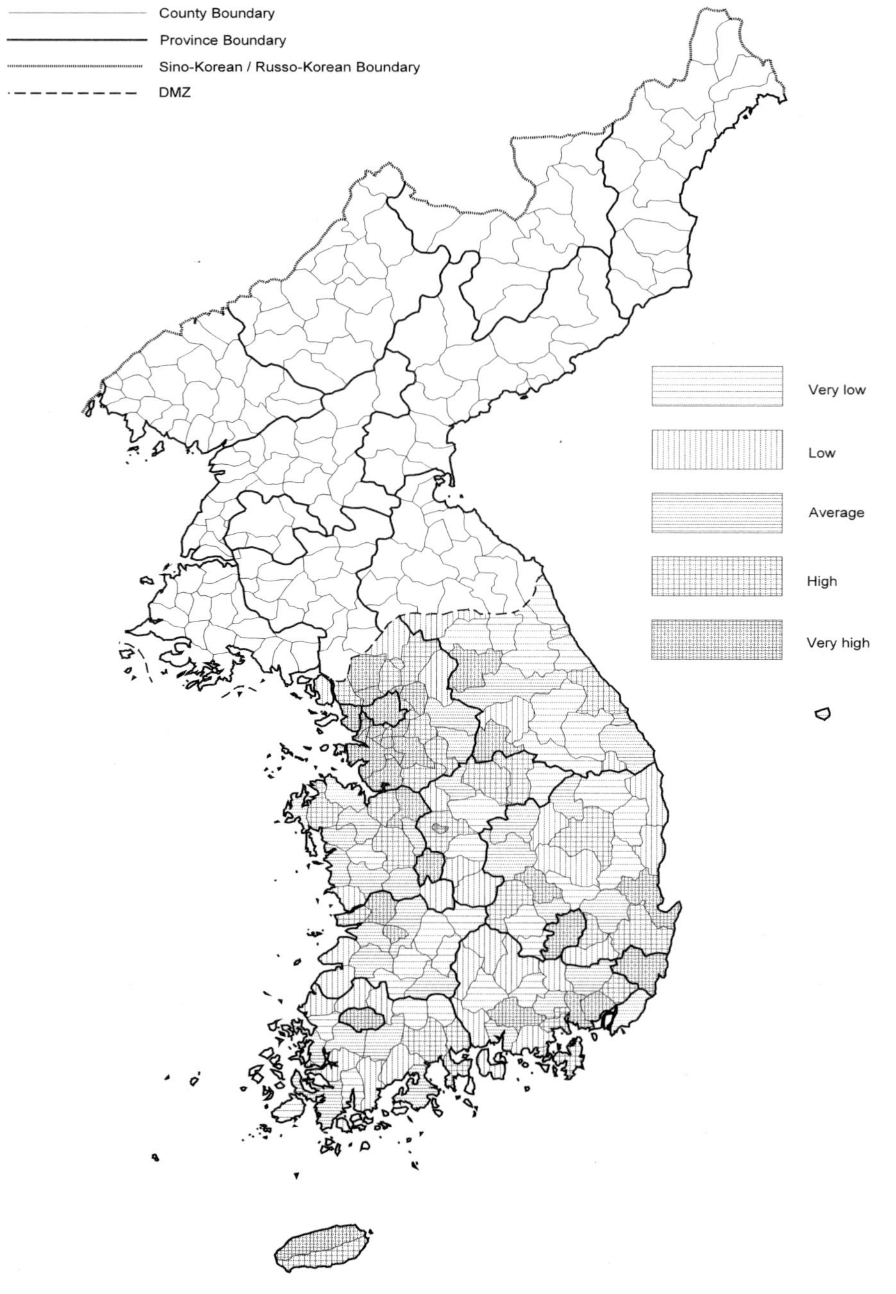

Notes: Unit = persons. Cut-offs = below 19029.4, 19029.4 to below 30027.0, 30027.0 to below 62241.1, 62241.1 to below 138354.2, 138354.2 or above.

Map 2.7 Sex ratio of the population of the Korean peninsula

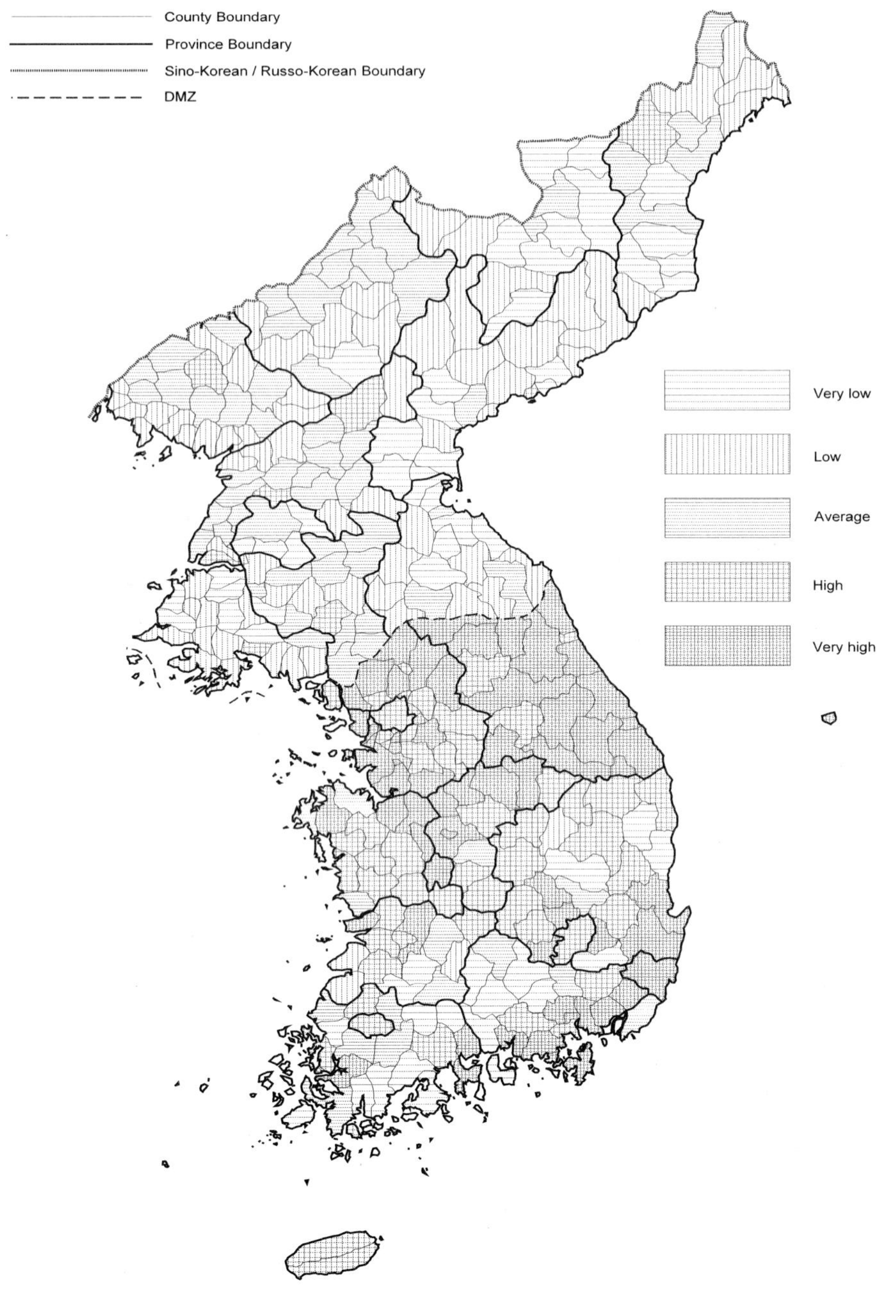

Notes: The sex ratio is the number of males and females for every 100 females. Cut-offs = below 88.60, 88.60 to below 90.00, 90.00 to below 92.20, 92.20 to below 99.03, 99.03 or above.

Map 2.8 Sex ratio of South Korea

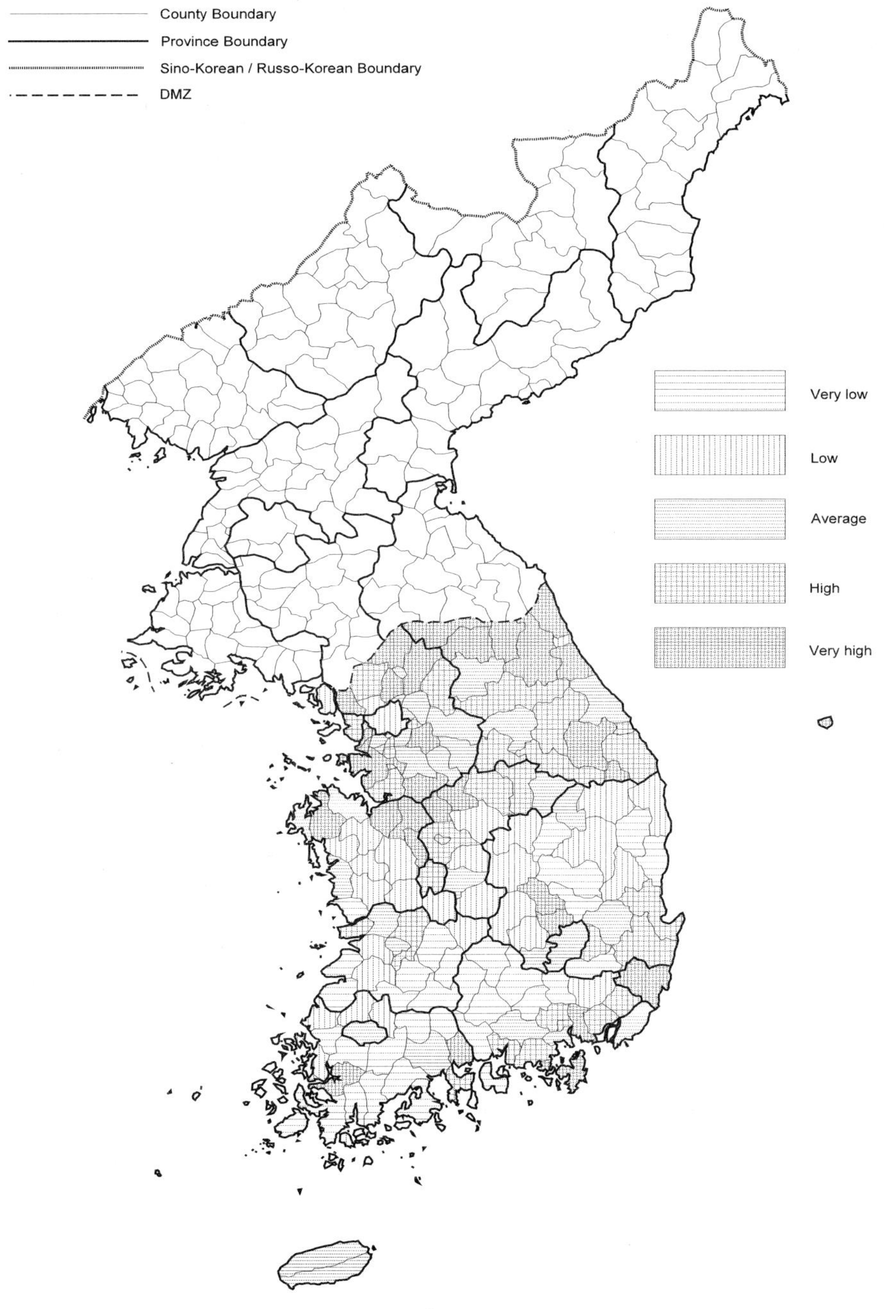

Notes: The sex ratio is the number of males and females for every 100 females.. Cut-offs = below 91.36, 91.36 to below 96.80, 96.80 to below 99.29, 99.29 to below 103.70, 103.70 or above.

Map 2.9 Total foreign population of South Korea

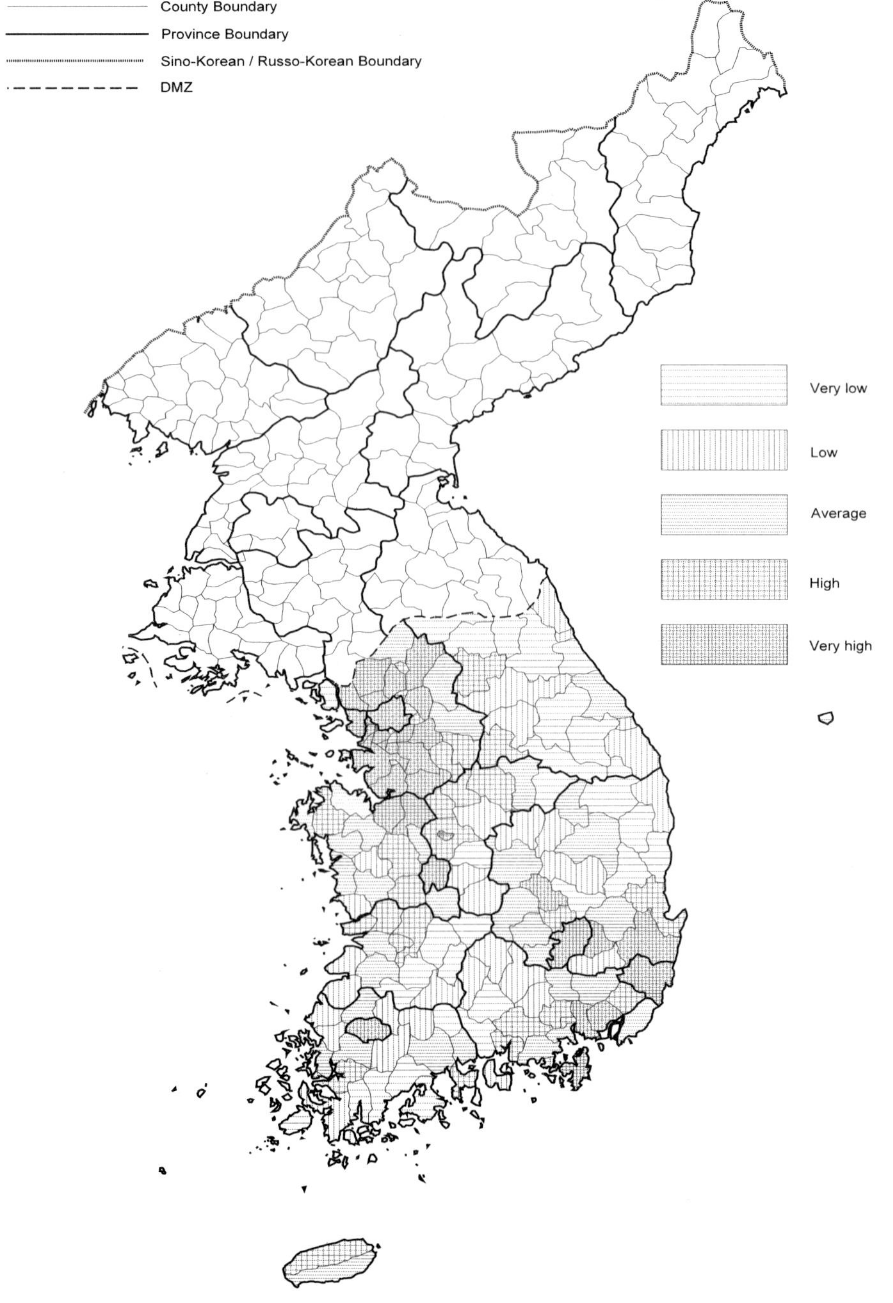

Notes: Unit = persons. Cut-offs = below 217.4, 217.4 to below 439.0, 439.0 to below 1148.2, 1148.2 to below 3246.1, 3246.1 or above.

Map 2.10 Male foreign population of South Korea

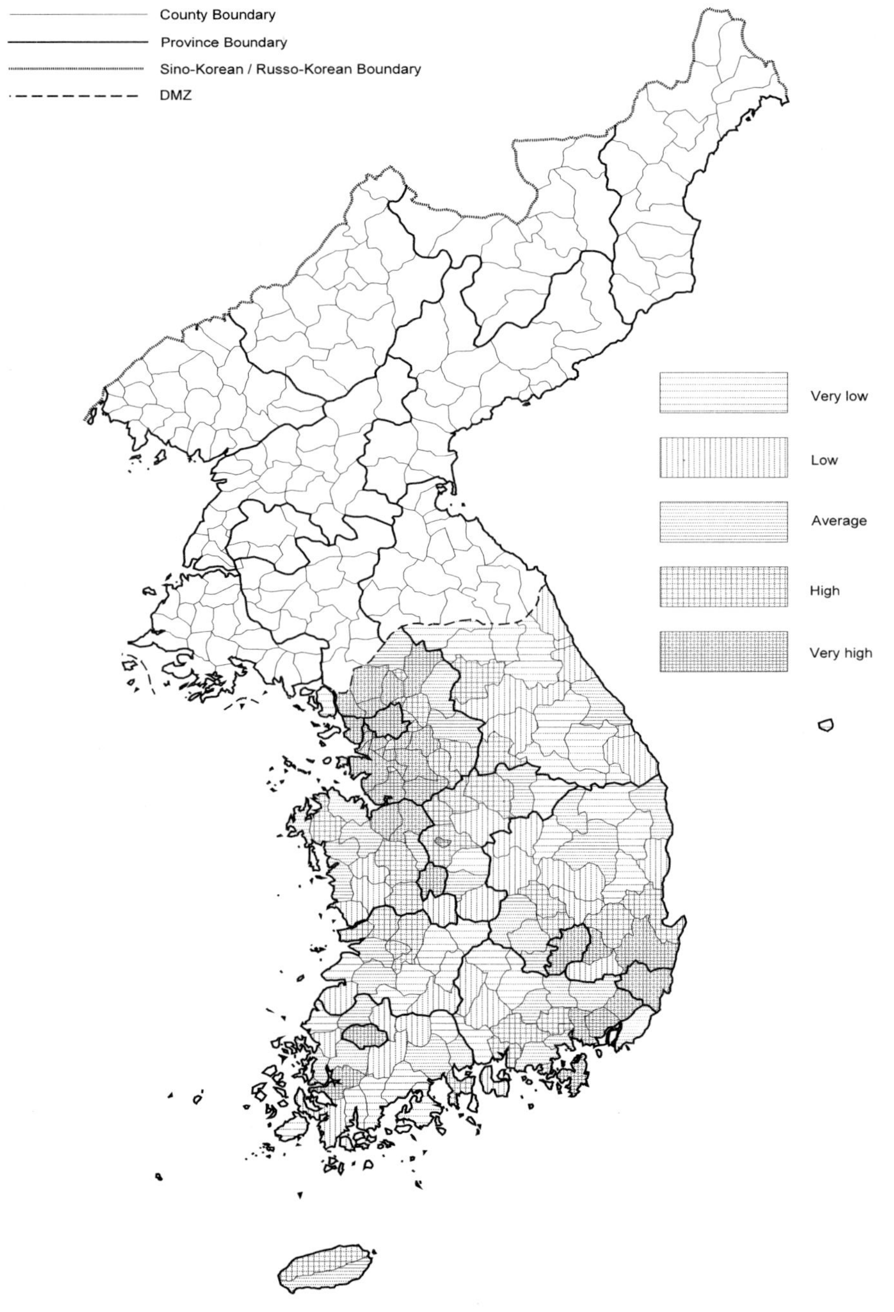

Notes: Unit = persons Cut-offs = below 79.3, 79.3 to below 229.0, 229.0 to below 650.4, 650.4 to below 1998.8, 1998.8 or above.

Map 2.11 Female foreign population of South Korea

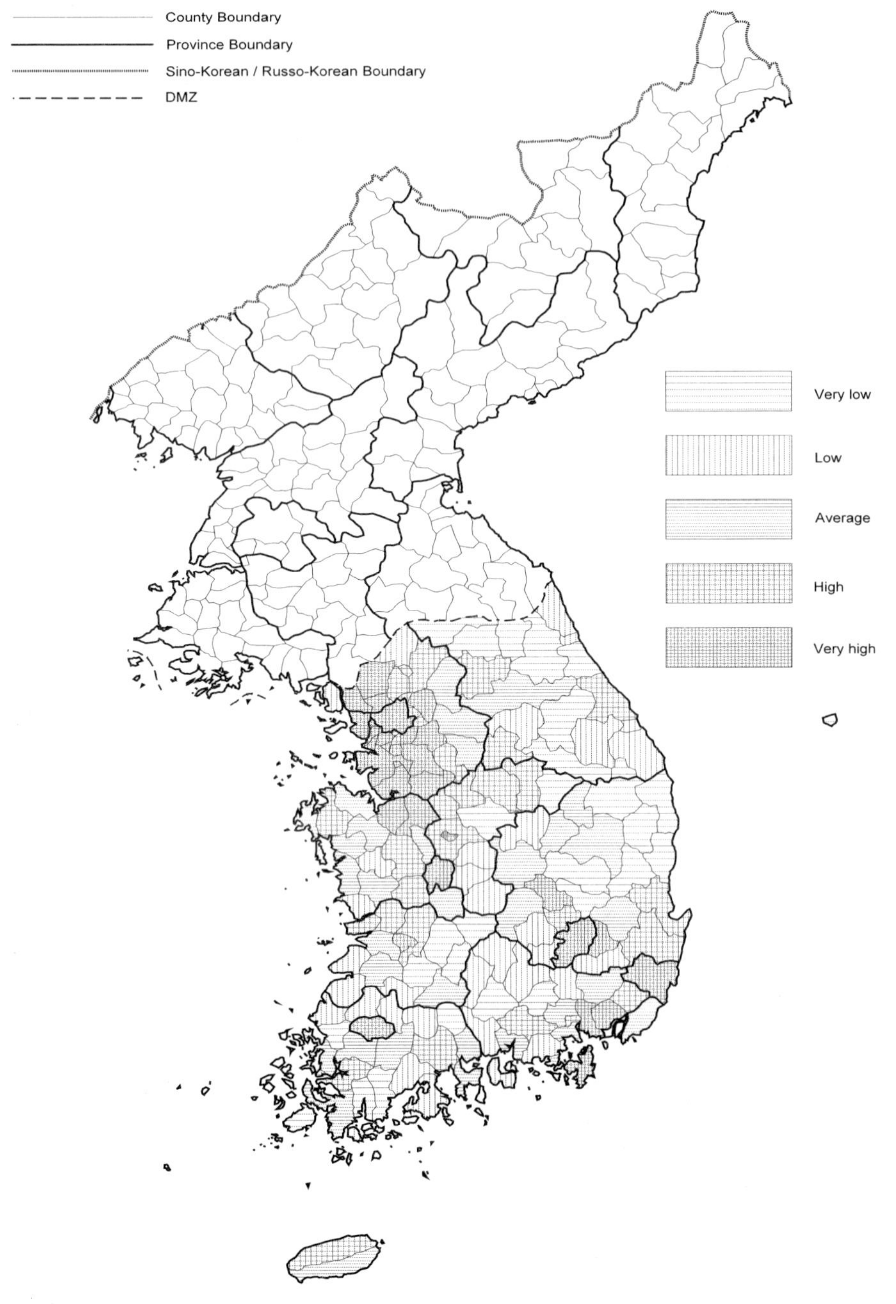

Notes: Unit = persons. Cut-offs = below 129.0, 129.0 to below 196.3, 196.3 to below 525.7, 525.7 to below 1418.6, 1418.6 or above. Notes: Unit = persons. Cut-offs = below 129.0, 129.0 to below 196.3, 196.3 to below 525.7, 525.7 to below 1418.6, 1418.6 or above

Map 2.12 Male population of the Korean peninsula (share)

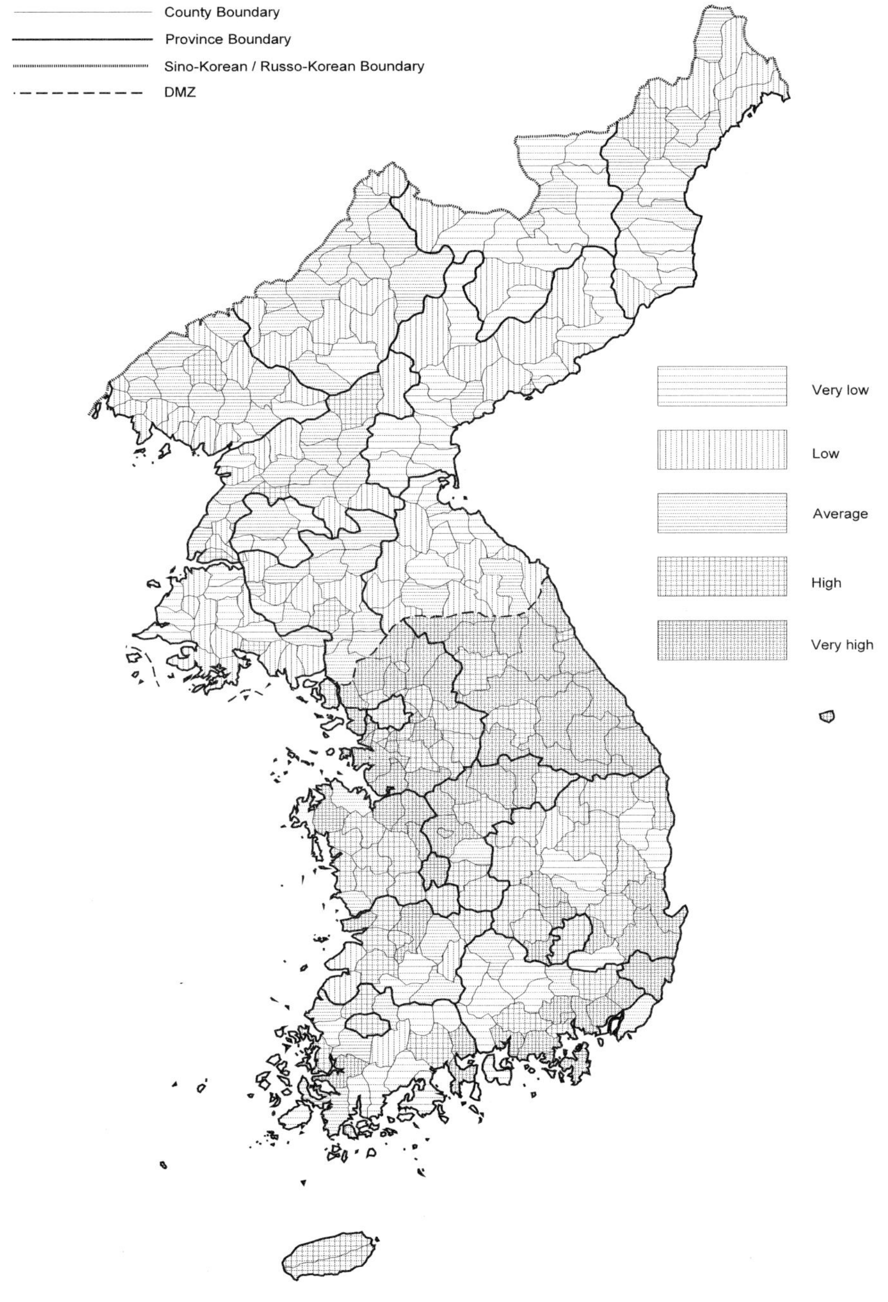

Notes: Unit = percent. Cut-offs = below 46.990, 46.990 to below 47.366, 47.366 to below 47.974, 47.974 to below 49.763, 49.763 or above.

Map 2.13 Female population of the Korean peninsula (share)

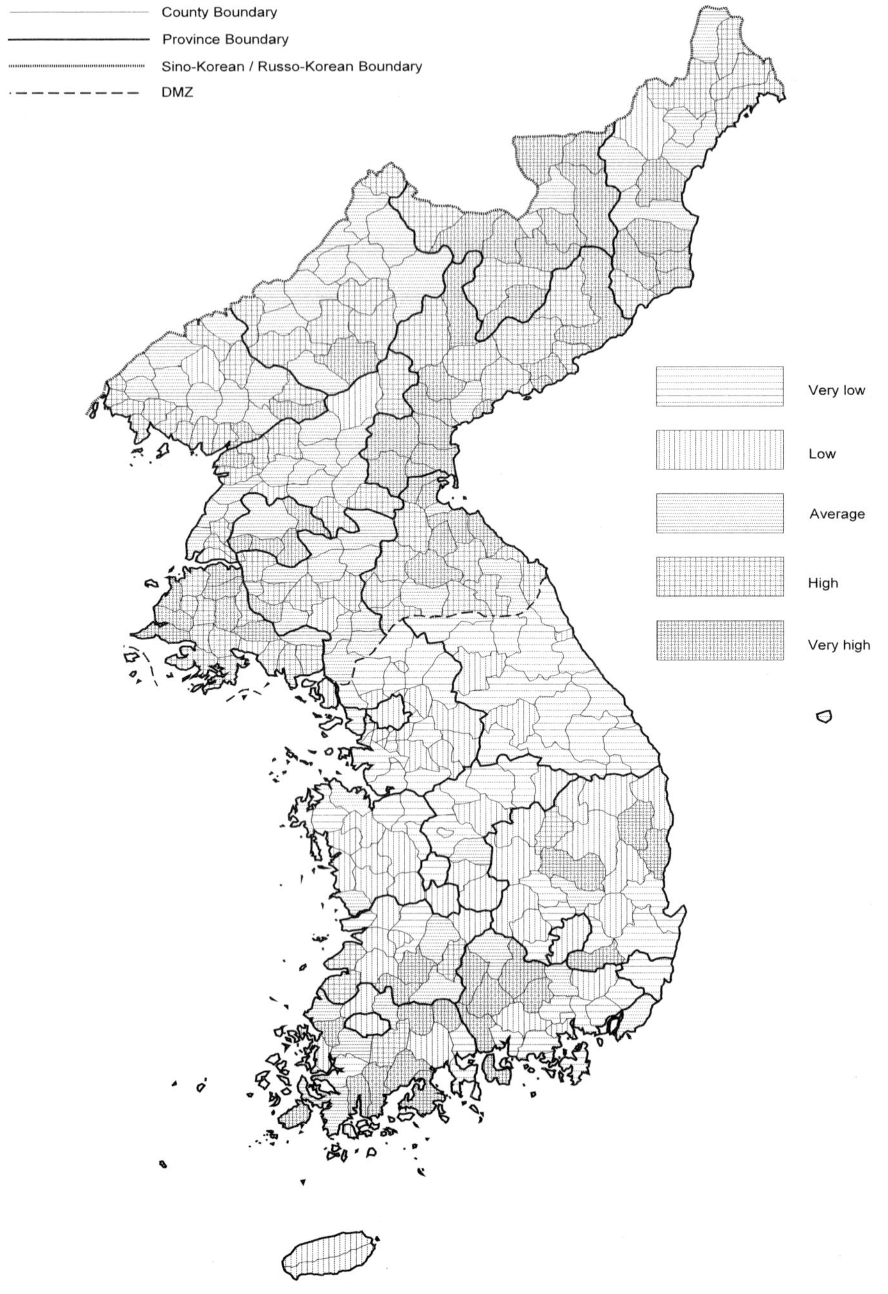

Notes: Unit = percent. Cut-offs = below 50.237, 50.237 to below 52.026, 52.026 to below 52.634, 52.634 to below 53.010, 53.010 or above.

Map 2.14 Male population of South Korea (share)

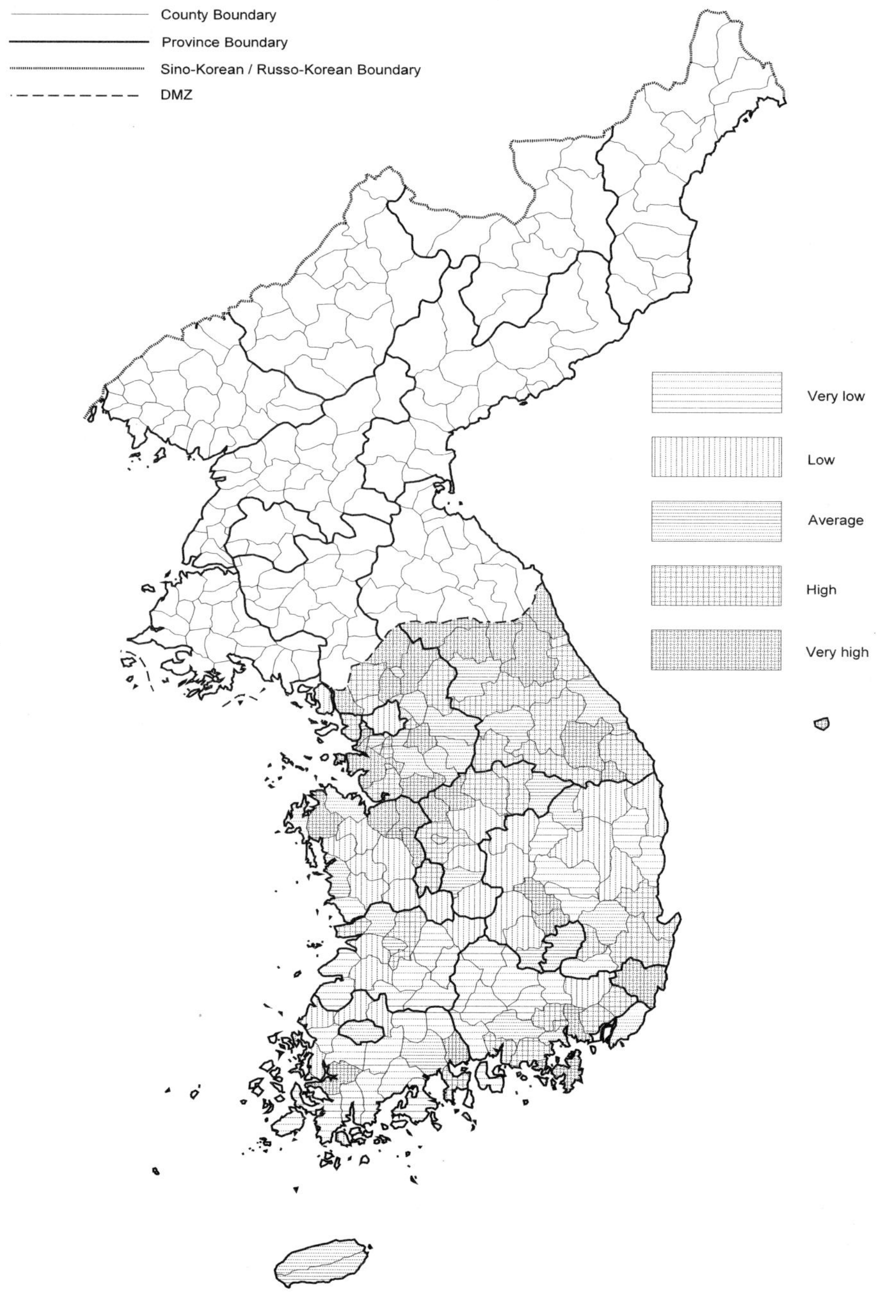

Notes: Unit = percent. Cut-offs = below 47.750, 47.750 to below 49.188, 49.188 to below 49.818, 49.818 to below 50.906, 50.906 or above.

Map 2.15 Female population of South Korea (share)

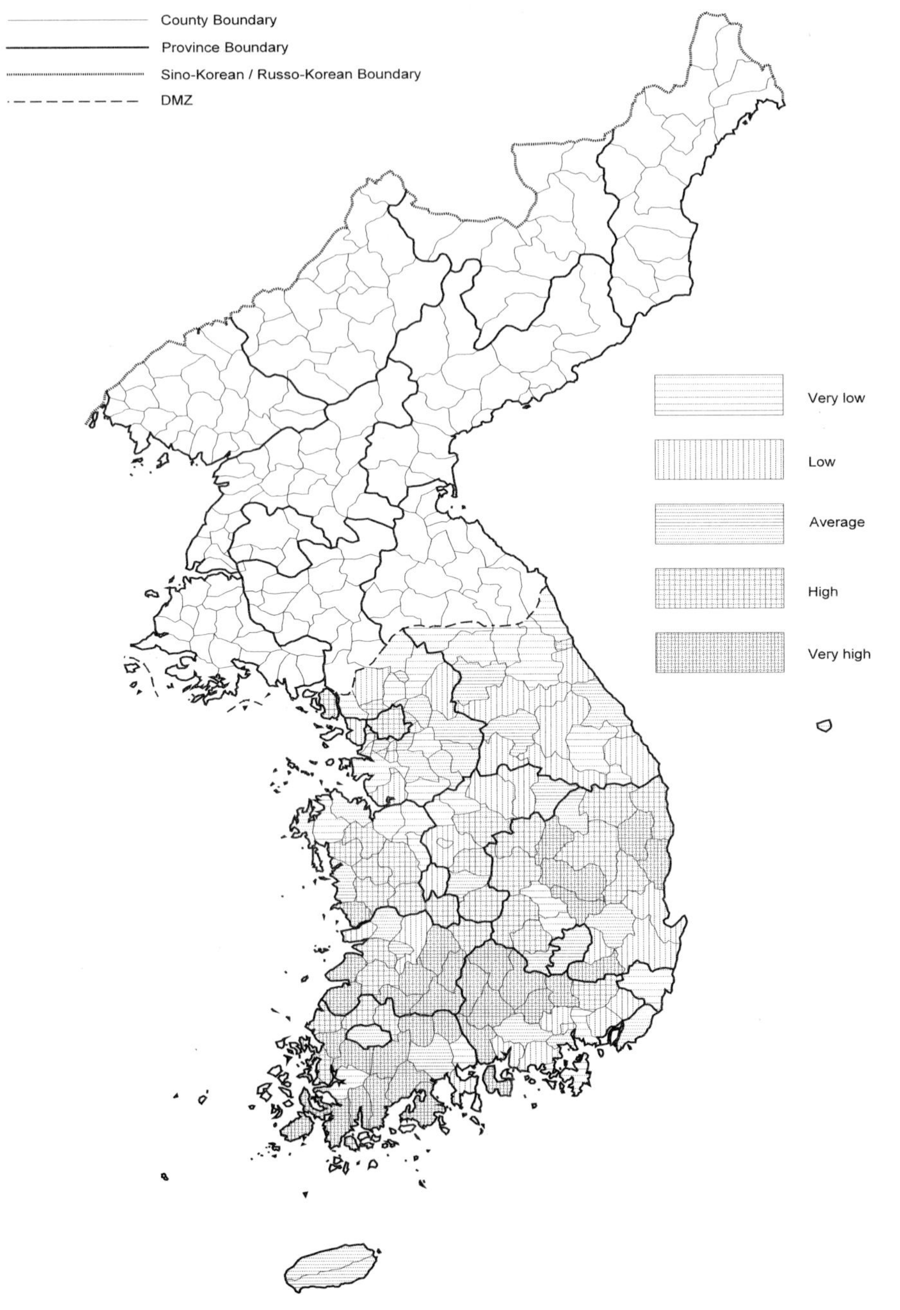

Notes: Unit = percent. Cut-offs = below 49.094, 49.094 to below 50.182, 50.182 to below 50.812, 50.812 to below 52.250, 52.250 tor above.

3. Households and Housing

Map 3.1 Households of the Korean peninsula

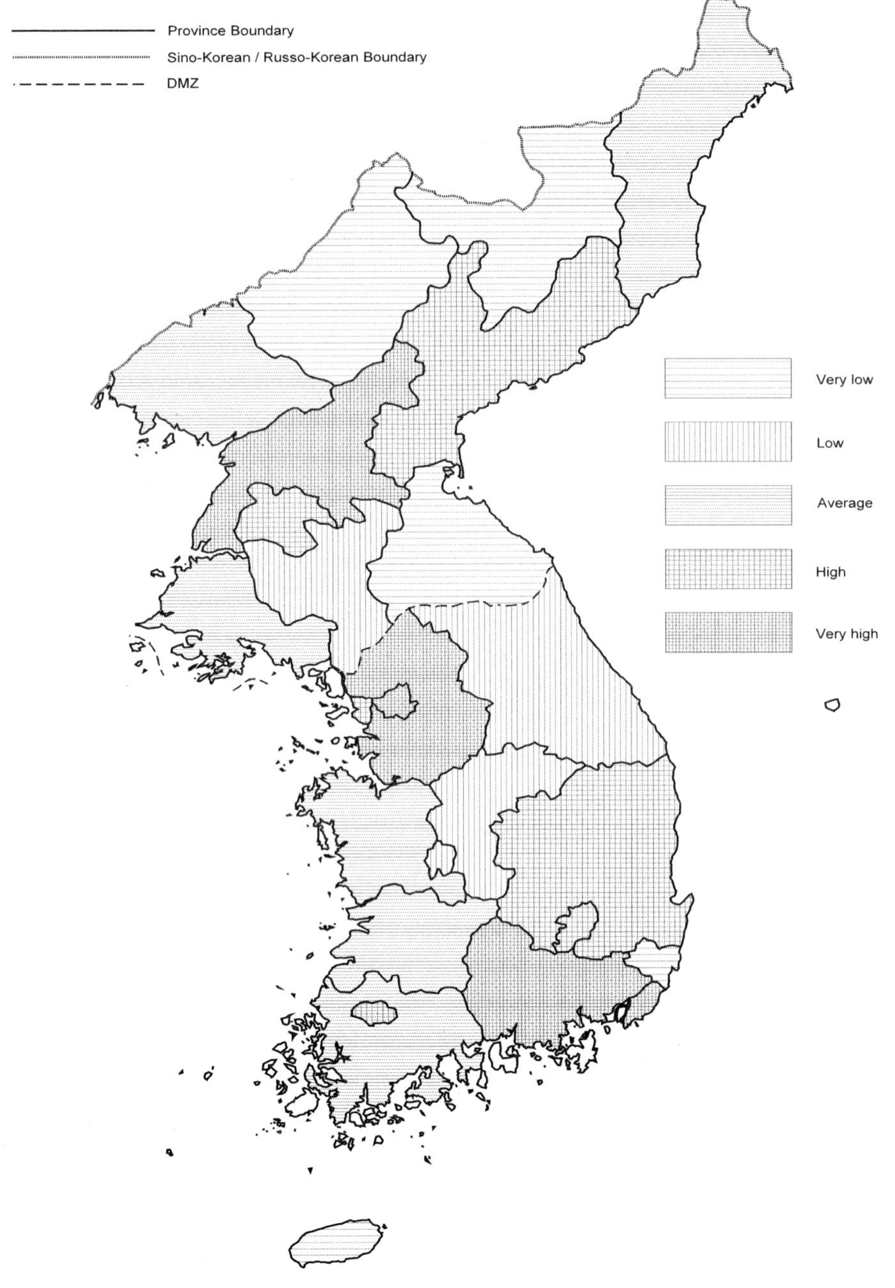

Notes: Unit = number of households. Cut-offs = below 476500.8, 476500.8 to below 576913.4, 576913.4 to below 760417.5, 760417.5 to below 1018359.6, 1018359.6 or above.

Map 3.2 Households of South Korea

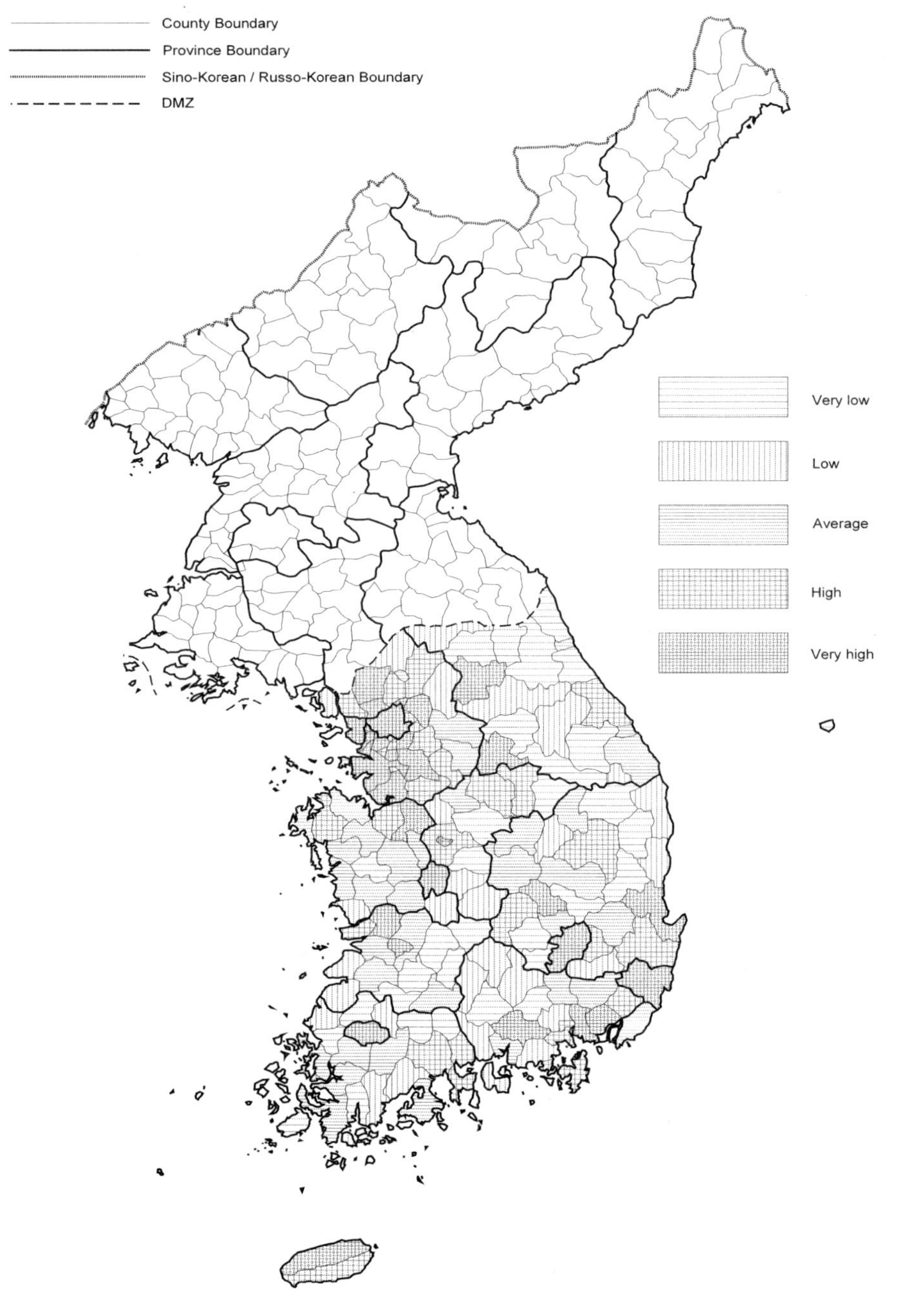

Notes: Unit = number of households. Cut-offs = below 15339.0, 15339.0 to below 24226.0, 24226.0 to below 45998.0, 45998.0 to below 103319.0, 103319.0 or above.

Map 3.3 Foreign population households of South Korea

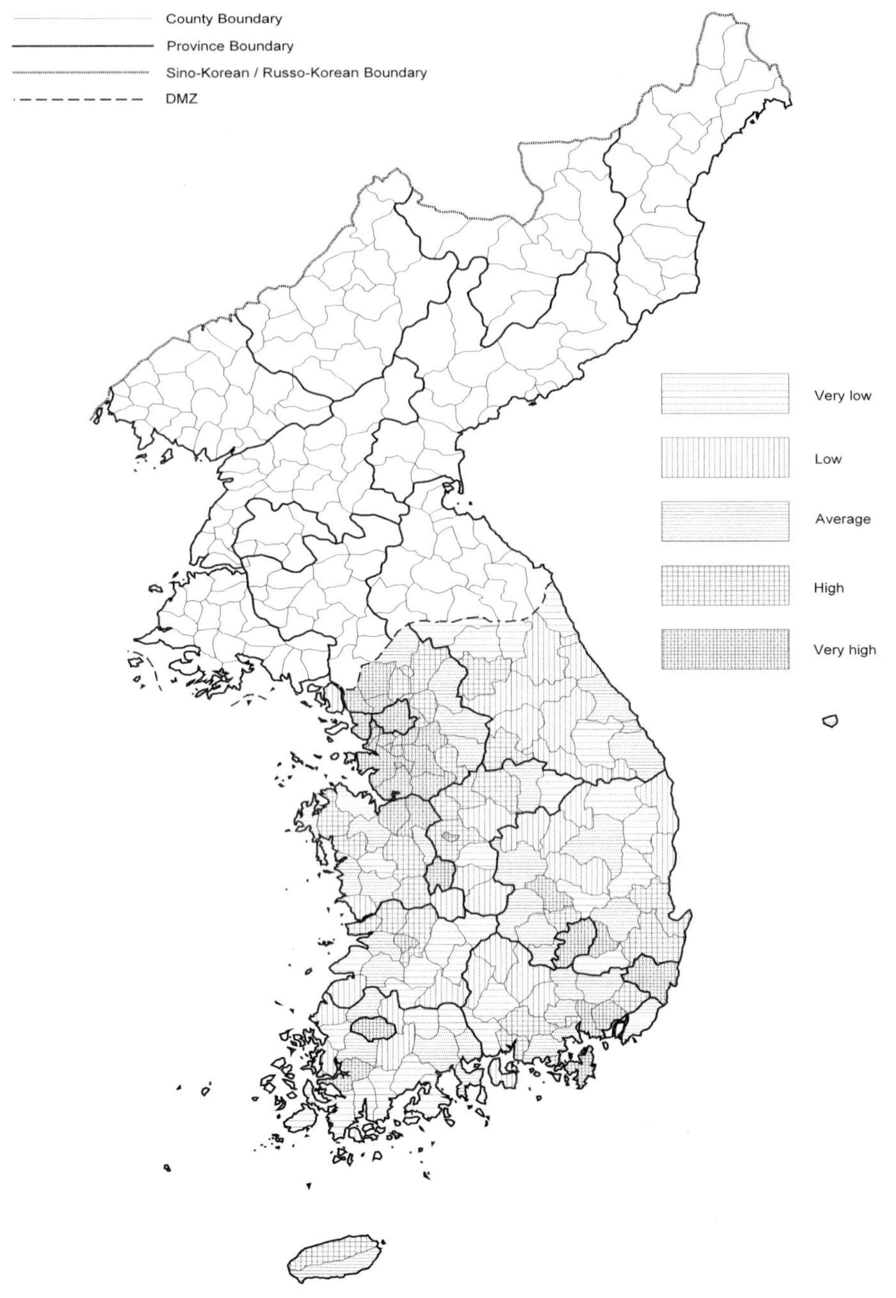

Notes: Unit = number of households. Cut-offs = below 36.3, 36.3 to below 81.1, 81.1 to below 338.6, 338.6 to below 992.7, 992.7 or above.

Map 3.4 Apartment residents of the Korean peninsula

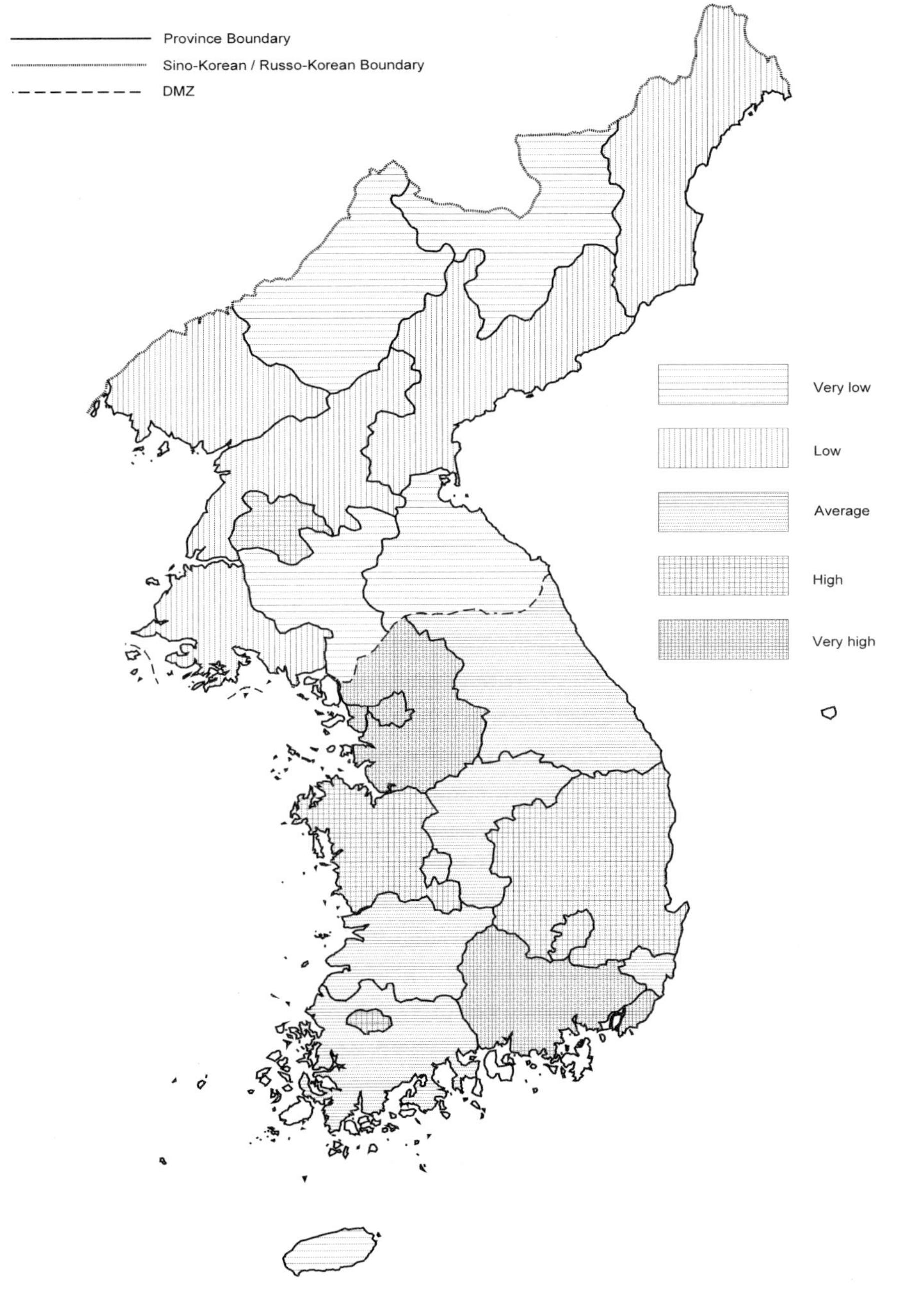

Notes: Unit = housing units. Cut-offs = below 70166.6, 70166.6 to below 216502.0, 216502.0 to below 322395.3, 322395.3 to below 470626.1, 470626.1 or above.

Map 3.5 Apartment residents of South Korea

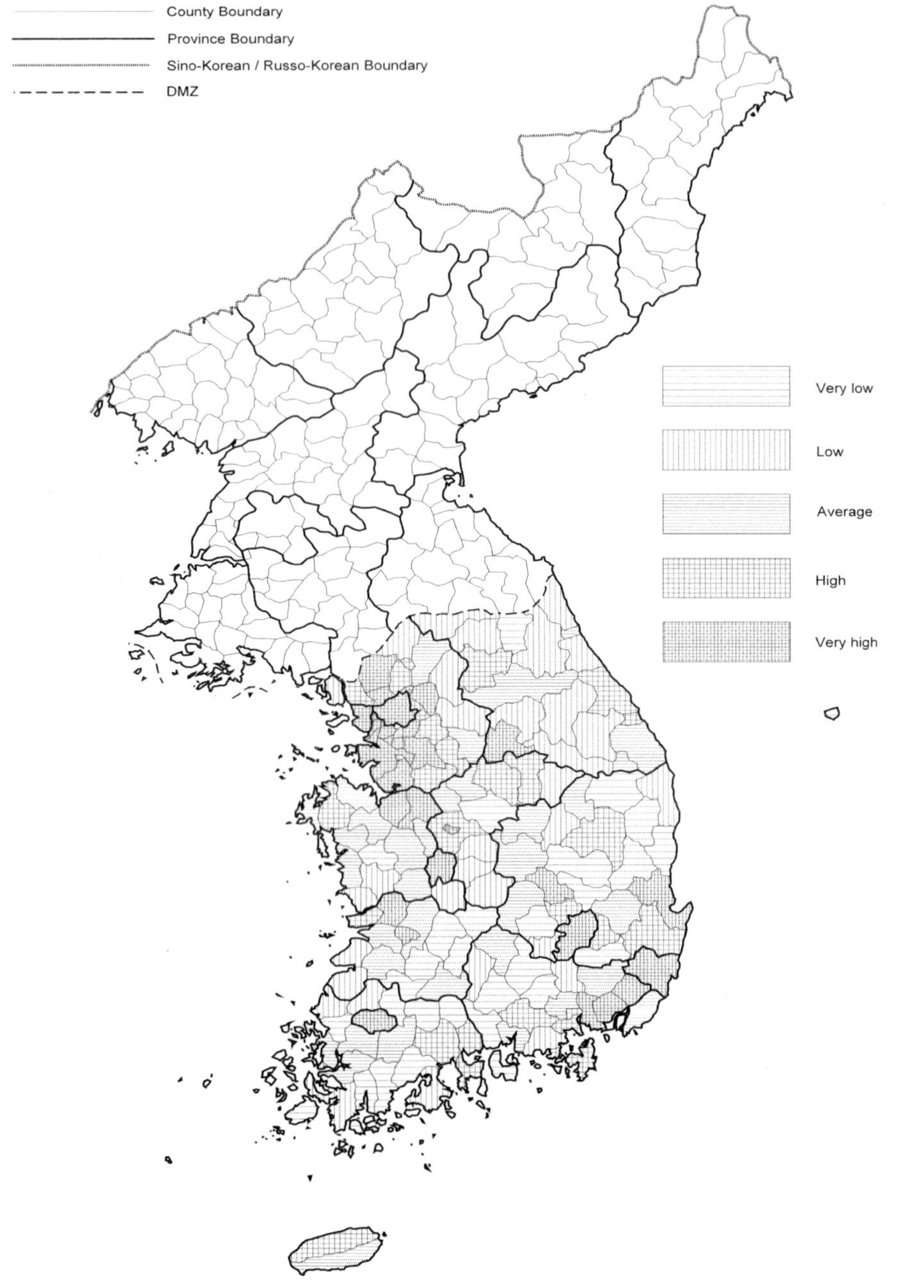

Notes: Unit = housing units. Cut-offs = below 1775.0, 1775.0 to below 5588.0, 5588.0 to below 19672.0, 19672.0 to below 61143.0, 61143.0 or above.

Map 3.6 Detached dwelling residents of the Korean peninsula

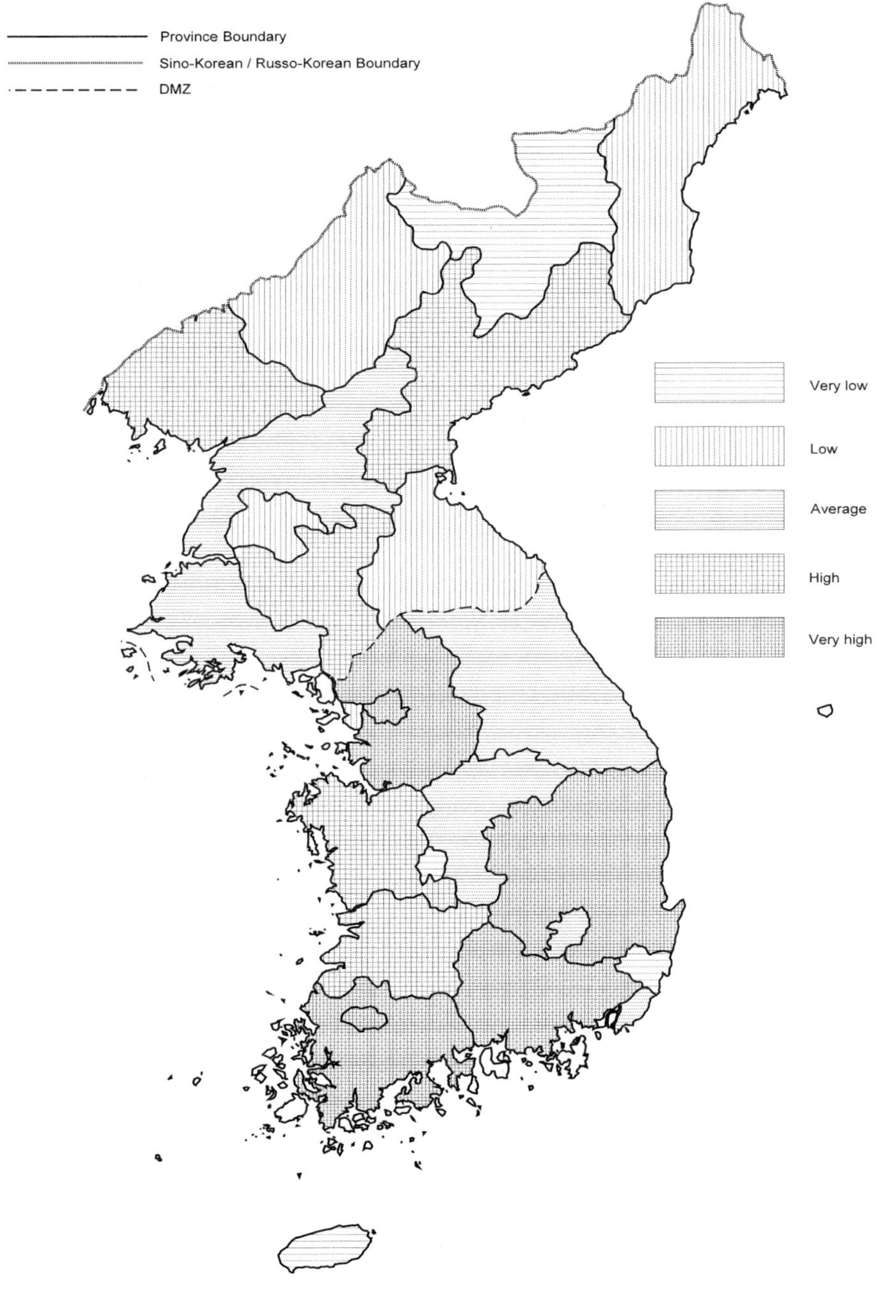

Notes: Unit = housing units. Cut-offs = below 95006.9, 95006.9 to below 164359.1, 164359.1 to below 267141.6, 267141.6 to below 390746.9, 390746.9 or above.

Map 3.7 Detached dwelling residents of South Korea

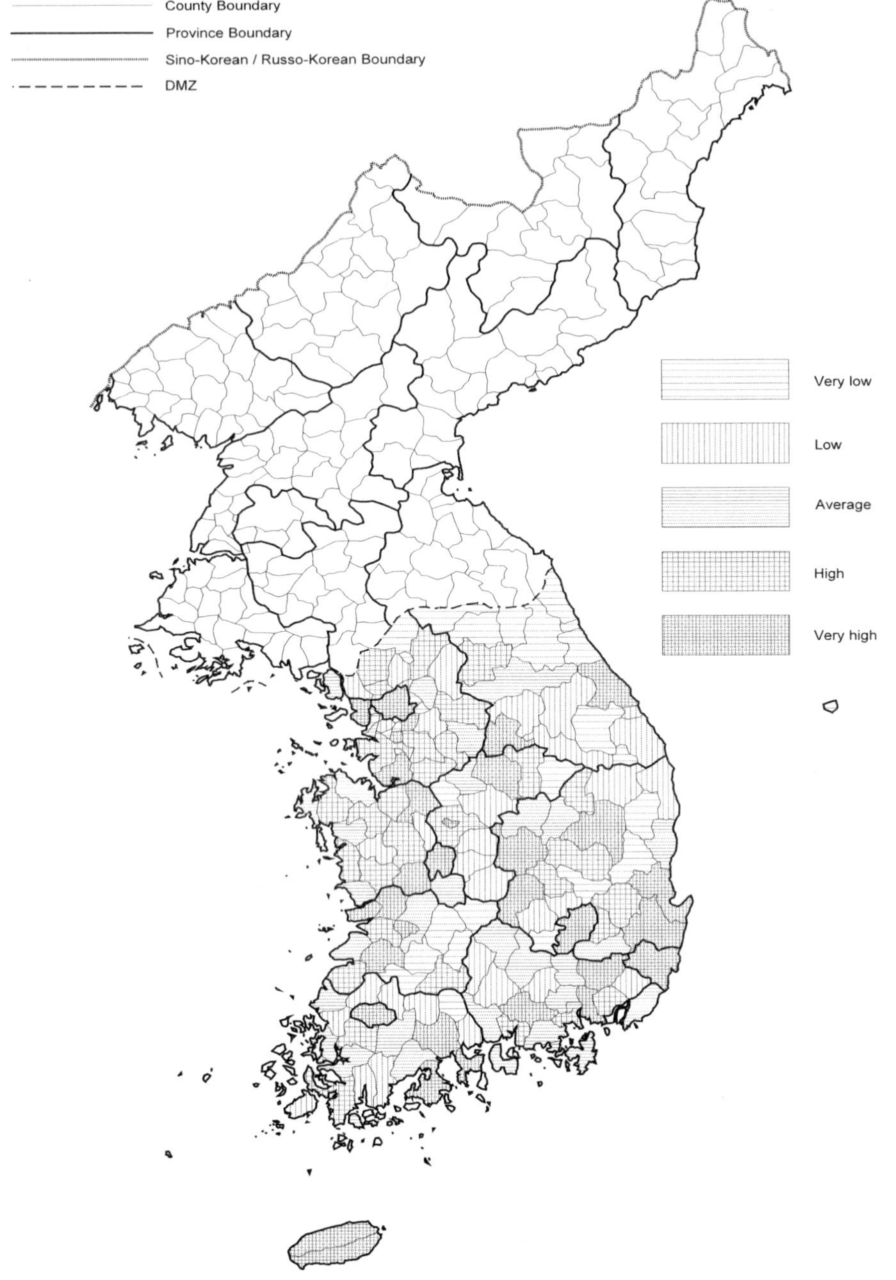

Notes: Unit = housing units. Cut-offs = below 10863.5, 10863.5 to below 15237.0, 15237.0 to below 19941.0, 19941.0 to below 26855.5, 26855.5 or above.

Map 3.8 Apartment residents of the Korean peninsula (share)

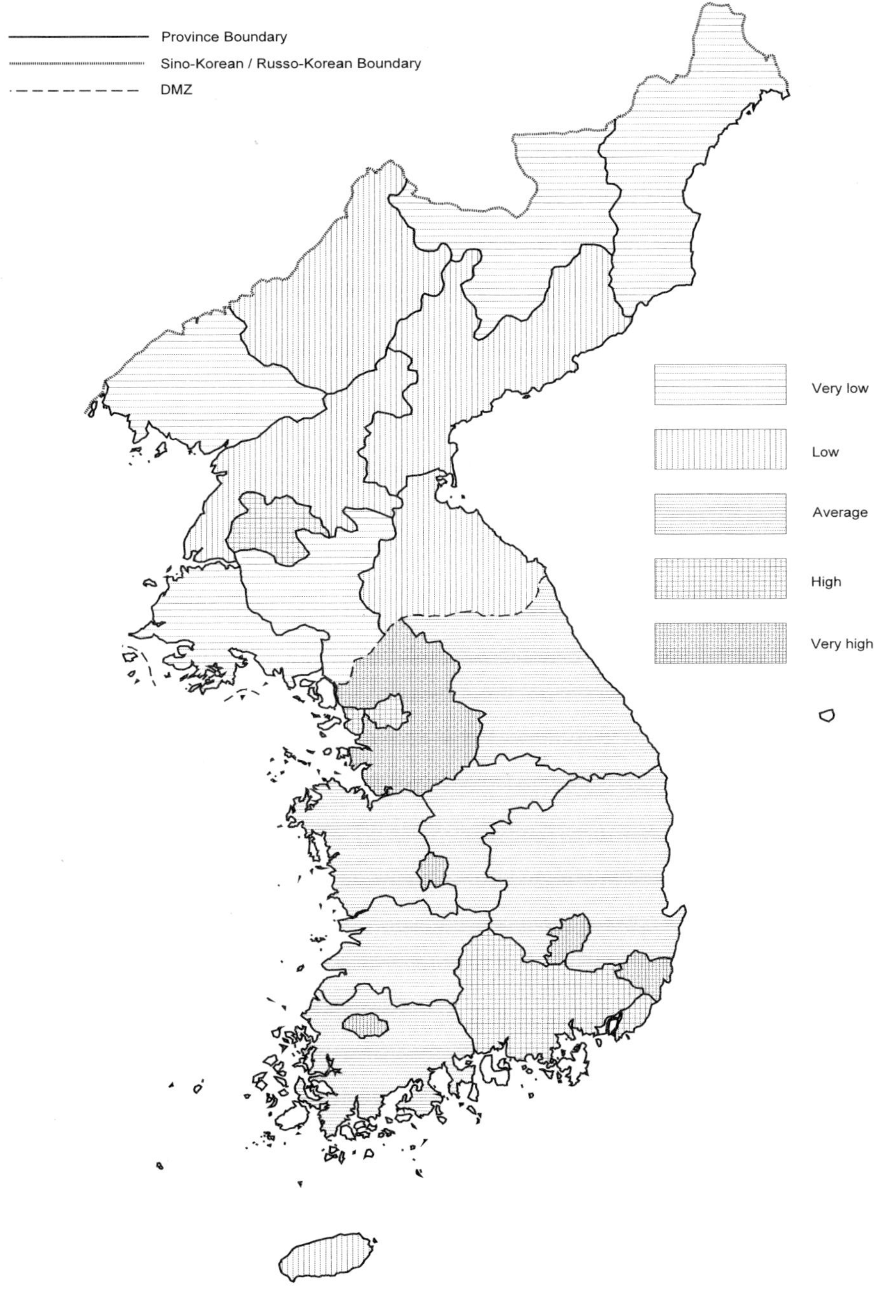

Notes: Unit = percentage of housing units. Cut-offs = below 17.44, 17.44 to below 36.06, 36.06 to below 53.51, 53.51 to below 63.67, 63.67 or higher.

Map 3.9 Apartment residents of South Korea (share)

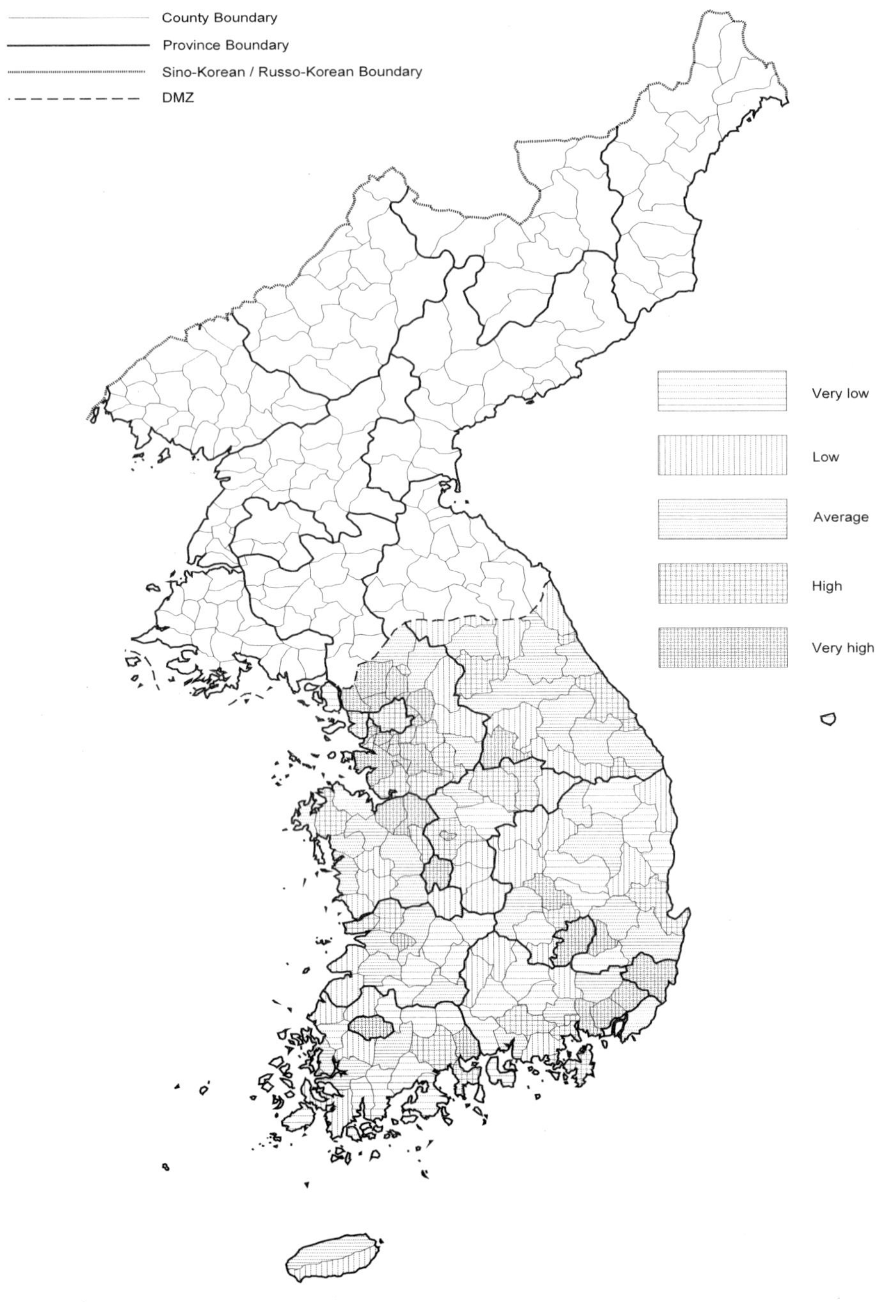

Notes: Unit = percentage of housing units. Cut-offs = below 11.00, 11.00 to below 24.90, 24.90 to below 44.20, 44.20 to below 65.90, 65.90 or above.

Map 3.10 Detached dwelling residents of the Korean peninsula (share)

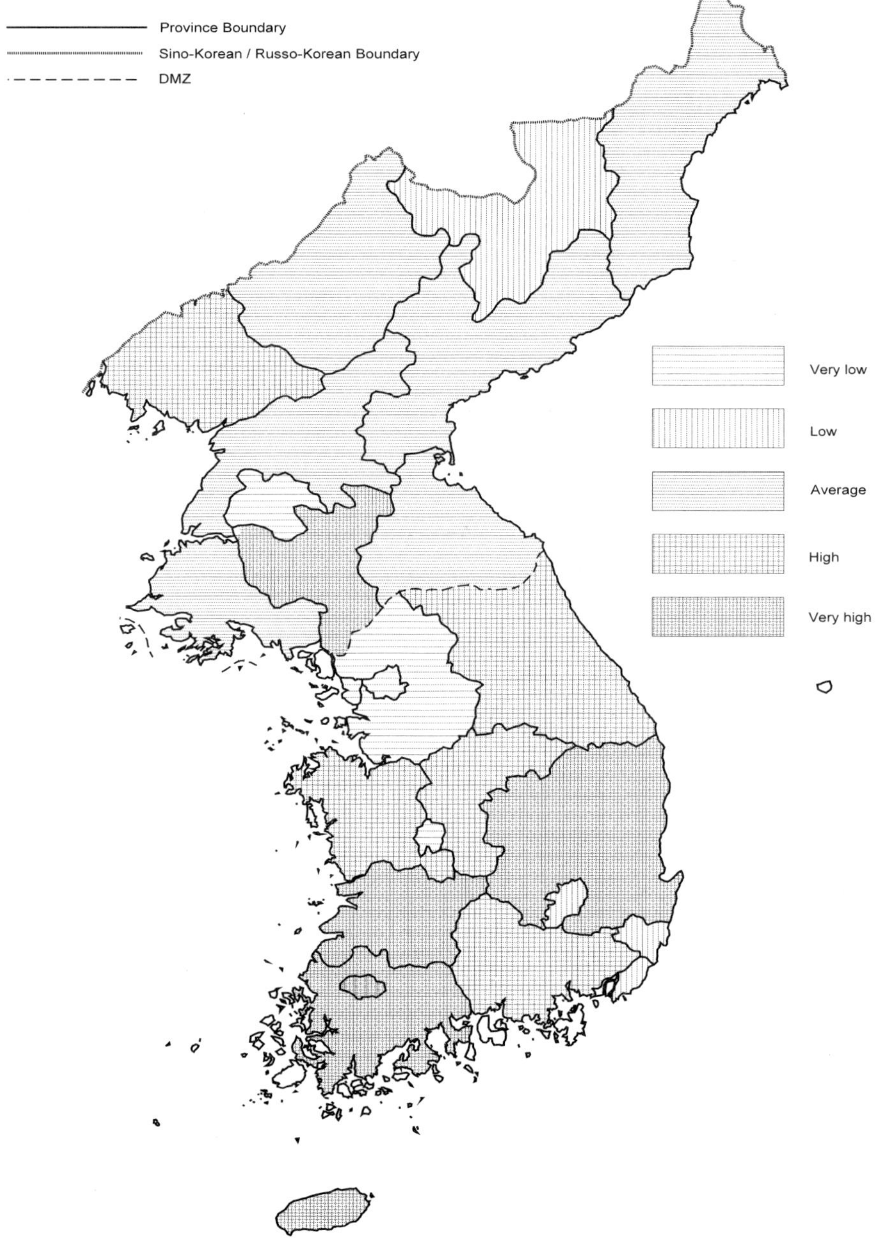

Notes: Unit = percentage of housing units. Cut-offs = below 20.02, 20.02 to below 24.88, 24.88 to below 39.94, 39.94 to below 45.45, 45.45 or above.

Map 3.11 Detached dwelling residents of South Korea (share)

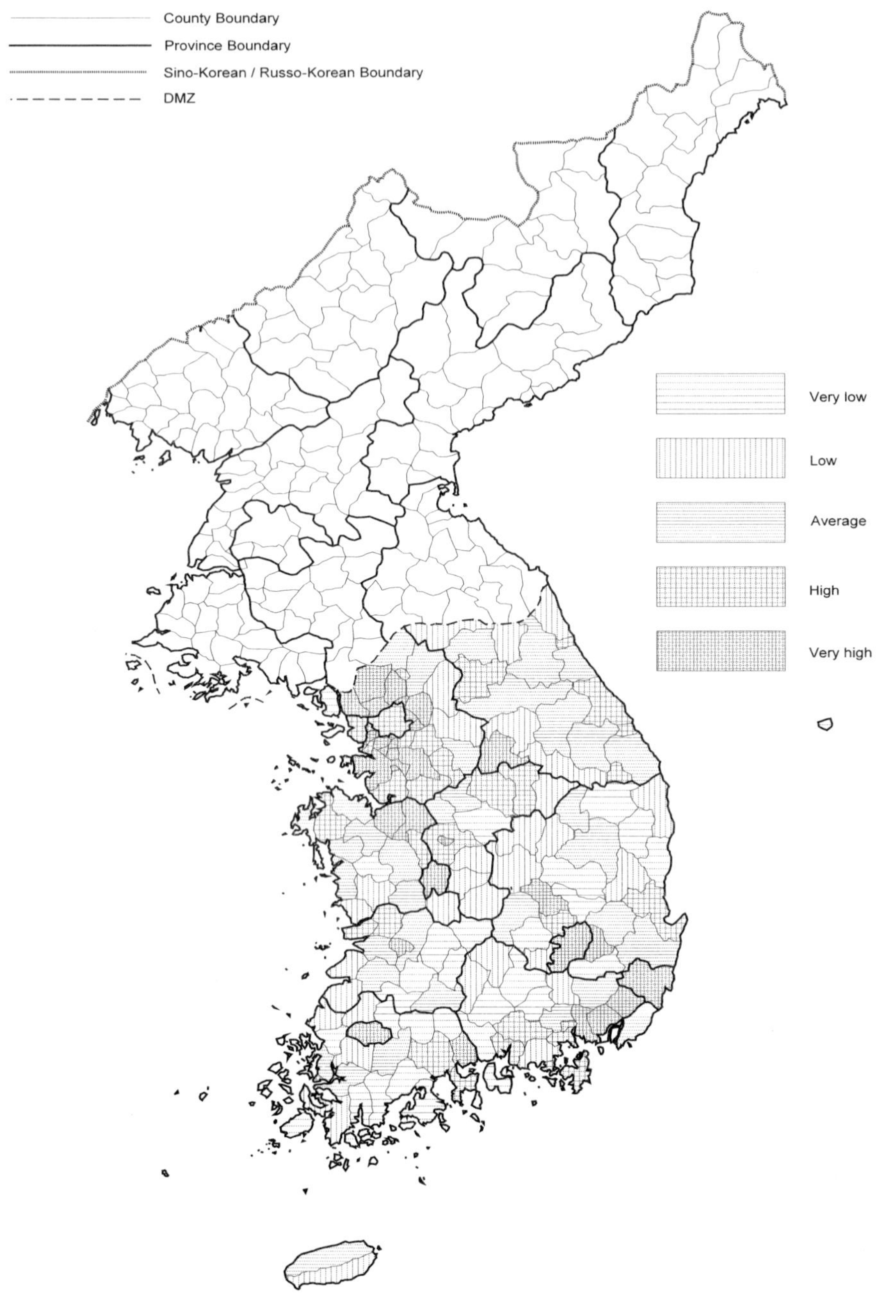

Notes: Unit = percentage of housing units. Cut-offs = below 11.03, 11.03 to below 24.87, 24.87 to below 44.17, 44.17 to below 65.91, 65.91 or above.

4. Age Structure

Map 4.1 Population aged 0-14 years of the Korean peninsula

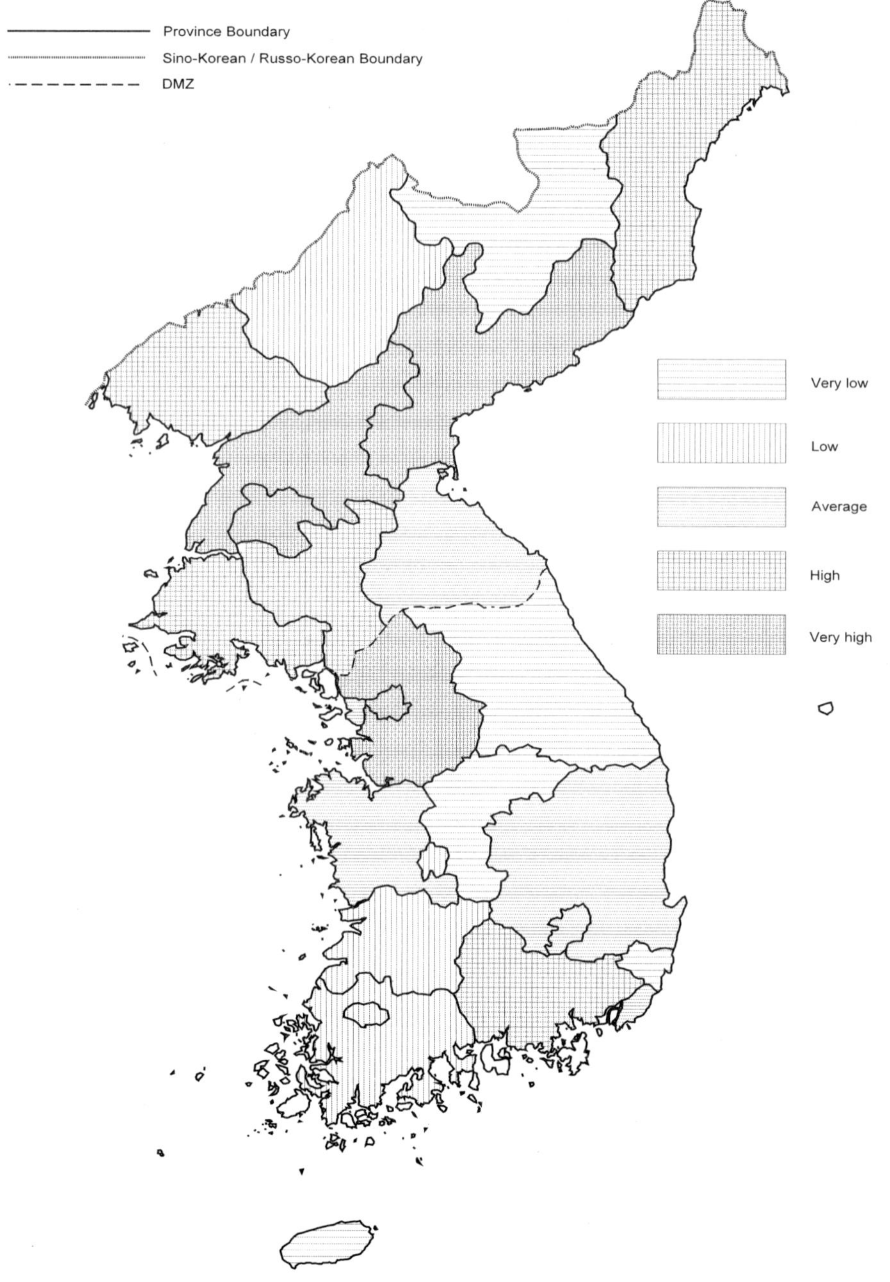

Notes: Unit = persons. Cut-offs = below 253729.1, 253729.1 to below 325915.6, 325915.6 to below 467672.7, 467672.7 to below 679112.8, 679112.8 or above.

Map 4.2 Population aged 0-14 years of South Korea

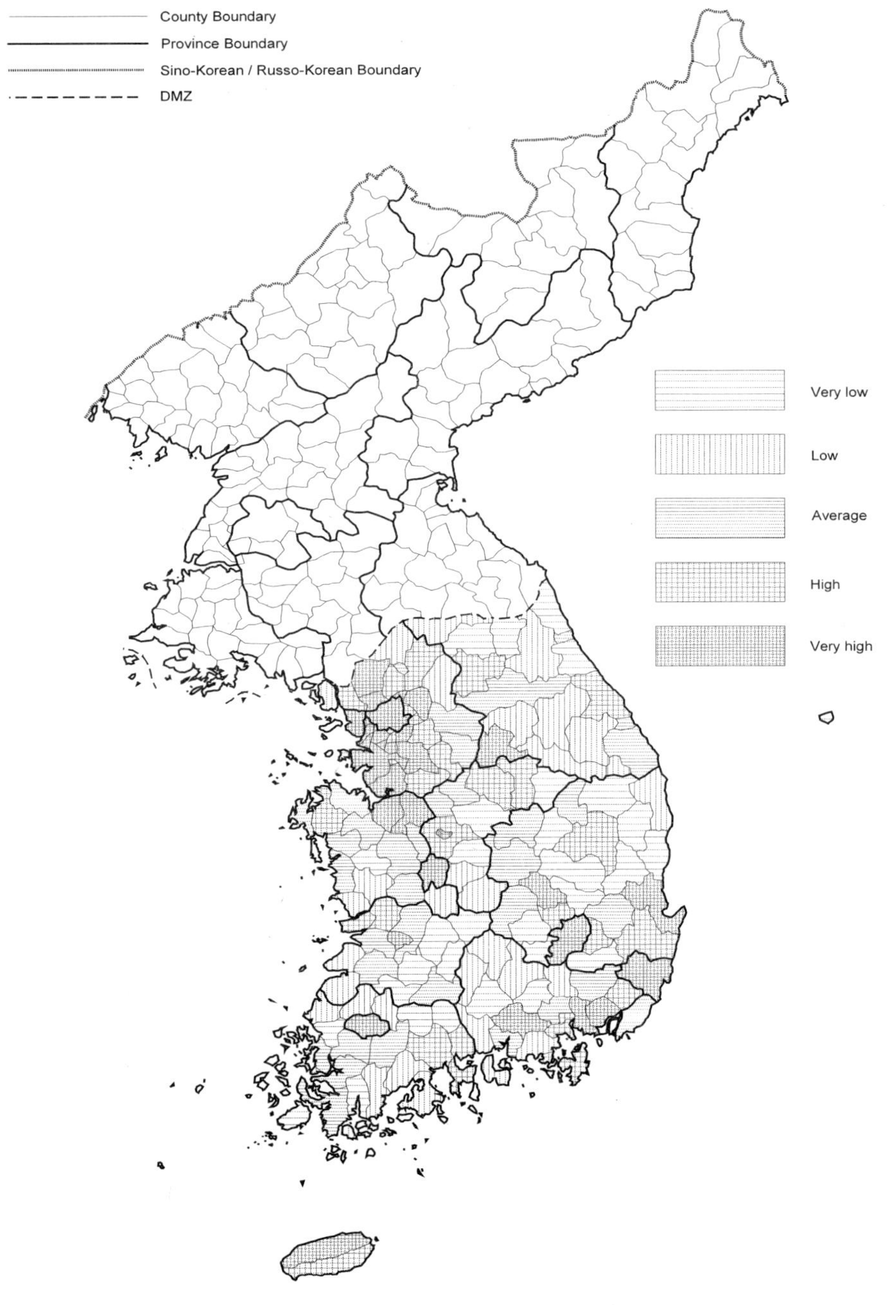

Notes: Unit = persons. Cut-offs = below 4306.0, 4306.0 to below 8582.0, 8582.0 to below 19061.0, 19061.0 to below 49146.5, 49146.5 or above.

Map 4.3 Sex ratio of population aged 0-14 years of the Korean peninsula

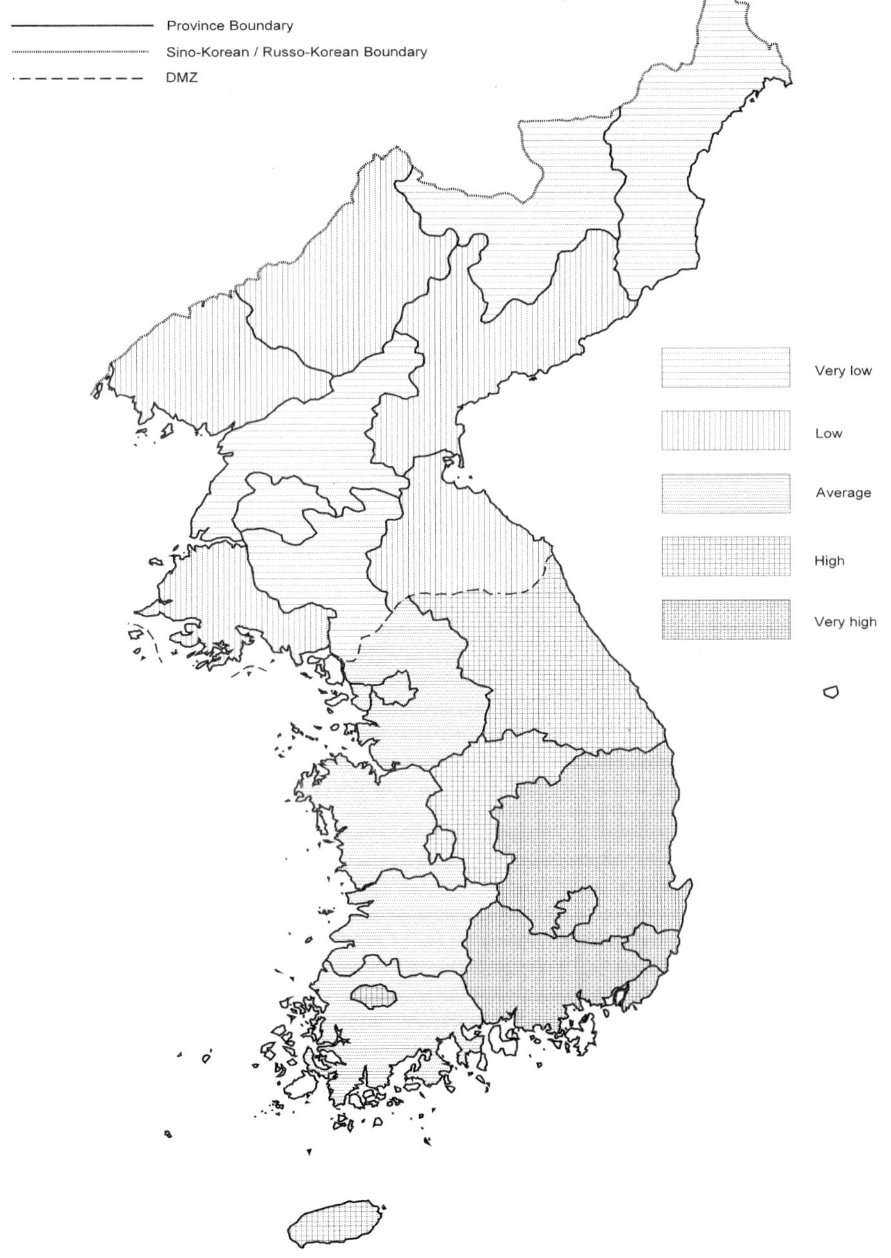

Notes: The sex ratio is the number of males and females for every 100 females.. Cut-offs = below 104.570, 104.570 to below 106.520, 106.520 to below 107.270, 107.270 to below 109.190, 109.190 or above.

Map 4.4 Sex ratio of population aged 0-14 years of South Korea

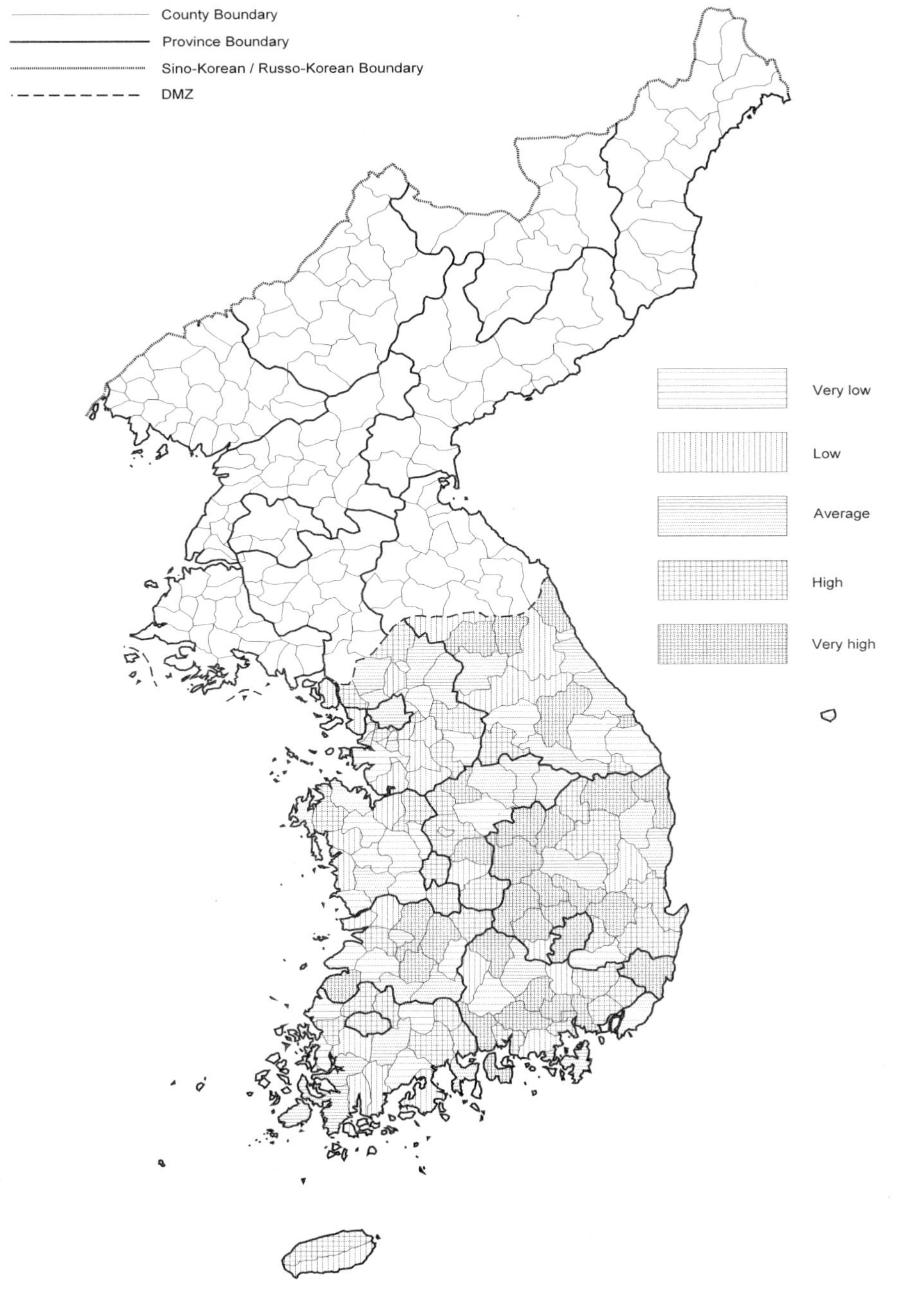

Notes: The sex ratio is the number of males and females for every 100 females. Cut-offs = below 105.750, 105.750 to below 106.900, 106.900 to below 107.900, 107.900 to below 109.850, 109.850 or above.

Map 4.5 Population aged 15-64 years of the Korean peninsula

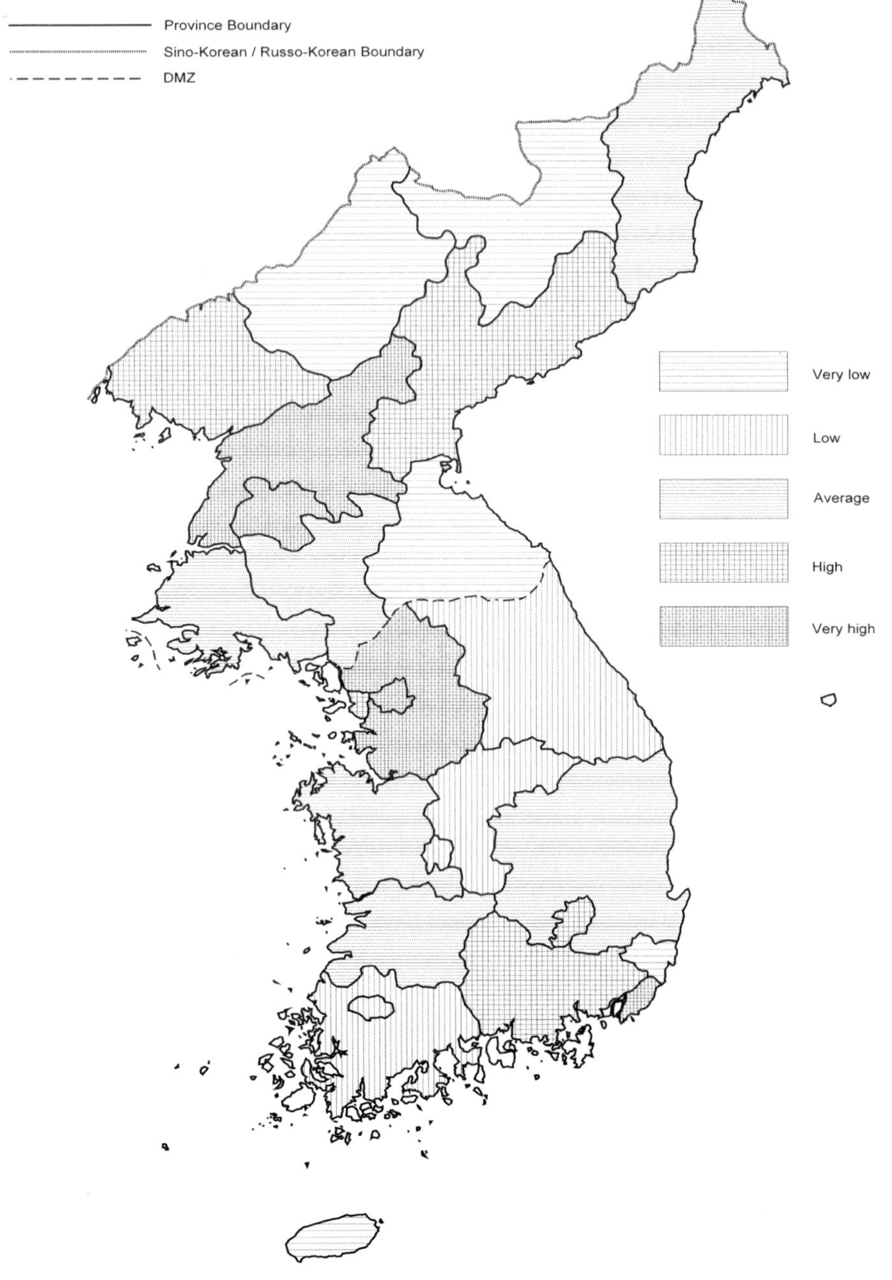

Notes: Unit = persons. Cut-offs = below 984498.1, 984498.1 to below 1179195.0, 1179195.0 to below 1762930.9, 1762930.9 to below 2196387.3, 2196387.3 or above.

Map 4.6 Population aged 15-64 years of South Korea

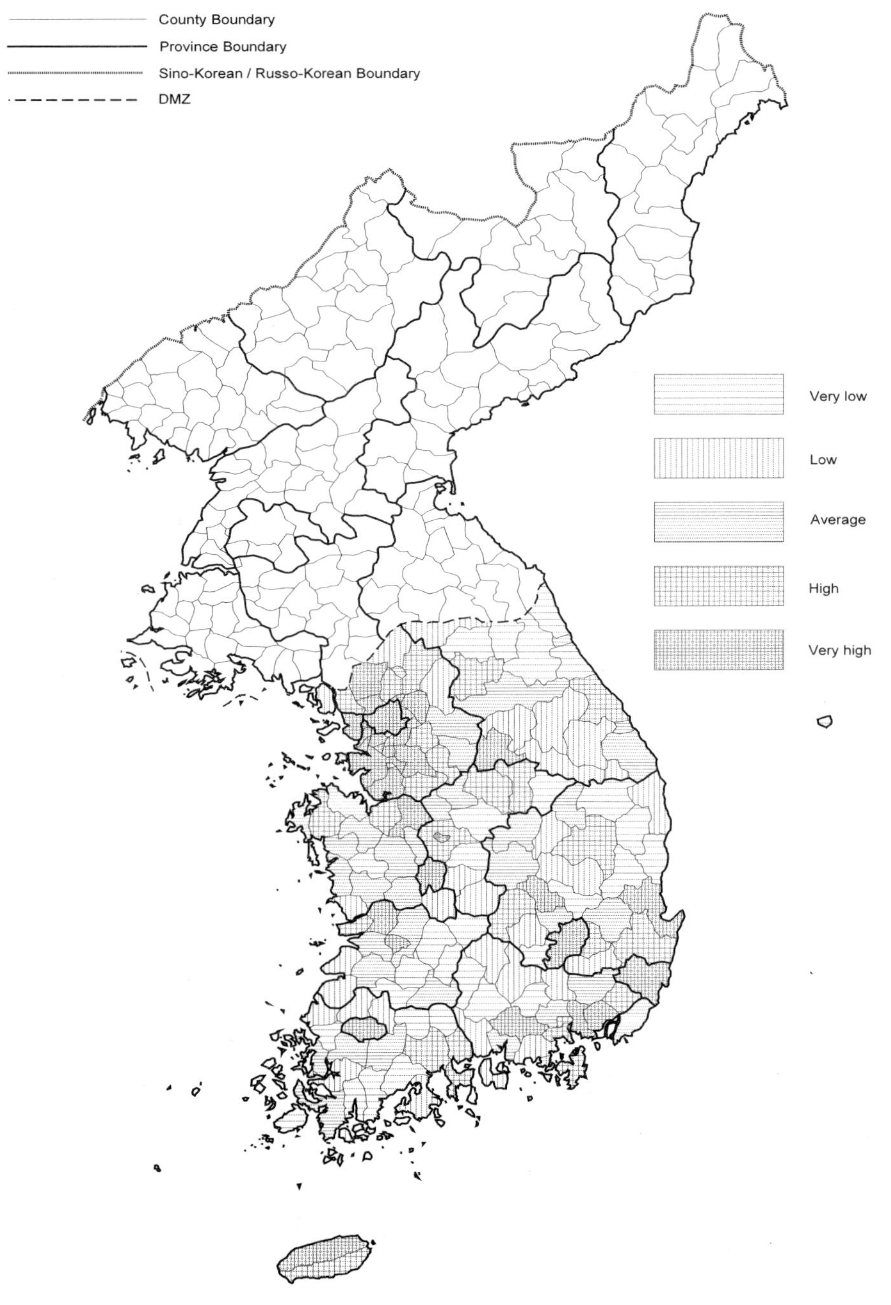

Notes: Unit = persons. Cut-offs = below 21404.0, 21404.0 to below 36121.5, 36121.5 to below 82385.0, 82385.0 to below 199222.5, 199222.5 or above.

Map 4.7 Sex ratio of population aged 15-64 years of the Korean peninsula

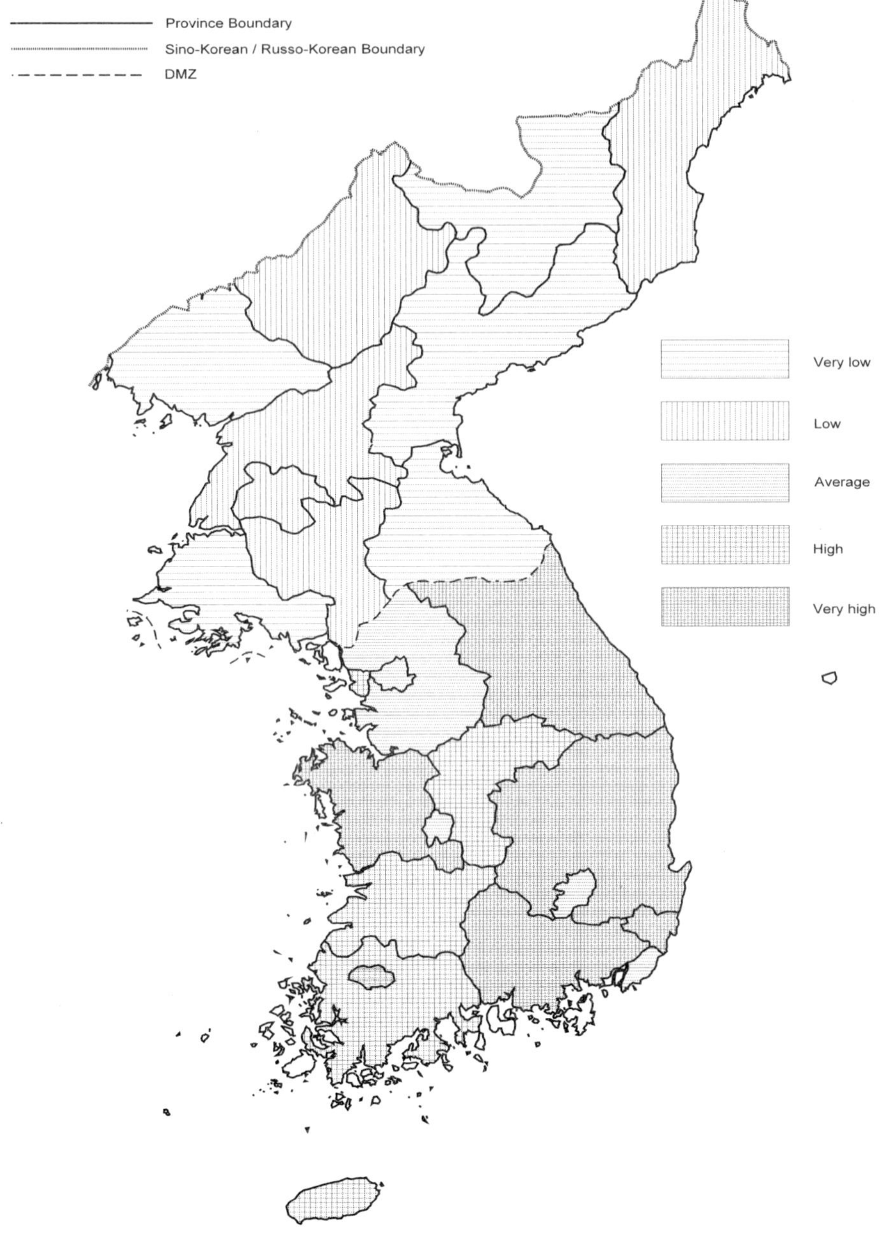

Notes The sex ratio is the number of males and females for every 100 females. Cut-offs = below 91.09, 91.09 to below 97.00, 97.00 to below 103.01, 103.01 to below 107.16, 107.16 or above.

Map 4.8 Sex ratio of population aged 15-64 years of South Korea

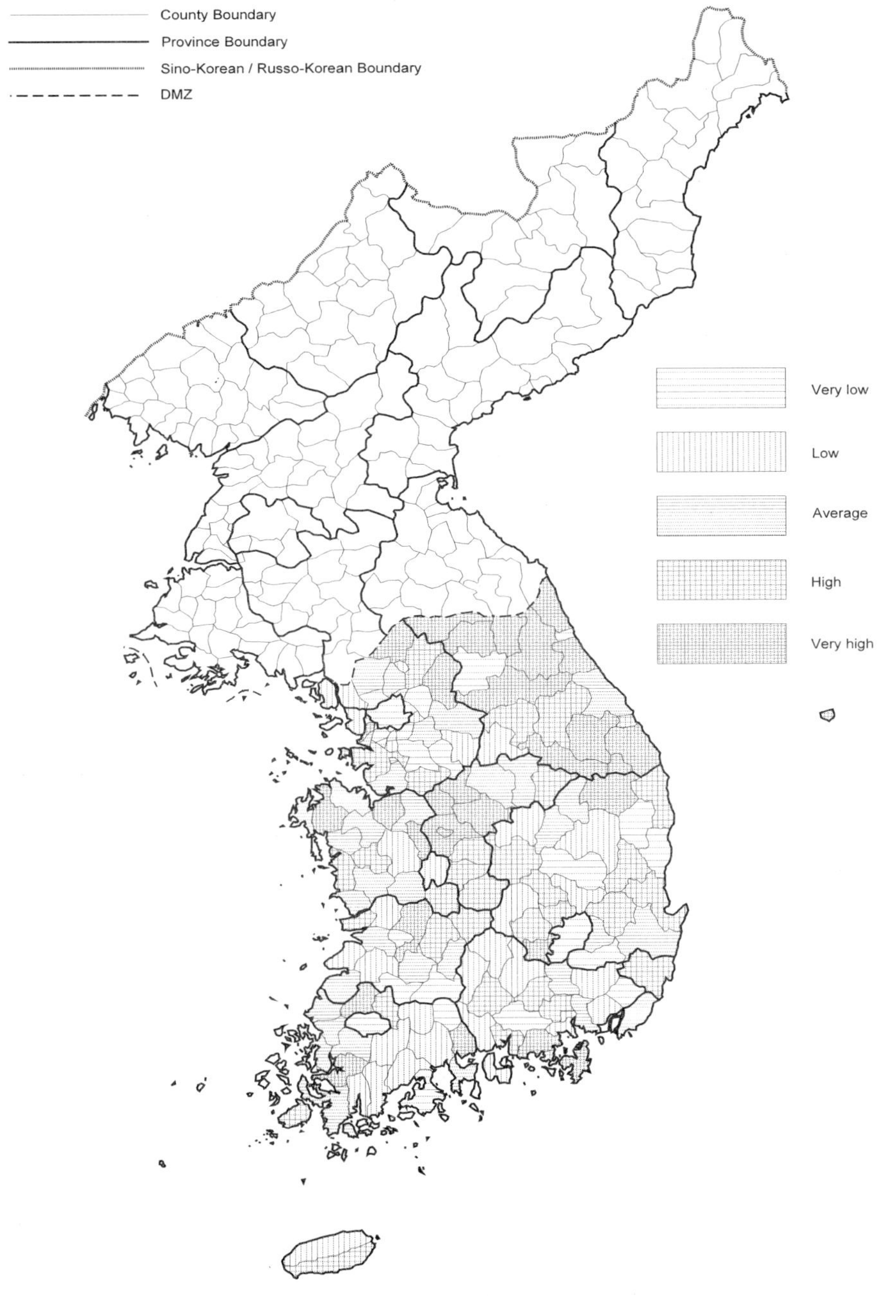

Notes: The sex ratio is the number of males and females for every 100 females. Cut-offs = below 102.60, 102.60 to below 105.50, 105.50 to below 108.05, 108.05 to below 112.10, 112.10 or above.

Map 4.9 Population aged 65 and over of the Korean peninsula

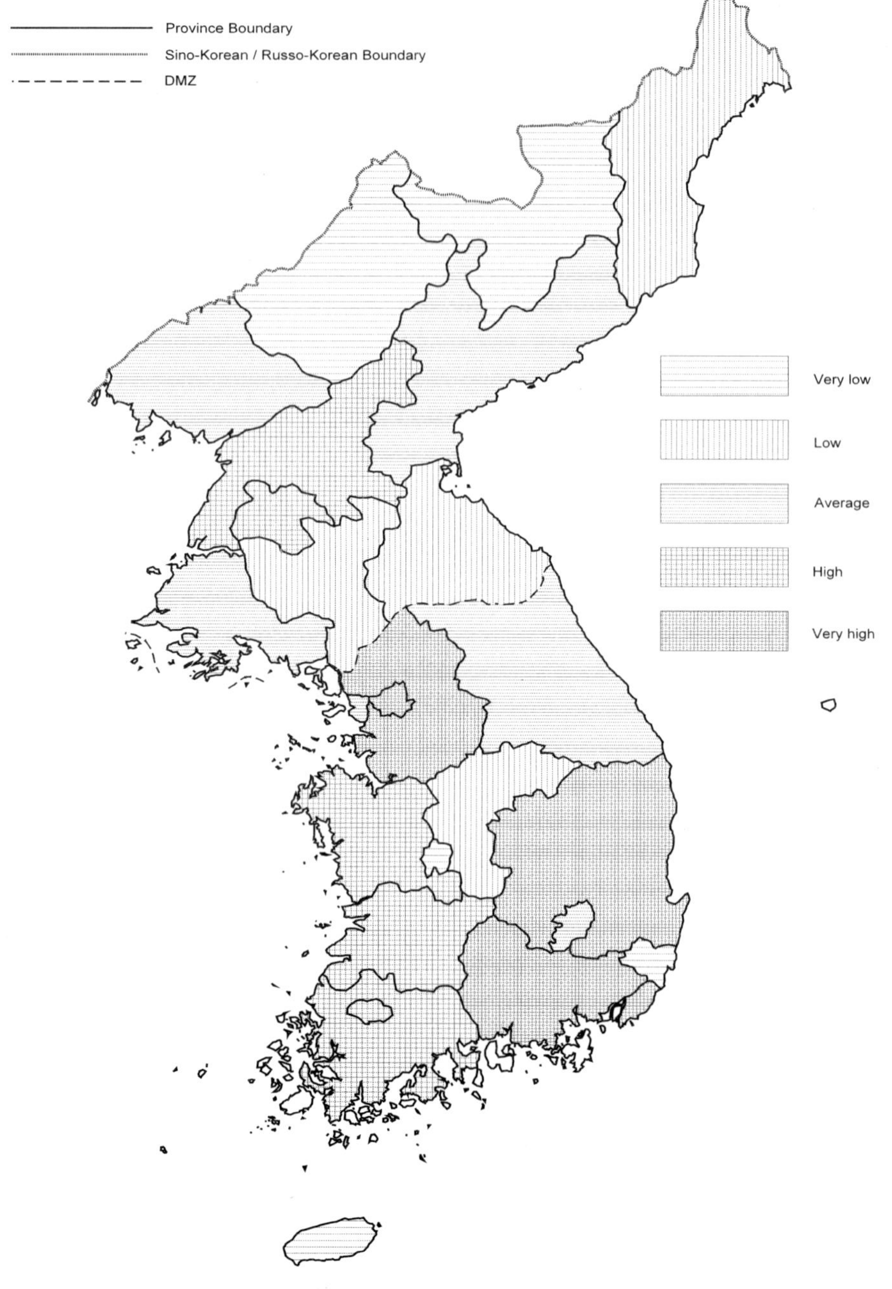

Notes: Unit = persons. Cut-offs = below 132500.4, 132500.4 to below 220878.8, 220878.8 to below 284548.5, 284548.5 to below 364476.4, 364476.4 or above.

Map 4.10 Population aged 65 and over of South Korea

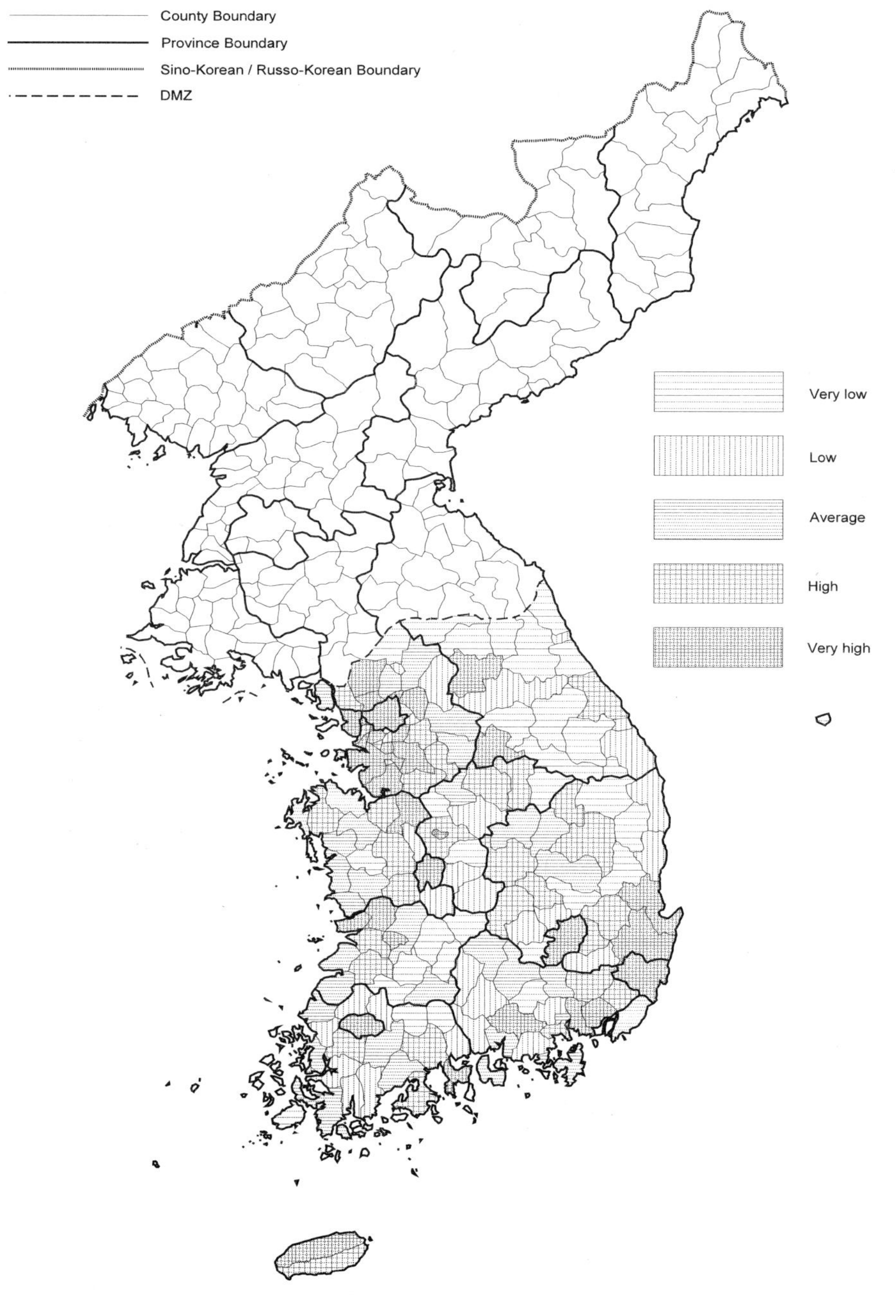

Notes: Unit = persons. Cut-offs = below 10347.0, 10347.0 to below 13482.0, 13482.0 to below 20224.5, 20224.5 to below 32669.5, 32669.5 or above.

Map 4.11 Sex ratio of population aged 65 and over of the Korean peninsula

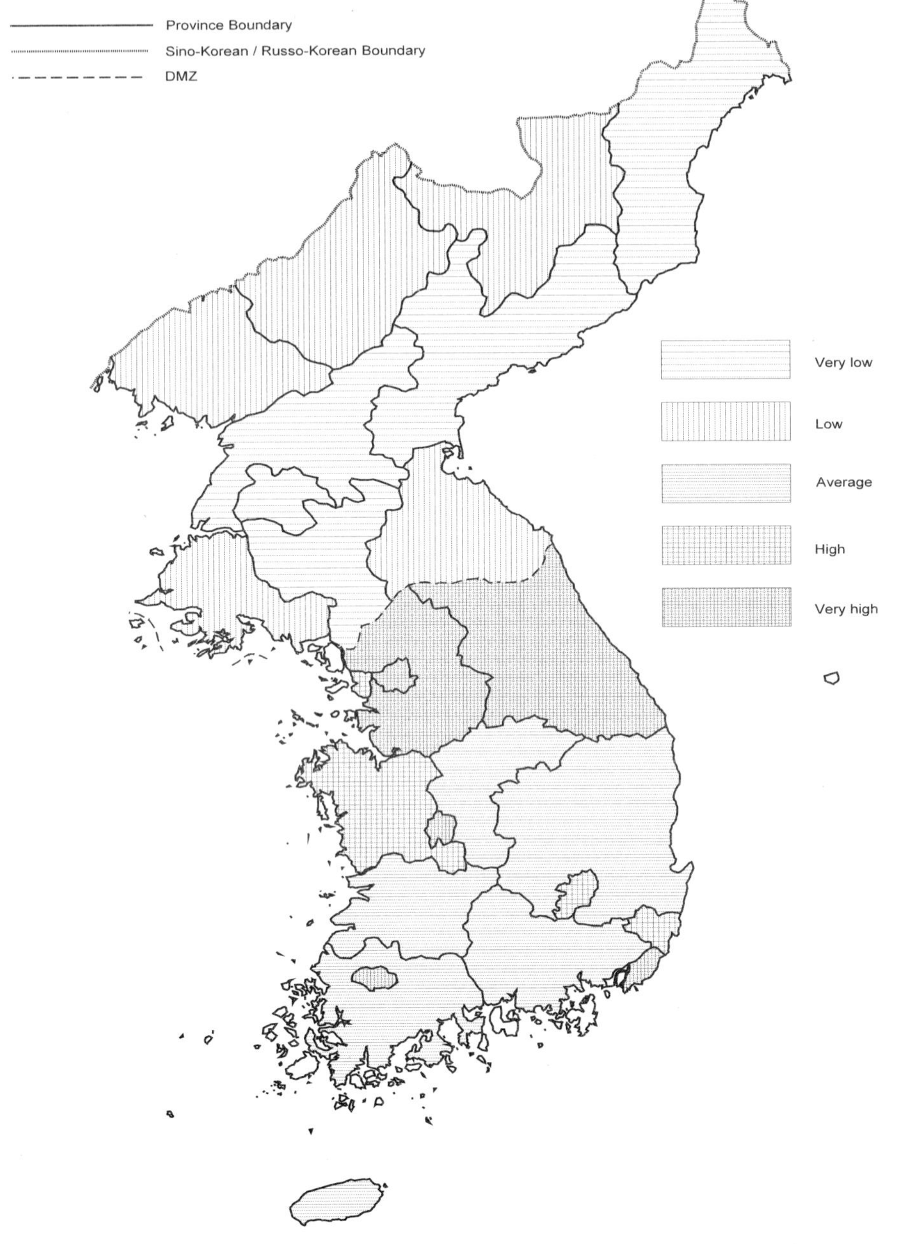

Notes: The sex ratio is the number of males and females for every 100 females. Cut-offs = below 52.33, 52.33 to below 59.69, 59.69 to below 66.52, 66.52 to below 68.80, 68.80 or above.

Map 4.12 Mean age of total population of South Korea

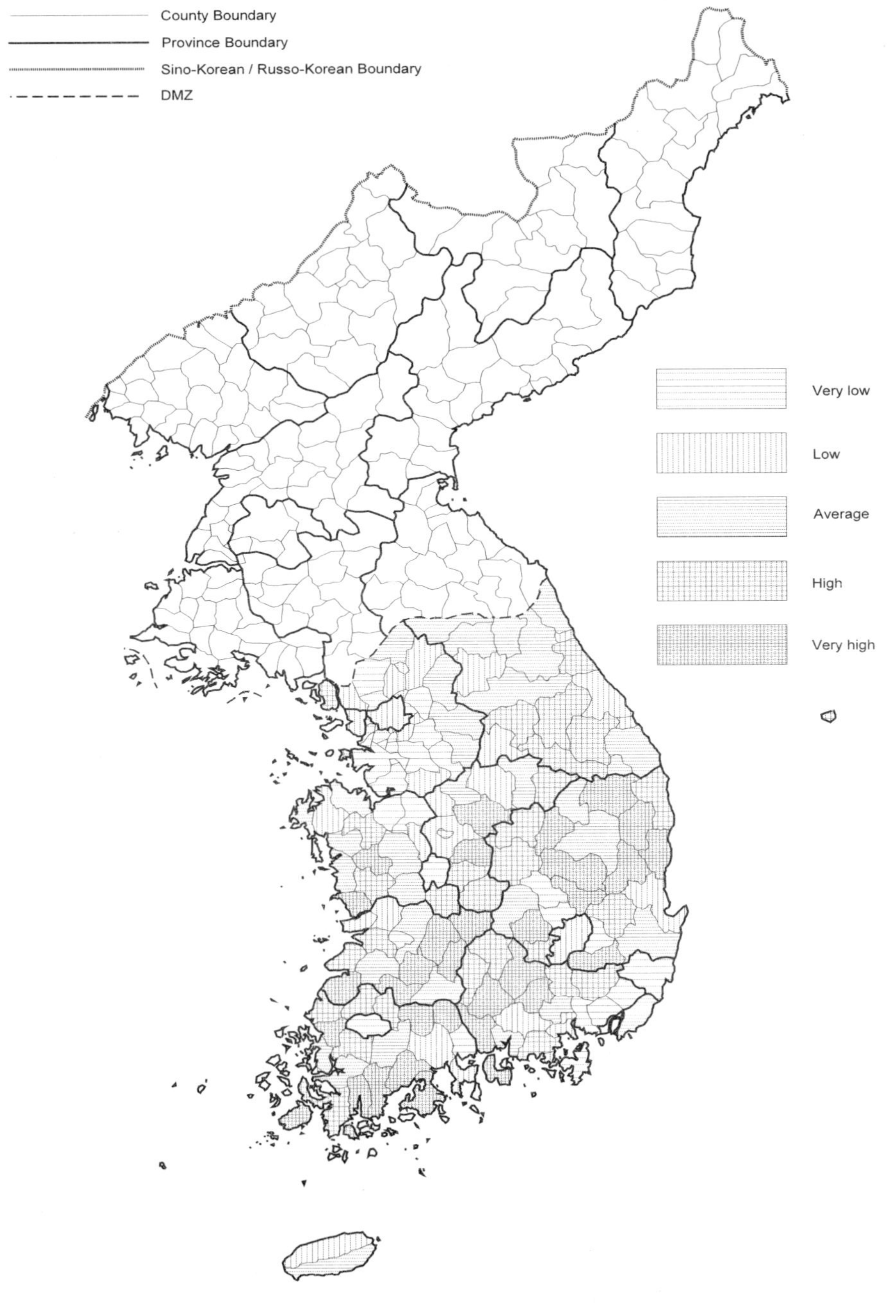

Notes: Unit = age in years. Cut-offs = below 36.83, 36.83 to below 40.52, 40.52 to below 45.06, 45.06 to below 49.20, 49.20 or above.

Map 4.13 Mean age of male population of South Korea

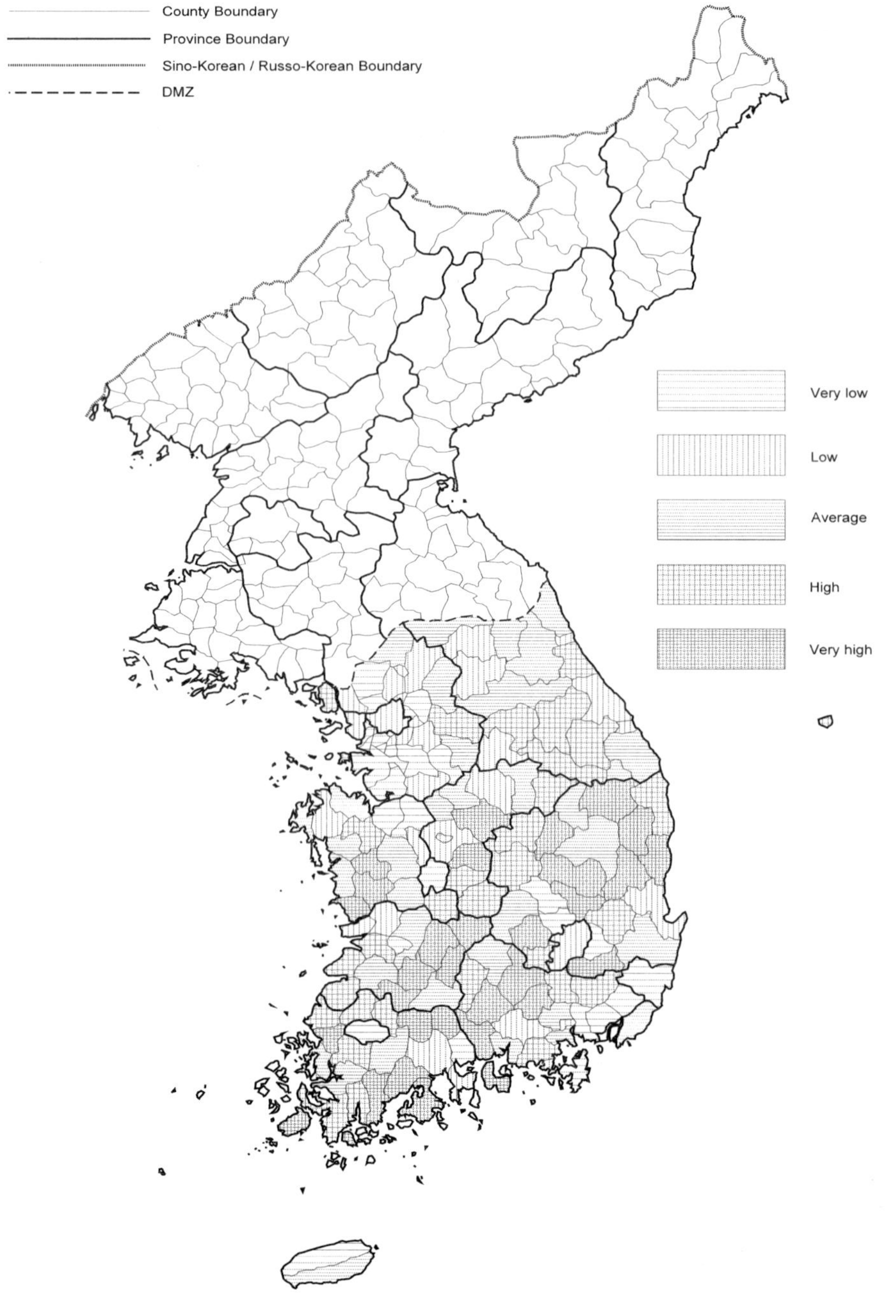

Notes: Unit = age in years. Cut-offs = below 35.630, 35.630 to below 38.700, 38.700 to below 42.380, 42.380 to below 46.040, 46.040 or above.

Map 4.14 Mean age of female population of South Korea

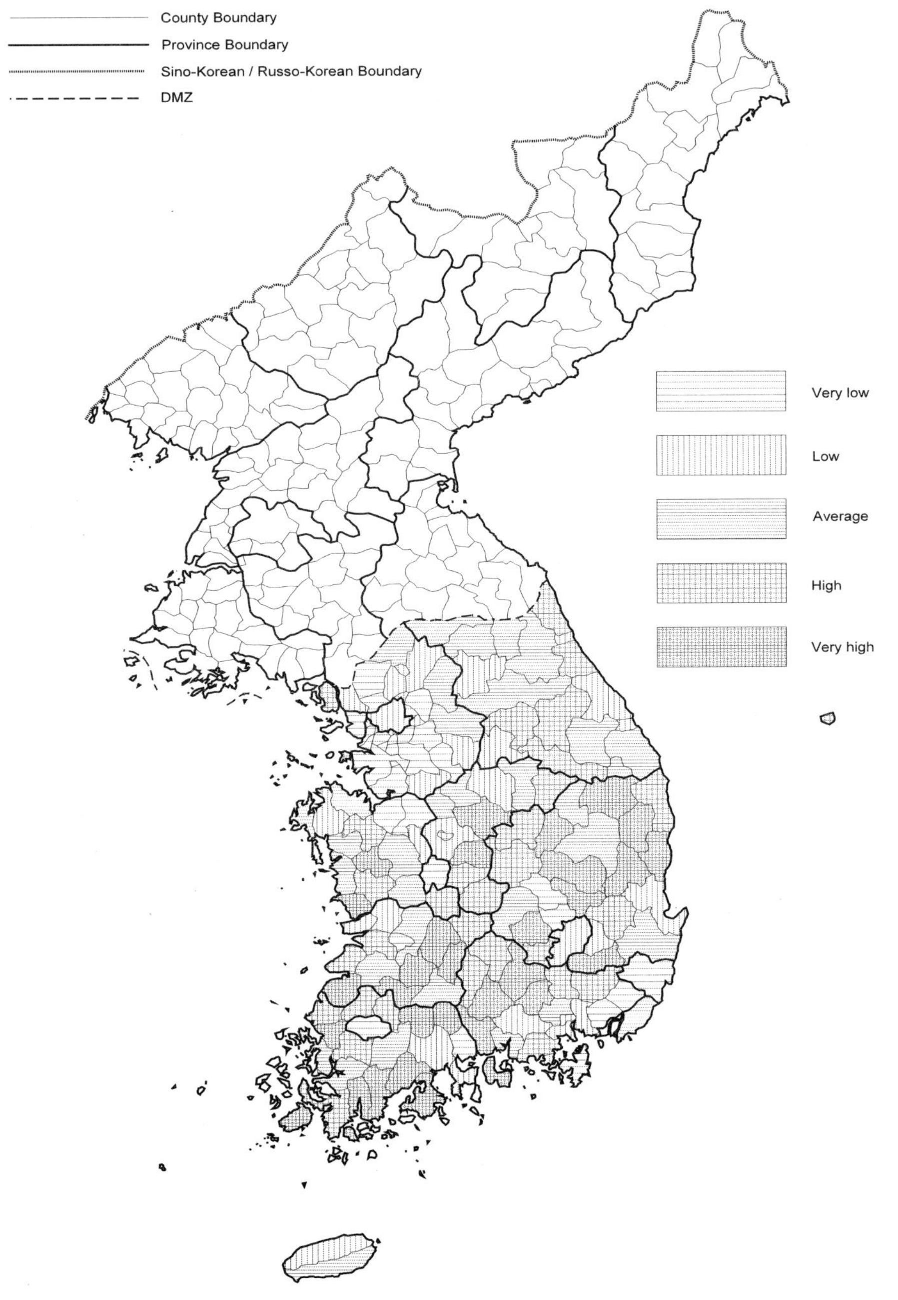

Notes: Unit = age in years. Cut-offs = below 37.93, 37.93 to below 42.21, 42.21 to below 47.29, 47.29 to below 51.87, 51.87 or above.

Map 4.15 Population aged 0-14 years of the Korean peninsula (share)

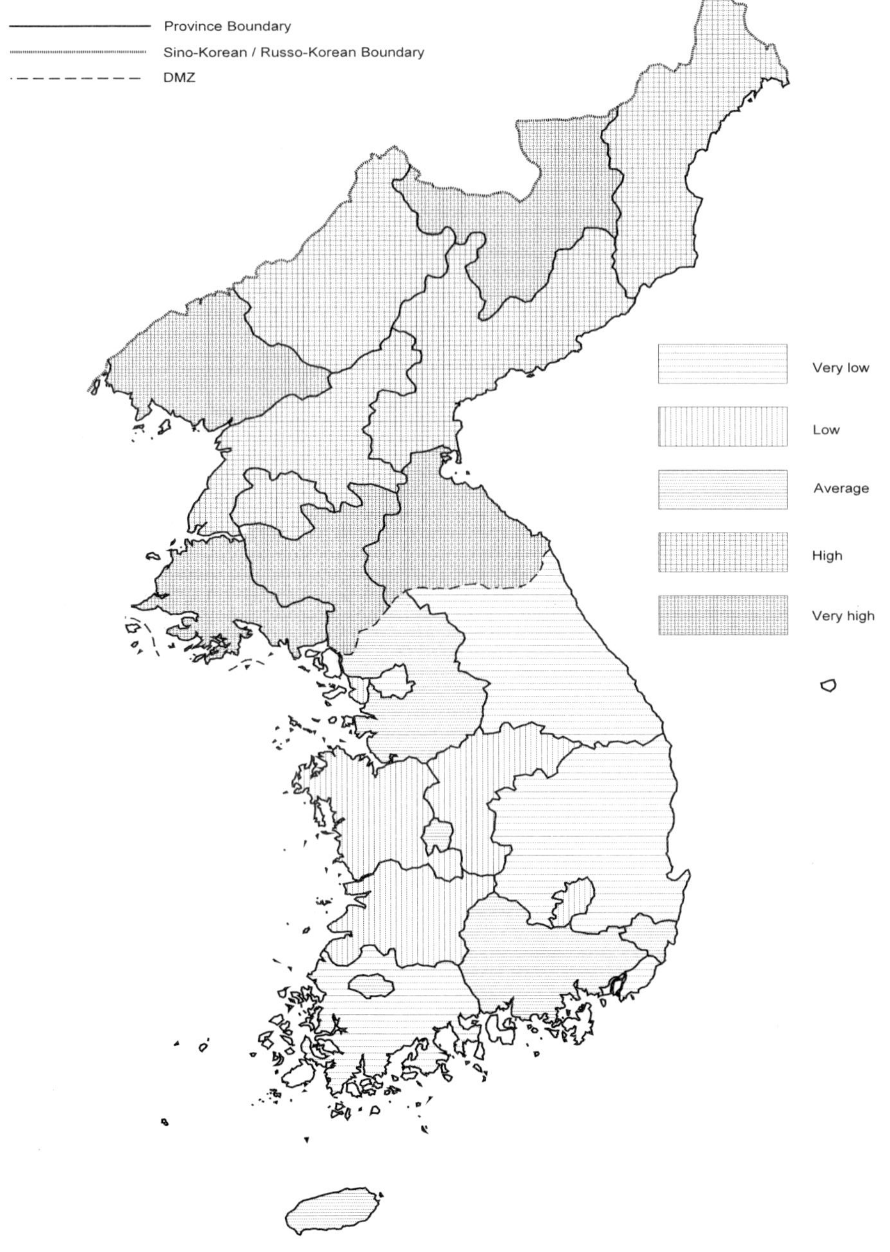

Notes: Unit = percent. Cut-offs = below 15.864, 15.864 to below 16.932, 16.932 to below 19.364, 19.364 to below 23.895, 23.895 or above.

Map 4.16 Population aged 0-14 years of South Korea (share)

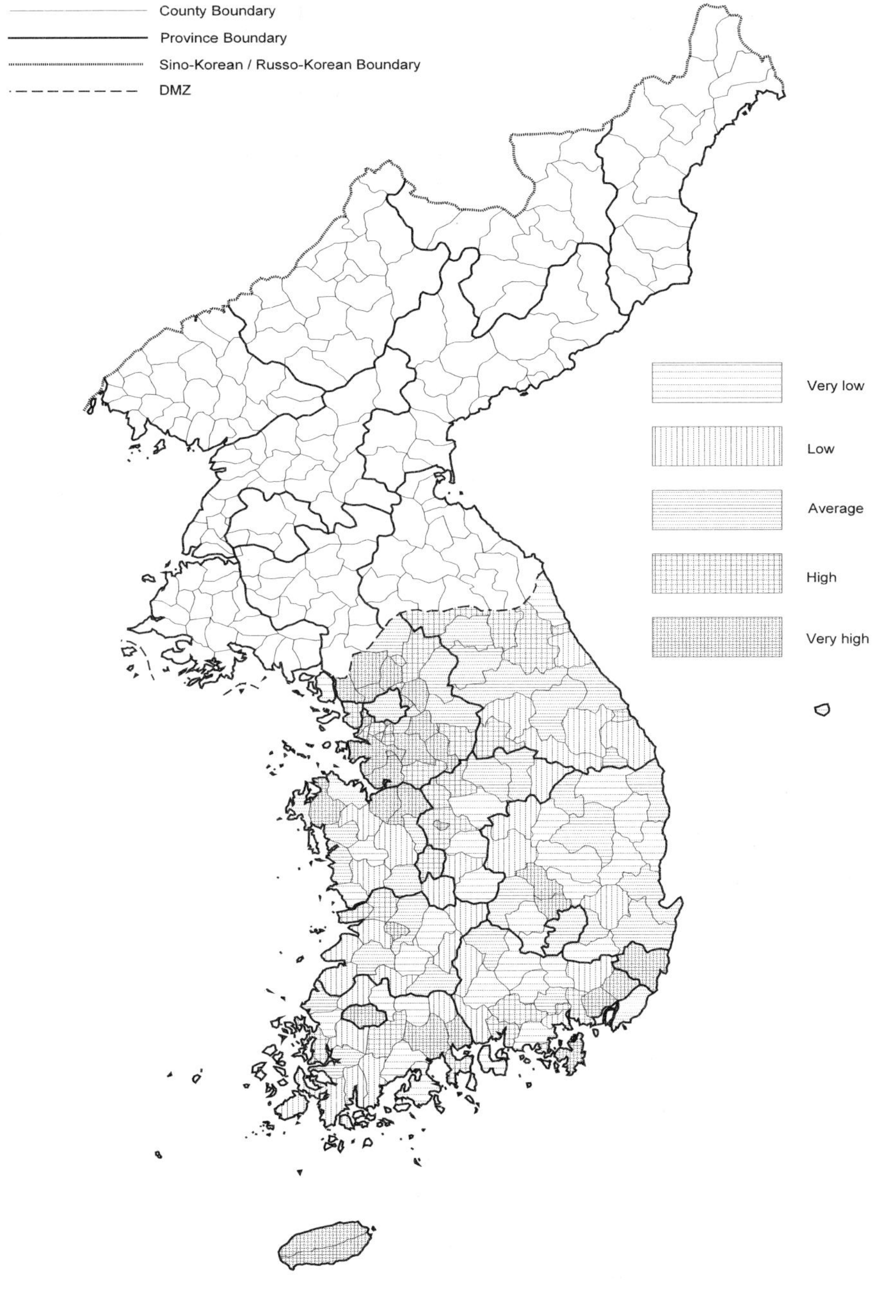

Notes: Unit = percent. Cut-offs = below 12.153, 12.153 to below 13.557, 13.557 to below 15.958, 15.958 to below 17.627, 17.627 or above.

Map 4.17 Population aged 15-64 years of the Korean peninsula (share)

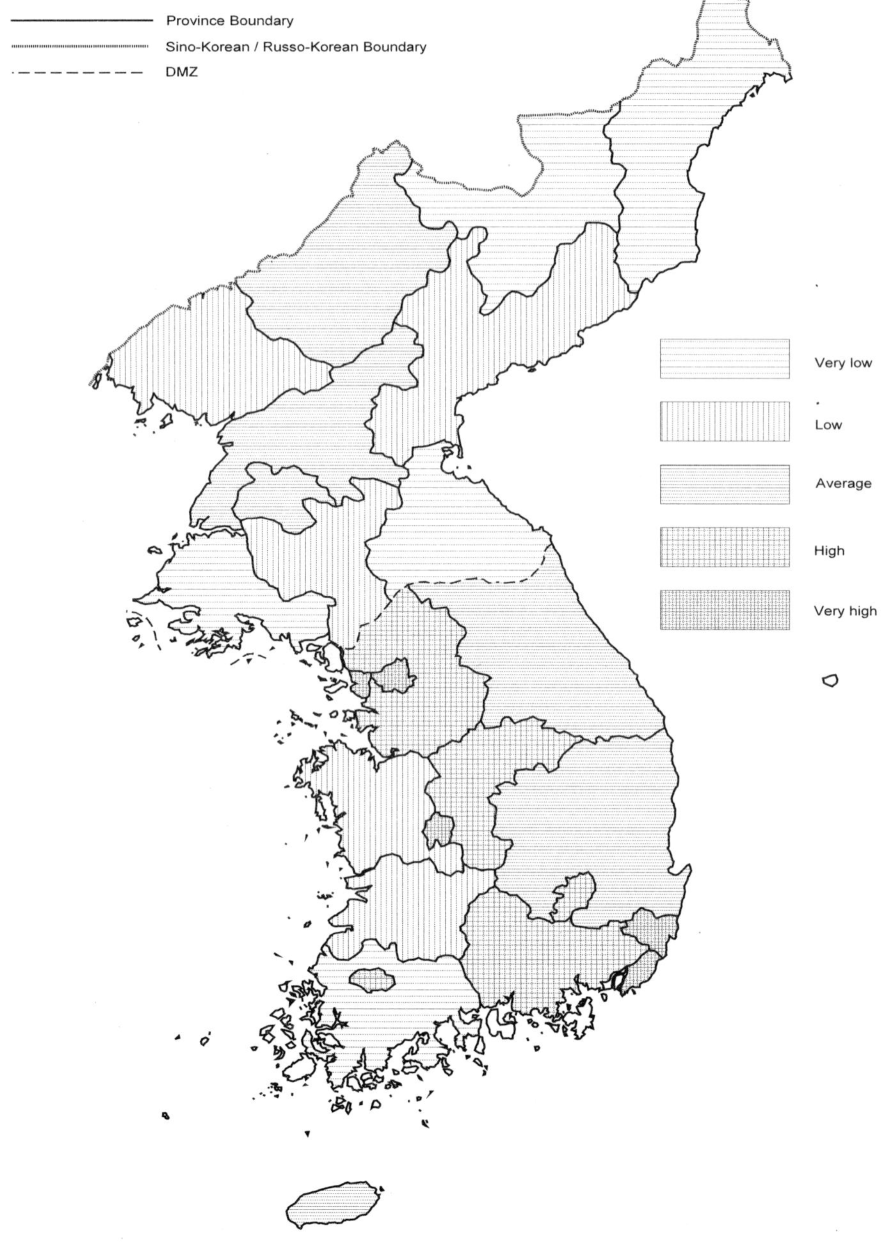

Notes: Unit = percent. Cut-offs = below 66.495, 66.495 to below 67.559, 67.559 to below 68.522, 68.522 to below 73.299, 73.299 or above.

Map 4.18 Population aged 15-64 years of South Korea (share)

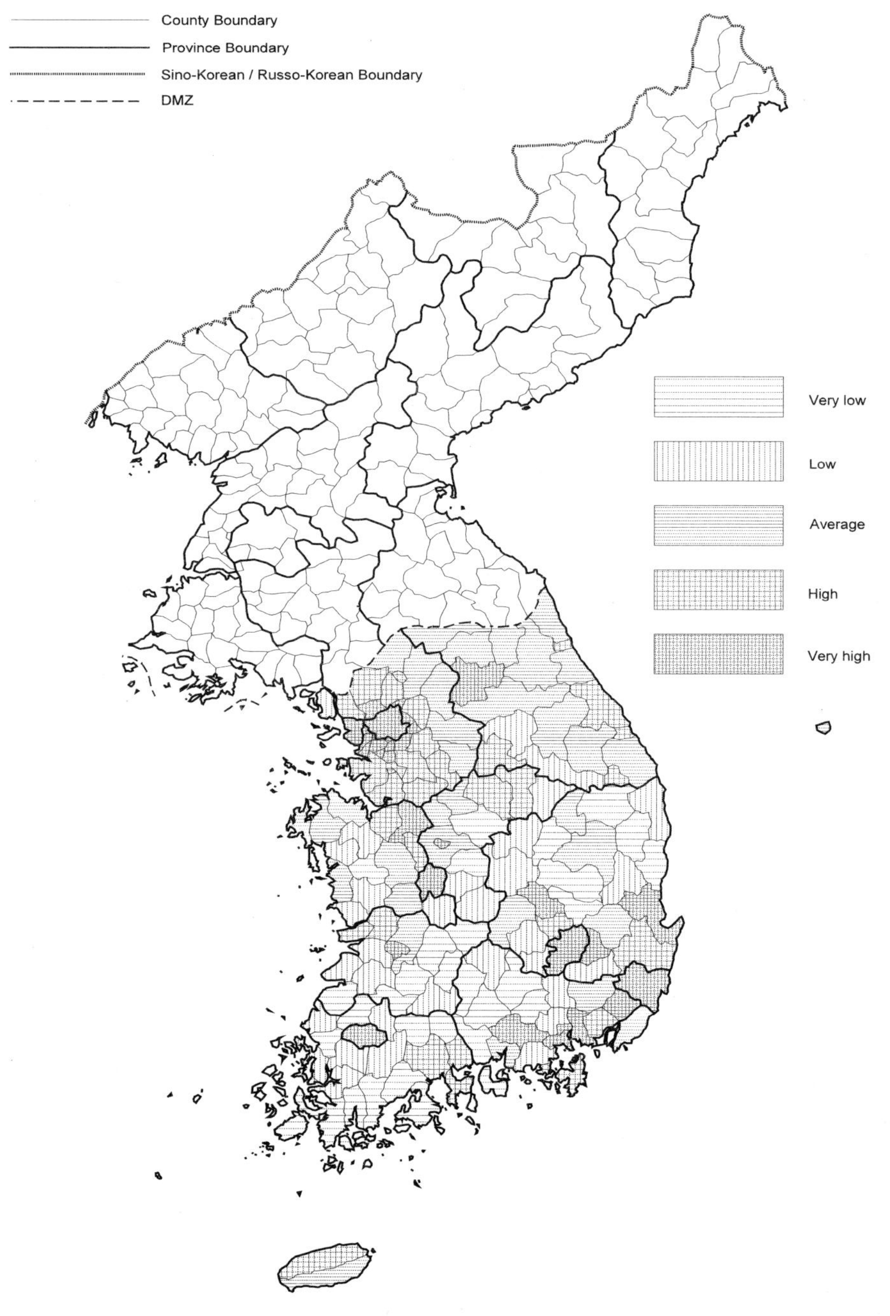

Notes: Unit = percent. Cut-offs = below 56.63, 56.63 to below 63.25, 63.25 to below 67.11, 67.11 to below 70.75, 70.75 or above.

Map 4.19 Population aged 65 and over of the Korean peninsula (share)

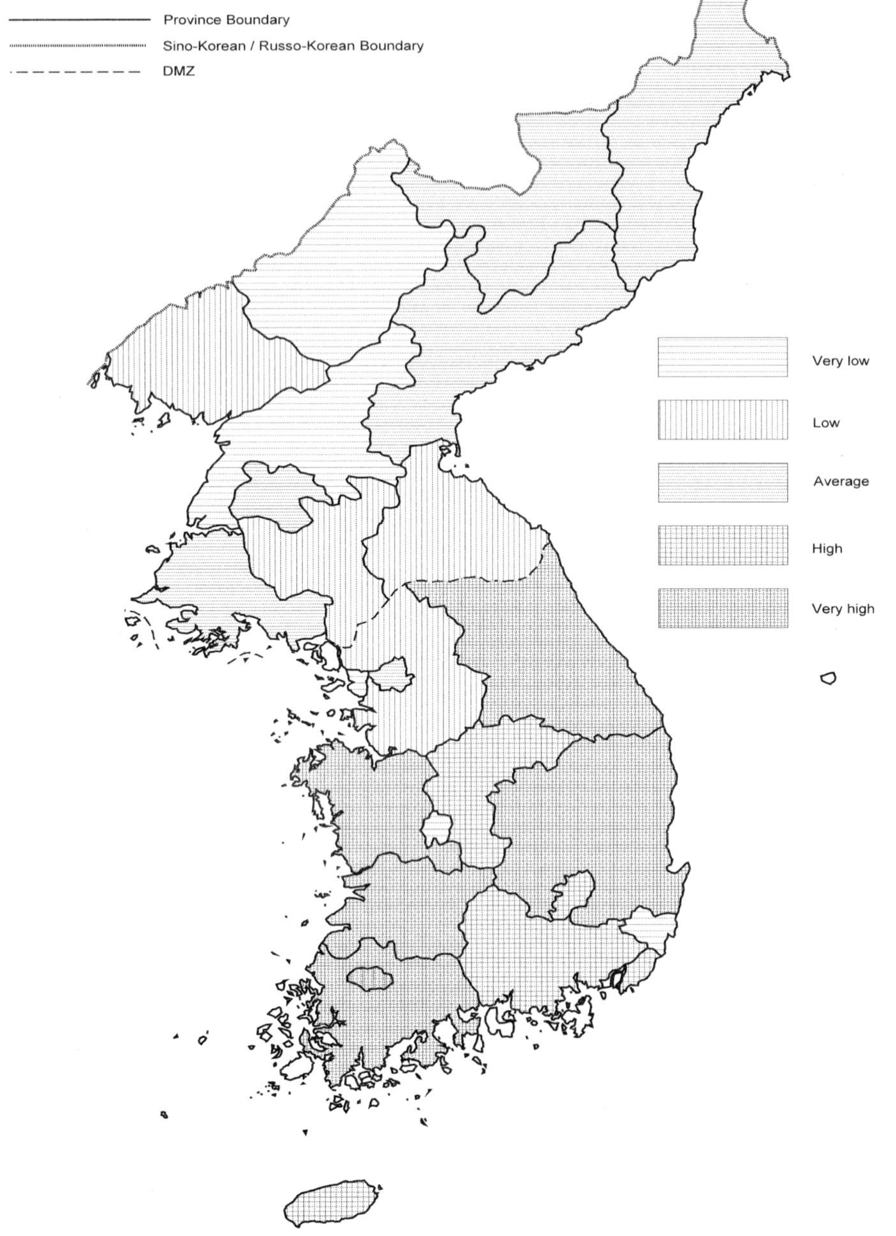

Notes: Unit = percent. Cut-offs = below 8.750, 8.750 to below 9.036, 9.036 to below 9.678, 9.678 to below 14.220, 14.220 or above.

Map 4.20 Population aged 65 and over of South Korea (share)

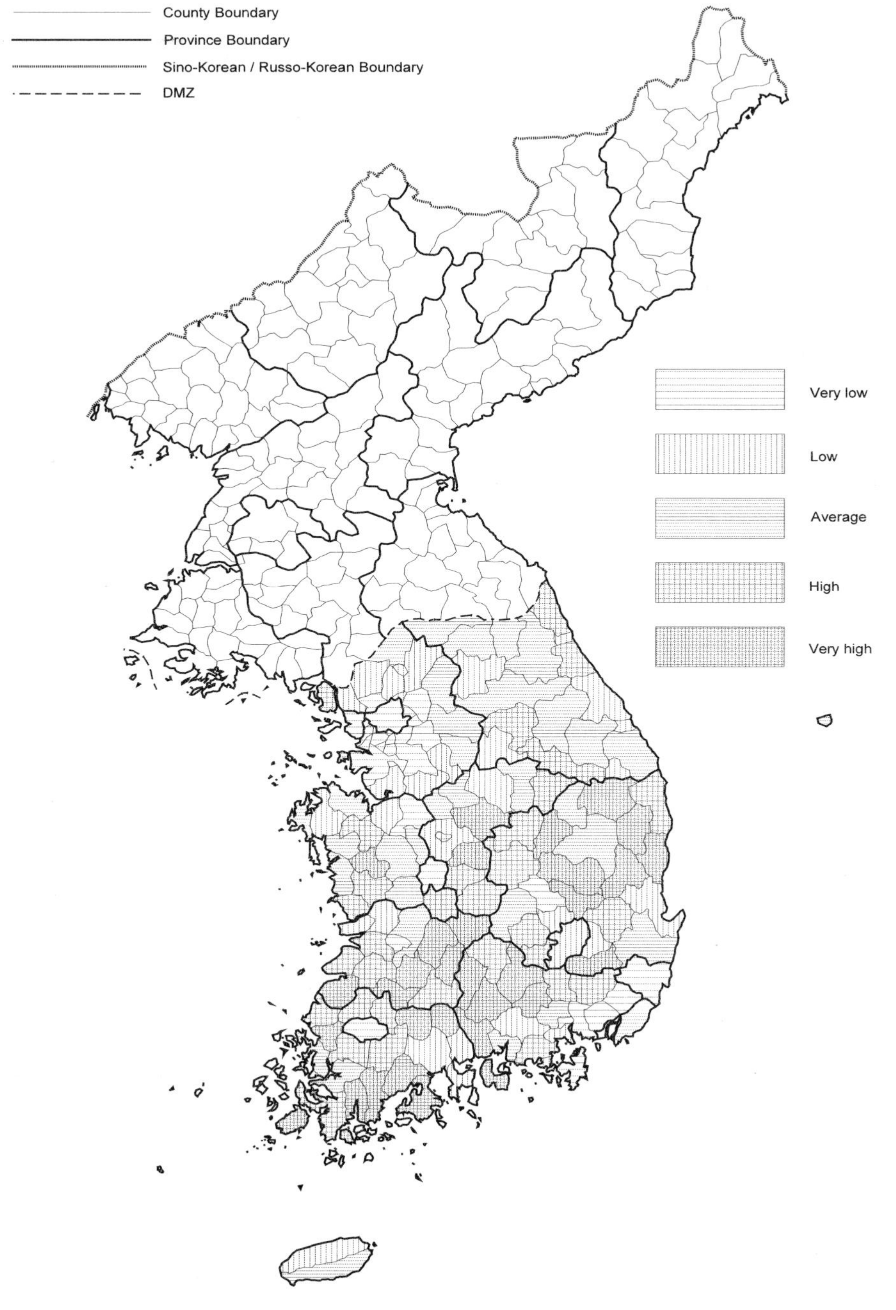

Notes: Unit = percent. Cut-offs = below 9.74, 9.74 to below 15.60, 15.60 to below 22.42, 22.42 to below 30.69, 30.69 or above.

5. Educational Status

Map 5.1 Elementary school graduates of South Korea

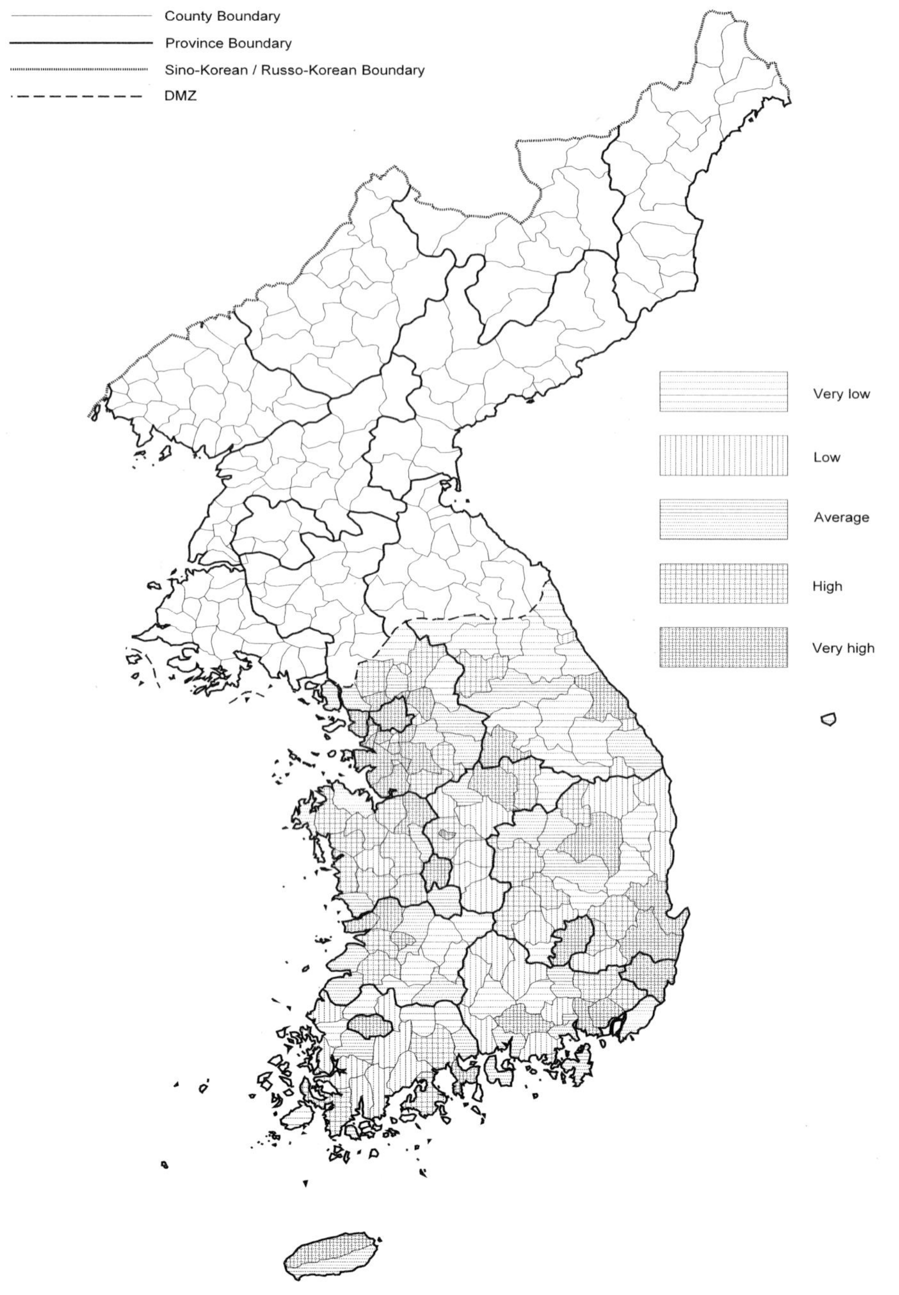

Notes: Unit = persons. Data pertain to people aged 6 years and over. Cut-offs = below 7193.3, 7193.3 to below 9917.1, 9917.1 to below 14762.9, 14762.9 to below 23139.4, 23139.4 or above.

Map 5.2 Middle school graduates of the Korean peninsula

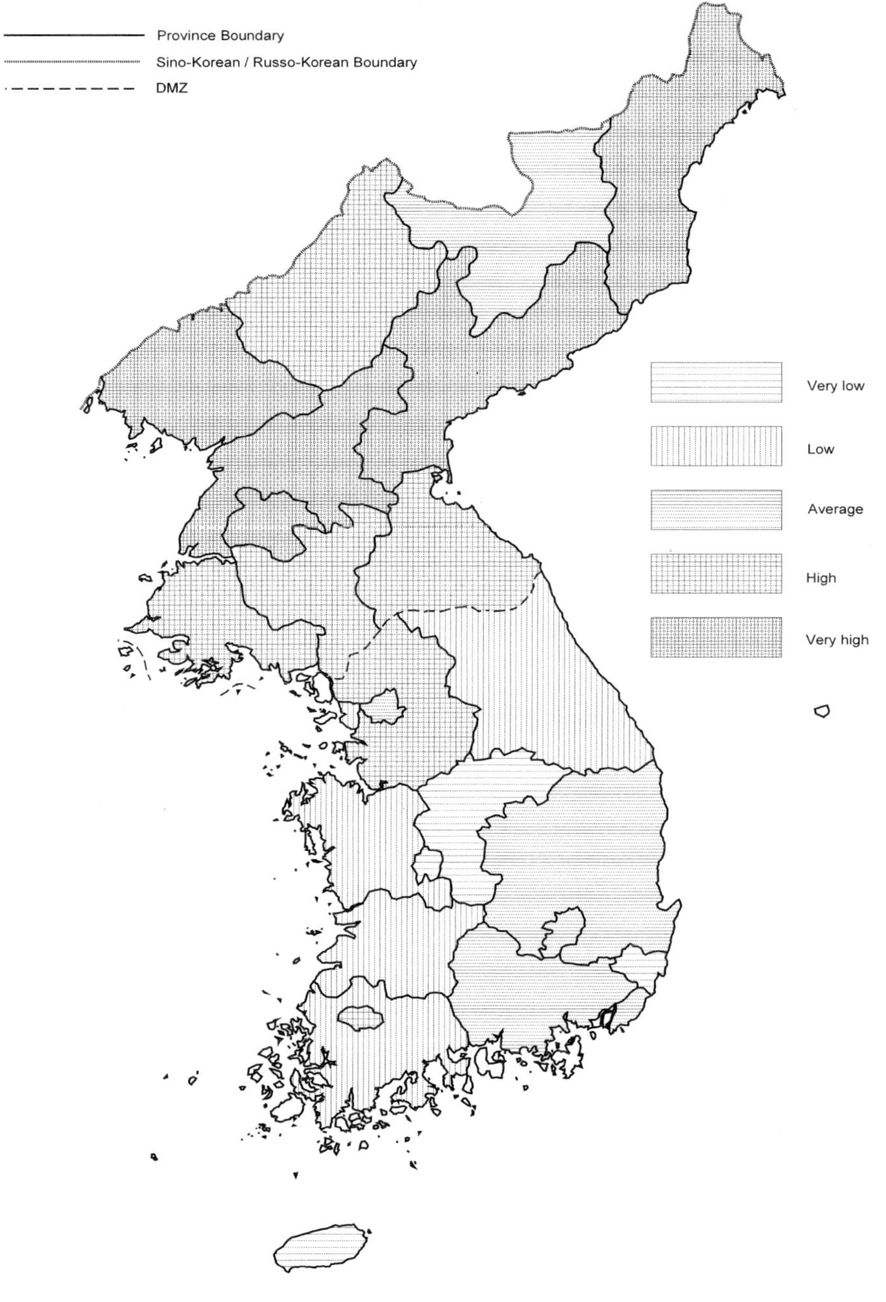

Notes: Unit = persons. Data pertain to people aged 6 years and over in South Korea and 5 years and over in North Korea. Cut-offs = below 113748.7, 113748.7 to below 181382.4, 181382.4 to below 566480.9, 566480.9 to below 1298019.1, 1298019.1 or above.

Map 5.3 Middle school graduates of South Korea

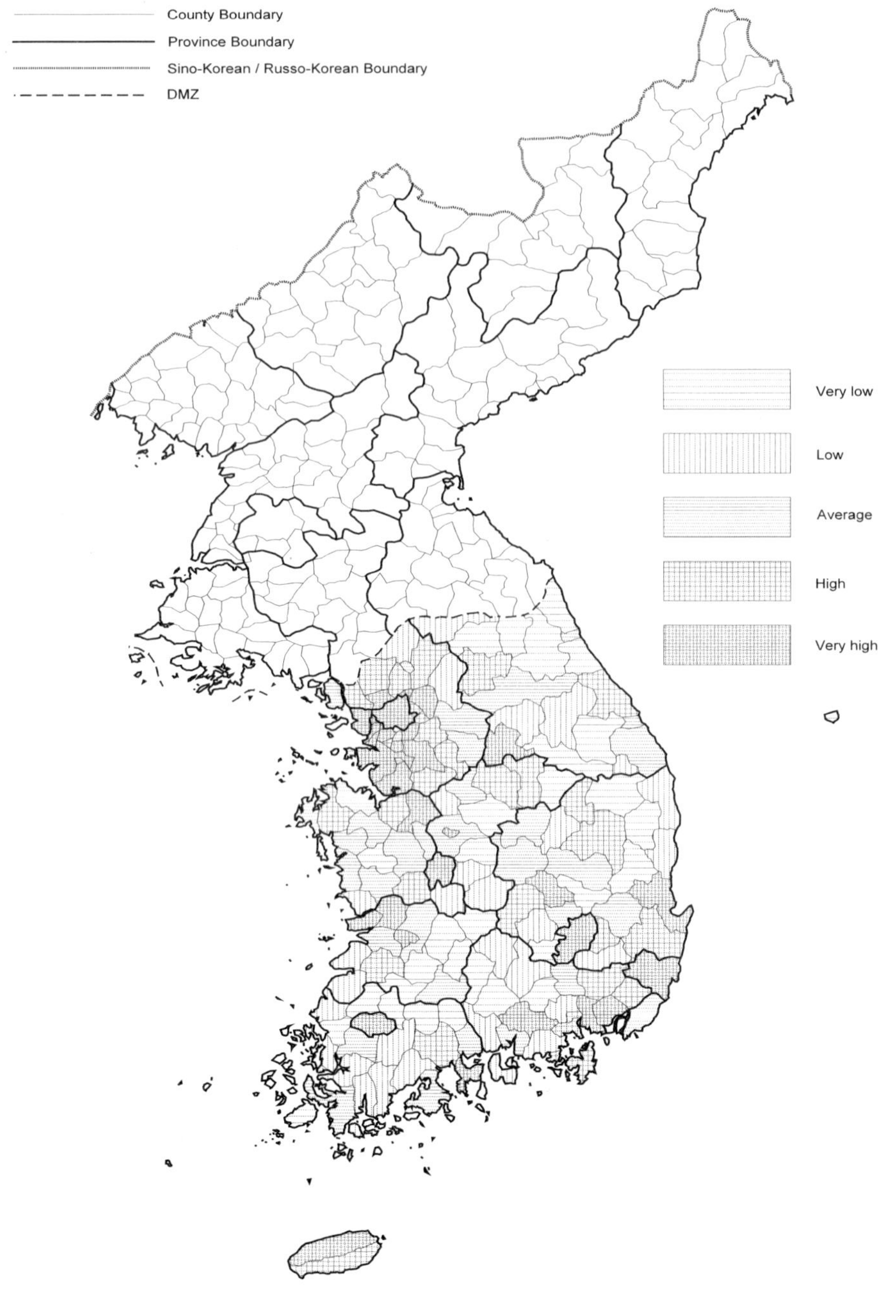

Notes: Unit = persons. Data pertain to people aged 6 years and over in South Korea and 5 years and over in North Korea. Cut-offs = below 3657.0, 3657.0 to below 5651.0, 5651.0 to below 9802.5, 9802.5 to below 19642.0, 19642.0 or above.

Map 5.4 High school graduates of South Korea

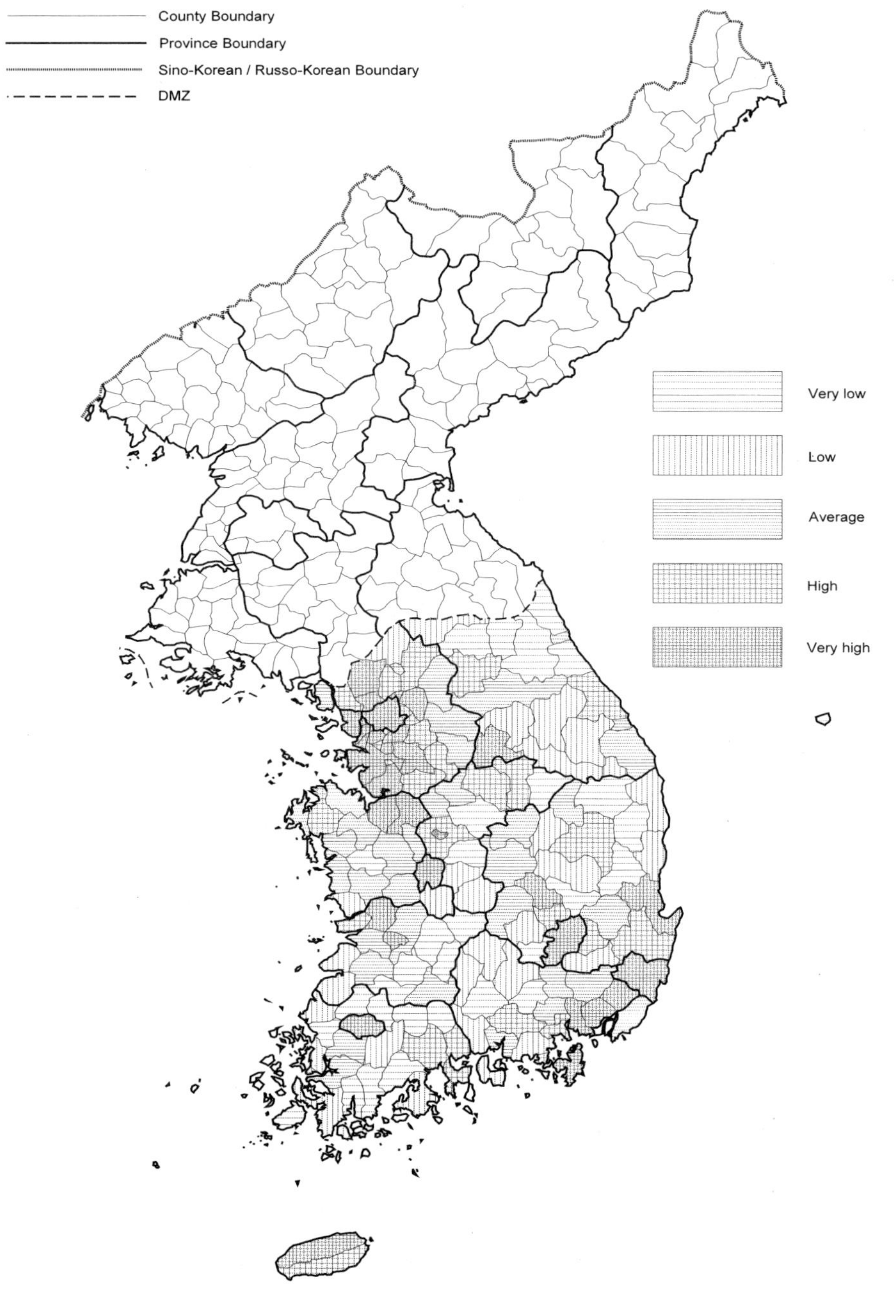

Notes: Unit = persons. Data pertain to people aged 6 years and over. Cut-offs = below 7047.2, 7047.2 to below 12226.0, 12226.0 to below 29740.3, 29740.3 to below 69343.9, 69343.9 or above.

Map 5.5 College or university graduates of the Korean peninsula

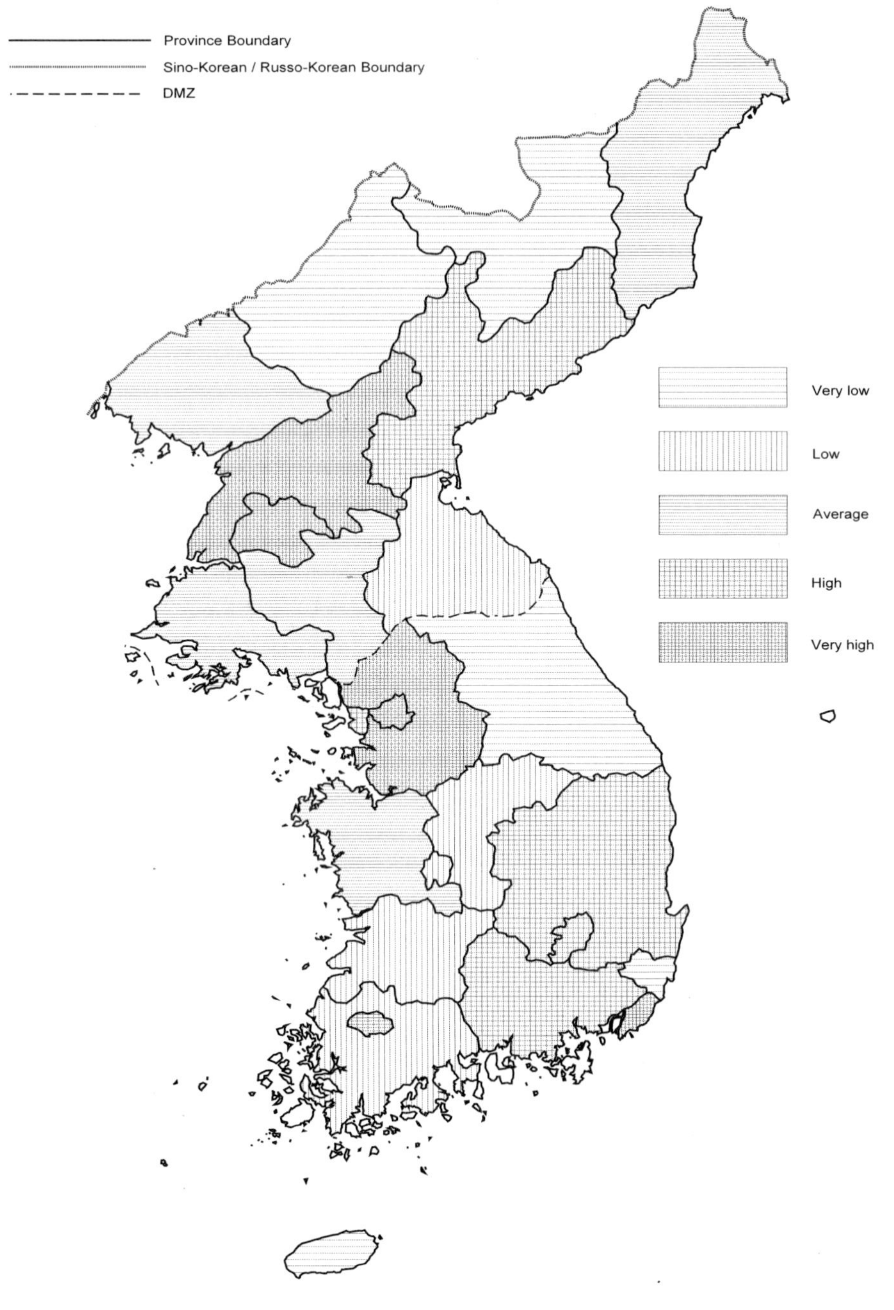

Notes: Unit = persons. Data pertain to people aged 6 years and over in South Korea and 5 years and over in North Korea. Cut-offs = below 103703.2, 103703.2 to below 136116.0, 136116.0 to below 191565.3, 191565.3 to below 271938.1, 271938.1 or above.

Map 5.6 College or university graduates of South Korea

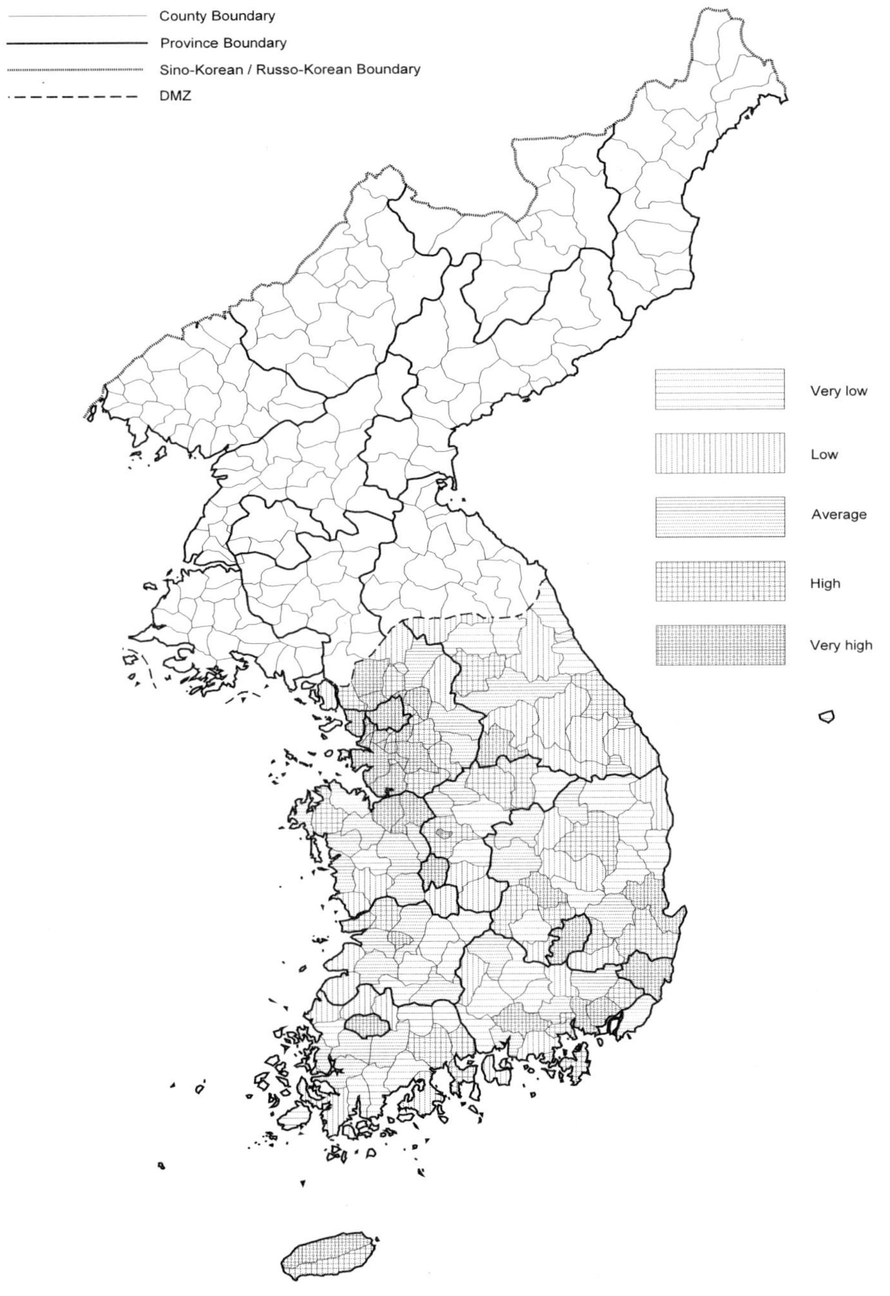

Notes: Unit = persons. Data pertain to people aged 6 years and over. Cut-offs = below 1949.5, 1949.5 to below 3405.5, 3405.5 to below 8906.5, 8906.5 to below 23857.5, 23857.5 or above.

Map 5.7 Population holding no formal education of the Korean peninsula

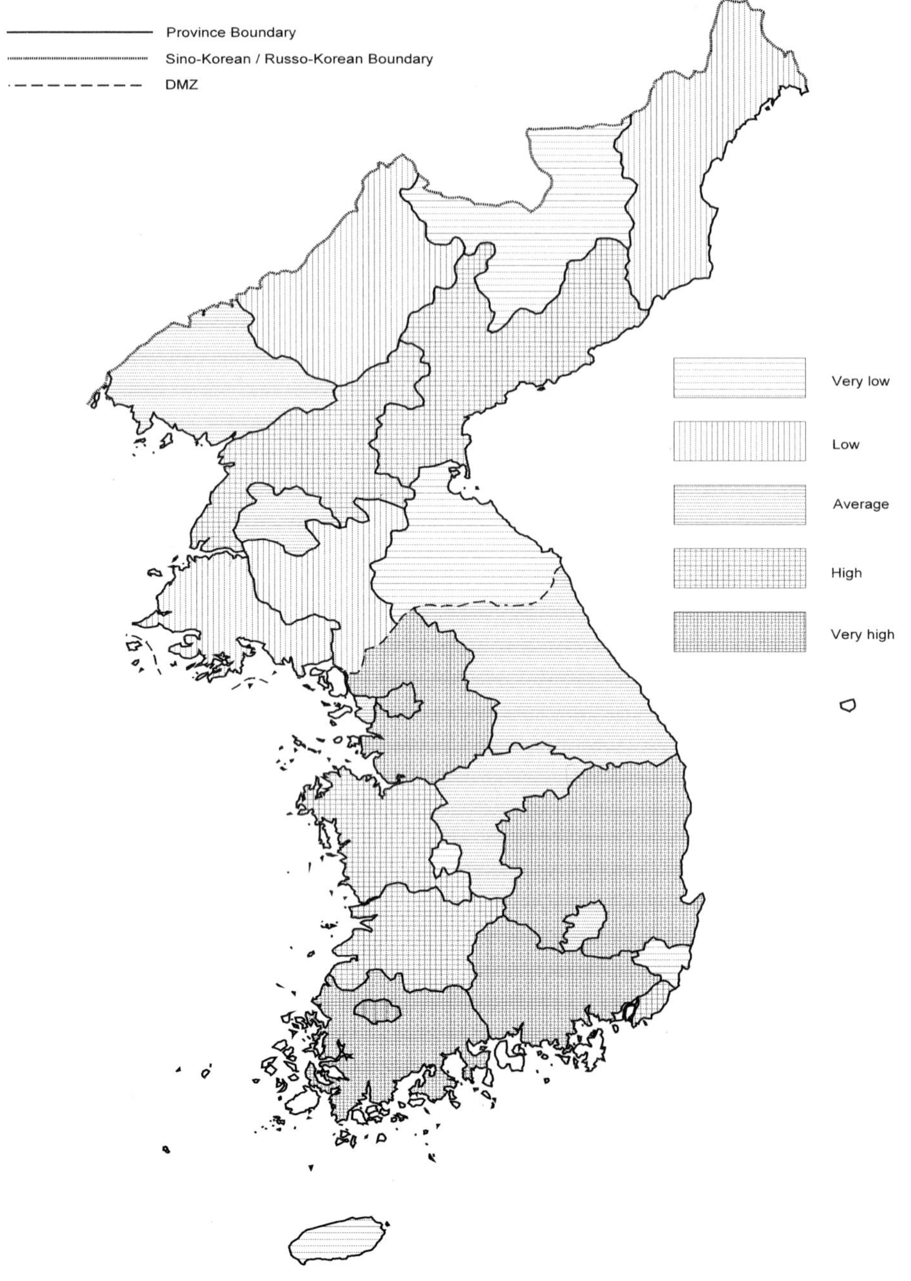

Notes: Unit = persons. Data pertain to people aged 6 years and over in South Korea and 5 years and over in North Korea. Cut-offs = below 47731.2, 47731.2 to below 77846.4, 77846.4 to below 103262.1, 103262.1 to below 147514.7, 147514.7 or above.

Map 5.8 Population holding no formal education of South Korea

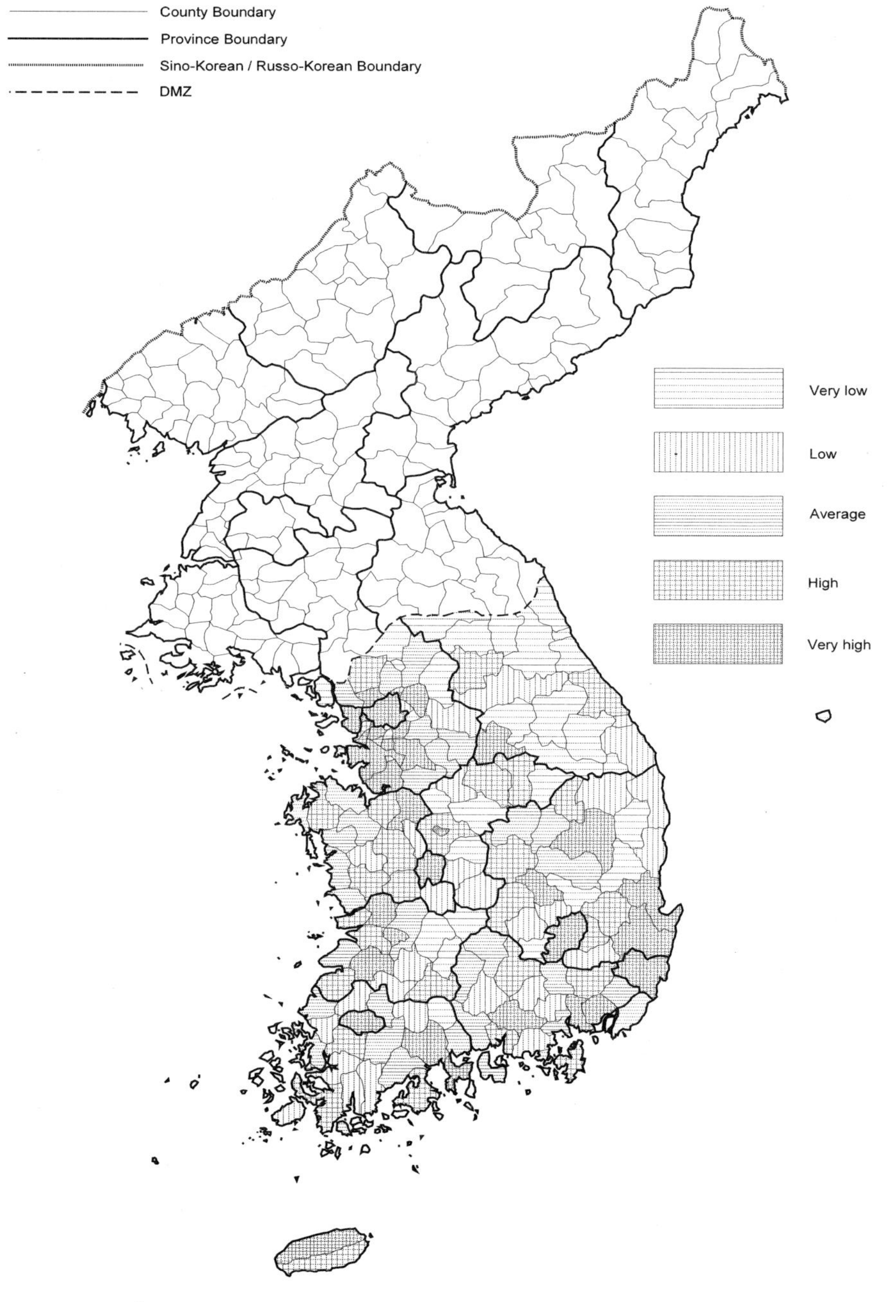

Notes: Unit = persons. Data pertain to people aged 6 years and over. Cut-offs = below 4602.5, 4602.5 to below 6461.0, 6461.0 to below 8919.5, 8919.5 to below 12466.0, 12466.0 or above.

Map 5.9 Middle school graduates of the Korean peninsula (share)

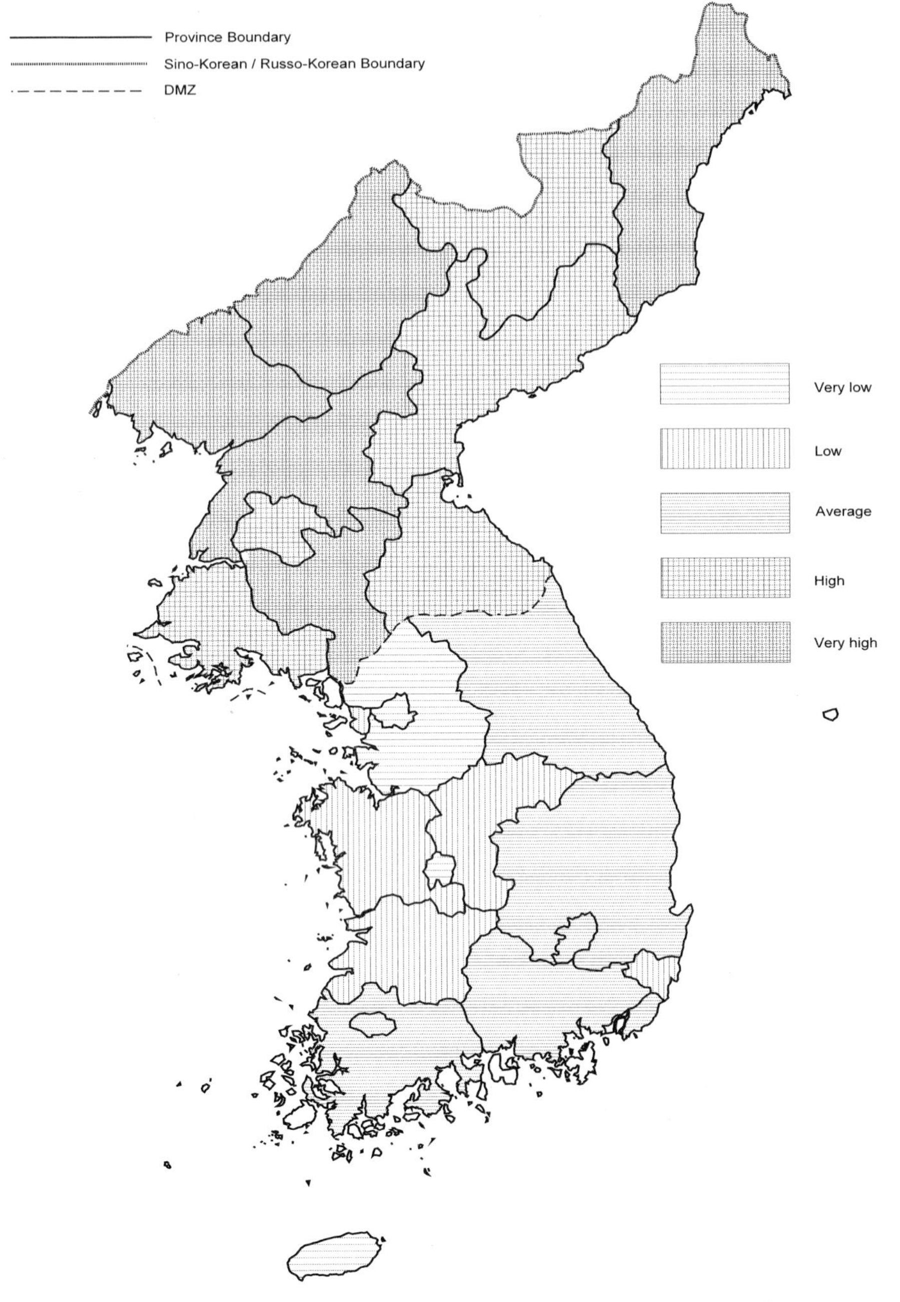

Notes: Unit = percent. Data pertain to people aged 6 years and over in South Korea and 5 years and over in North Korea. Cut-offs = below 7.10, 7.10 to below 7.87, 7.87 to below 13.17, 13.17 to below 60.41, 60.41 or above.

Map 5.10 Middle school graduates of South Korea (share)

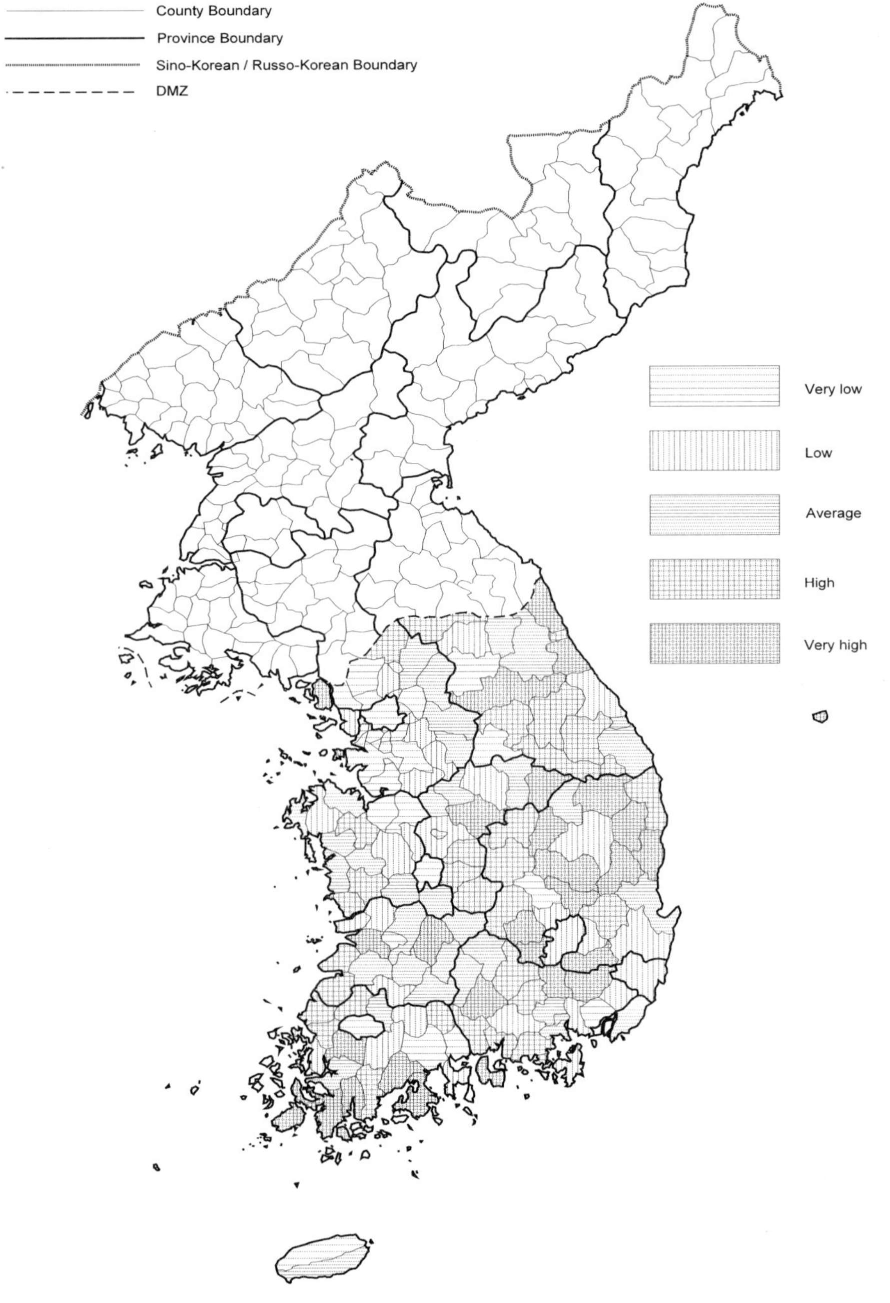

Notes: Unit = percent. Data pertain to people aged 6 years and over. Cut-offs = below 6.97, 6.97 to below 8.58, 8.58 to below 9.68, 9.68 to below 10.93, 10.93 or above.

Map 5.11 College or university graduates of the Korean peninsula (share)

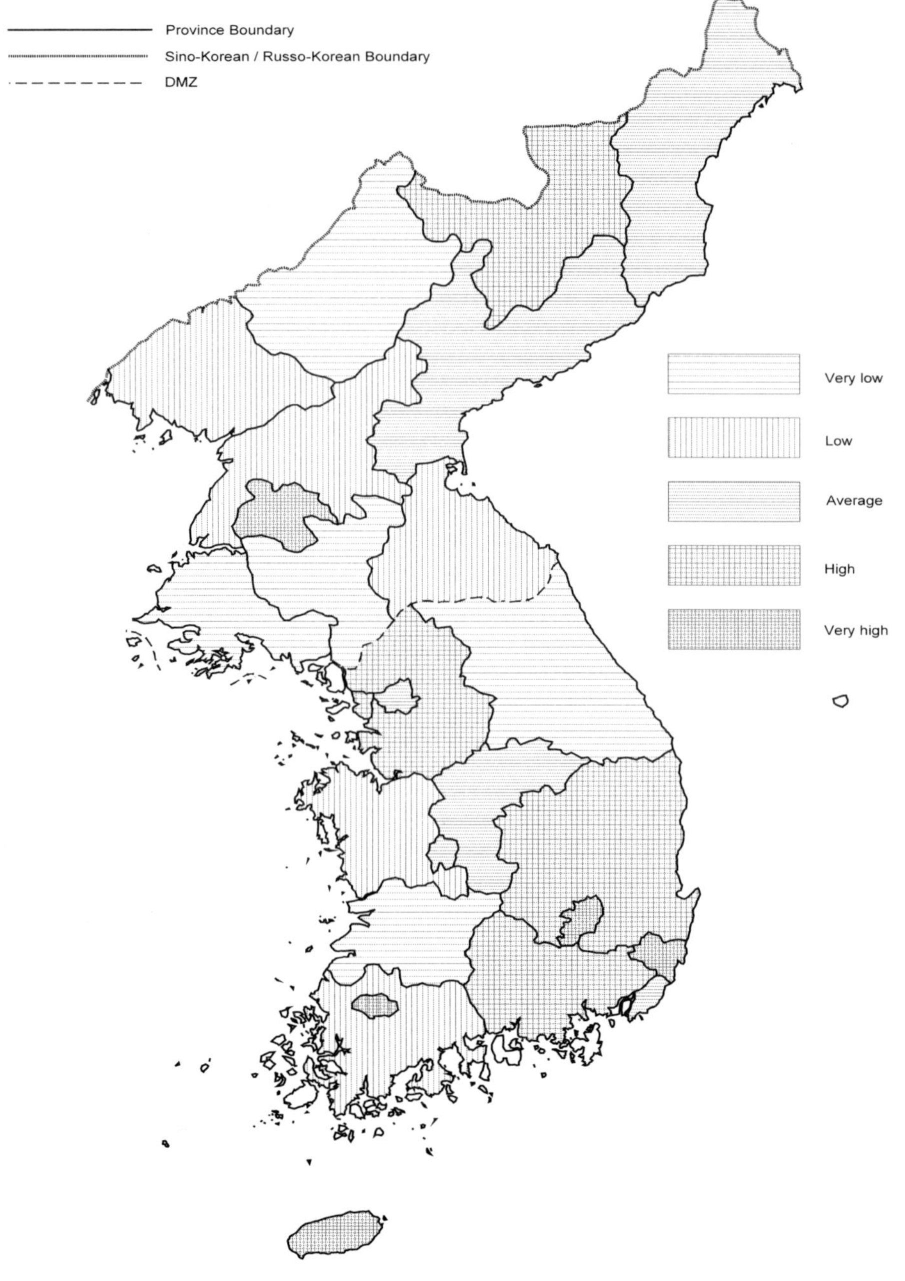

Notes: Unit = percent. Data pertain to people aged 6 years and over in South Korea and 5 years and over in North Korea. Cut-offs = below 7.391, 7.391 to below 7.876, 7.876 to below 8.835, 8.835 to below 9.663, 9.663 or above.

Map 5.12 College or university graduates of South Korea (share)

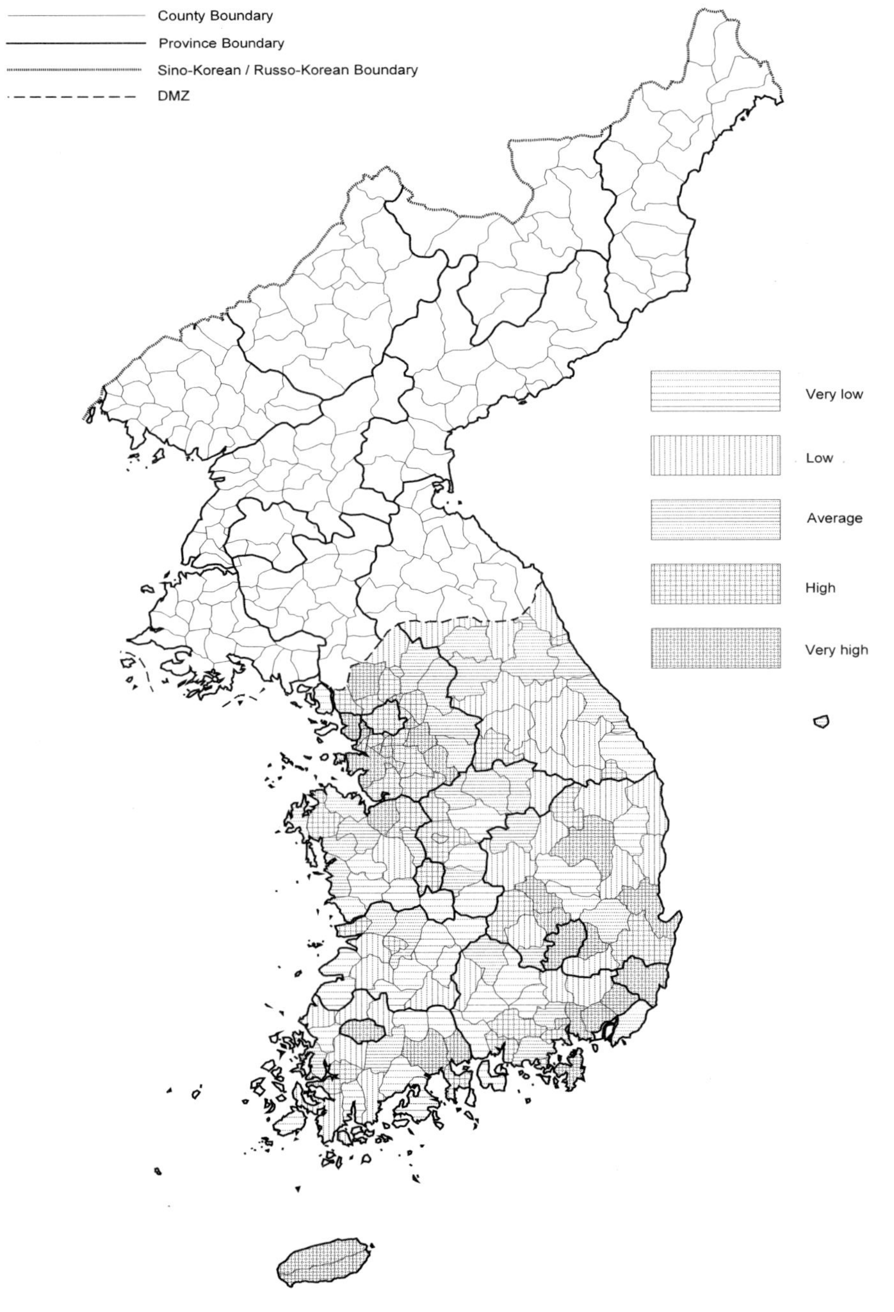

Notes: Unit = percent. Data pertain to people aged 6 years and over. Cut-offs = below 5.090, 5.090 to below 6.379, 6.379 to below 7.802, 7.802 to below 9.431, 9.431 or above.

Map 5.13 Population holding no formal education of the Korean peninsula (share)

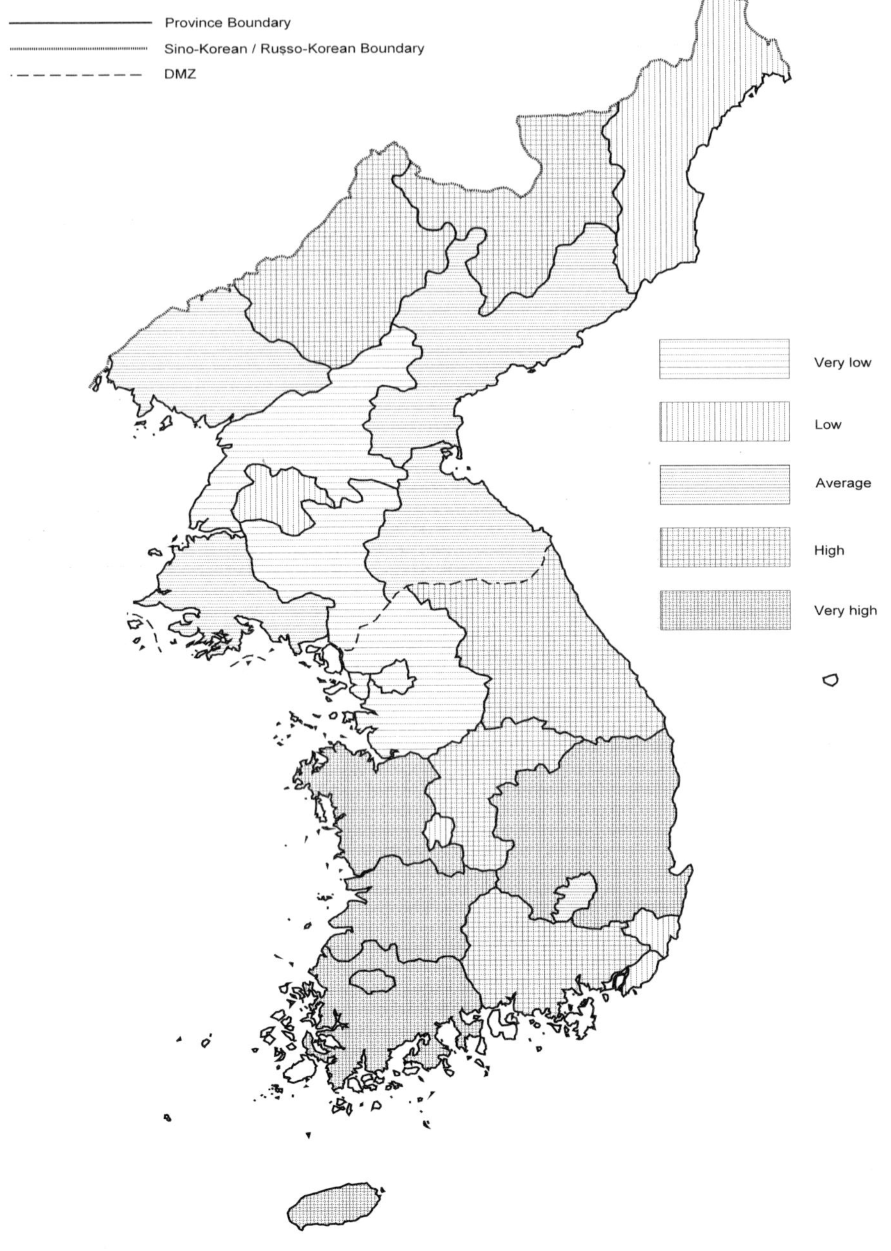

Notes: Unit = percent. Data pertain to people aged 6 years and over in South Korea and 5 years and over in North Korea. Cut-offs = below 3.220, 3.220 to below 3.437, 3.437 to below 3.789, 3.789 to below 6.416, 6.416 or above.

Map 5.14 Population holding no formal education of South Korea (share)

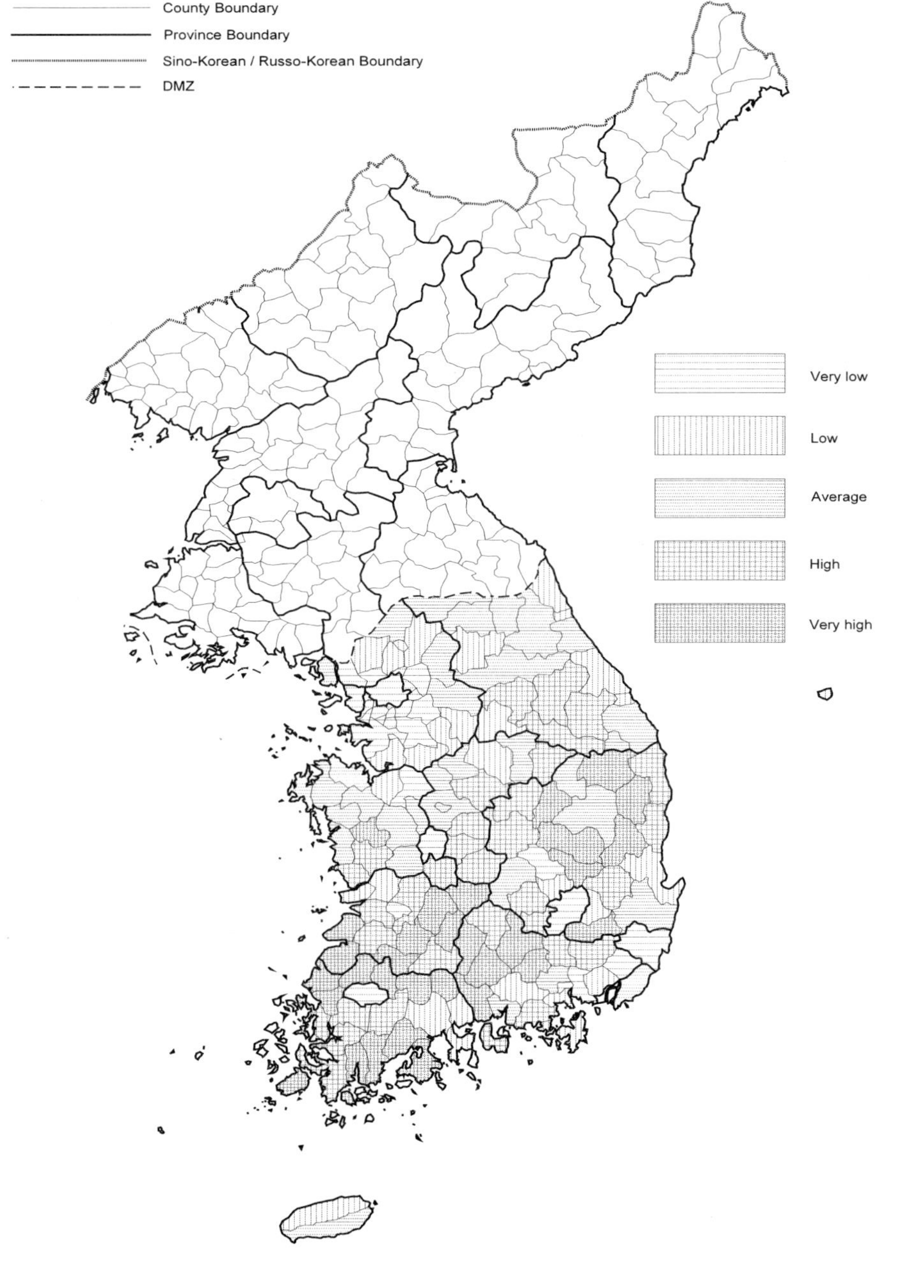

Notes: Unit = percent. Data pertain to people aged 6 years and over. Cut-offs = below 3.77, 3.77 to below 7.17, 7.17 to below 10.71, 10.71 to below 15.61, 15.61 or above.

6. Marital Status

Map 6.1 Never married population of South Korea

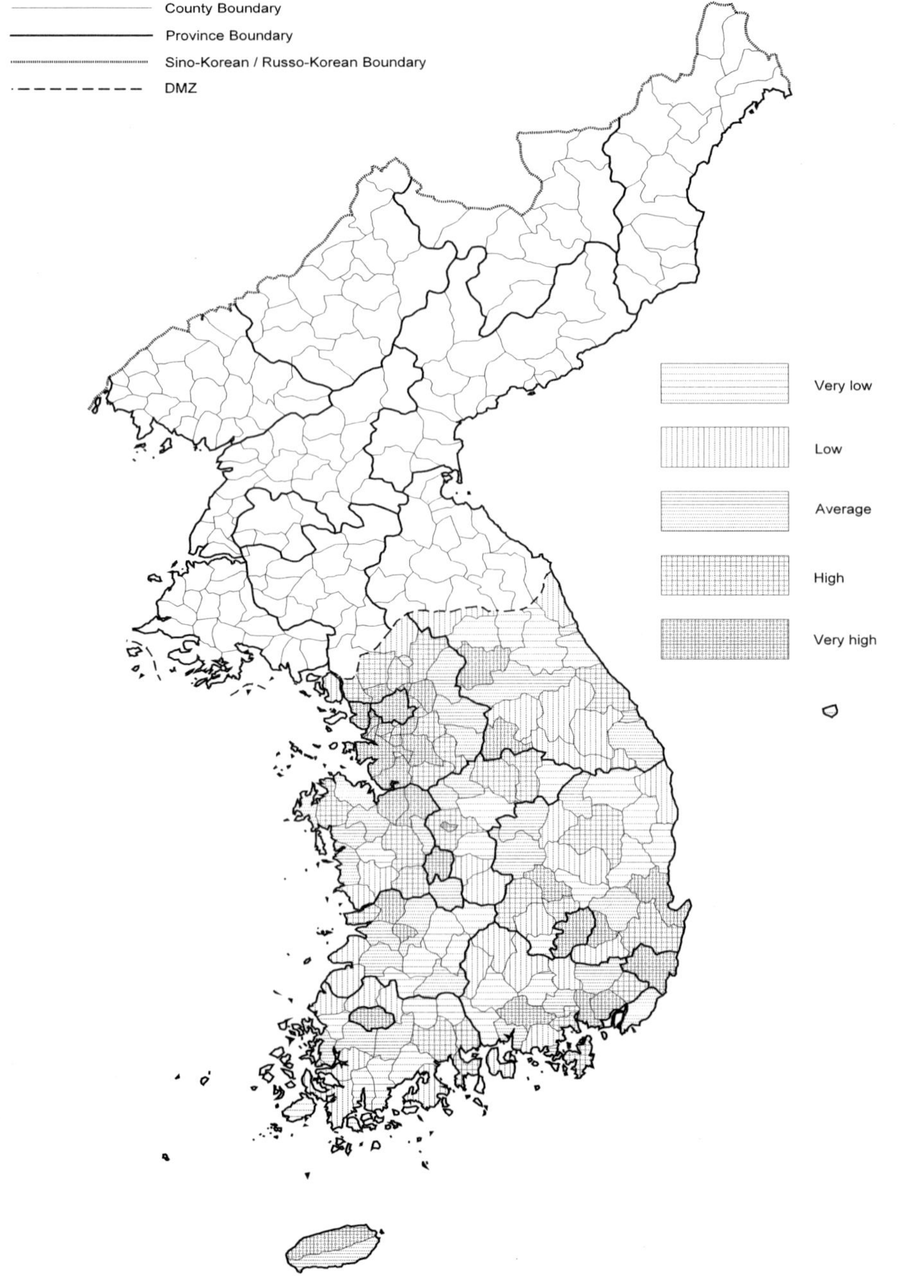

Notes: Unit = persons. Data pertain to people aged 15 years and older. Cut-offs = below 5458.2, 5458.2 to below 10393.0, 10393.0 to below 25346.1, 25346.1 to below 74106.2, 74106.2 or above.

Map 6.2 Married population of the Korean peninsula

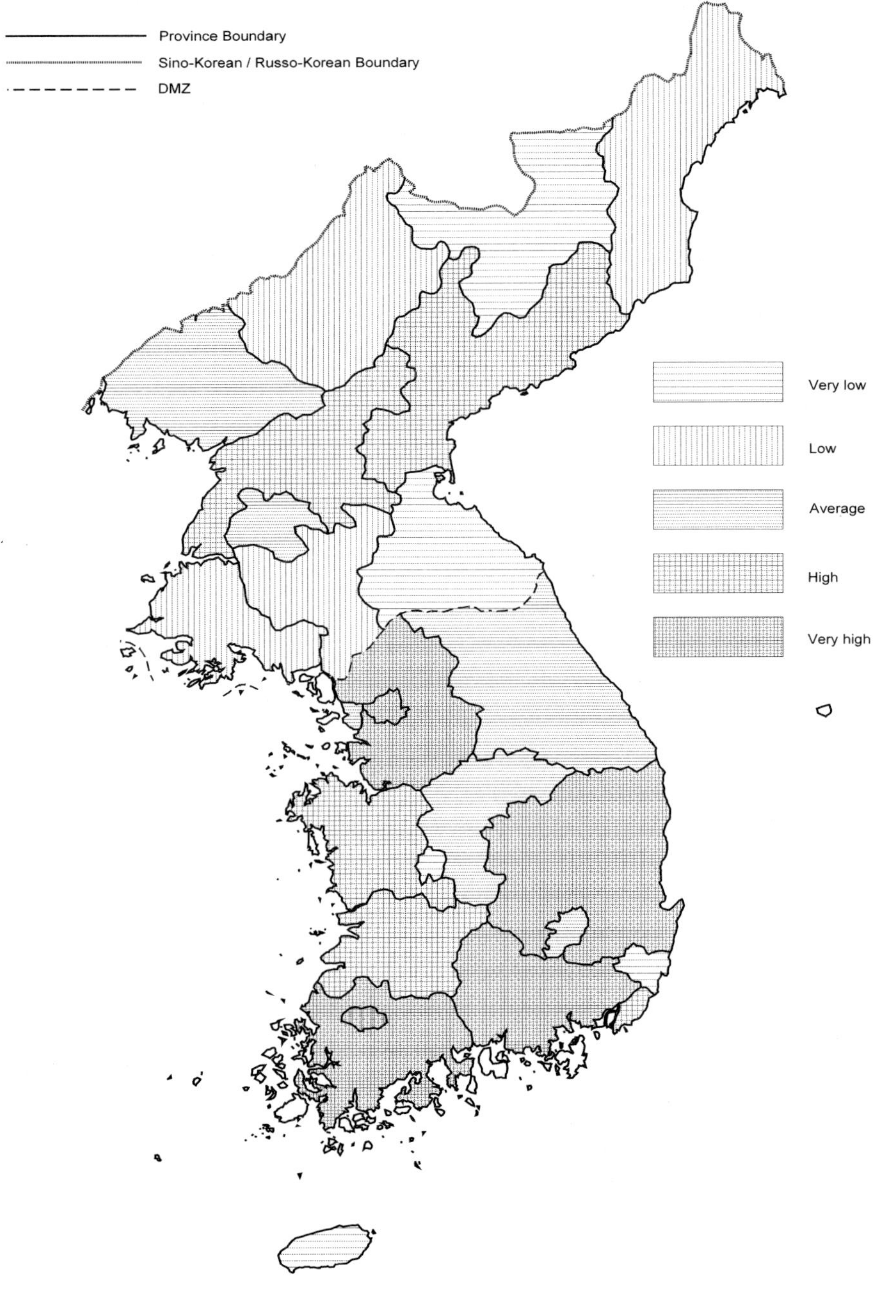

Notes: Unit = persons. Data pertain to people aged 15 years and older. Cut-offs = below 47731.2, 47731.2 to below 77846.4, 77846.4 to below 103262.1, 103262.1 to below 147514.7, 147514.7 or above.

Map 6.3 Married population of South Korea

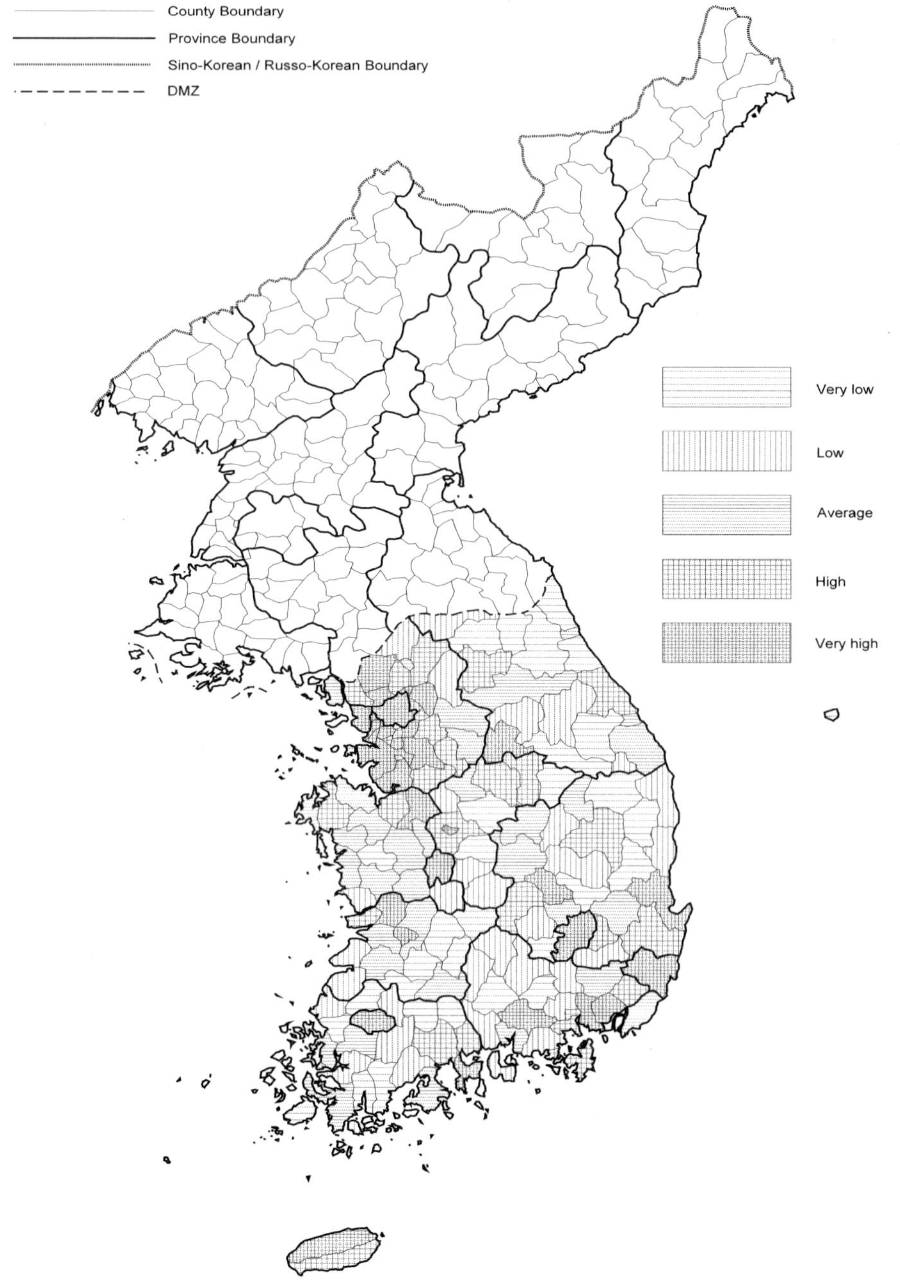

Notes: Unit = persons. Data pertain to people aged 15 years and older. Cut-offs = below 20112.5, 20112.5 to below 31078.0, 31078.0 to below 61891.0, 61891.0 to below 136359.5, 136359.5 or above.

Map 6.4 Widowed population of the Korean peninsula

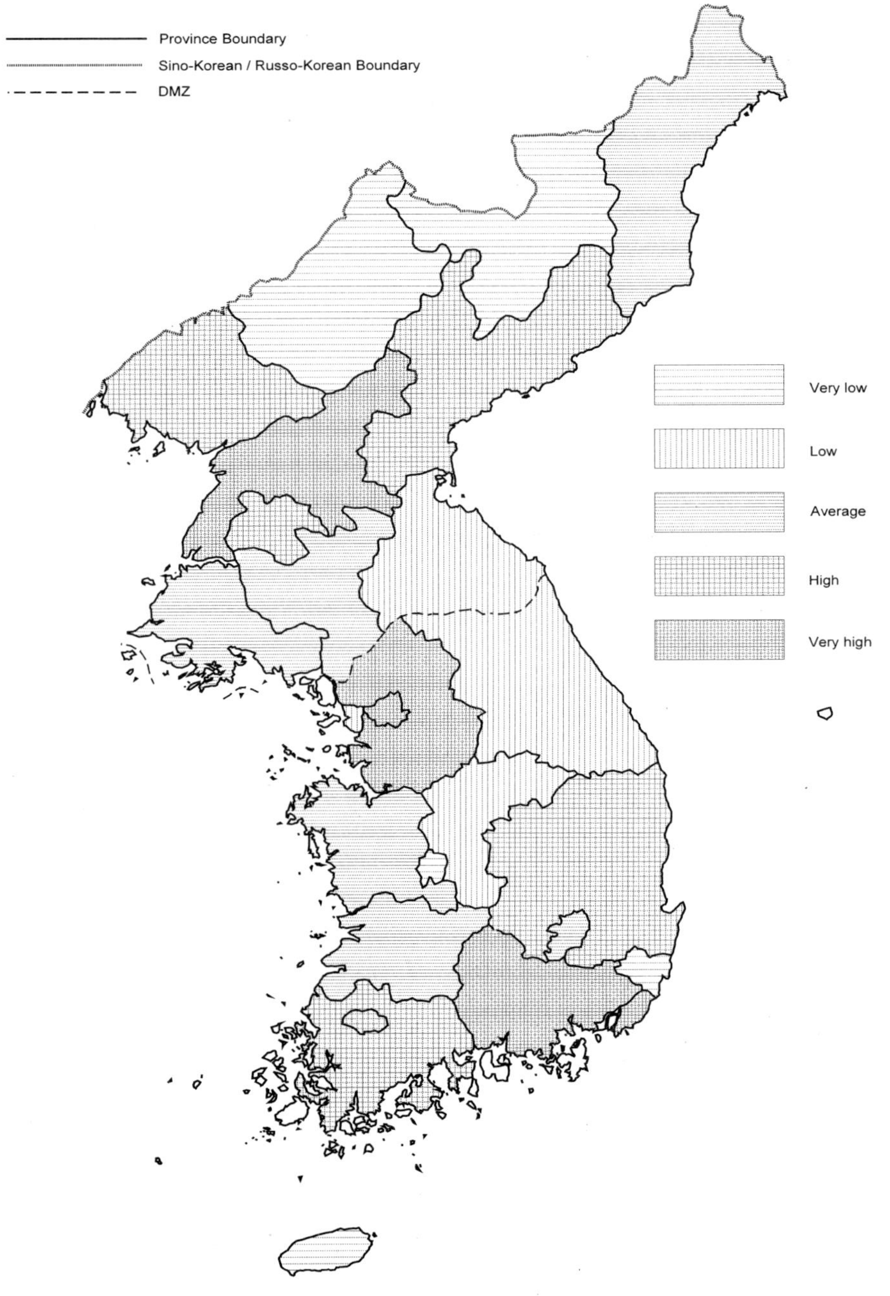

Notes: Unit = persons. Data pertain to people aged 15 years and older. Cut-offs = below 82202.2, 82202.2 to below 152708.7, 152708.7 to below 167396.4, 167396.4 to below 241346.9, 241346.9 or above.

Map 6.5 Widowed population of South Korea

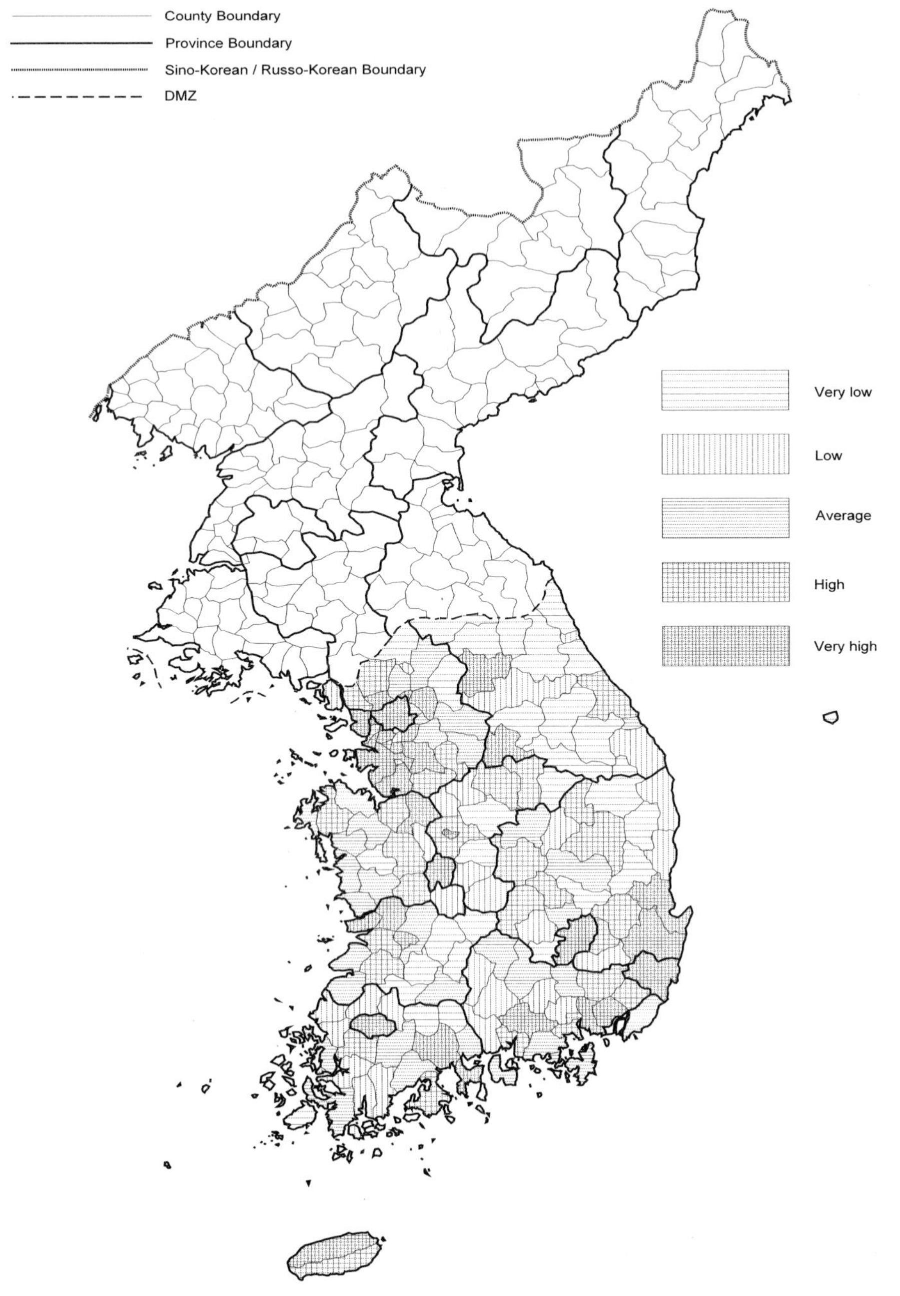

Notes: Unit = persons. Data pertain to people aged 15 years and older. Cut-offs = below 5025.0, 5025.0 to below 7356.5, 7356.5 to below 10951.0, 10951.0 to below 18371.5, 18371.5 or above.

Map 6.6 Divorced population of the Korean peninsula

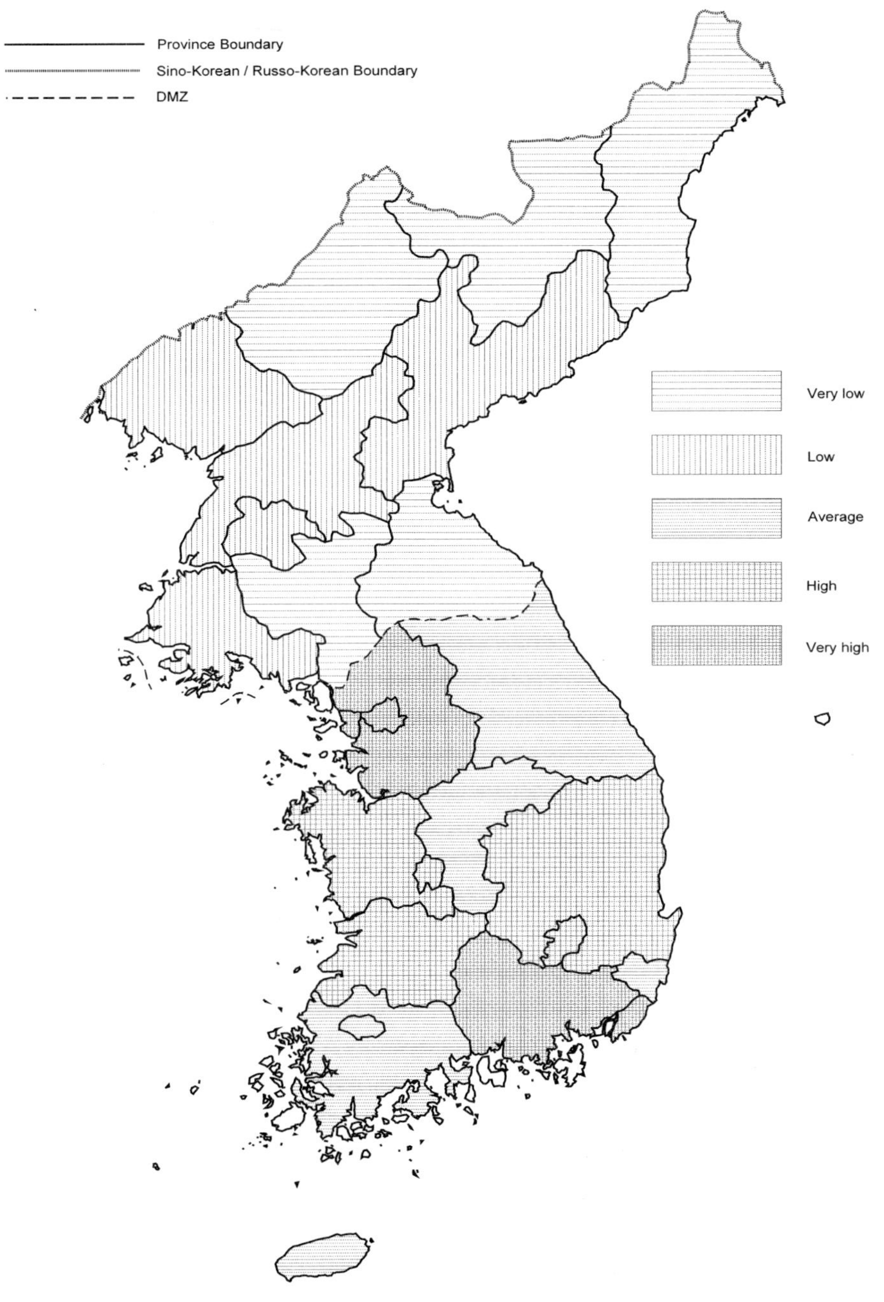

Notes: Unit = persons. Data pertain to people aged 15 years and older. North Korean data pertain to 'separated', a term that is not further explained but likely means the same as divorce. Cut-offs = below 7509.5, 7509.5 to below 20502.9, 20502.9 to below 48387.2, 48387.2 to below 89113.0, 89113.0 or above.

Map 6.7 Divorced population of South Korea

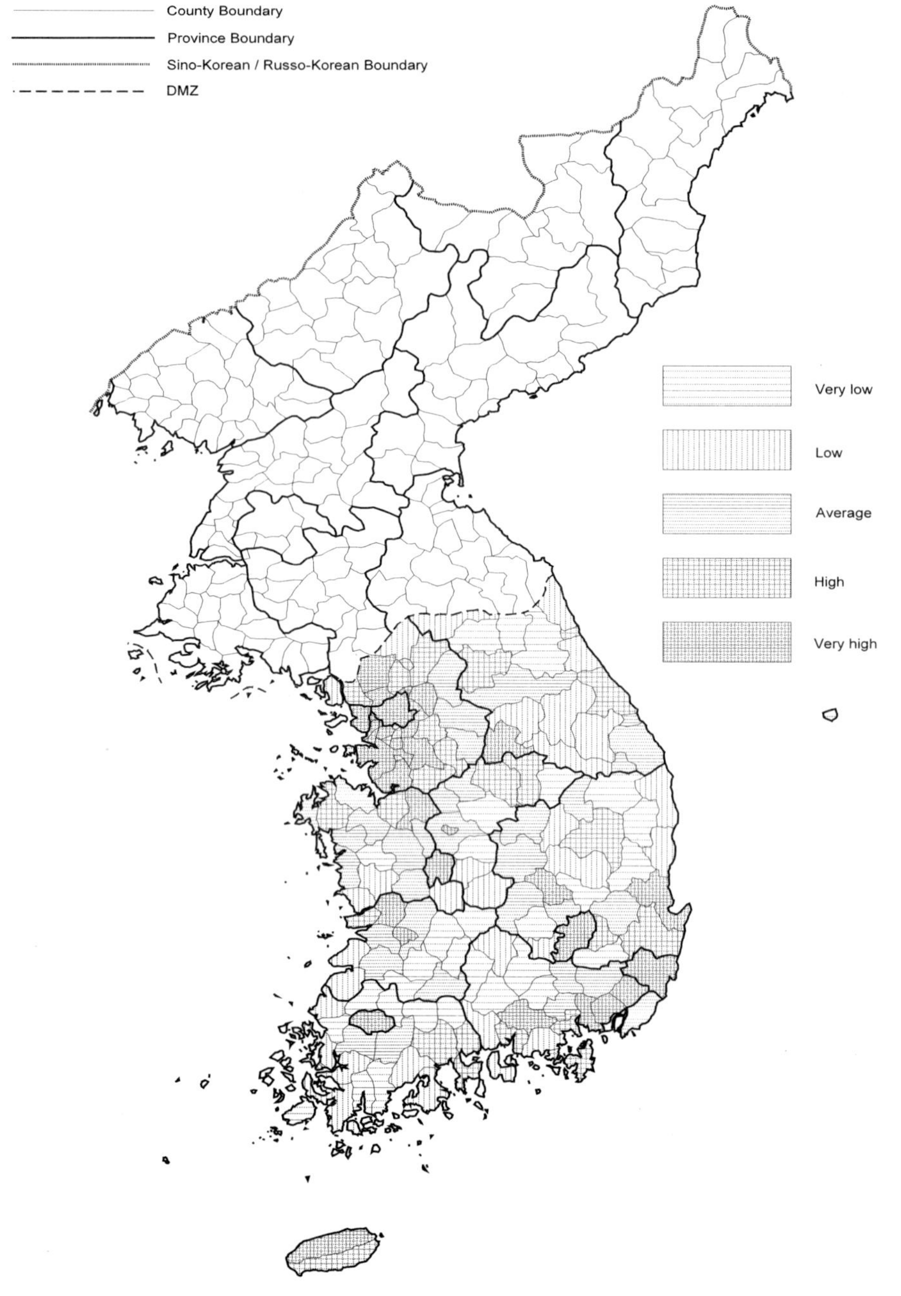

Notes: Unit = persons. Data pertain to people aged 15 years and older. Cut-offs = below 766.0, 766.0 to below 1443.0, 1443.0 to below 3384.0, 3384.0 to below 9014.0, 9014.0 or above.

Map 6.8 Male never married population of South Korea

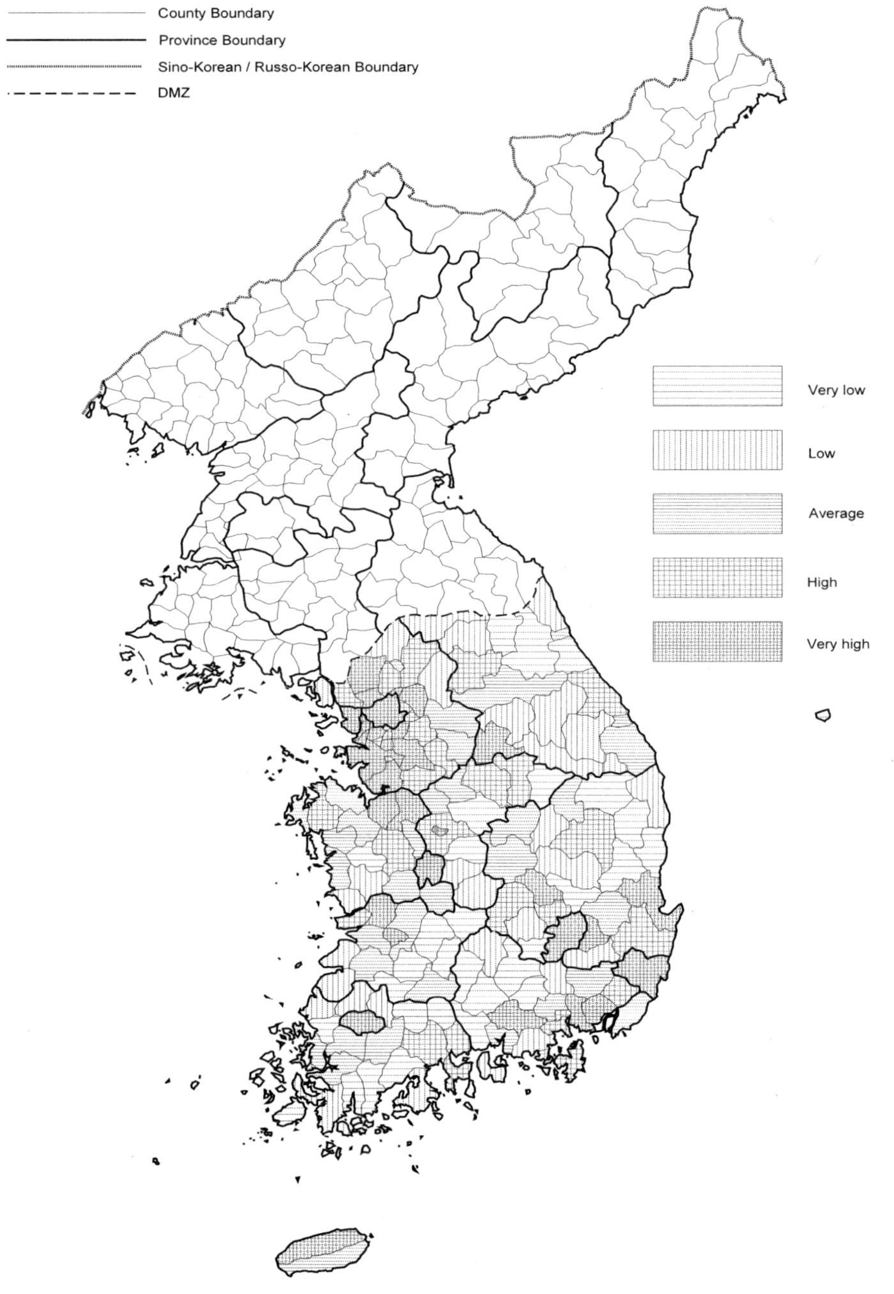

Notes: Unit = persons. Data pertain to people aged 15 years and older. Cut-offs = below 3611.9, 3611.9 to below 6619.1, 6619.1 to below 15430.9, 15430.9 to below 43352.6, 43352.6 or above.

Map 6.9 Male married population of South Korea

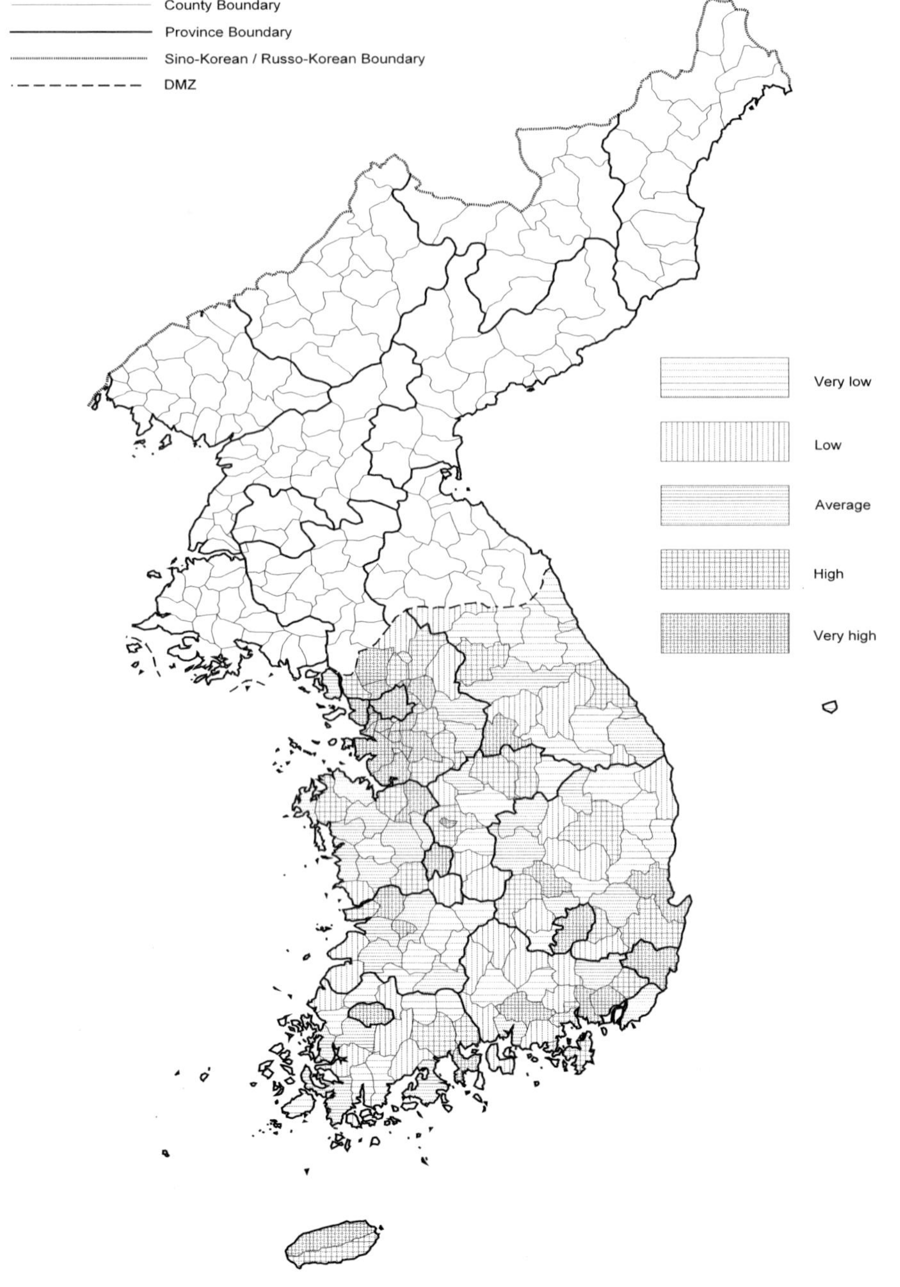

Notes: Unit = persons. Data pertain to people aged 15 years and older. Cut-offs = below 10369.6, 10369.6 to below 15948.1, 15948.1 to below 29991.9, 29991.9 to below 66314.8, 66314.8 or above.

Map 6.10 Male widowed population of South Korea

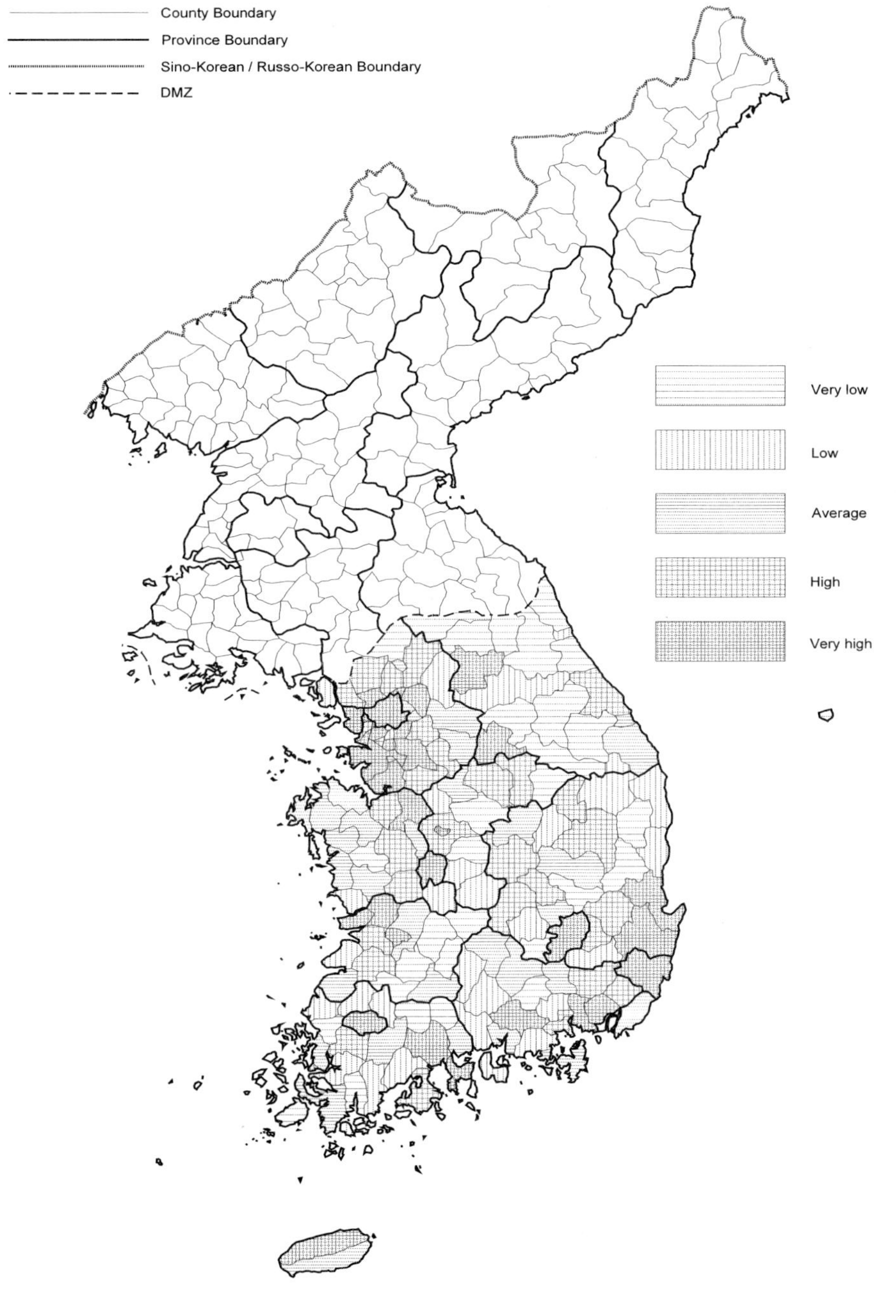

Notes: Unit = persons. Data pertain to people aged 15 years and older. Cut-offs = below 739.5, 739.5 to below 1004.4, 1004.4 to below 1540.8, 1540.8 to below 2638.9, 2638.9 or above.

Map 6.11 Male divorced population of South Korea

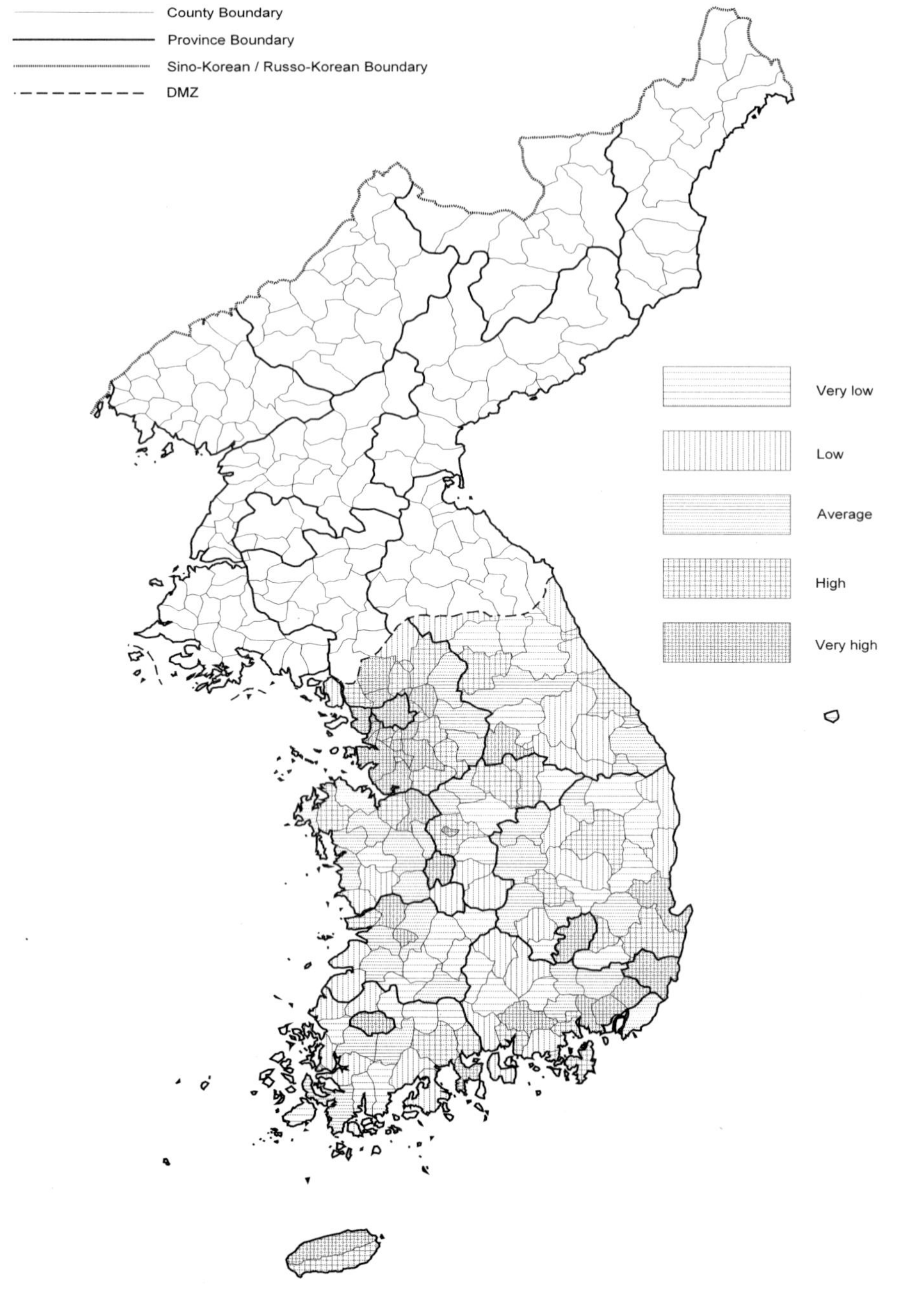

Notes: Unit = persons. Data pertain to people aged 15 years and older. Cut-offs = below 482.0, 482.0 to below 845.2, 845.2 to below 1771.4, 1771.4 to below 4256.7, 4256.7 or above.

Map 6.12 Female never married population of South Korea

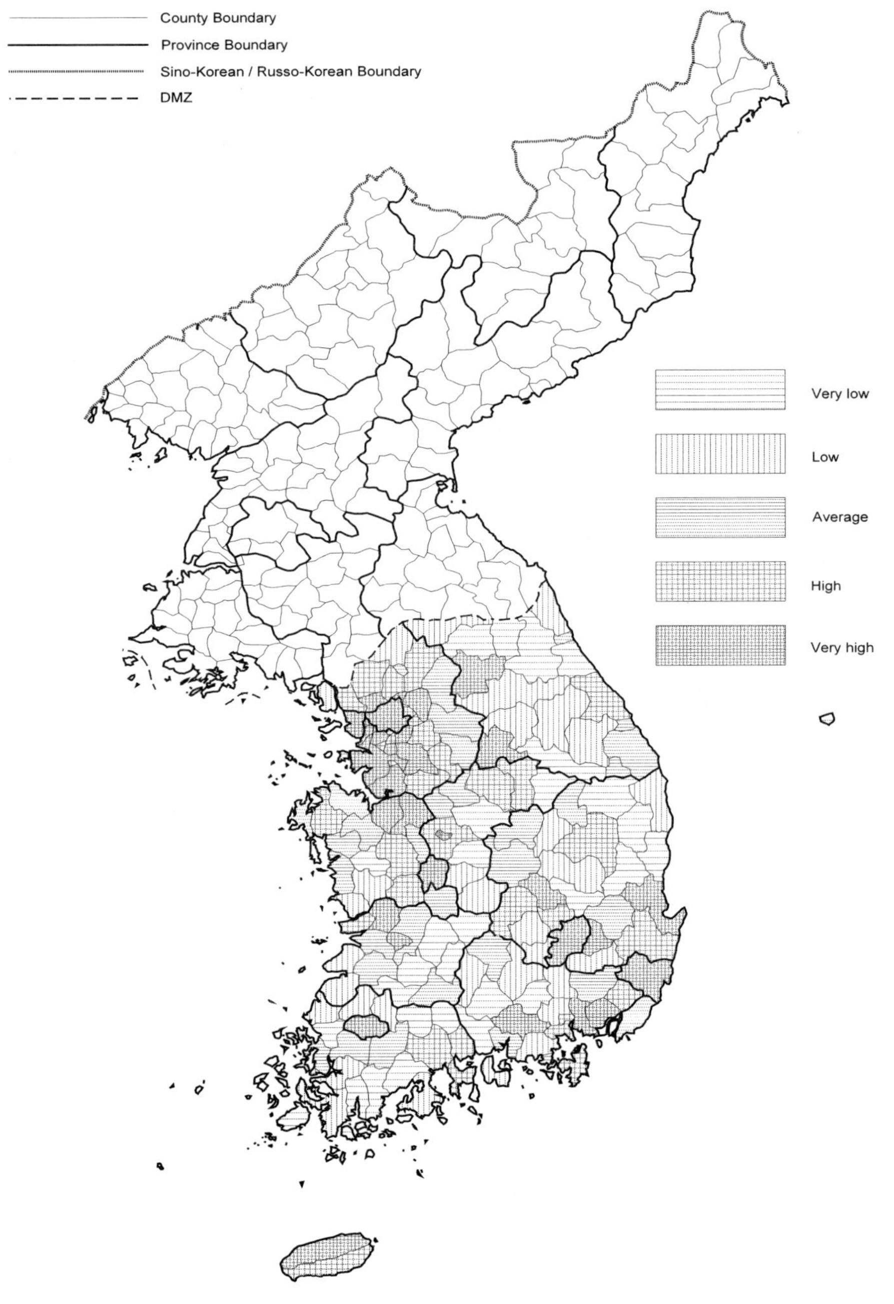

Notes: Unit = persons. Data pertain to people aged 15 years and older. Cut-offs = below 1857.3, 1857.3 to below 3762.1, 3762.1 to below 9372.2, 9372.2 to below 30249.9, 30249.9 or above.

Map 6.13 Female married population of South Korea

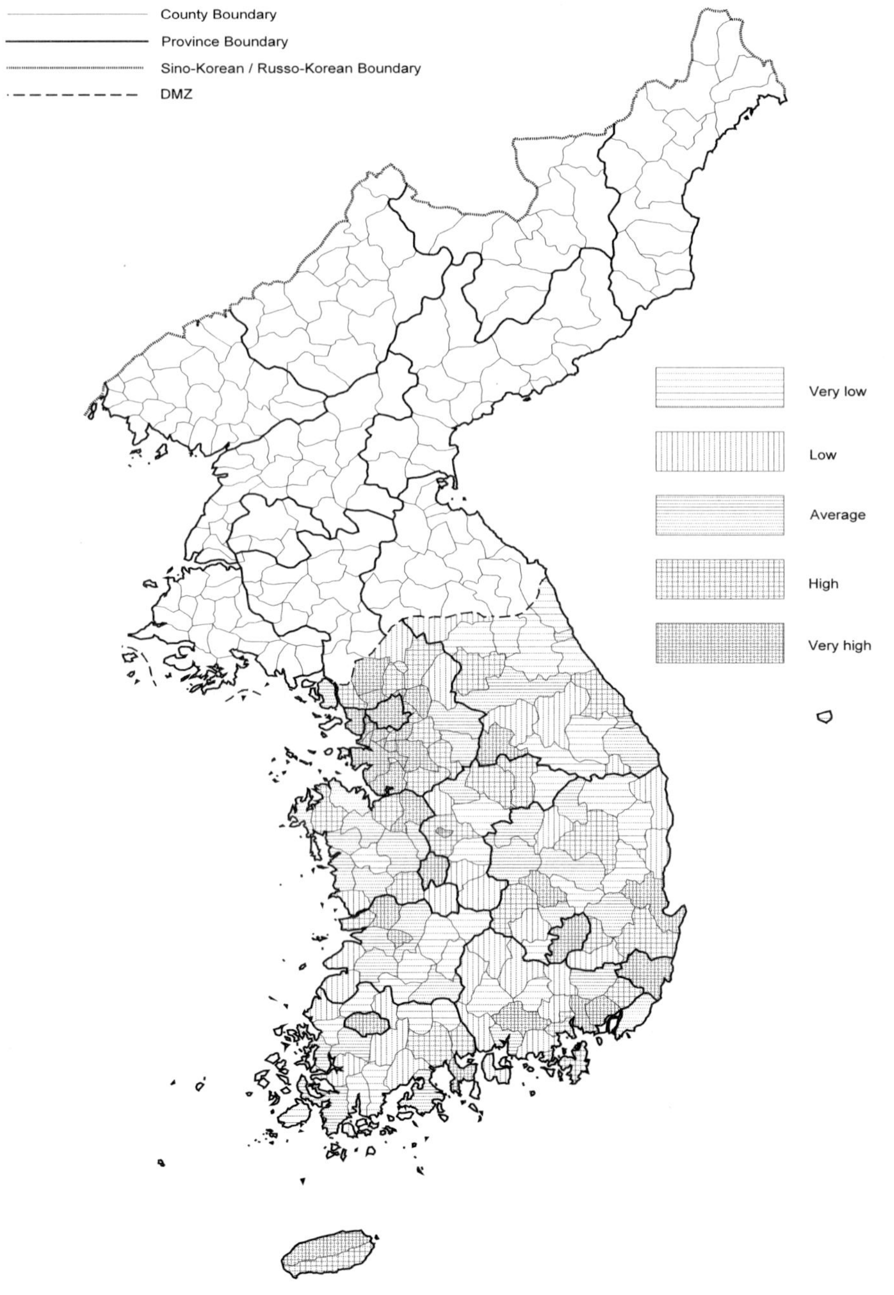

Notes: Unit = persons. Data pertain to people aged 15 years and older. Cut-offs = below 9769.5, 9769.5 to below 15156.8, 15156.8 to below 29038.6, 29038.6 to below 66959.3, 66959.3 or above.

Map 6.14 Female widowed population of South Korea

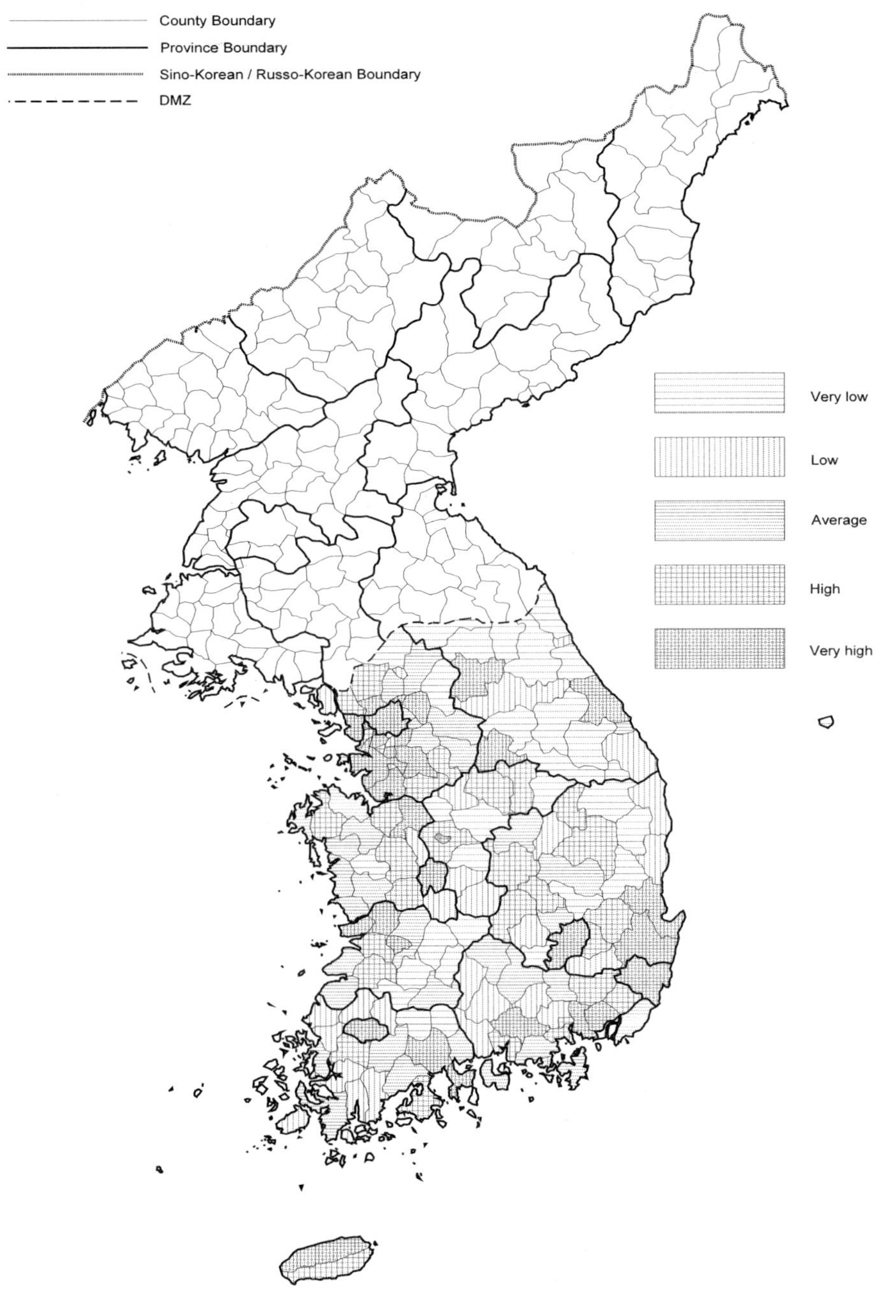

Notes: Unit = persons. Data pertain to people aged 15 years and older. Cut-offs = below 4337.4, 4337.4 to below 6348.3, 6348.3 to below 9192.9, 9192.9 to below15614.1, 15614.1 or above.

Map 6.15 Female divorced population of South Korea

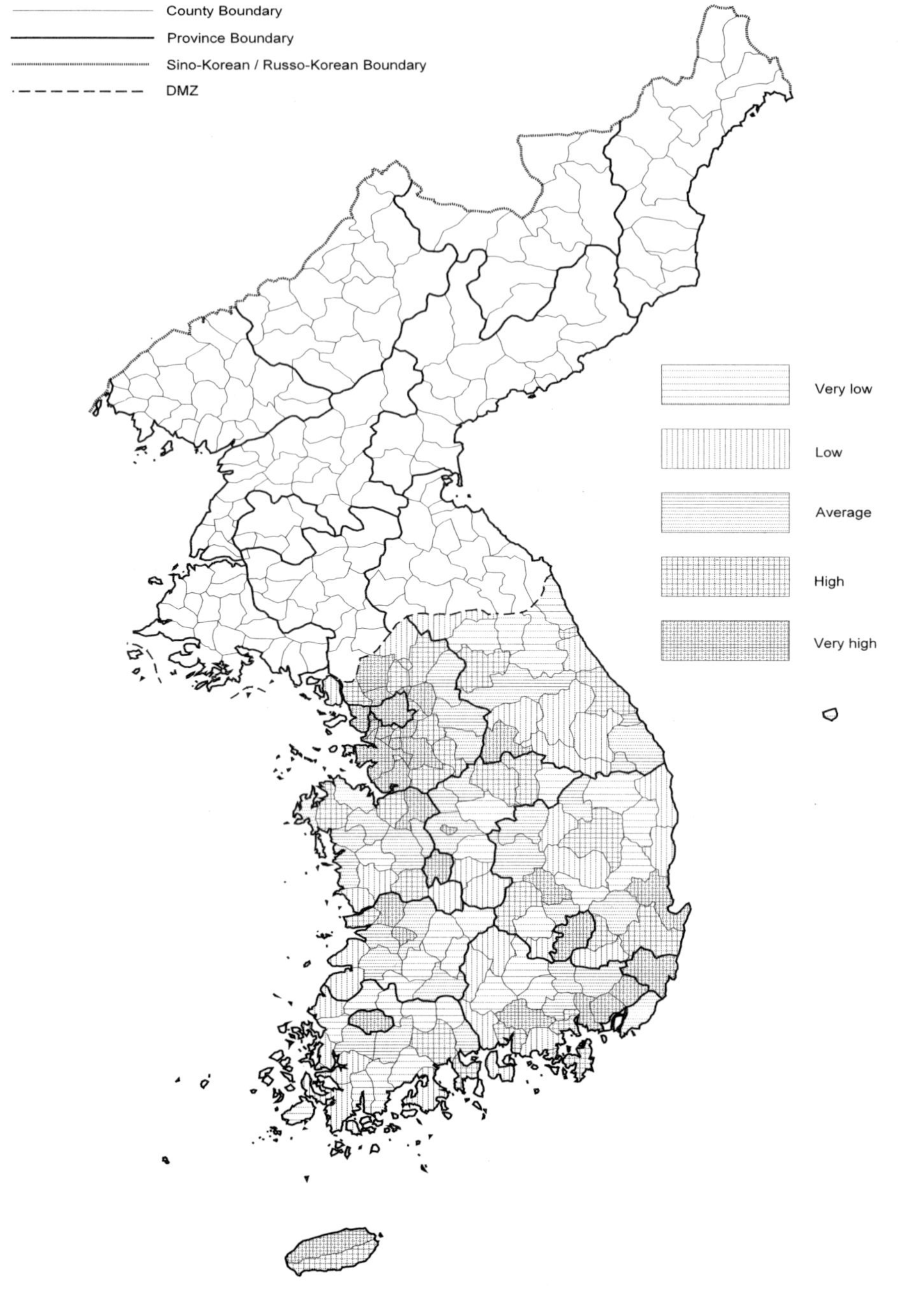

Notes: Unit = persons. Data pertain to people aged 15 years and older. Cut-offs = below 274.6, 274.6 to below 627.4, 627.4 to below1609.9, 1609.9 to below 4951.3, 4951.3 or above.

Map 6.16 Married population of the Korean peninsula (share)

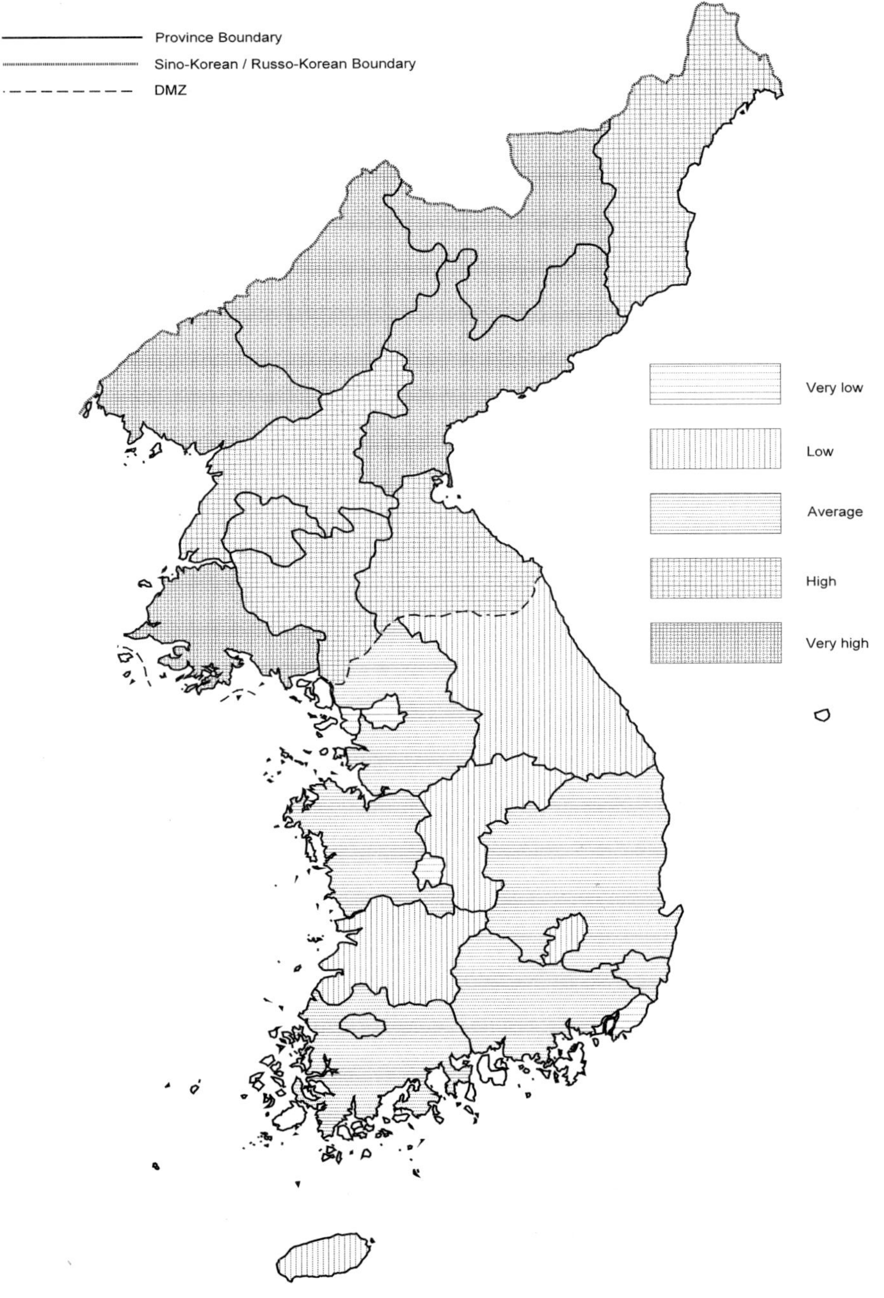

Notes: Unit = percent. Data pertain to people aged 15 years and older. Cut-offs = below 57.12, 57.12 to below 59.35, 59.35 to below 68.98, 68.98 to below 146.87, 146.87 or above.

Map 6.17 Married population of South Korea (share)

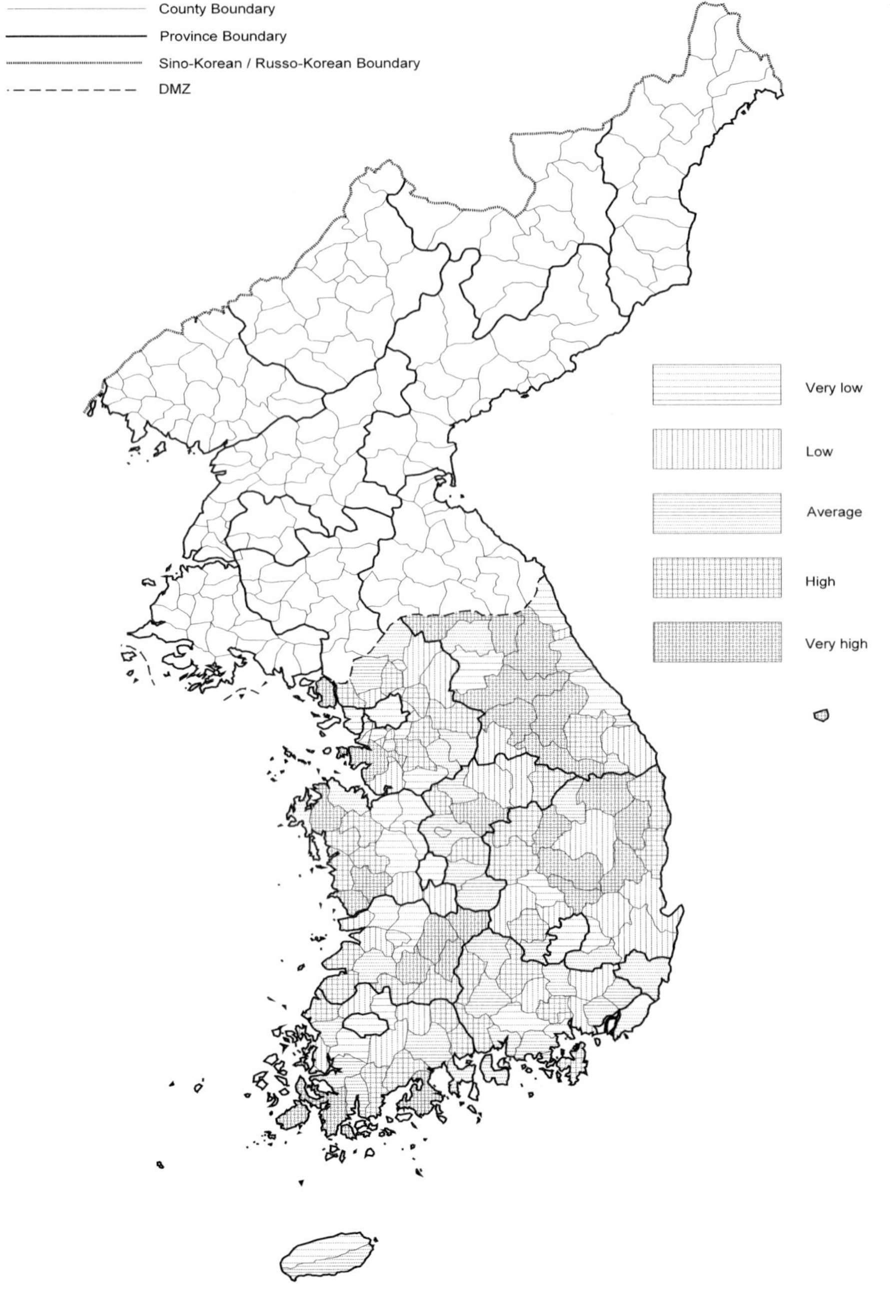

Notes: Unit = percent. Data pertain to people aged 15 years and older. Cut-offs = below 58.24, 58.24 to below 60.46, 60.46 to below 61.79, 61.79 to below 64.38, 64.38 or above.

Map 6.18 Widowed population of the Korean peninsula (share)

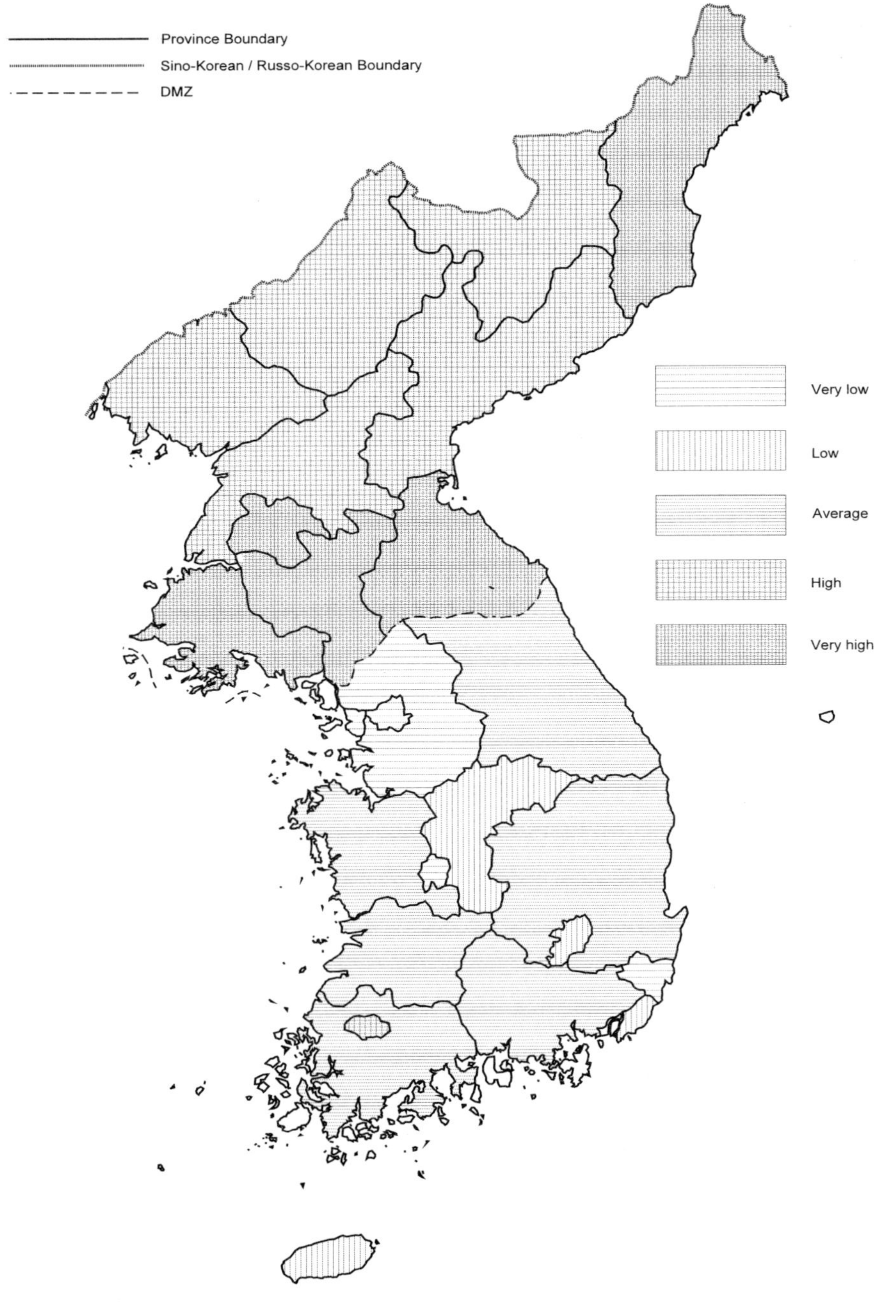

Notes: Unit = percent. Data pertain to people aged 15 years and older. Cut-offs = below 6.758, 6.758 to below 9.351, 9.351 to below 13.829, 13.829 to below 19.589, 19.589 or above.

Map 6.19 Widowed population of South Korea (share)

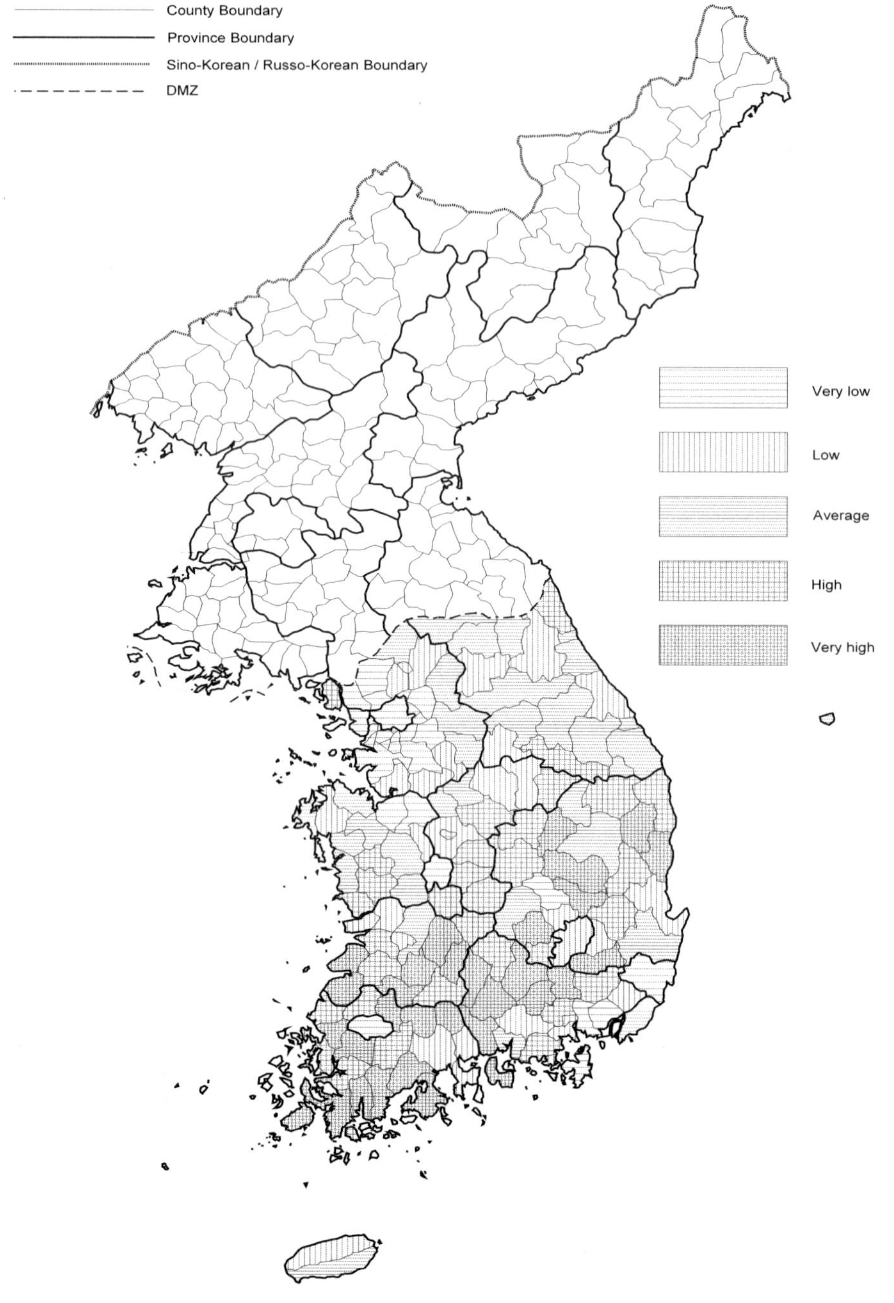

Notes: Unit = percent. Data pertain to people aged 15 years and older. Cut-offs = below 7.014, 7.014 to below 10.055, 10.055 to below 13.474, 13.474 to below 17.639, 17.639 or above.

Map 6.20 Divorced population of the Korean peninsula (share)

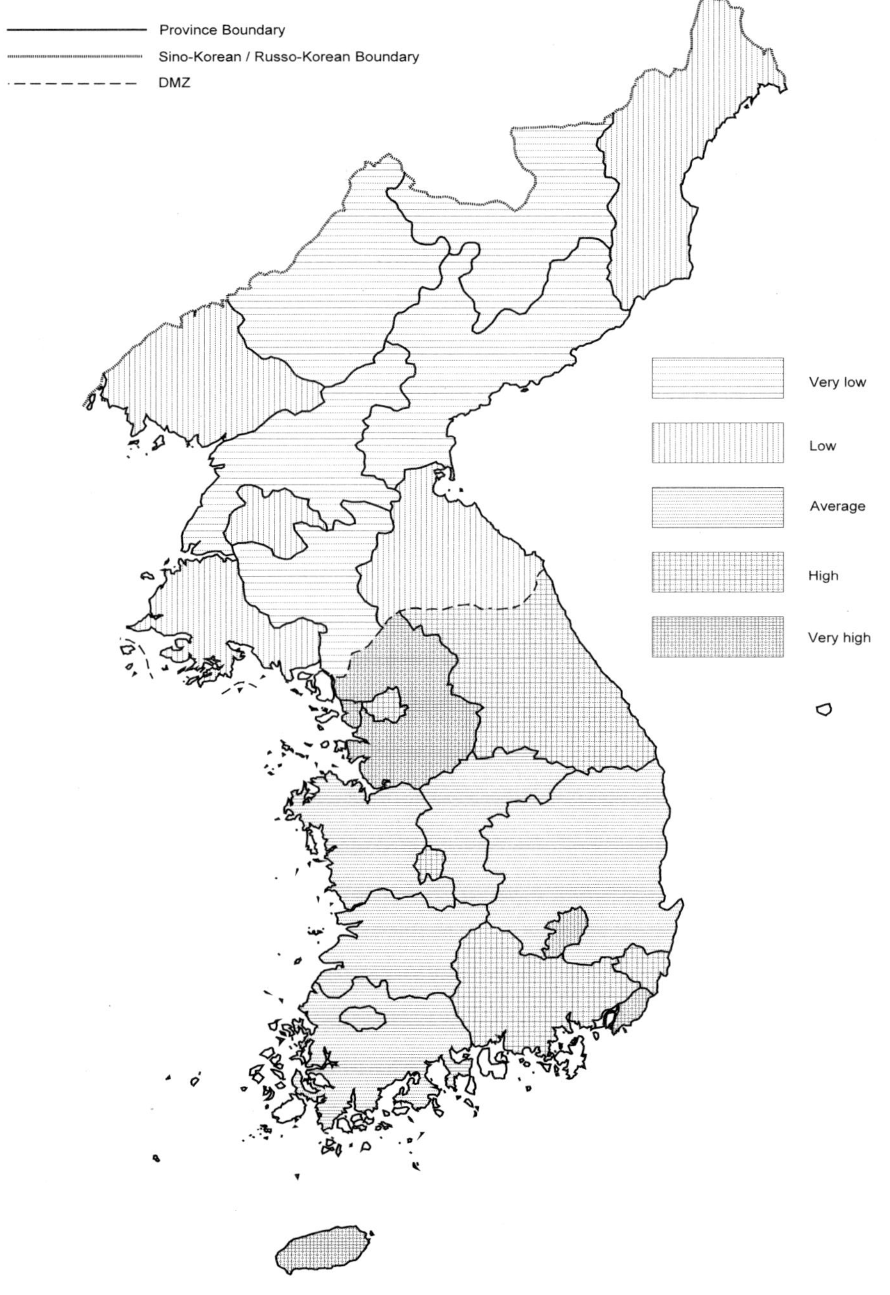

Notes: Unit = percent. Data pertain to people aged 15 years and older. Cut-offs = below 0.917, 0.917 to below 2.801, 2.801 to below 3.688, 3.688 to below 4.103, 4.103 or above.

Map 6.21 Divorced population of South Korea (share)

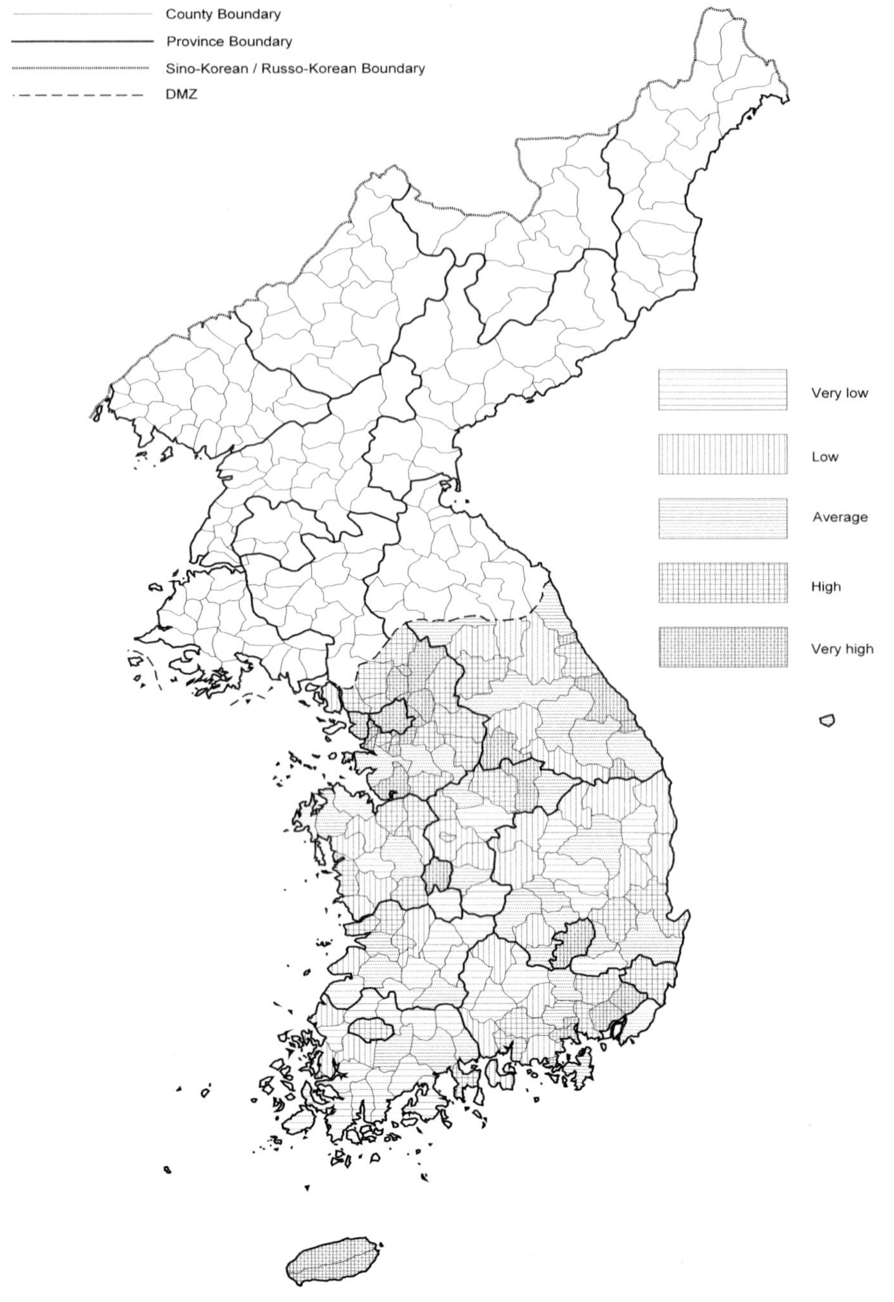

Notes: Unit = percent. Data pertain to people aged 15 years and older. Cut-offs = below 2.311, 2.311 to below 2.808, 2.808 to below 3.330, 3.330 to below 4.047, 4.047 or above.

7. Family Composition

Map 7.1 One generation households of South Korea

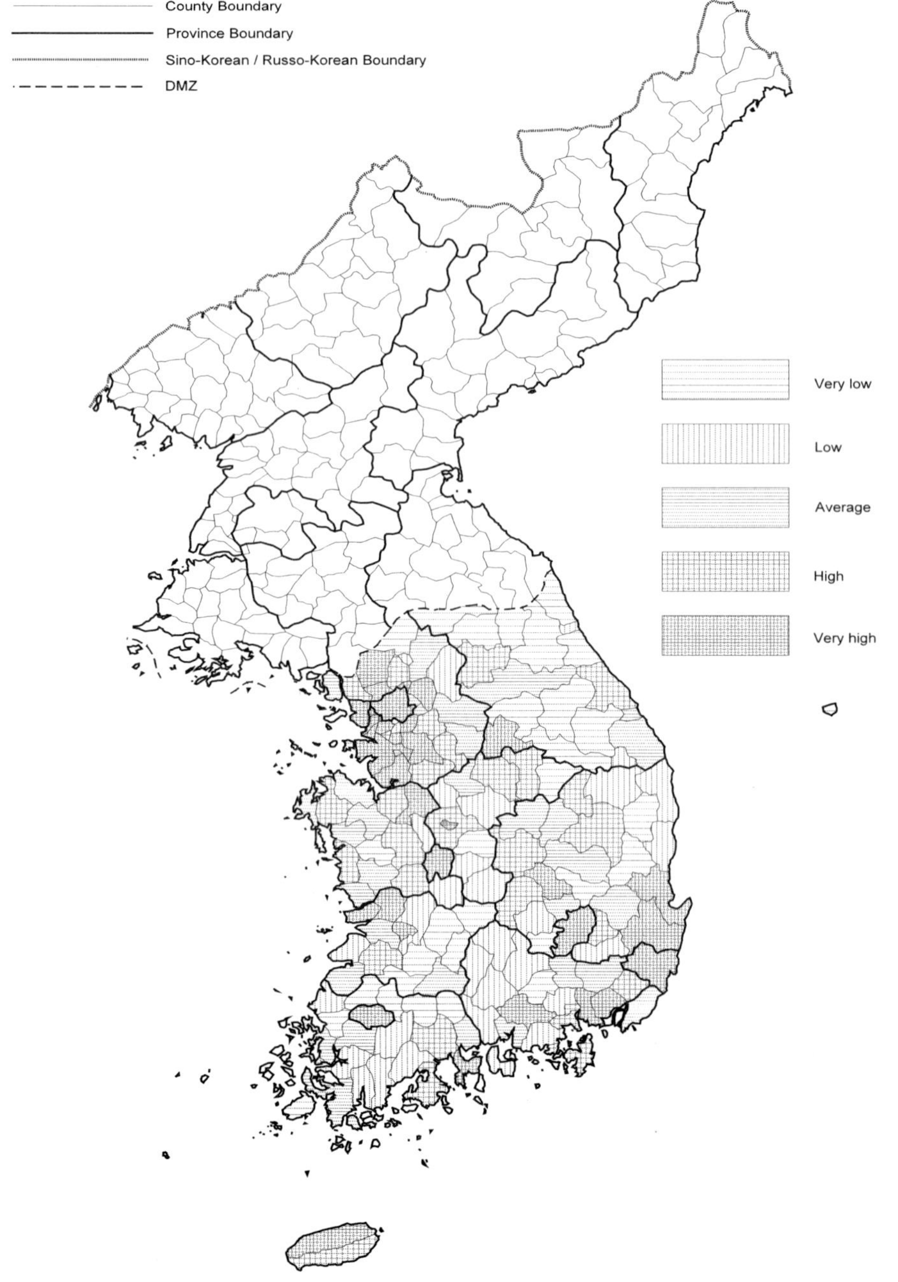

Notes: Unit = number of households. Cut-offs = below 9183.5, 9183.5 to below 13625.1, 13625.1 to below 21181.0, 21181.0 to below 37216.2, 37216.2 or above.

Map 7.2 Two generation households of South Korea

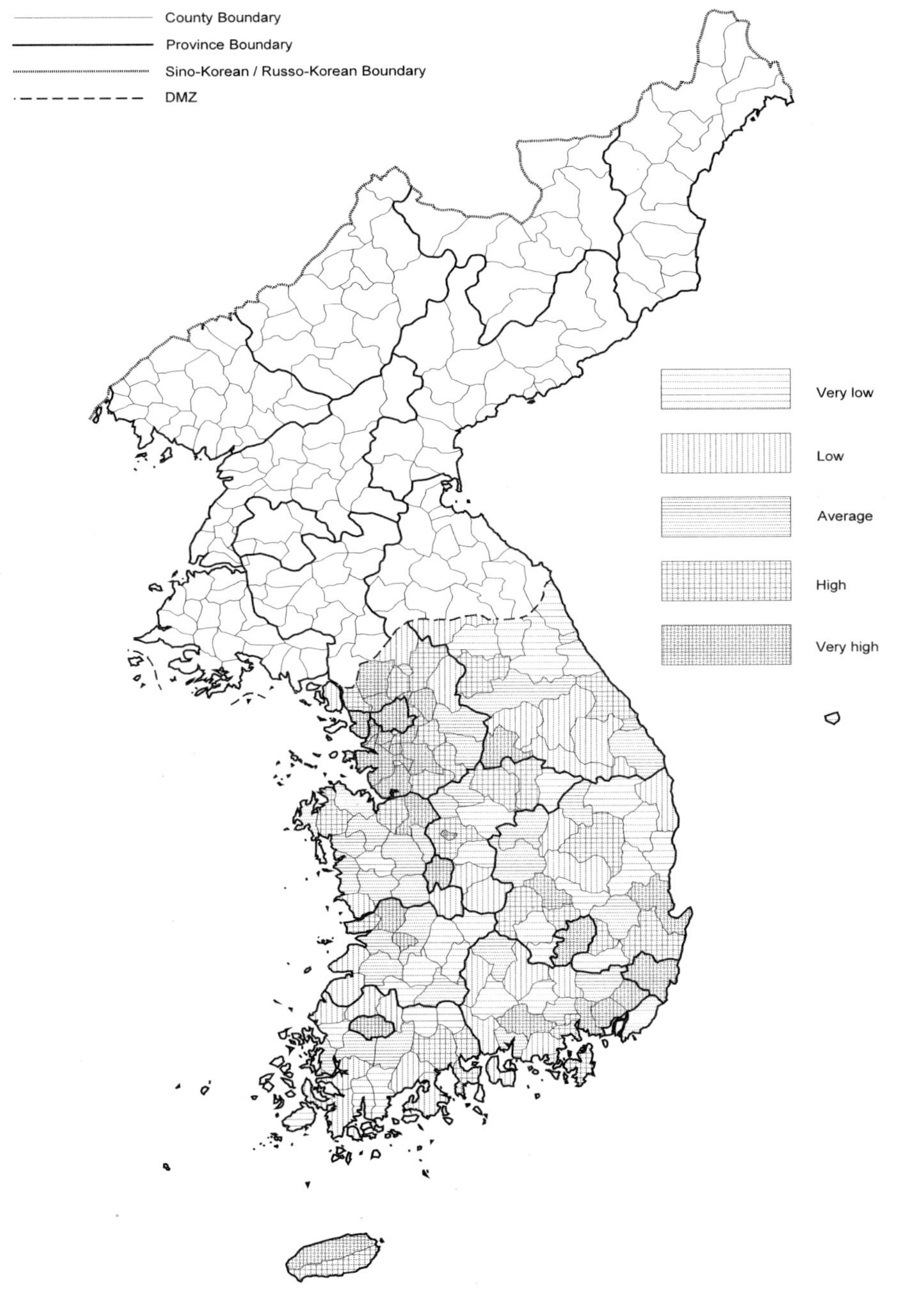

Notes: Unit = number of households. Cut-offs = below 15276.6, 15276.6 to below 27803.7, 27803.7 to below 65374.3, 65374.3 to below 166134.7, 166134.7 or above.

Map 7.3 Three generation households of South Korea

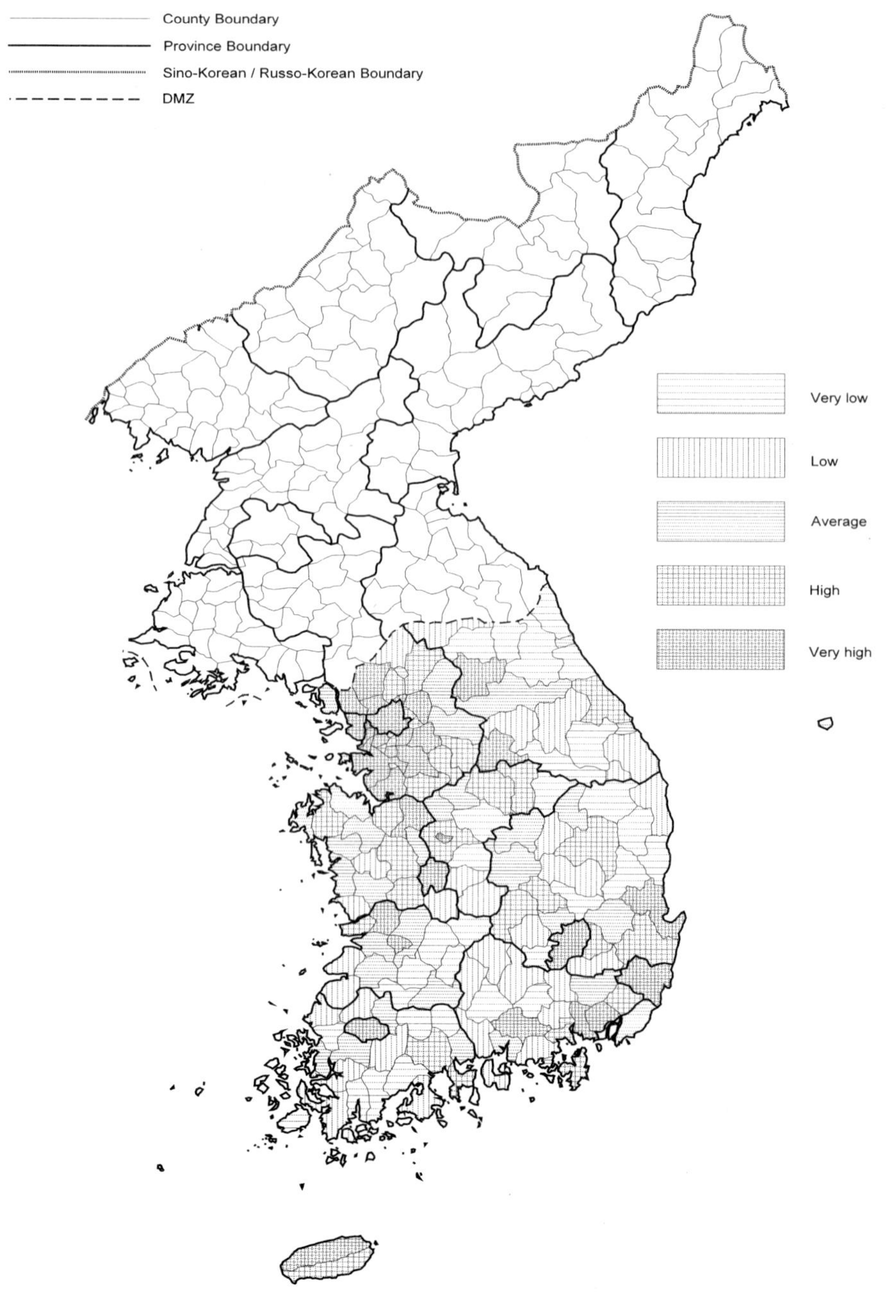

Notes: Unit = number of households. Cut-offs = below 4306.2, 4306.2 to below 6866.7, 6866.7 to below 14394.2, 14394.2 to below 31320.2, 31320.2 or above.

Map 7.4 Four or more generation households of South Korea

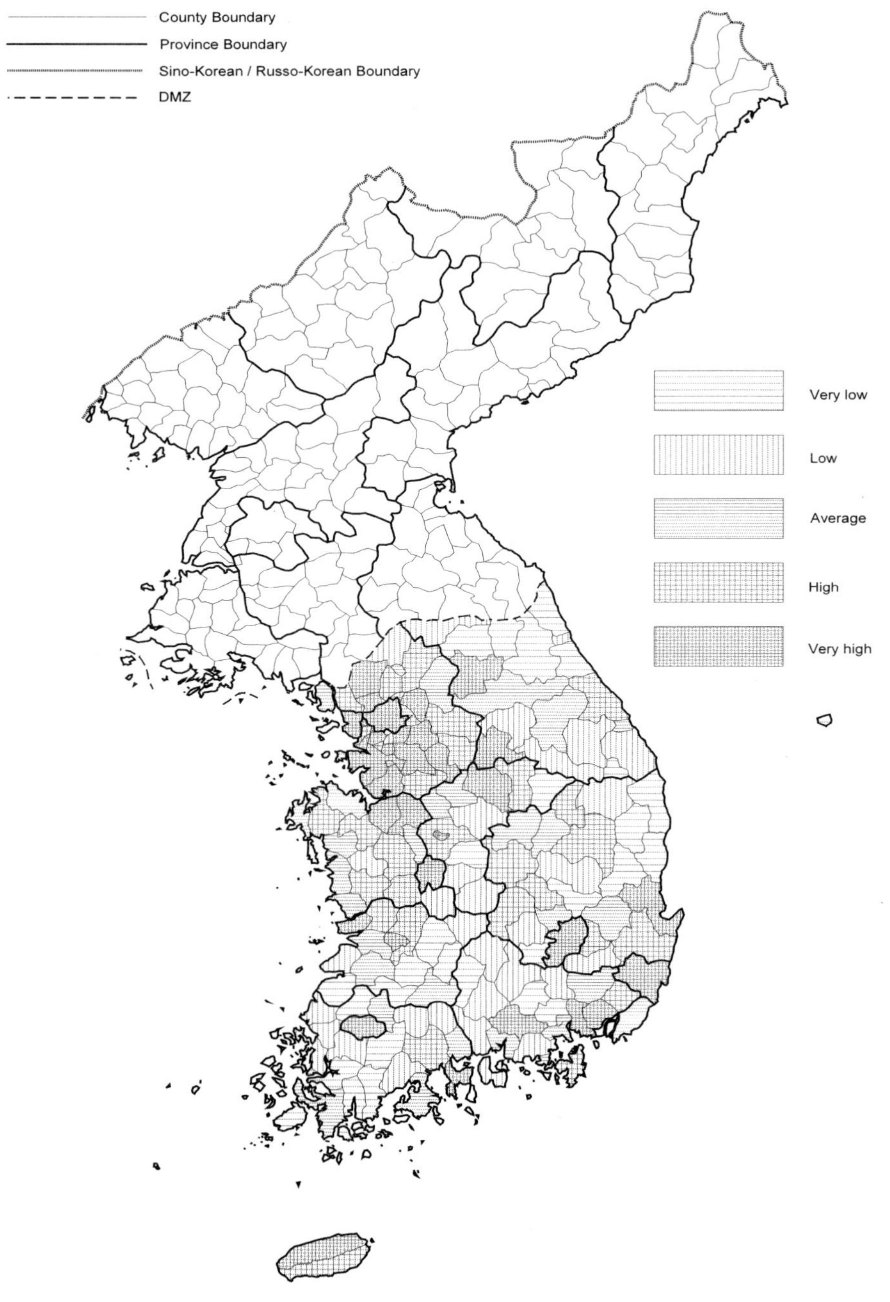

Notes: Unit = number of households. Cut-offs = below 104.9, 104.9 to below 178.3, 178.3 to below 272.8, 272.8 to below 560.8, 560.8 or above.

Map 7.5 One person households of the Korean peninsula

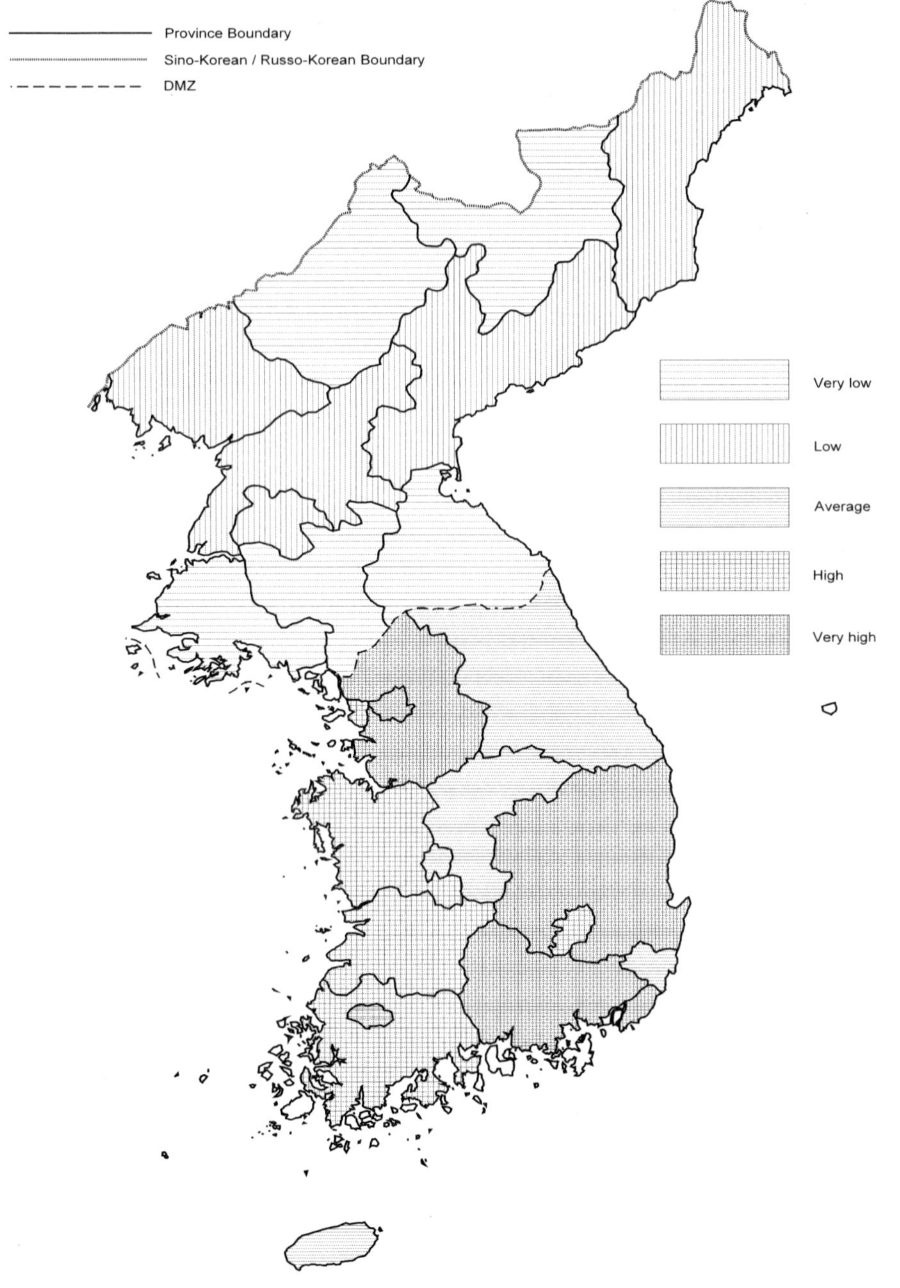

Notes: Unit = number of households. Cut-offs = below 7528.6, 7528.6 to below 42524.2, 42524.2 to below 157410.3, 157410.3 to below 227258.0, 227258.0 or above.

Map 7.6 One person households of South Korea

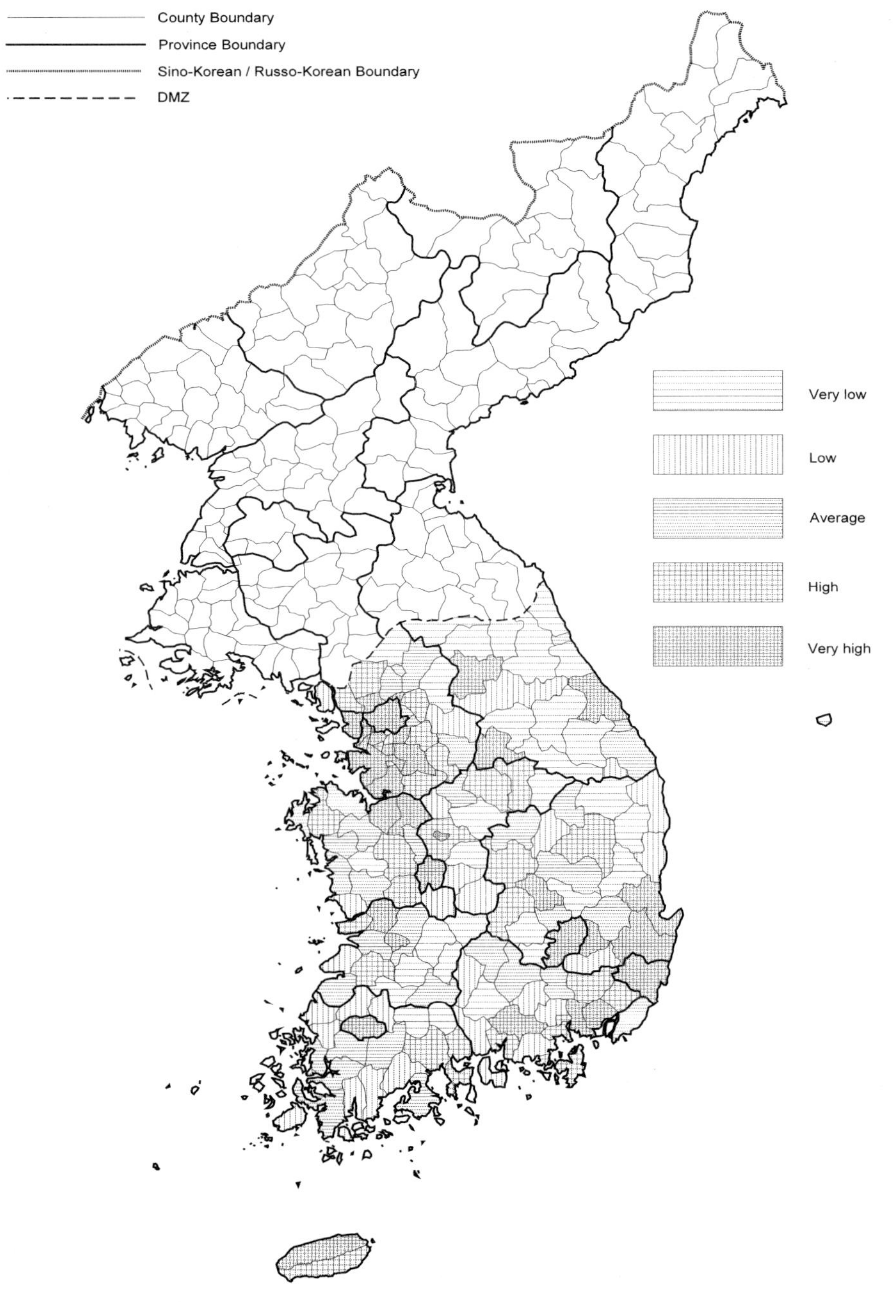

Notes: Unit = number of households. Cut-offs = below 4549.0, 4549.0 to below 7308.5, 7308.5 to below 11347.5, 11347.5 to below 24705.5, 24705.5 or above.

Map 7.7 Male one person households of South Korea

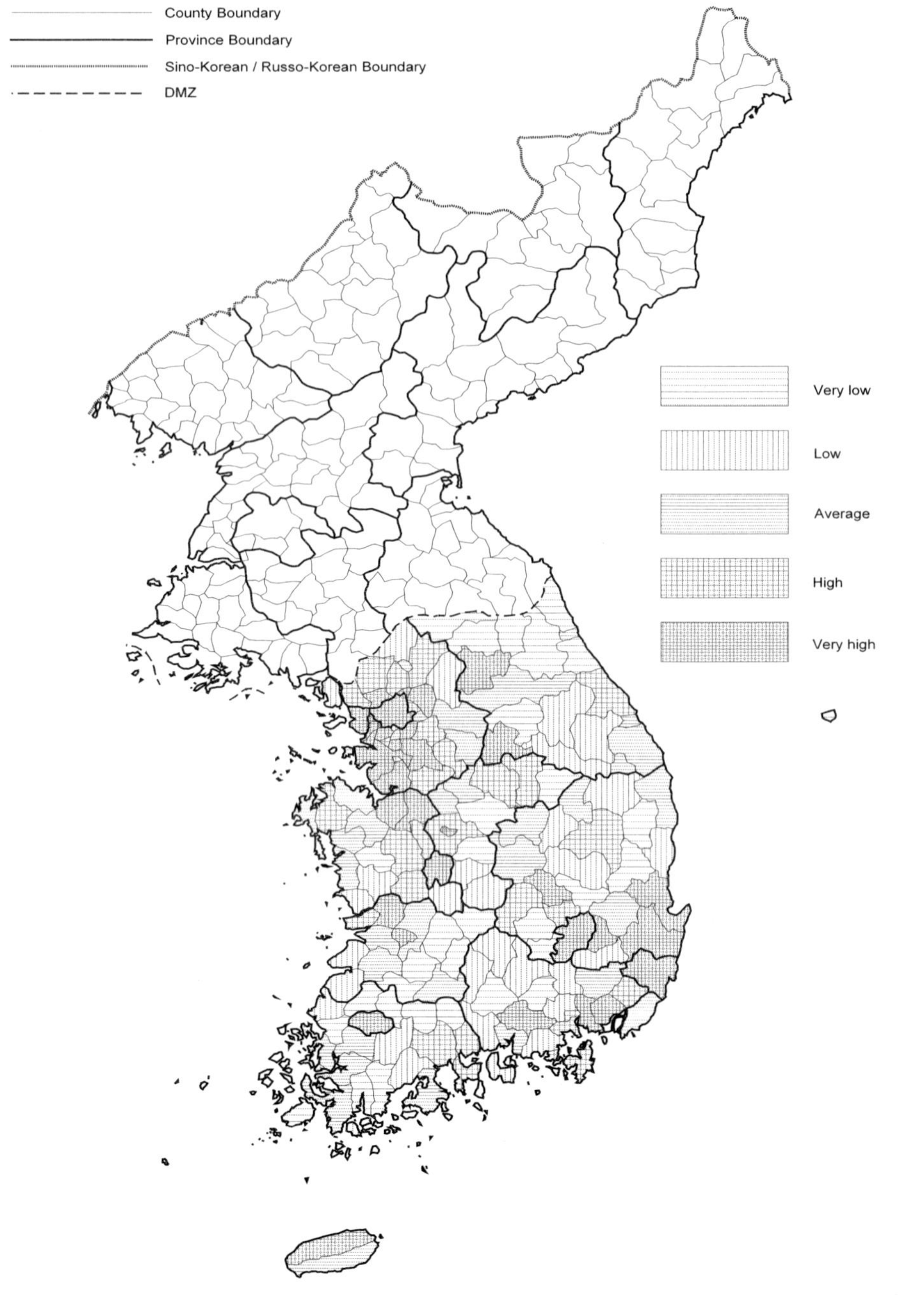

Notes: Unit = number of households. Cut-offs = below 1468.4, 1468.4 to below 2430.2, 2430.2 to below 4509.8, 4509.8 to below 11674.5, 11674.5 or above.

Map 7.8 Female one person households of South Korea

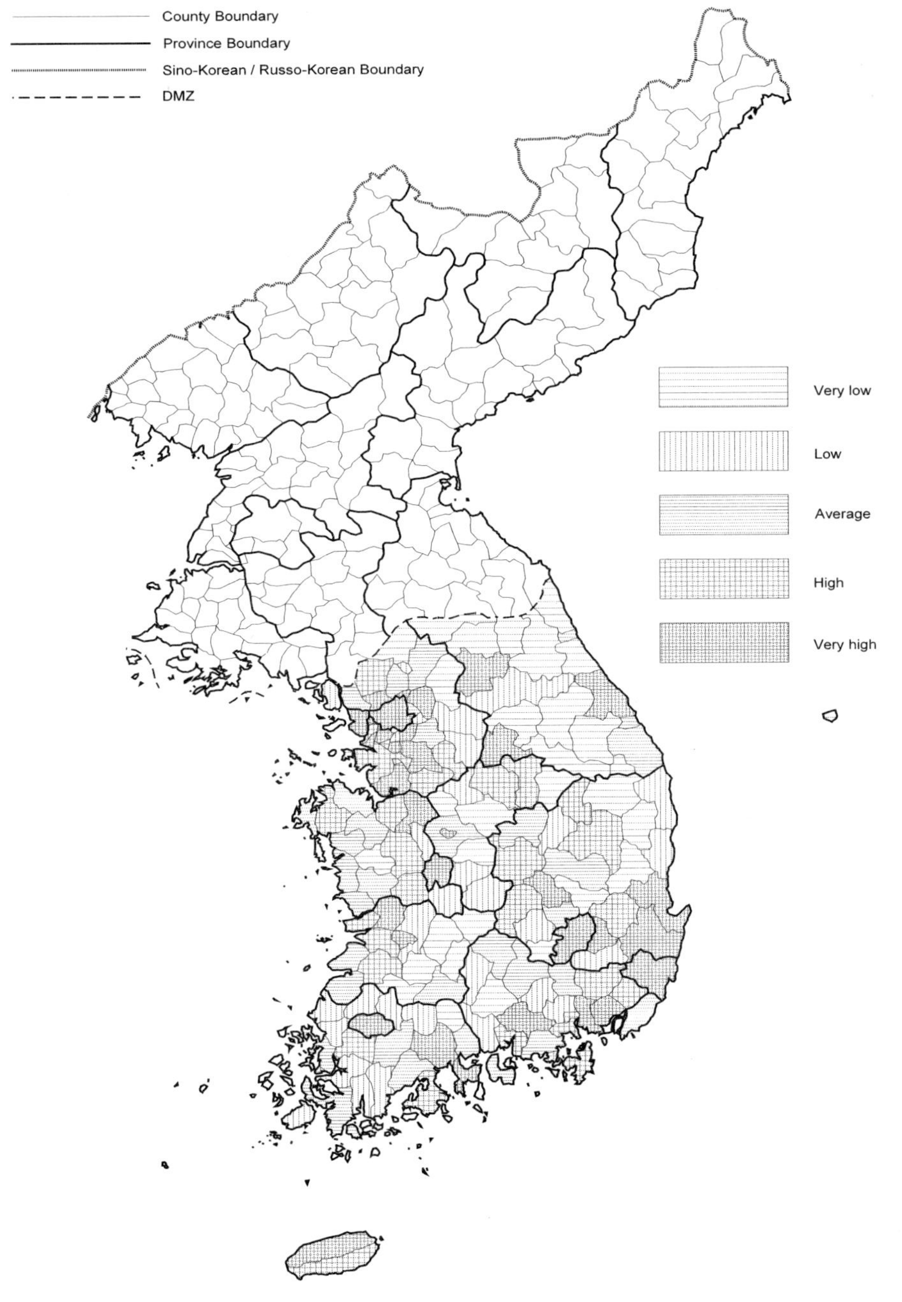

Notes: Unit = number of households. Cut-offs = below 3082.0, 3082.0 to below 4561.2, 4561.2 to below 6912.7, 6912.7 to below 12530.5, 12530.5 or above.

Map 7.9 One person households of the Korean peninsula (share)

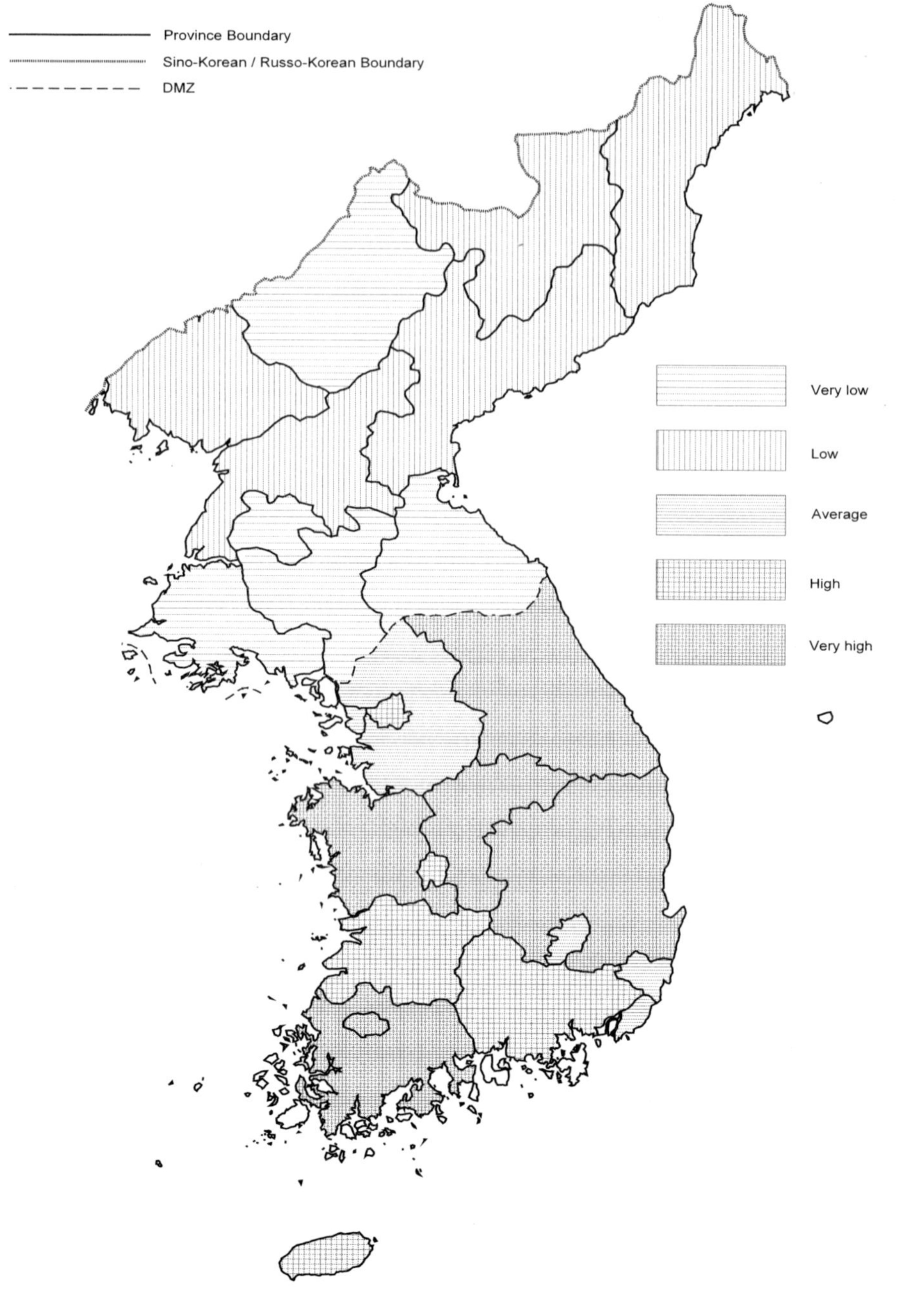

Notes: Unit = percent. Cut-offs = below 1.63, 1.63 to below 18.25, 18.25 to below 23.64, 23.64 to below 26.44, 26.44 or above.

Map 7.10 One person households of South Korea (share)

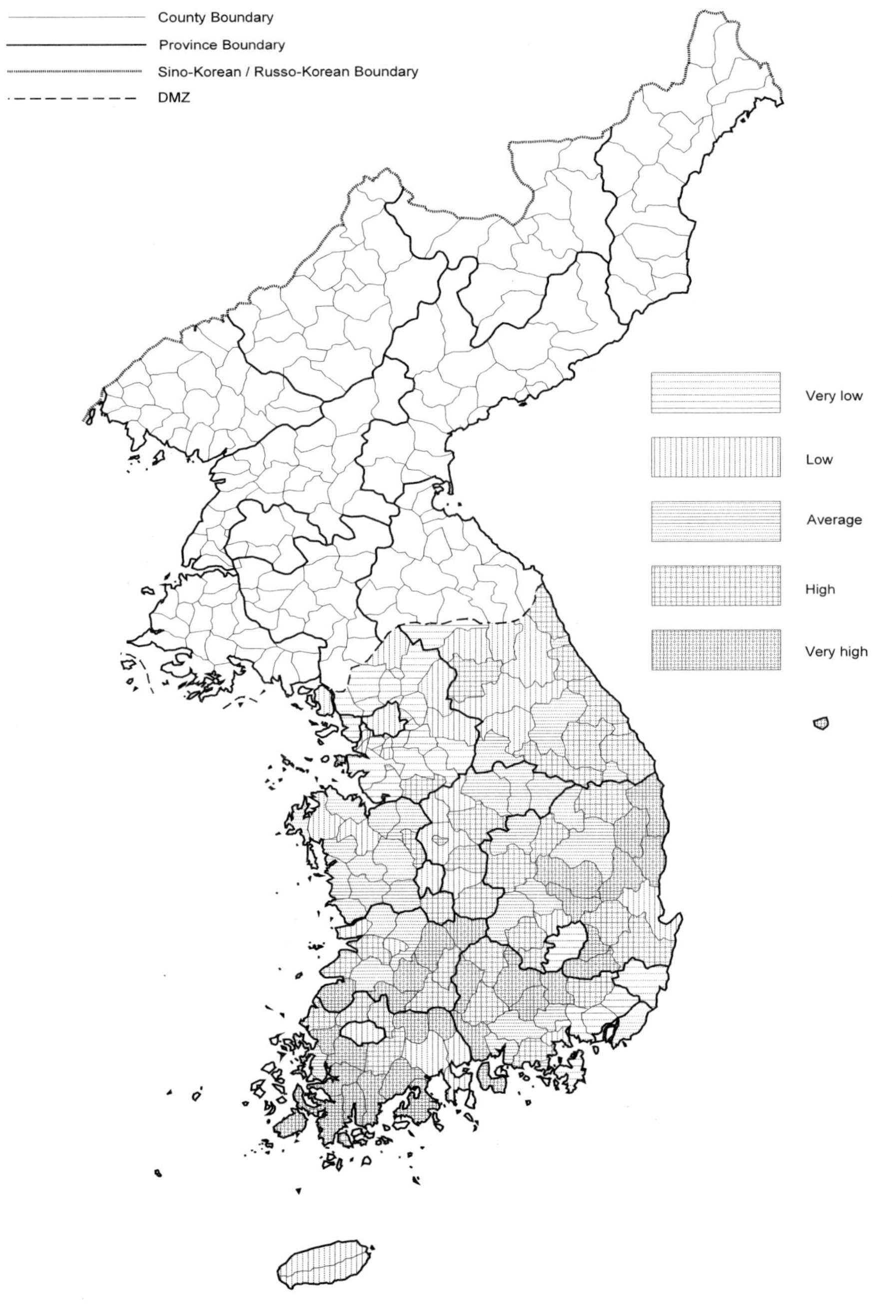

Notes: Unit = percent. Cut-offs = below 22.62, 22.62 to below 25.82, 25.82 to below 29.01, 29.01 to below 32.22, 32.22 or above.

8. Mobility

Map 8.1 Non-commuting population of South Korea

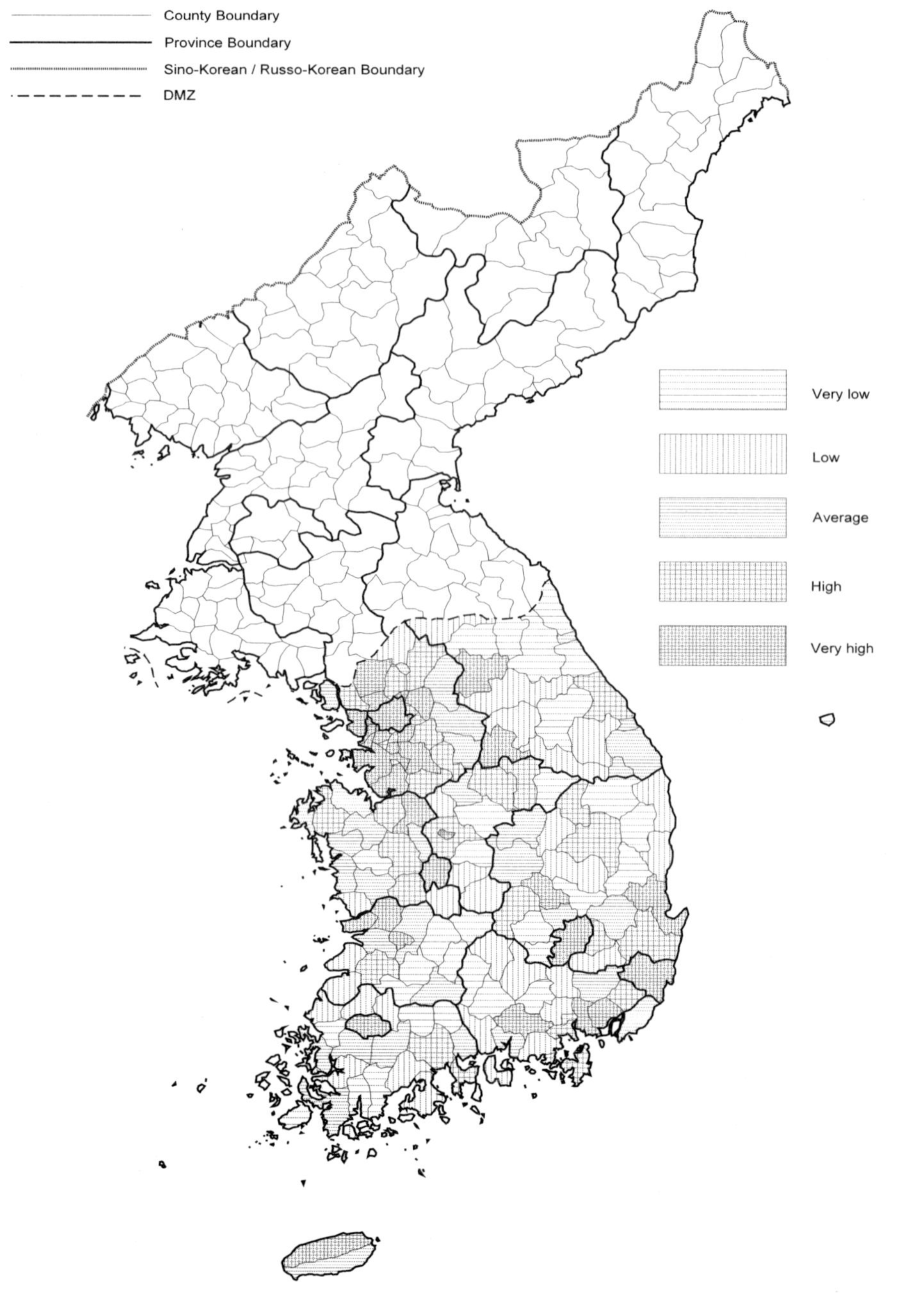

Notes: Unit = persons. Data pertain to people aged 12 years and over. Cut-offs = below 10146.5, 10146.5 to below 16380.8, 16380.8 to below 32670.7, 32670.7 to below 77759.6, 77759.6 or above.

Map 8.2 Commuting population of South Korea

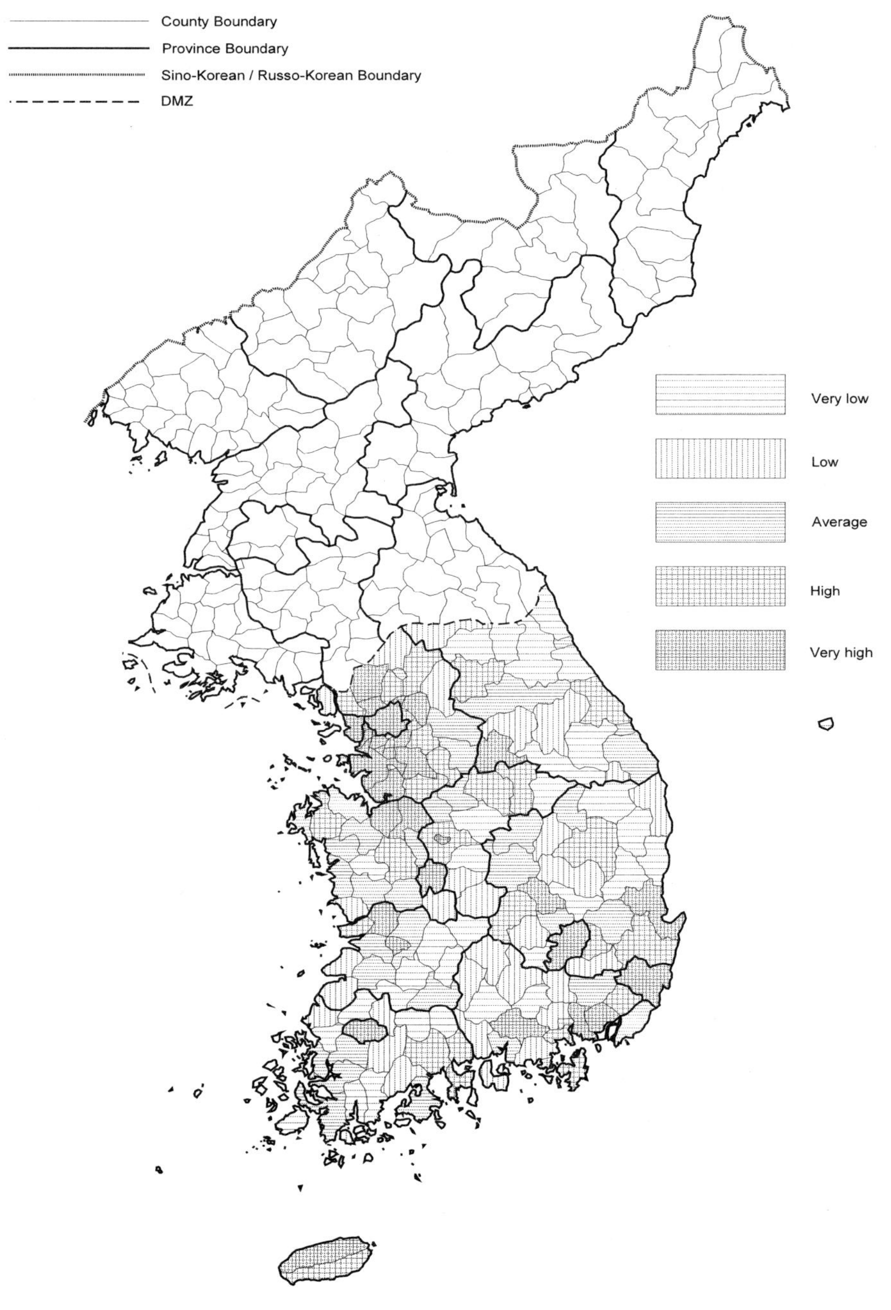

Notes: Unit = persons. Data pertain to people aged 12 years and over. Commuters are defined as people who commute to school or work. Cut-offs = below 22088.6, 22088.6 to below 36062.8, 36062.8 to below 71771.1, 71771.1 to below 161213.8, 161213.8 or above.

Map 8.3 Walking commuters of South Korea

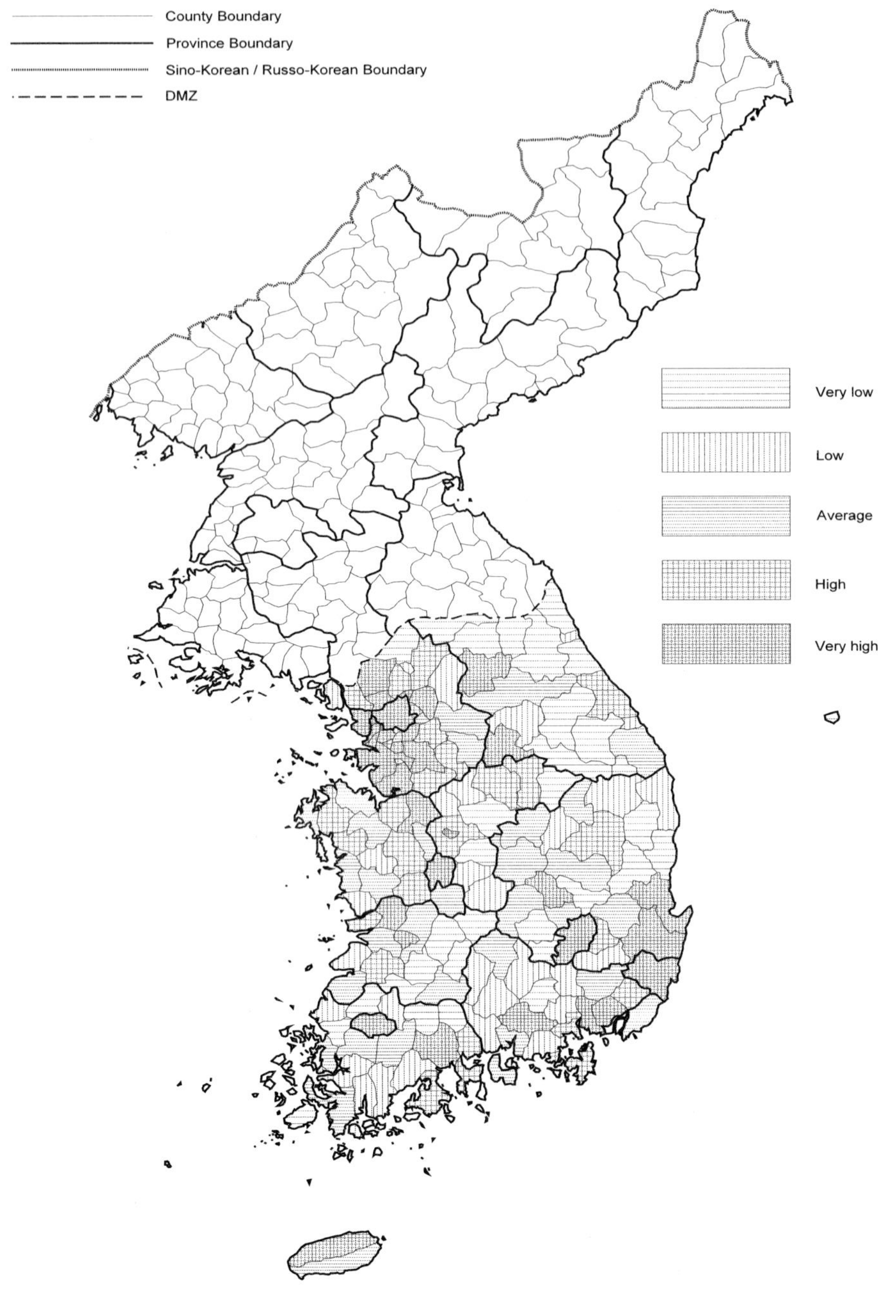

Notes: Unit = persons. Data pertain to people aged 12 years and over. Commuters are defined as people who commute to school or work. Cut-offs = below 8754.3, 8754.3 to below 13376.0, 13376.0 to below 19445.9, 19445.9 to below 42825.2, 42825.2 or above.

Map 8.4 Private car commuters of South Korea

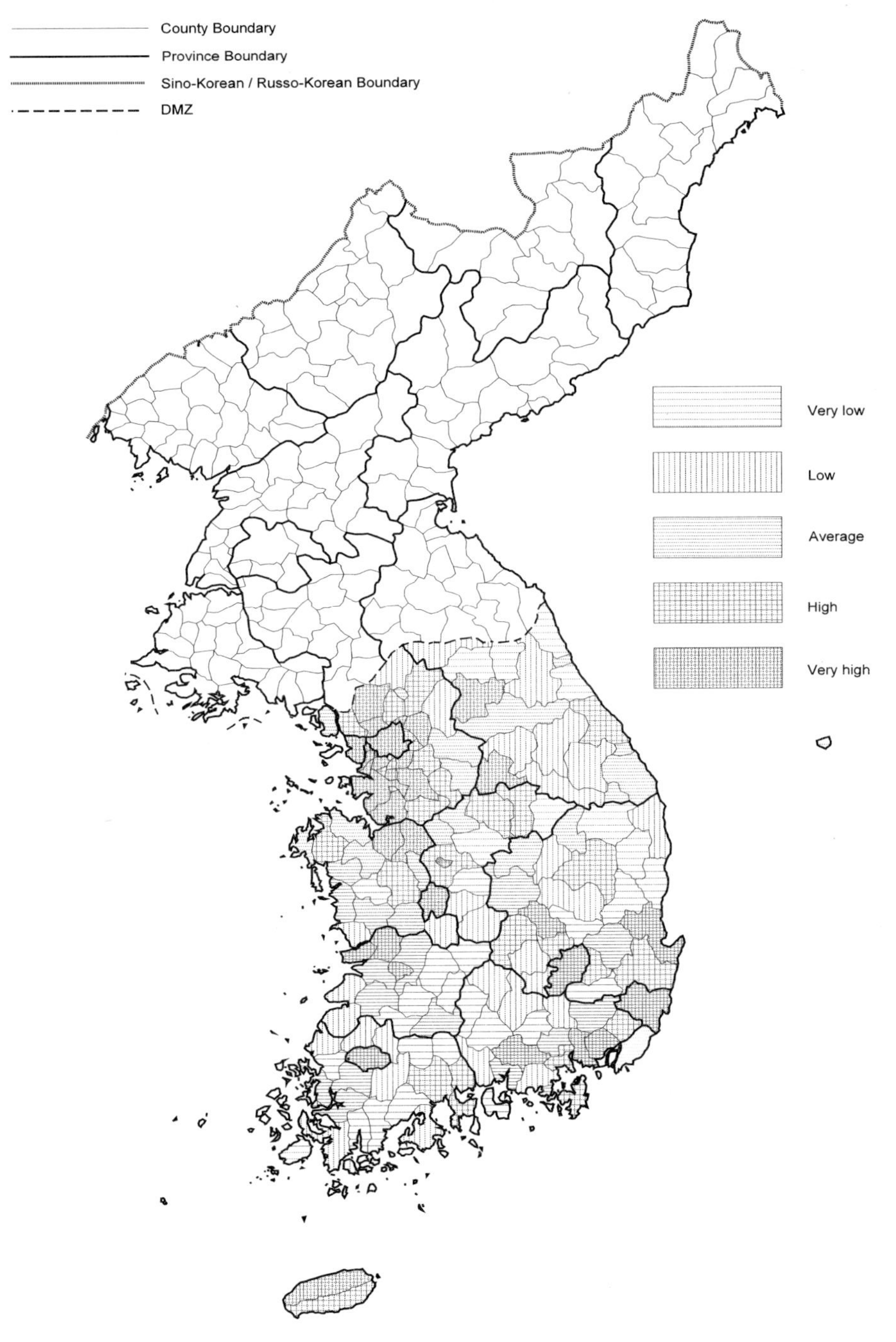

Notes: Unit = persons. Data pertain to people aged 12 years and over. Commuters are defined as people who commute to school or work. Cut-offs = below 6579.2, 6579.2 to below 12263.4, 12263.4 to below 27027.3, 27027.3 to below 63321.5, 63321.5 or above.

Map 8.5 Intra-city bus commuters of South Korea

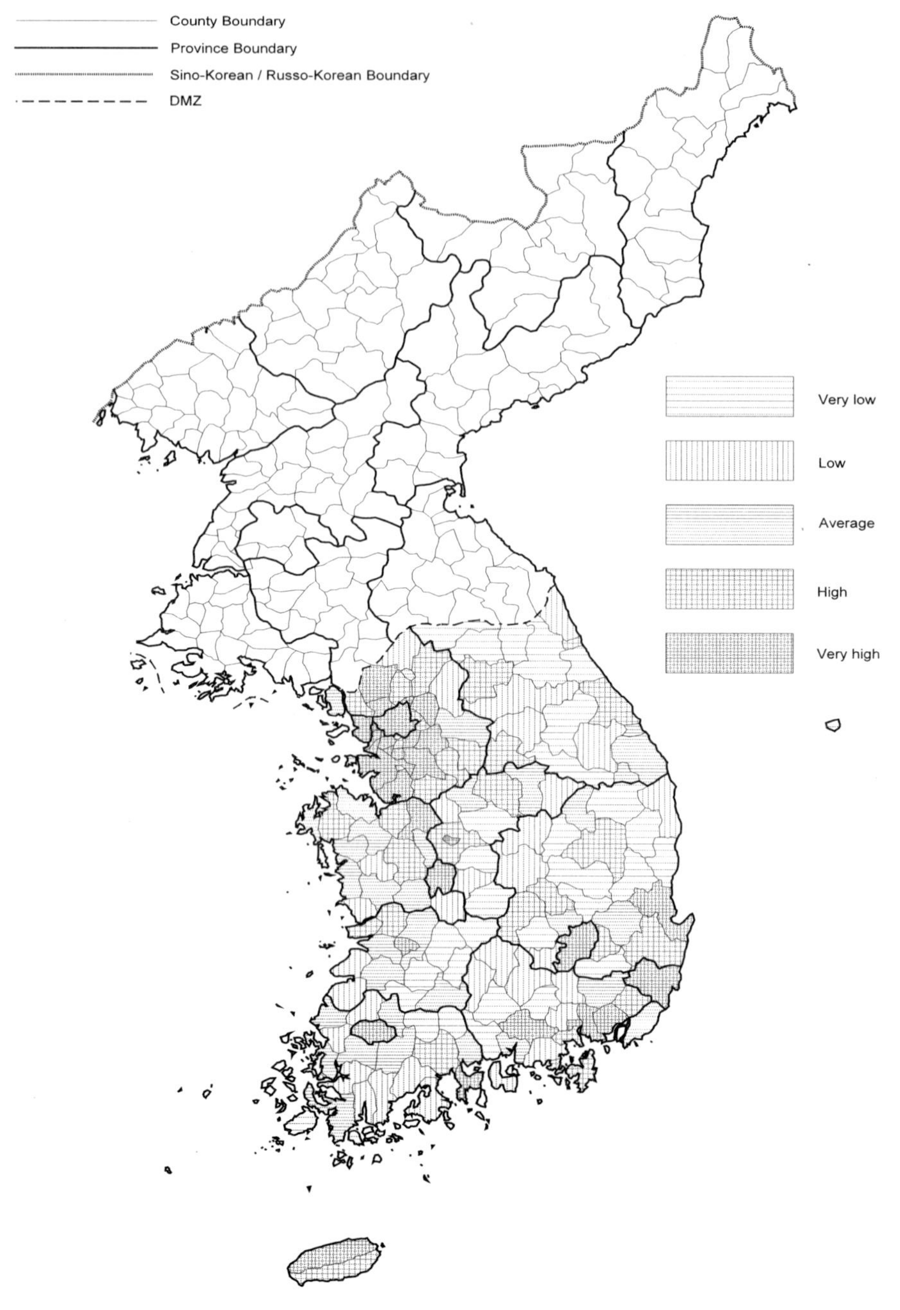

Notes: Unit = persons. Data pertain to people aged 12 years and over. Commuters are defined as people who commute to school or work. Cut-offs = below 1288.0, 1288.0 to below 2387.0, 2387.0 to below 7452.5, 7452.5 to below 26060.0, 26060.0 or above.

Map 8.6 Express and suburban bus commuters of South Korea

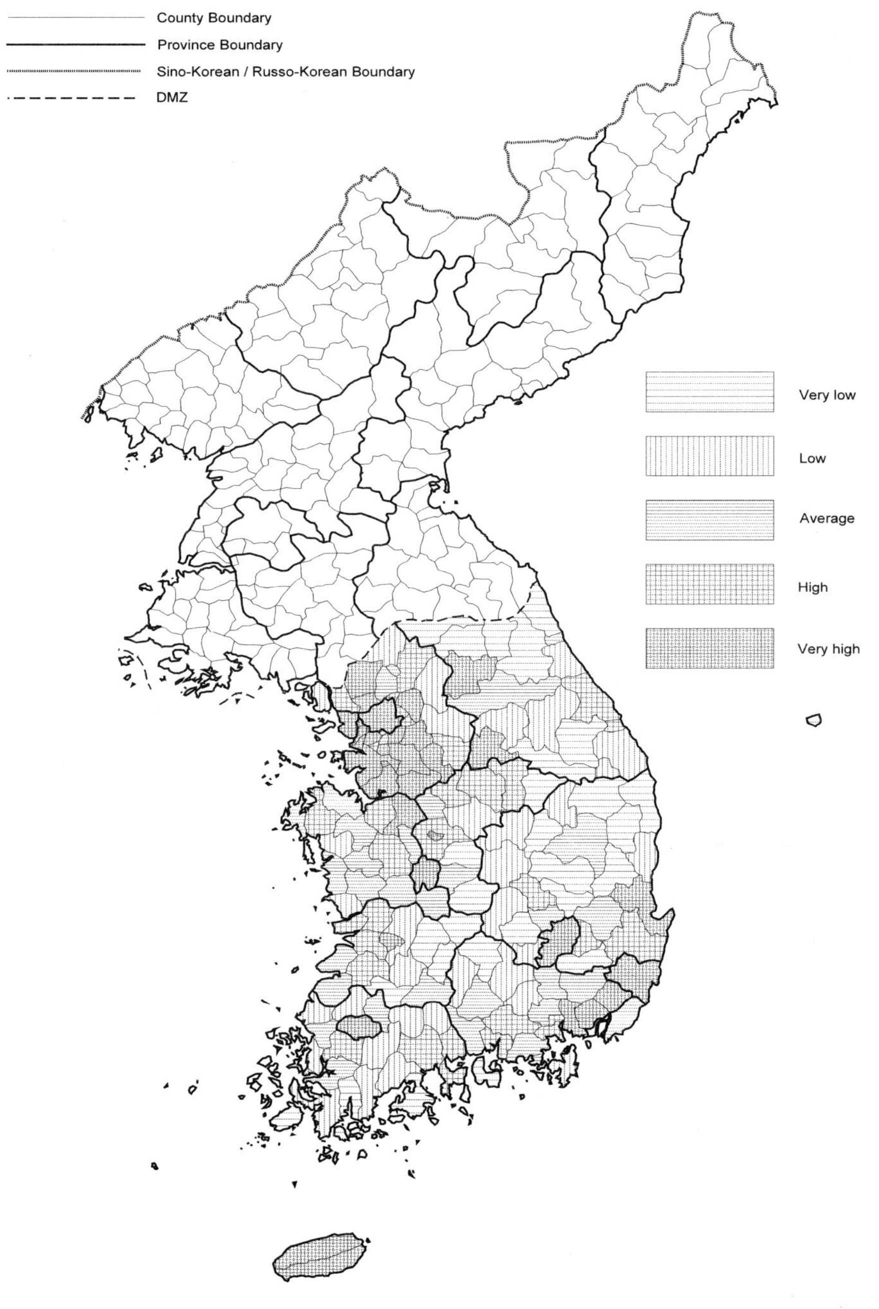

Notes: Unit = persons. Data pertain to people aged 12 years and over. Commuters are defined as people who commute to school or work. Cut-offs = below 96.0, 96.0 to below 191.3, 191.3 to below 403.8, 403.8 to below 1079.3, 1079.3 or above.

Map 8.7 Subway commuters of South Korea

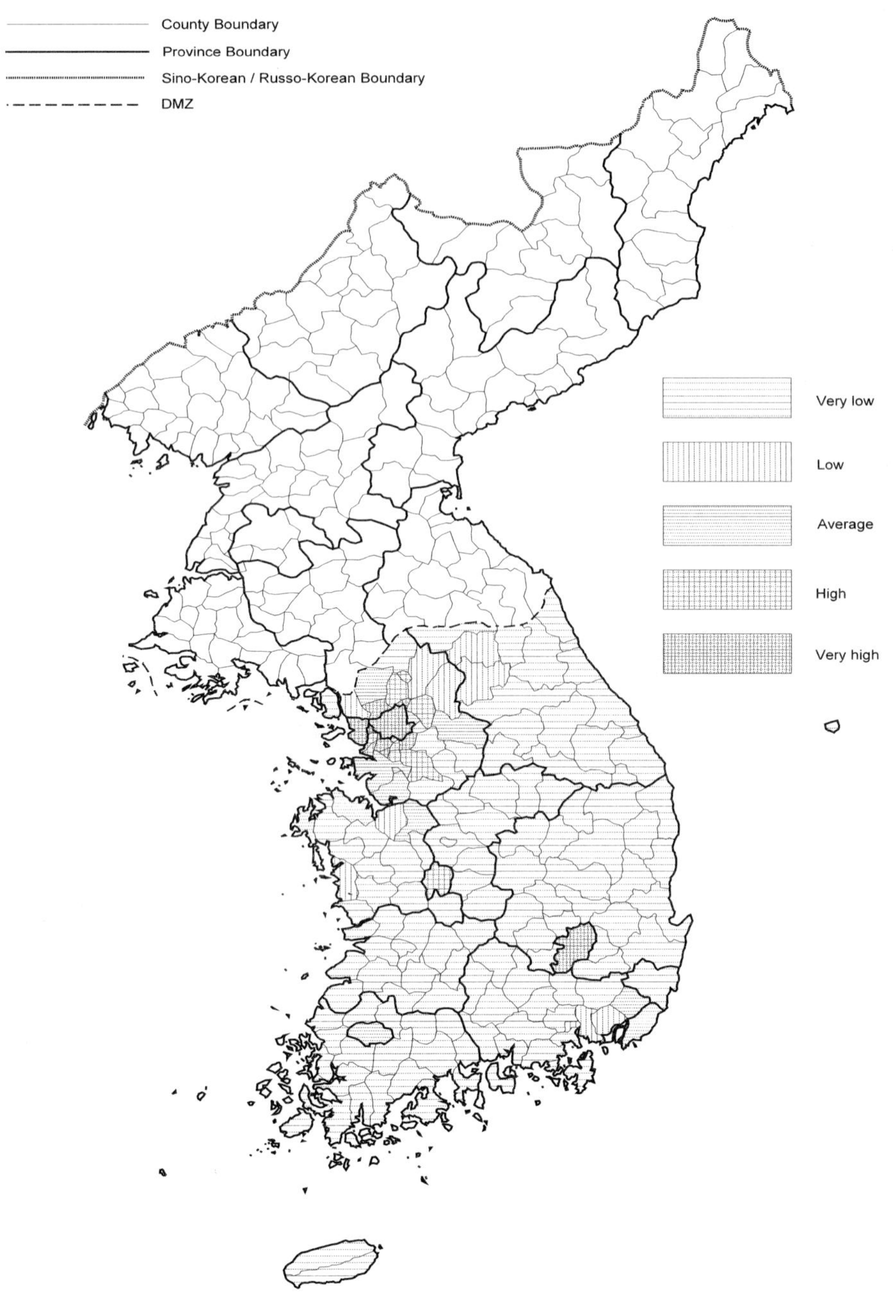

Notes: Unit = persons. Data pertain to people aged 12 years and over. Commuters are defined as people who commute to school or work. This is not an equivalent map with balanced classes because 125 counties had a value below 1.0. The cut-offs were chosen freely with about 10 counties per class for the remaining four classes above 0.00. Cut-offs = below 1.0, 1.0 to below 2200.0, 2200.0 to below 5650.0, 5650.0 to below 23000.9, 23000.9 or above.

Map 8.8 Train commuters of South Korea

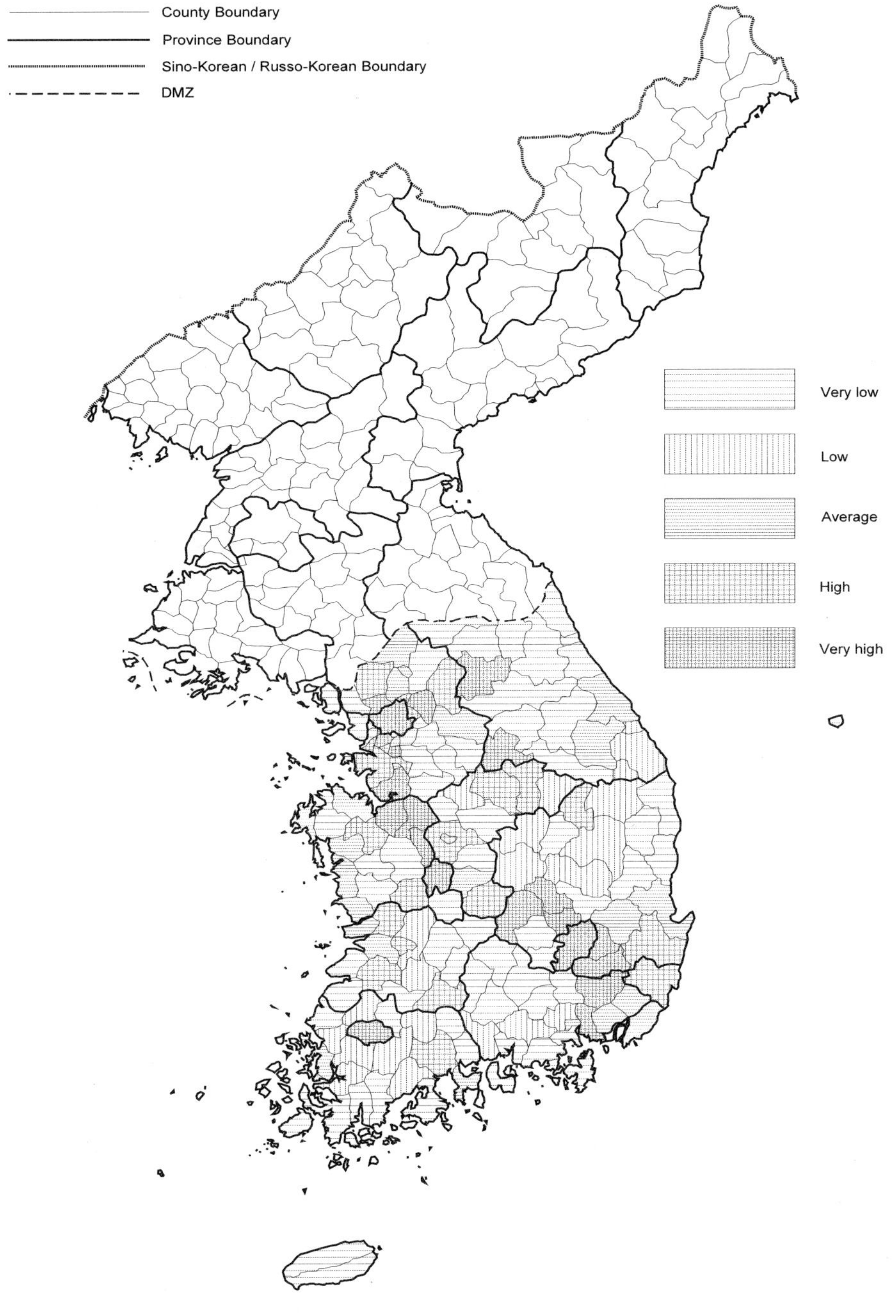

Notes: Unit = persons. Data pertain to people aged 12 years and over. Commuters are defined as people who commute to school or work. This is not an equivalent map with balanced classes because 76 counties had a value below 1.0. The cut-offs were chosen freely with about 22 counties per class the remaining four classes above 0.0. Cut-offs = below 1.0, 1.0 to below 38.0, 38.0 to below 118.0, 118.0 to below 240, 240 or above.

Map 8.9 Taxi commuters of South Korea

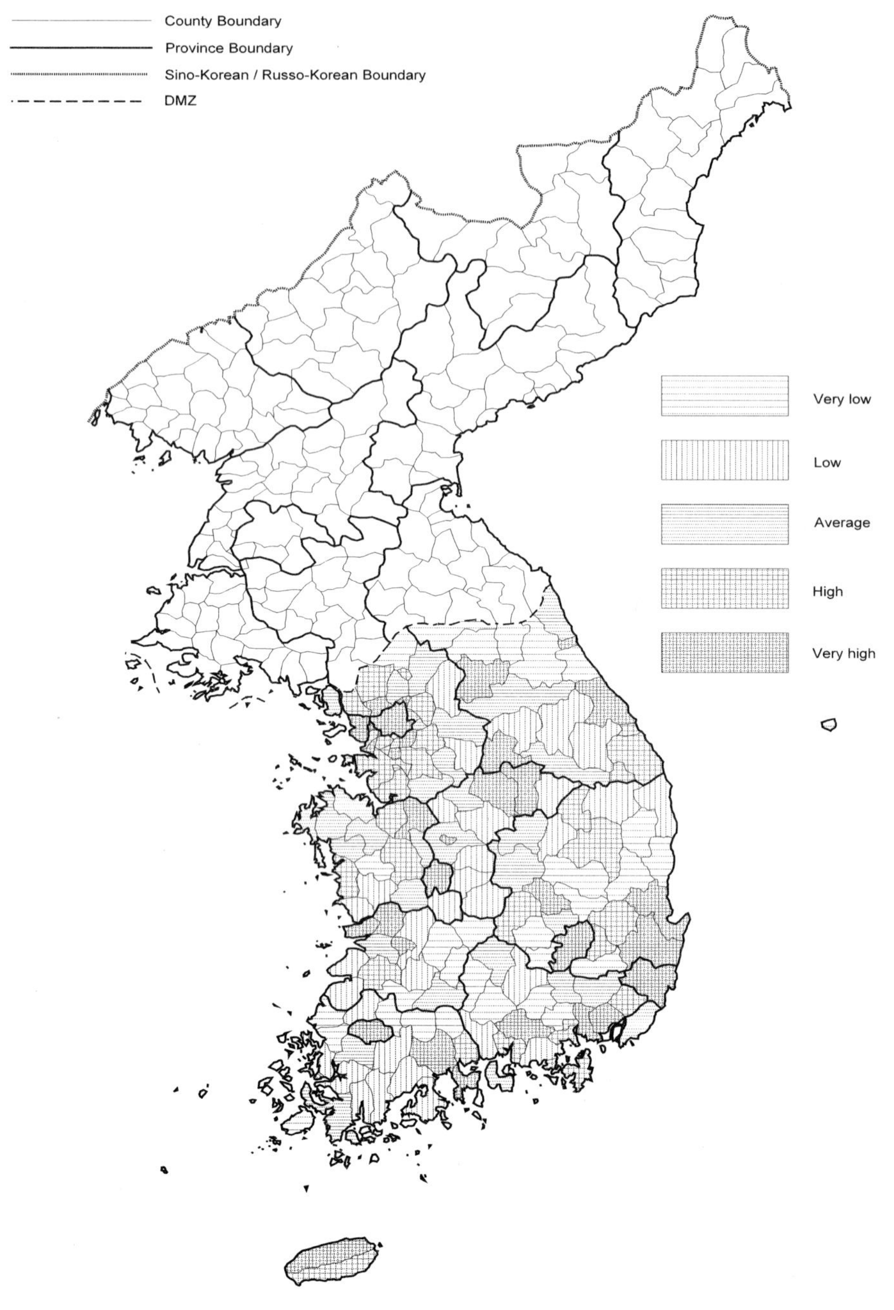

Notes: Unit = persons. Data pertain to people aged 12 years and over. Commuters are defined as people who commute to school or work. Cut-offs = below 41.3, 41.3 to below 99.2, 99.2 to below 323.7, 323.7 to below 996.3, 996.3 or above.

Map 8.10 Bicycle commuters of South Korea

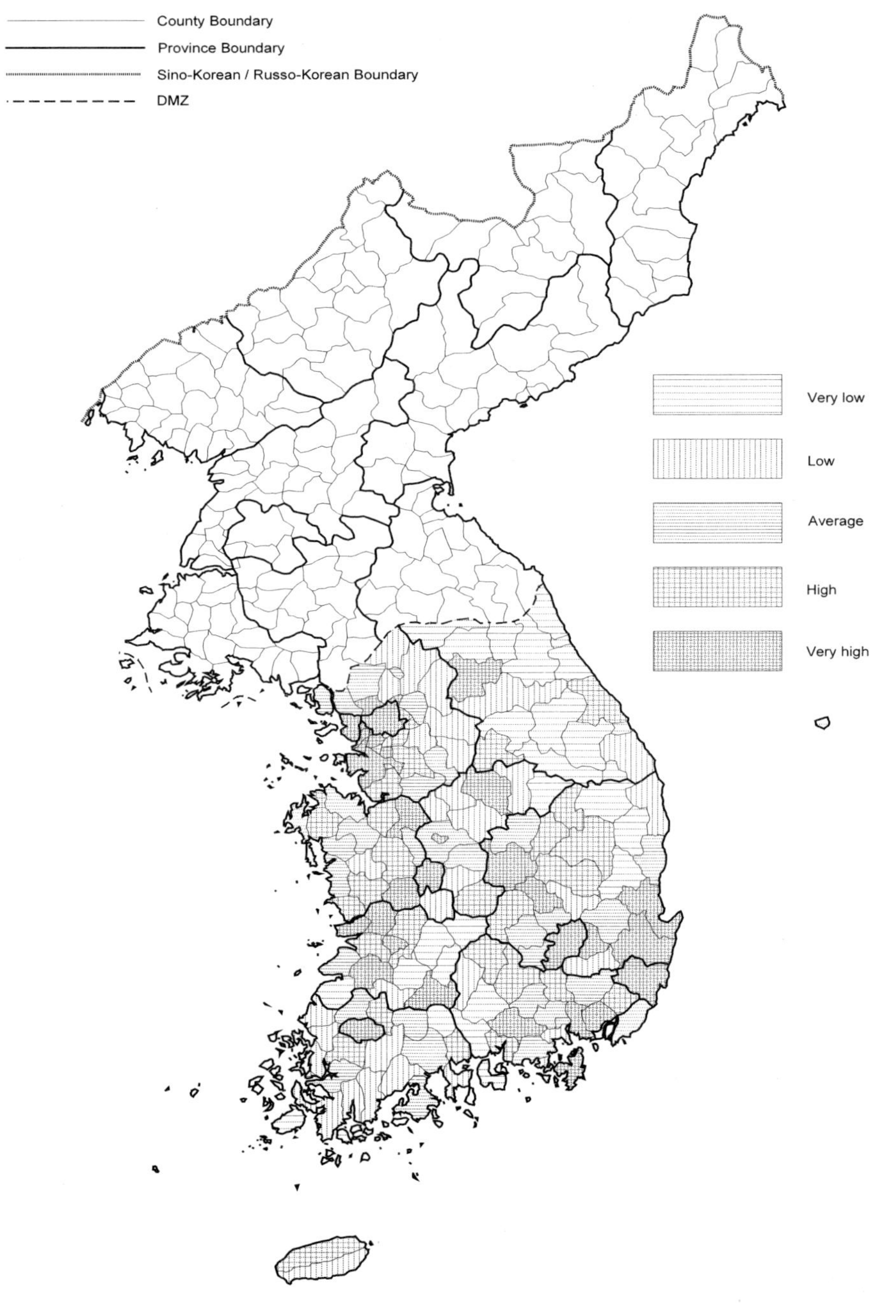

Notes: Unit = persons. Data pertain to people aged 12 years and over. Commuters are defined as people who commute to school or work. Cut-offs = below 490.0, 490.0 to below 823.1, 823.1 to below 1330.6, 1330.6 to below 2439.4, 2439.4 or above.

Map 8.11 Multi-transportation means commuters of South Korea

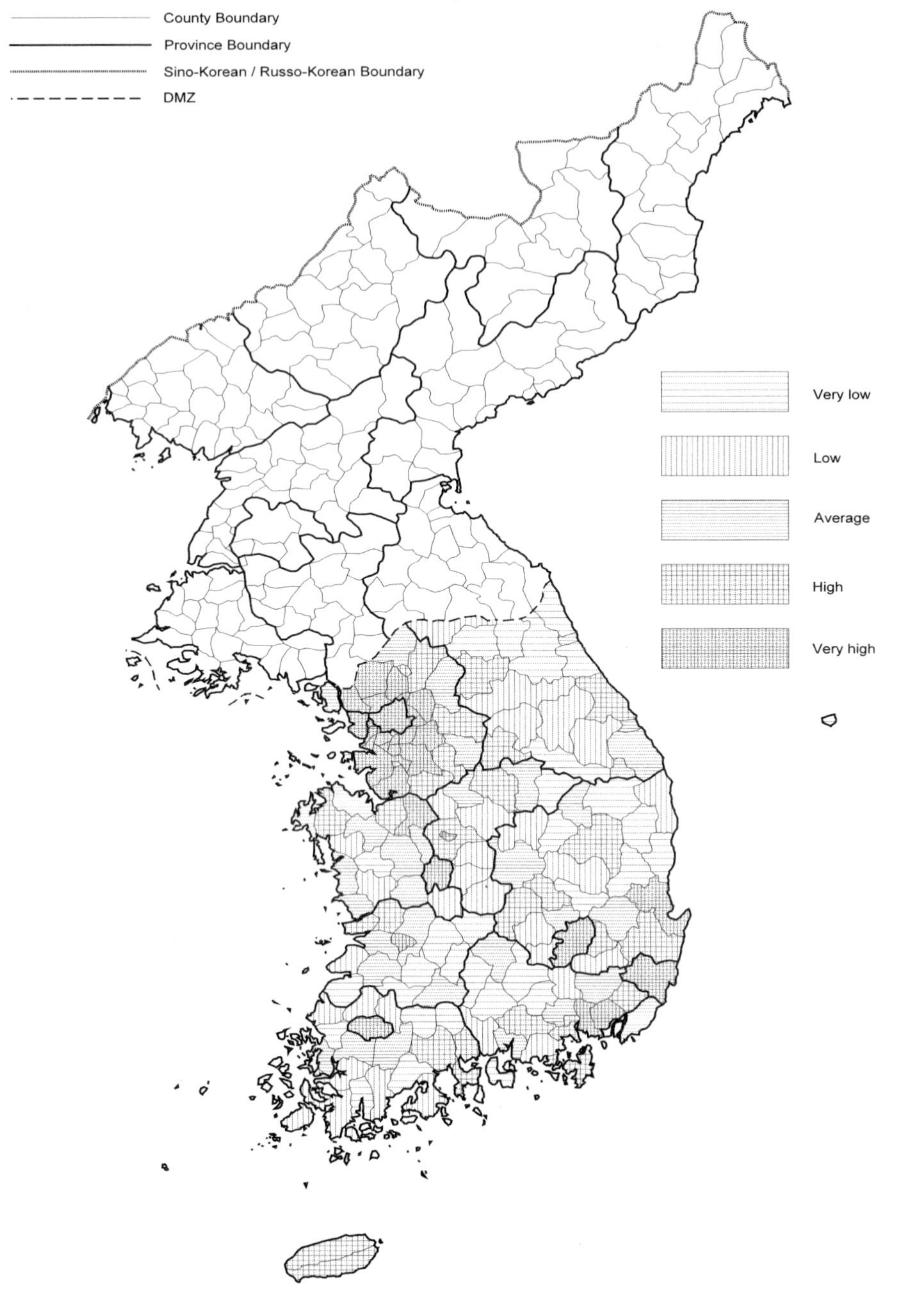

Notes: Unit = persons. Data pertain to people aged 12 years and over. Commuters are defined as people who commute to school or work. Cut-offs = below 203.1, 203.1 to below 508.4, 508.4 to below 1552.4, 1552.4 to below 8247.8, 8247.8 or above.

Map 8.12 Below 15 minute commuters of South Korea

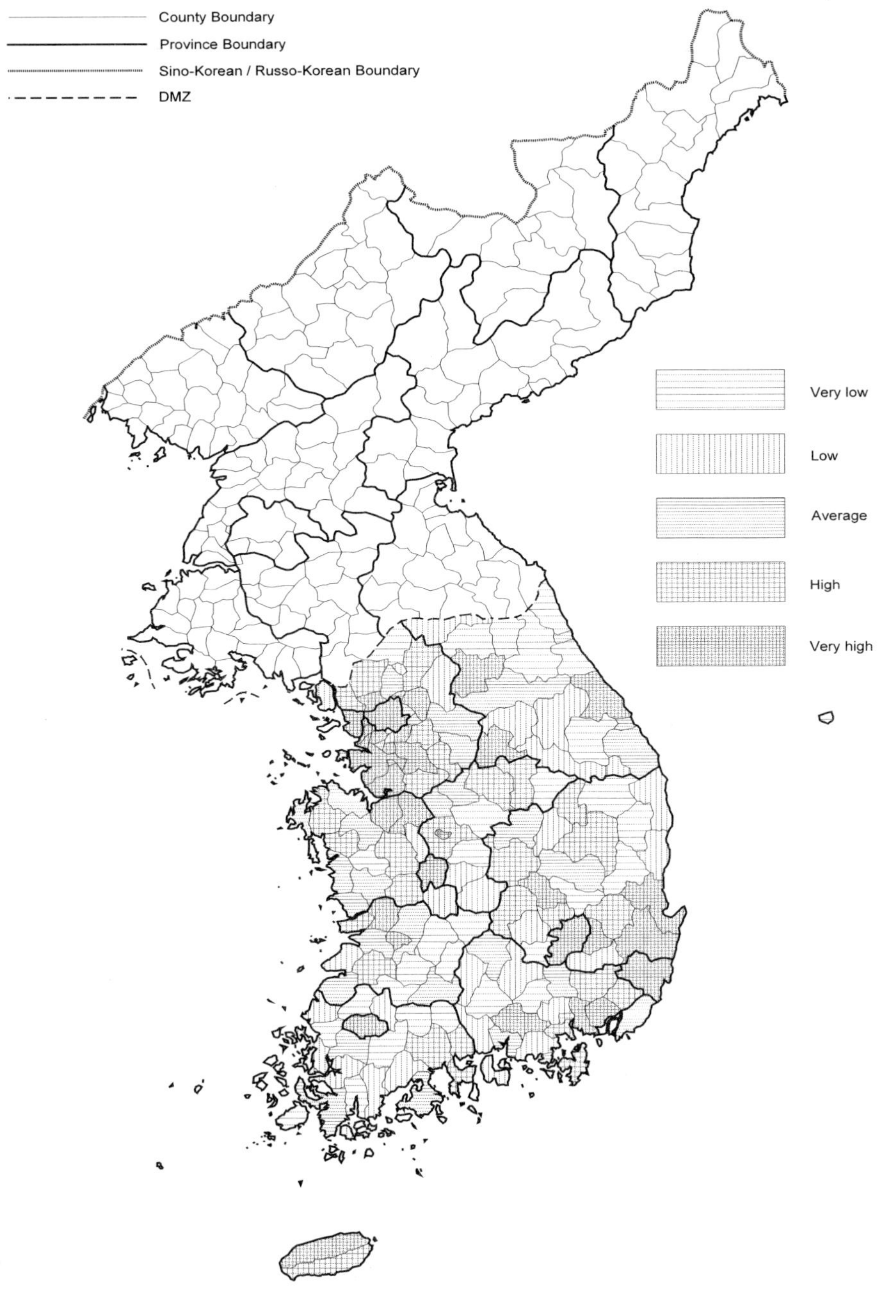

Notes: Unit = persons. Data pertain to people aged 12 years and over. Commuters are defined as people who commute to school or work. Cut-offs = below 11663.6, 11663.6 to below 18409.5, 18409.5 to below 28041.4, 28041.4 to below 51935.5, 51935.5 or above.

Map 8.13 Two hours and over commuters of South Korea

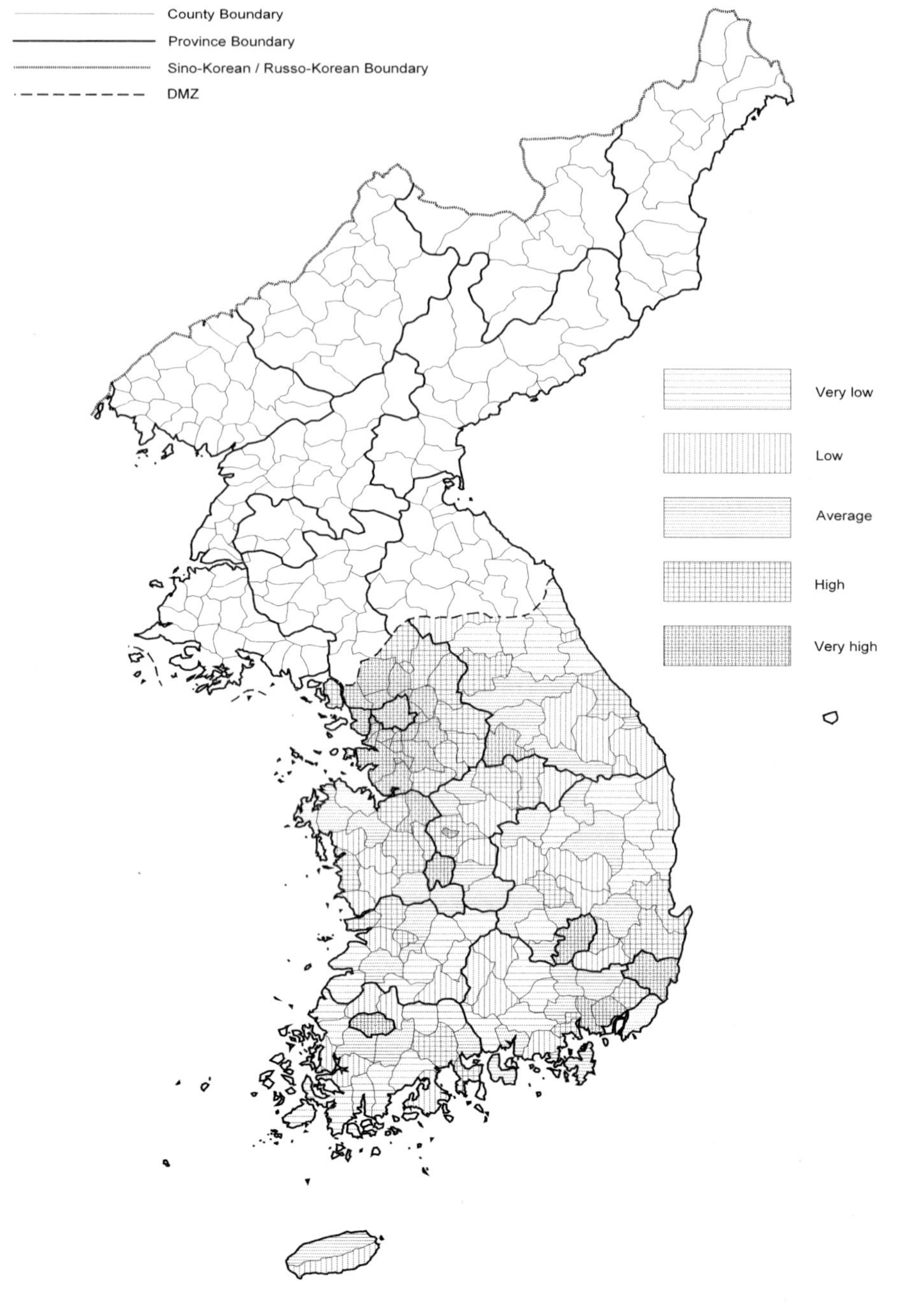

Notes: Unit = persons. Data pertain to people aged 12 years and over. Commuters are defined as people who commute to school or work. Cut-offs = below 43.2, 43.2 to below 118.0, 118.0 to below 335.1, 335.1 to below 1792.2, 1792.2 or above.

Map 8.14 Daytime inflow population of South Korea

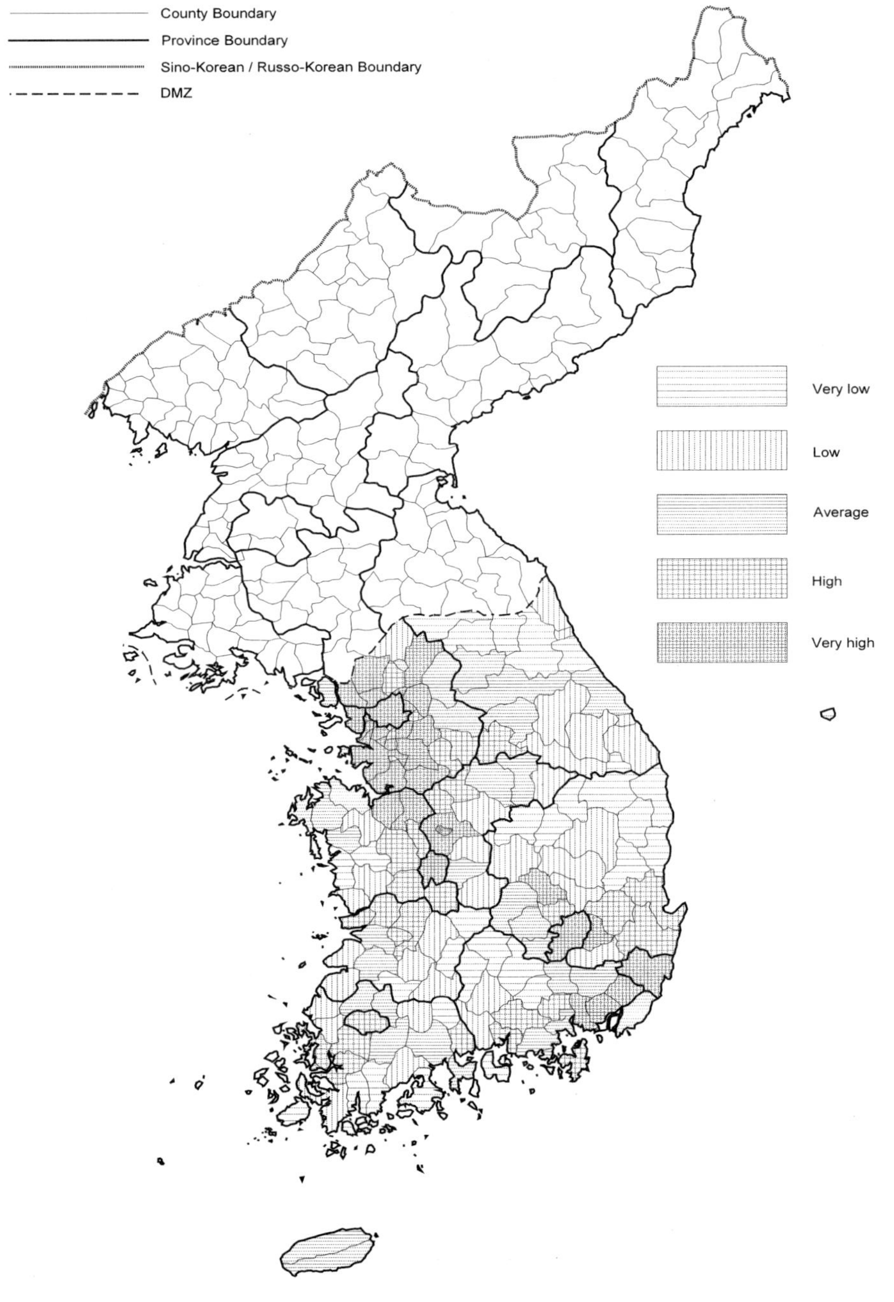

Notes: Unit = persons. Data pertain to people aged 12 years and over. Commuters are defined as people who commute to school or work. Cut-offs = below 2717.4, 2717.4 to below 4849.8, 4849.8 to below 11419.2, 11419.2 to below 30033.6, 30033.6 or above.

Map 8.15 Daytime outflow population of South Korea

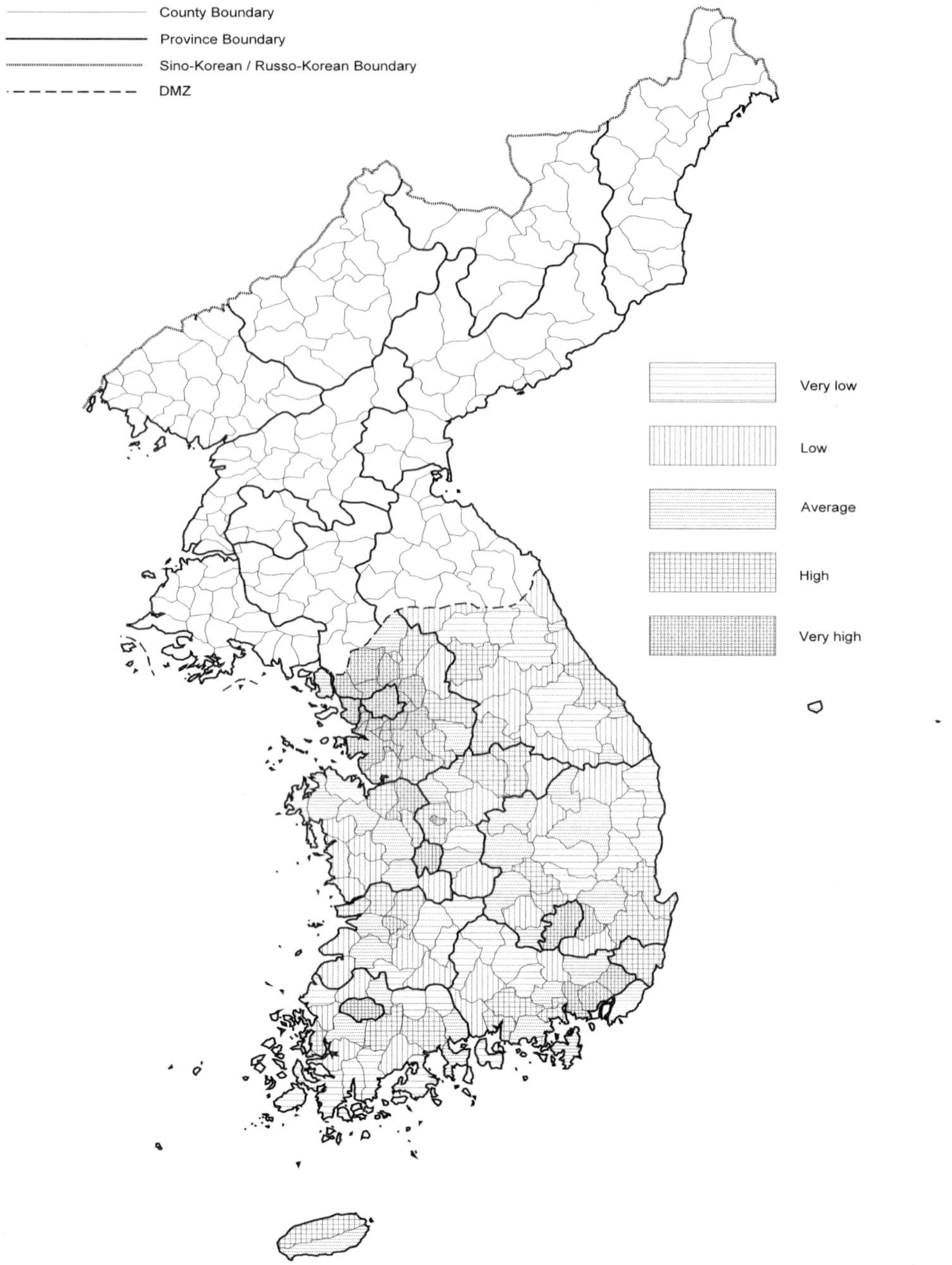

Notes: Unit = persons. Data pertain to people aged 12 years and over. Commuters are defined as people who commute to school or work. Cut-offs = below 682.0, 682.0 to below 2210.4, 2210.4 to below 6730.1, 6730.1 to below 32471.4, 32471.4 or above.

Map 8.16 Intra-migrants of South Korea

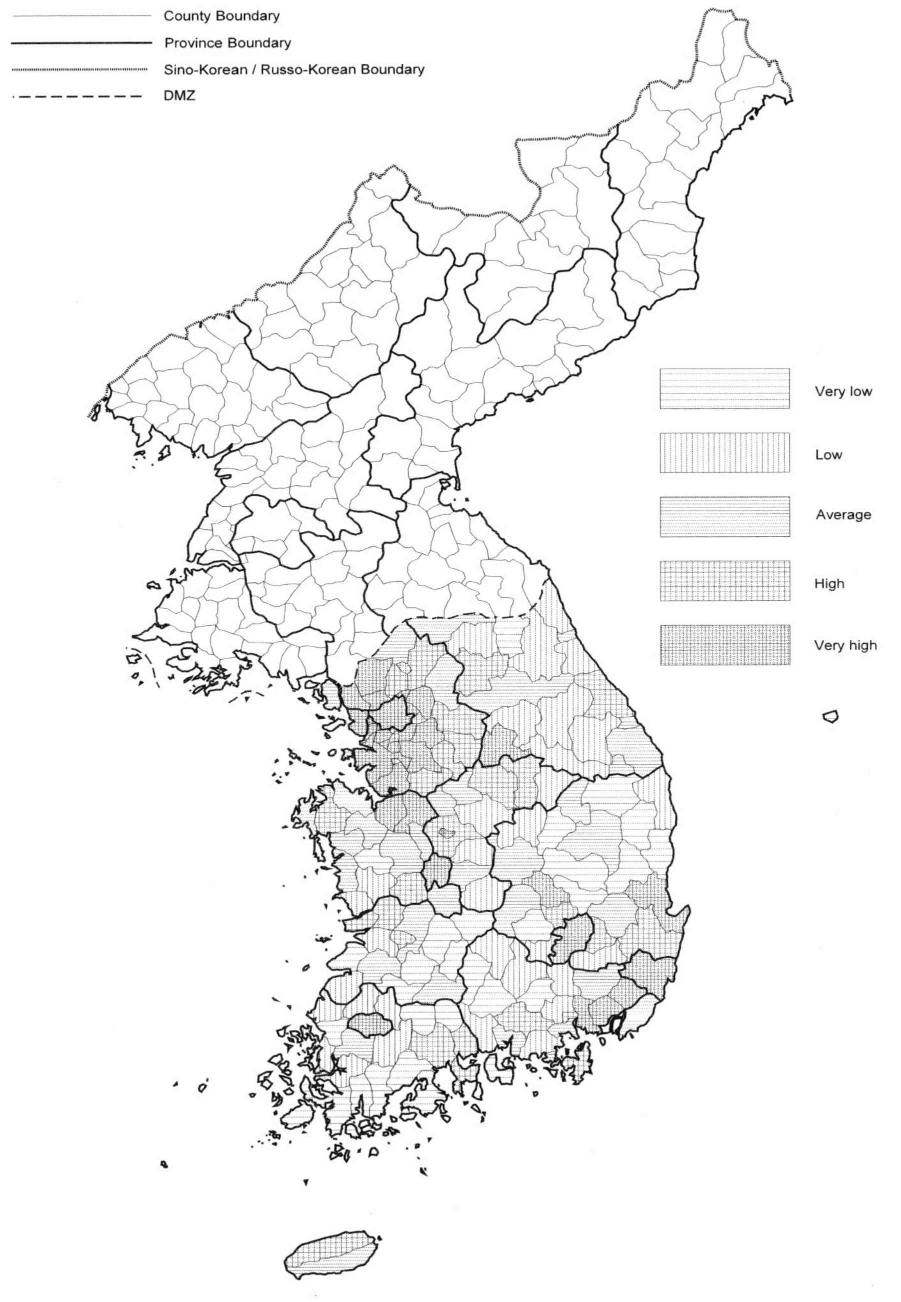

Notes: Unit = persons. Data pertain to people currently live in district than is different from their native district. Cut-offs = below 6004.9, 6004.9 to below 12736.4, 12736.4 to below 34359.5, 34359.5 to below 101534.2, 101534.2 or above.

Map 8.17 Non-commuting population of South Korea (share)

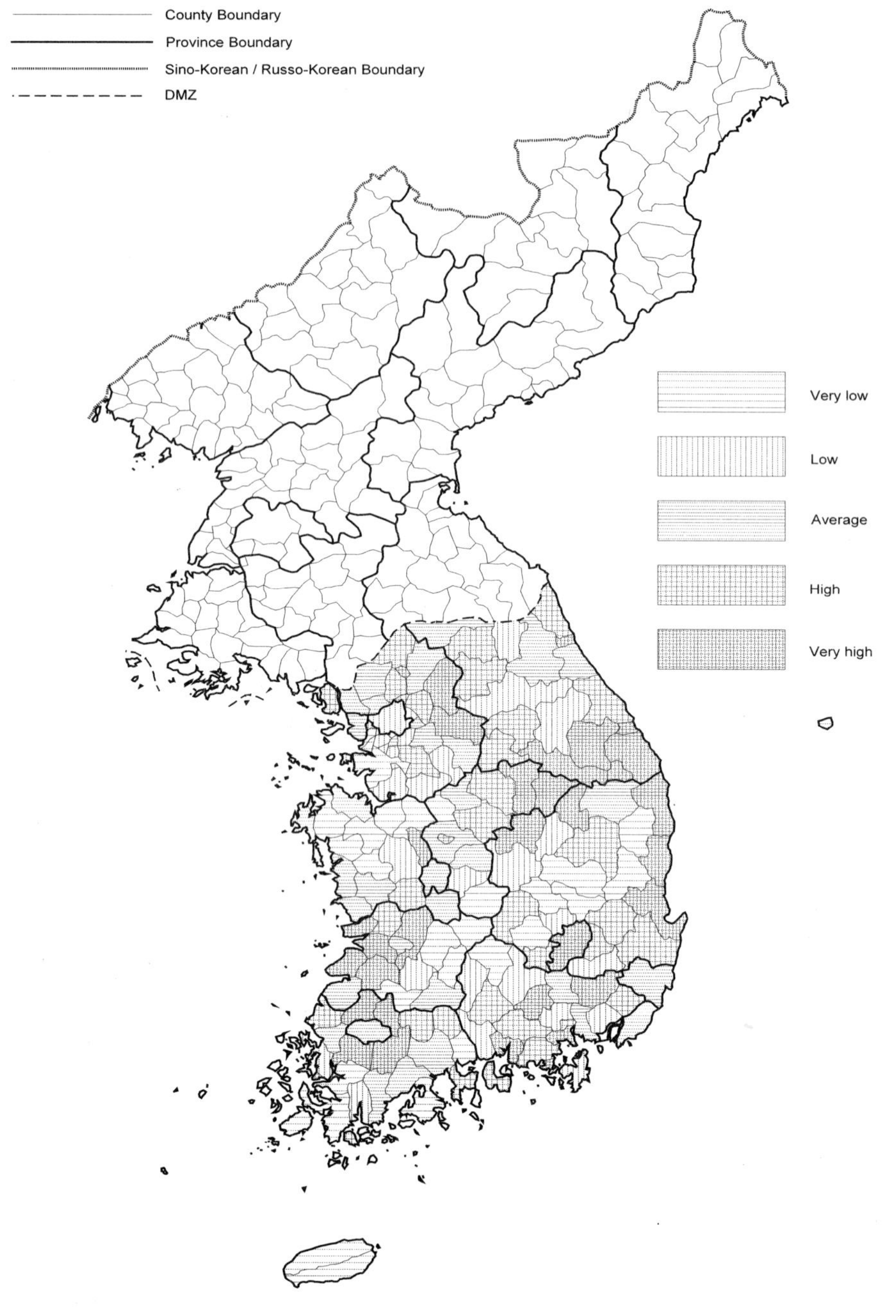

Notes: Unit = percent. Data pertain to people aged 12 years and over. Cut-offs = below 28.627, 28.627 to below 30.816, 30.816 to below 32.049, 32.049 to below 34.090, 34.090 or above.

Map 8.18 Commuting population of South Korea (share)

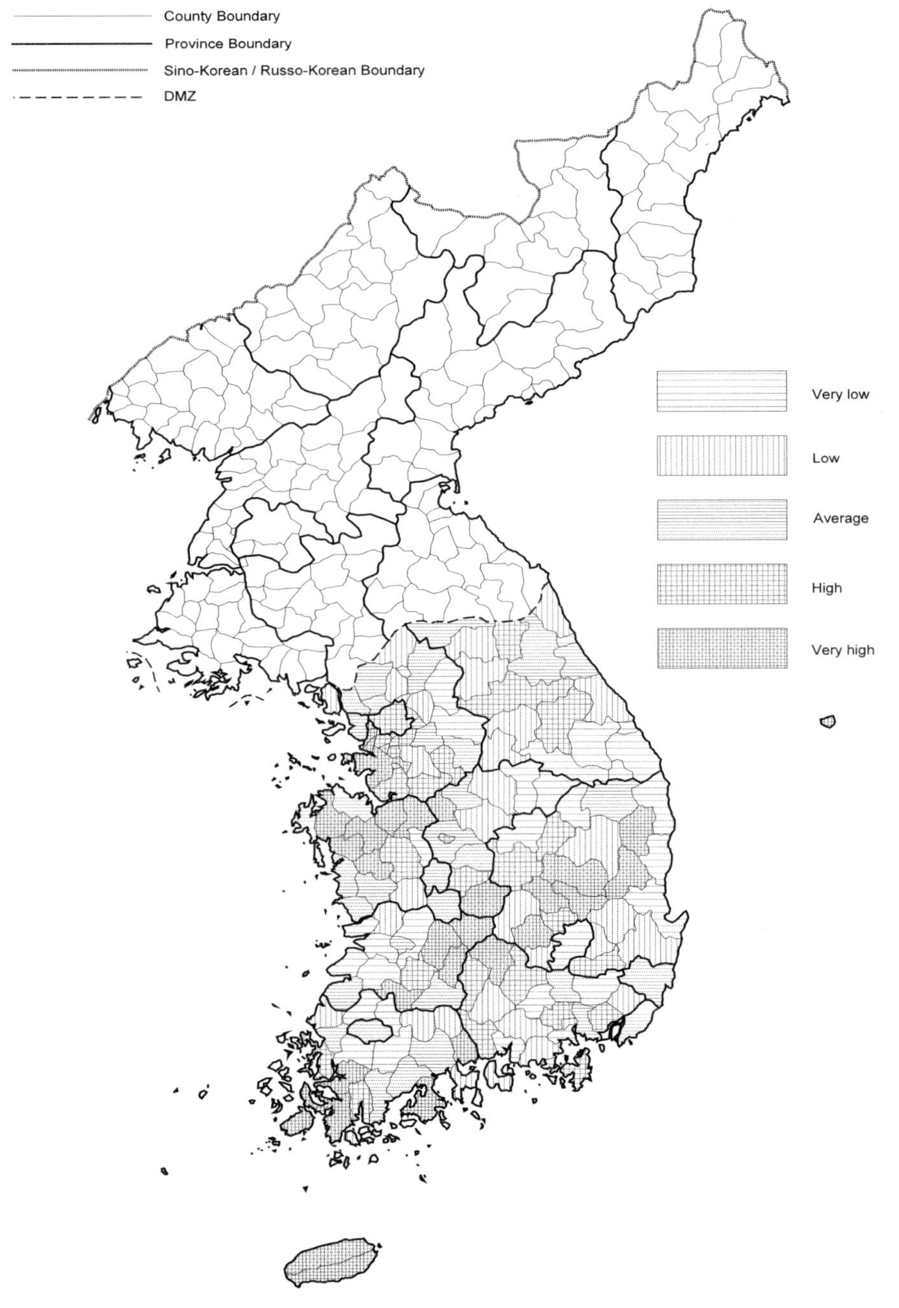

Notes: Unit = percent. Data pertain to people aged 12 years and over. Cut-offs = below 65.910, 65.910 to below 67.951, 67.951 to below 69.184, 69.184 to below 71.373, 71.373 or above.

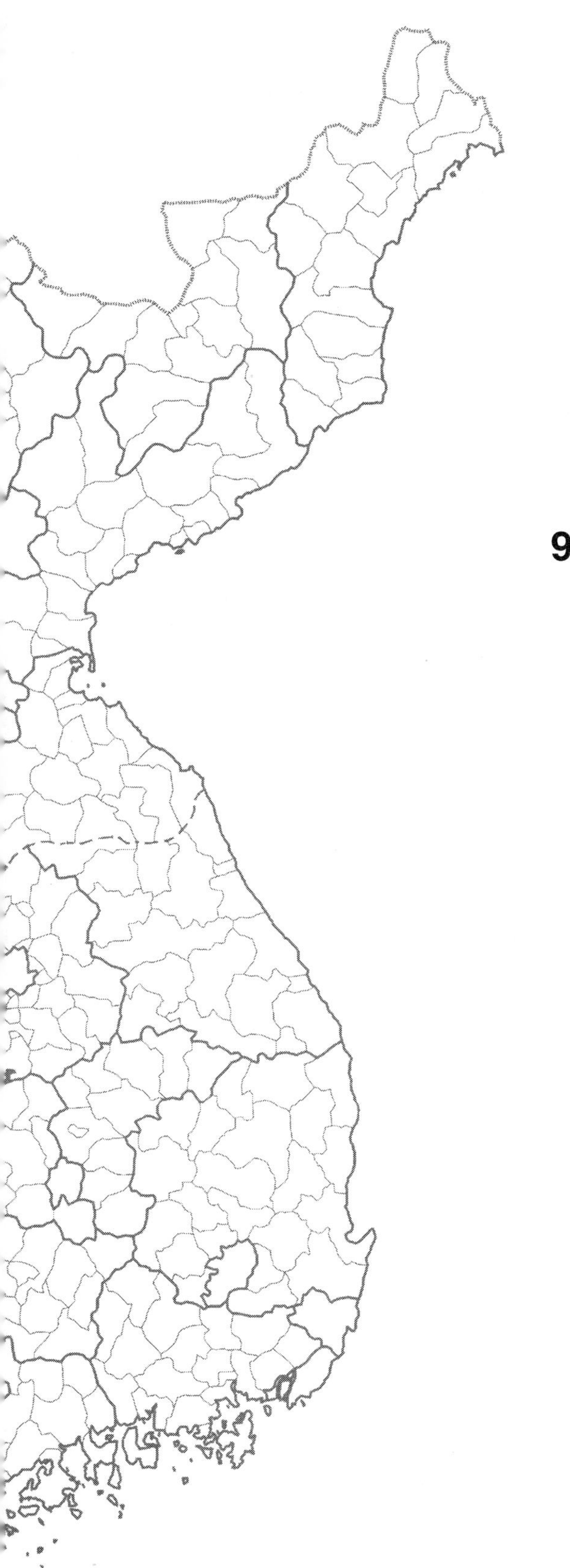

9. Population with Restrictions

Map 9.1 Total population with restrictions in activity of the Korean peninsula

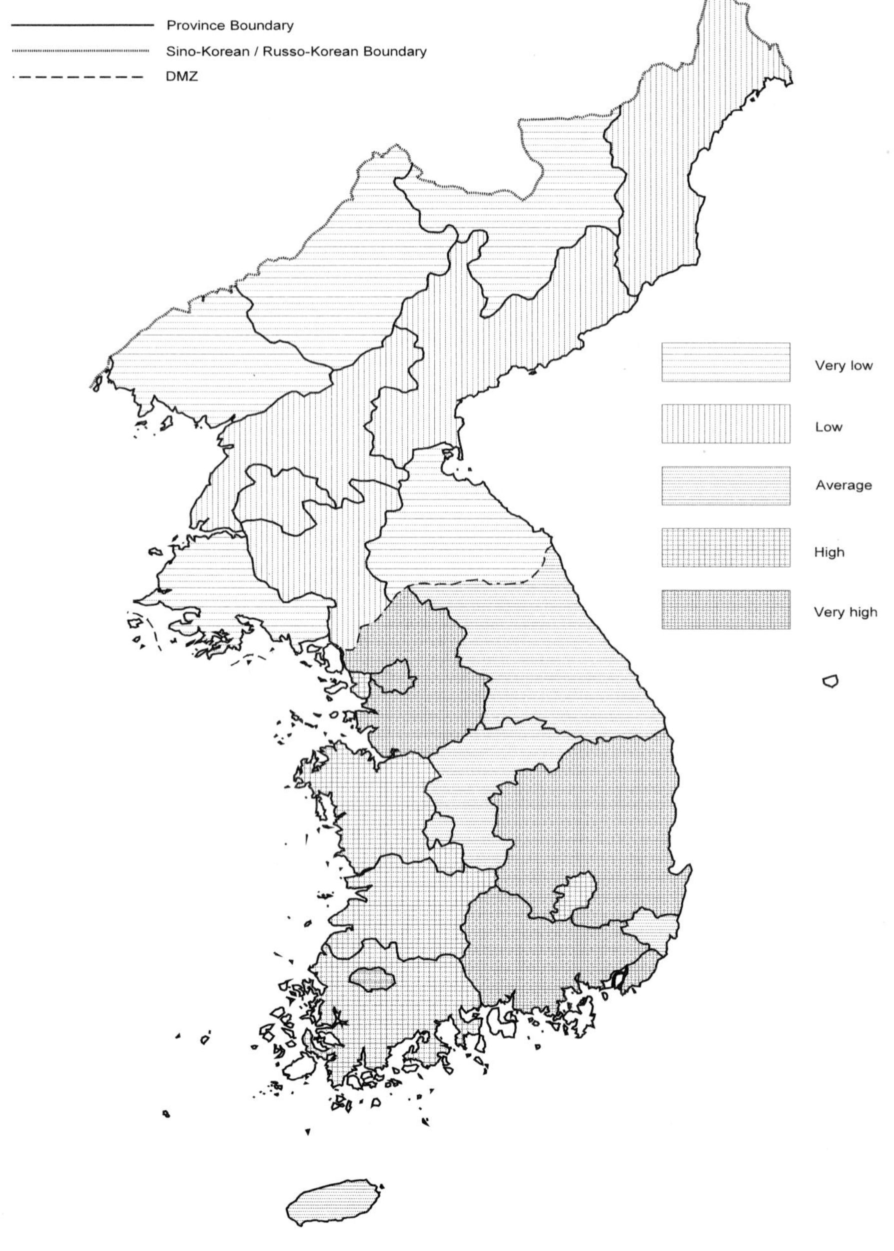

Notes: Unit = persons. South Korean data pertain to people with restrictions in activity aged 5 years and older, North Korean data to 'disabled' people aged 16 years and older. Cut-offs = below 14985.3, 14985.3 to below 43750.0, 43750.0 to below 145693.3, 145693.3 to below 226225.9, 226225.9 or above.

Map 9.2 Total population with restrictions in activity of South Korea

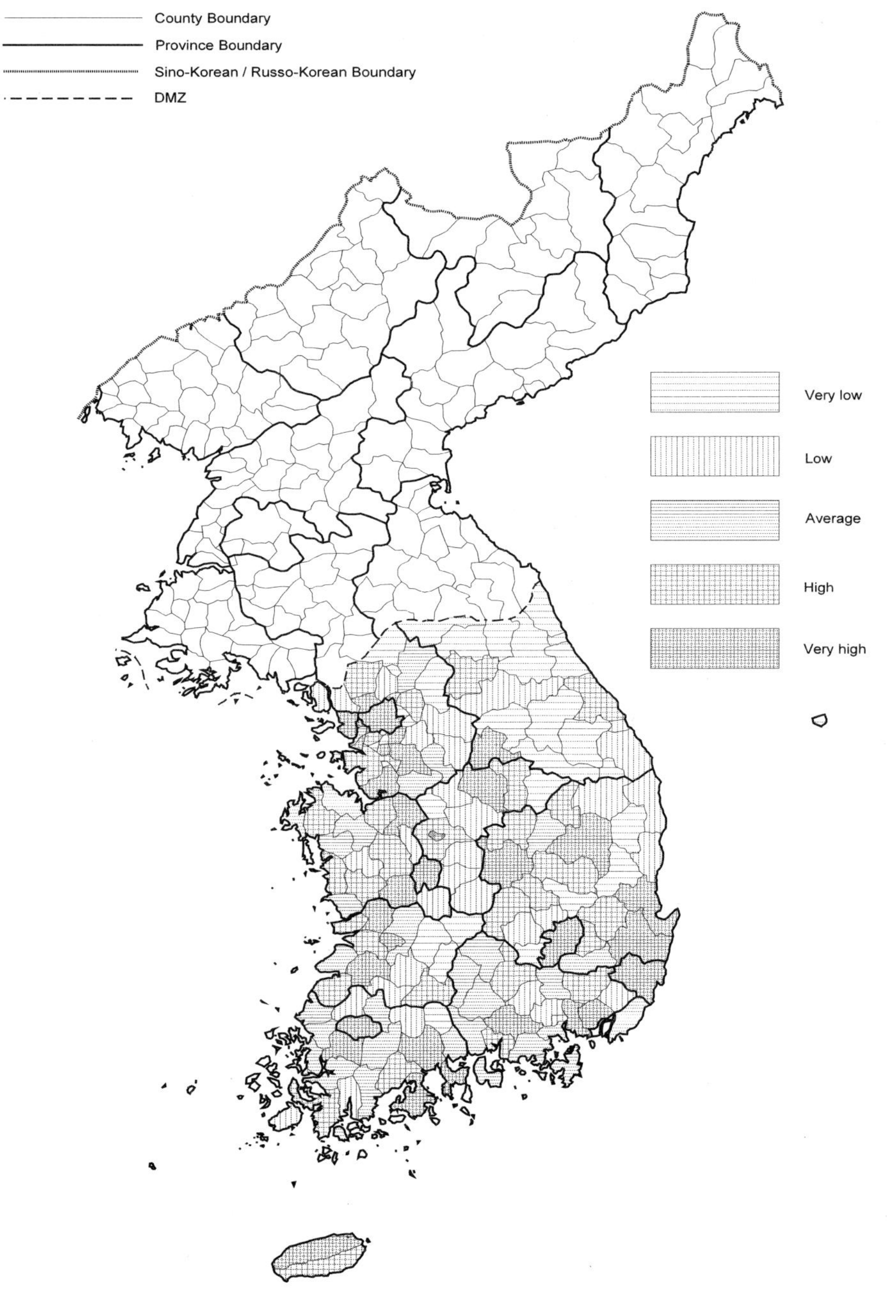

Notes: Unit = persons. Data pertain to people with restrictions in activity aged 5 years and older. Cut-offs = below 3871.1, 3871.1 to below 5423.1, 5423.1 to below 7235.5, 7235.5 to below 9430.6, 9430.6 or above.

Map 9.3 Male population with restrictions in activity of the Korean peninsula

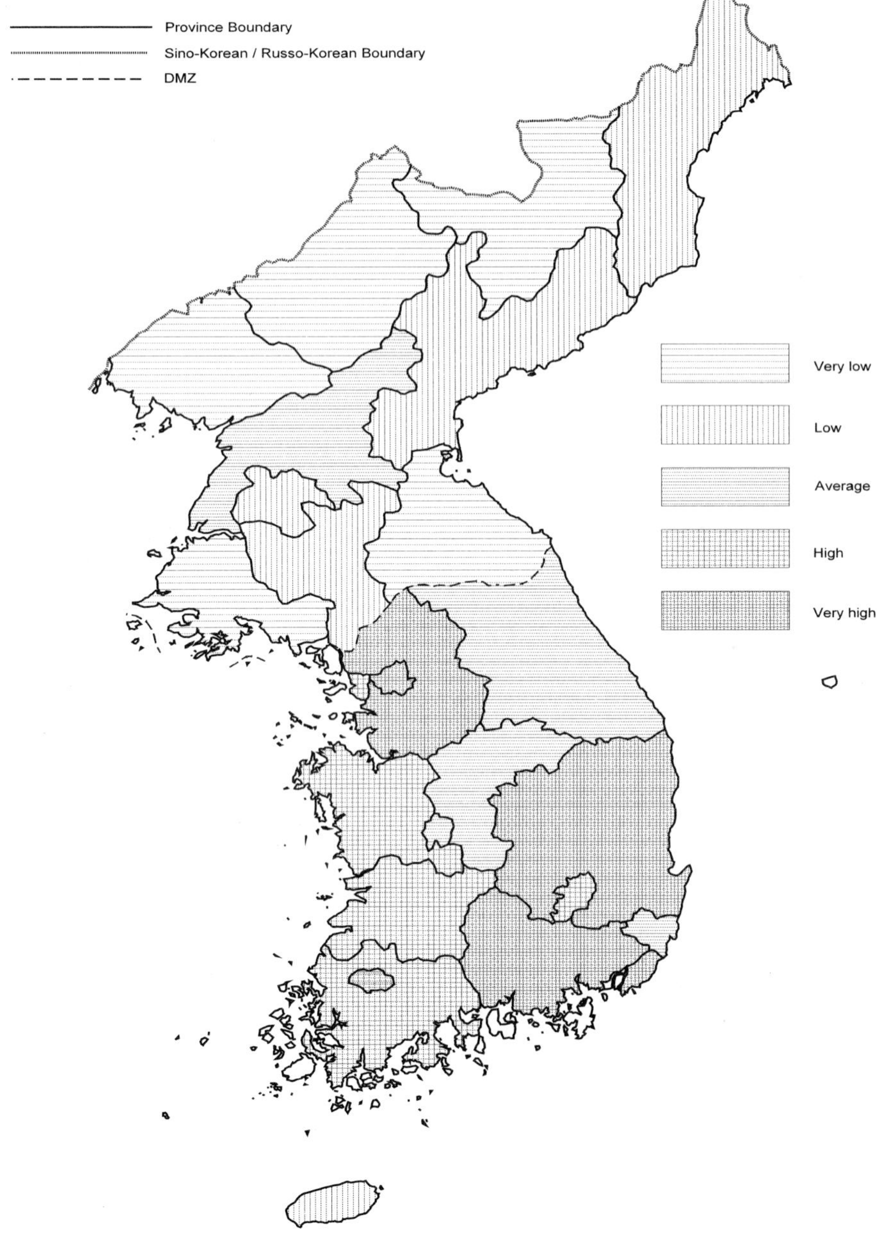

Notes: Unit = persons. South Korean data pertain to people with restrictions in activity aged 5 years and older, North Korean data to 'disabled' people aged 16 years and older. Cut-offs = below 9104.8, 9104.8 to below 19268.5, 19268.5 to below 59100.3, 59100.3 to below 86519.4, 86519.4 or above.

Map 9.4 Male population with restrictions in activity of South Korea

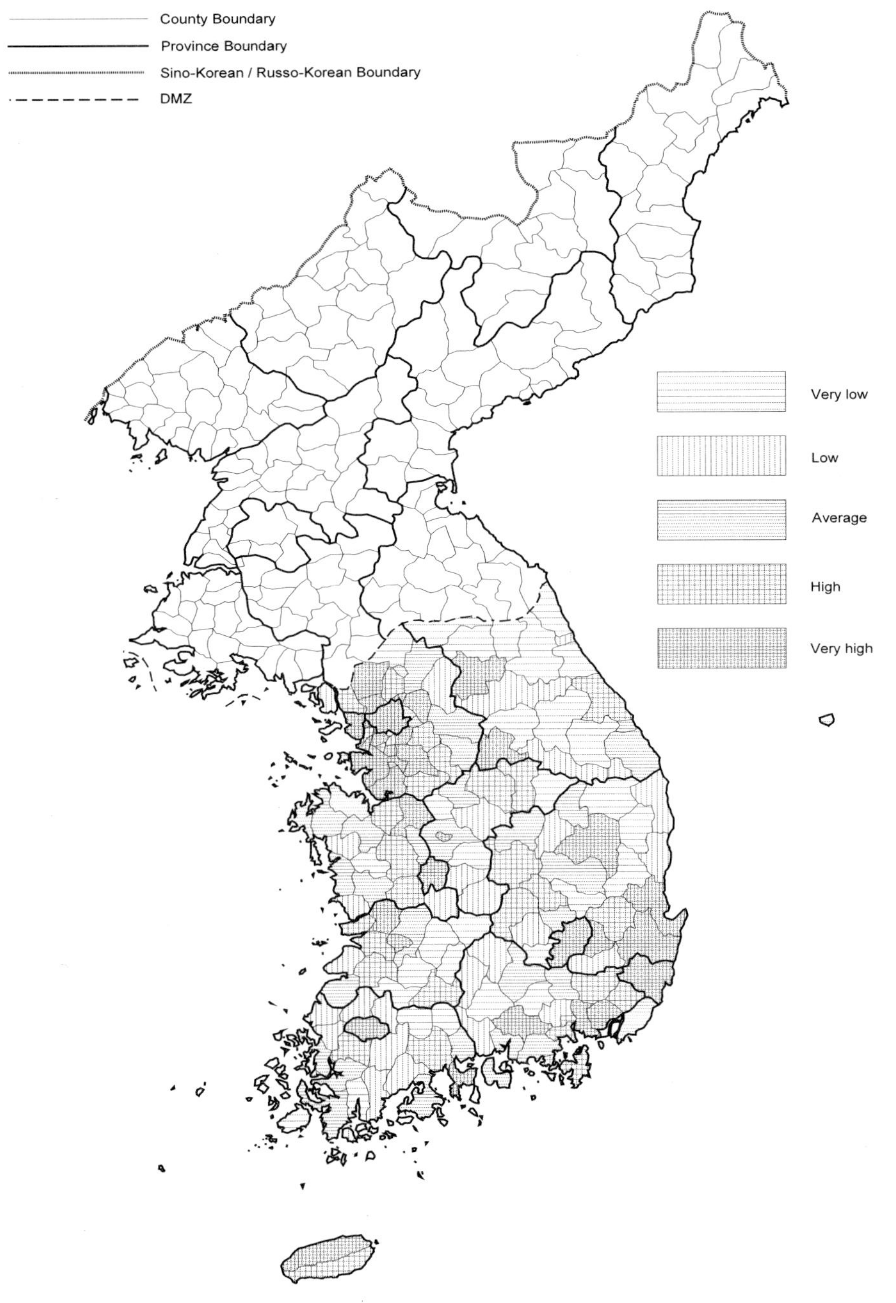

Notes: Unit = persons. Data pertain to people with restrictions in activity aged 5 years and older. Cut-offs = below 2108.0, 2108.0 to below 3139.5, 3139.5 to below 4914.0, 4914.0 to below 8594.0, 8594.0 or above.

Map 9.5 Female population with restrictions in activity of the Korean peninsula

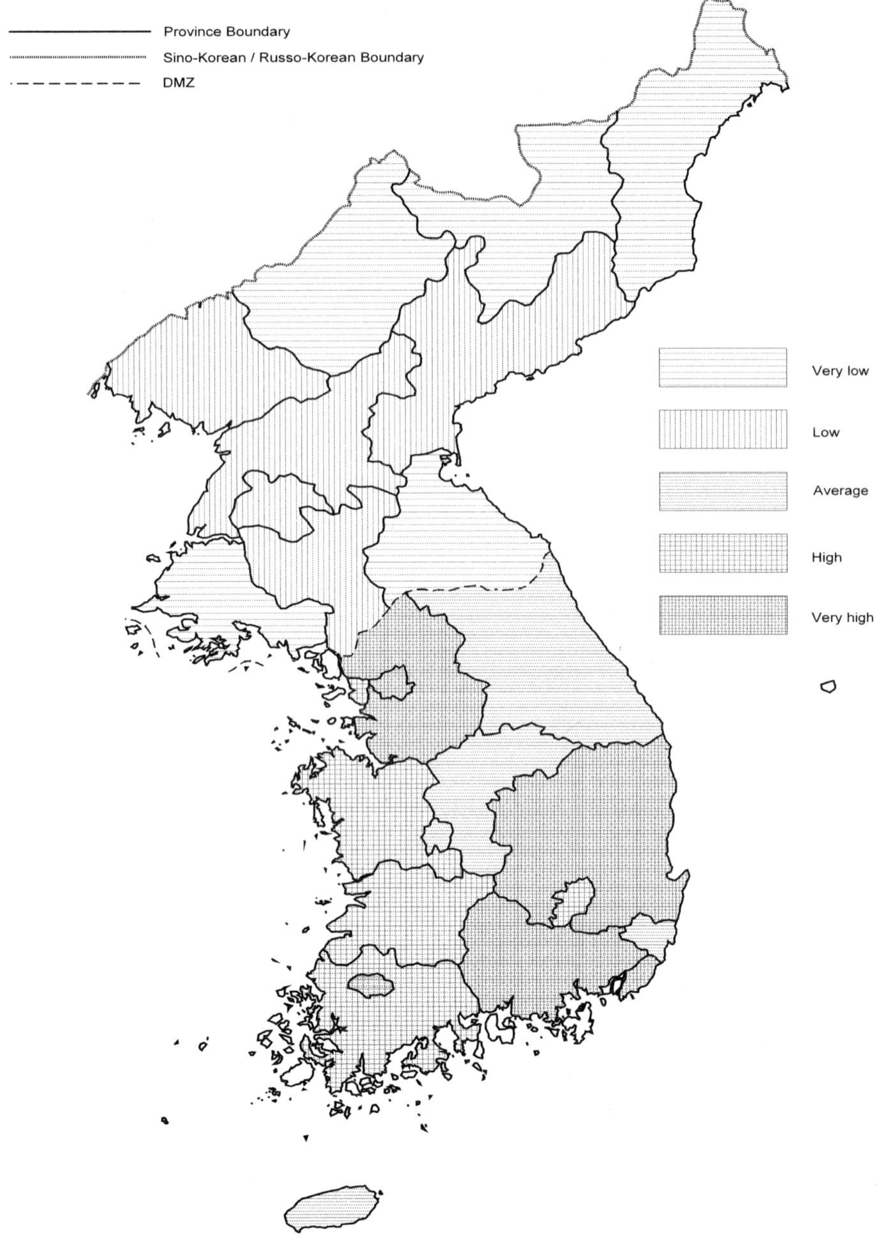

Notes: Unit = persons. South Korean data pertain to people with restrictions in activity aged 5 years and older, North Korean data to 'disabled' people aged 16 years and older. Cut-offs = below 5481.9, 5481.9 to below 26277.5, 26277.5 to below 86593.0, 86593.0 to below 139648.6, 139648.6 or above.

Map 9.6 Female population with restrictions in activity of South Korea

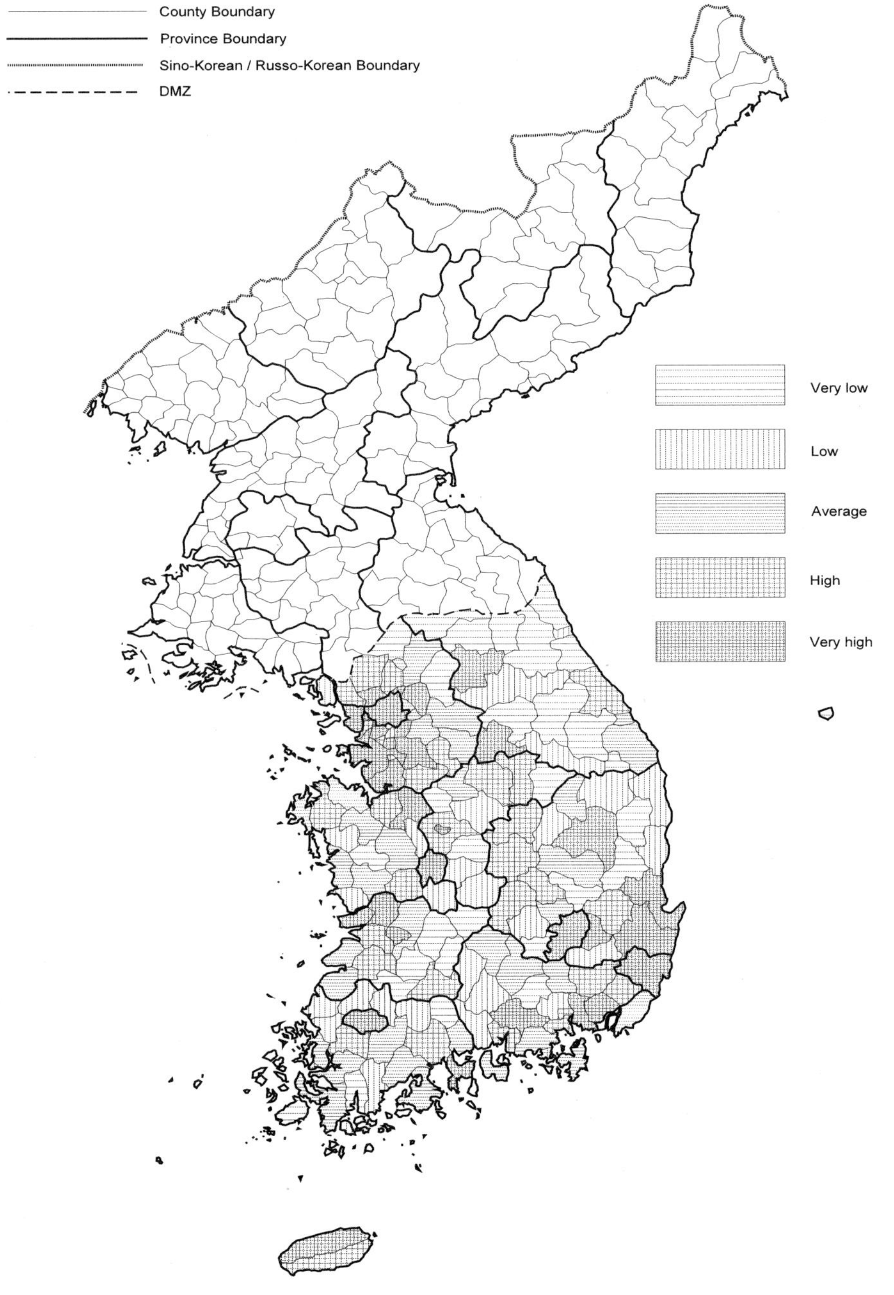

Notes: Unit = persons. Data pertain to people with restrictions in activity aged 5 years and older. Cut-offs = below 3505.0, 3505.0 to below 5055.5, 5055.5 to below 7170.0, 7170.0 to below 12516.0, 12516.0 or above.

Map 9.7 Total population with restrictions in activity of the Korean peninsula (share)

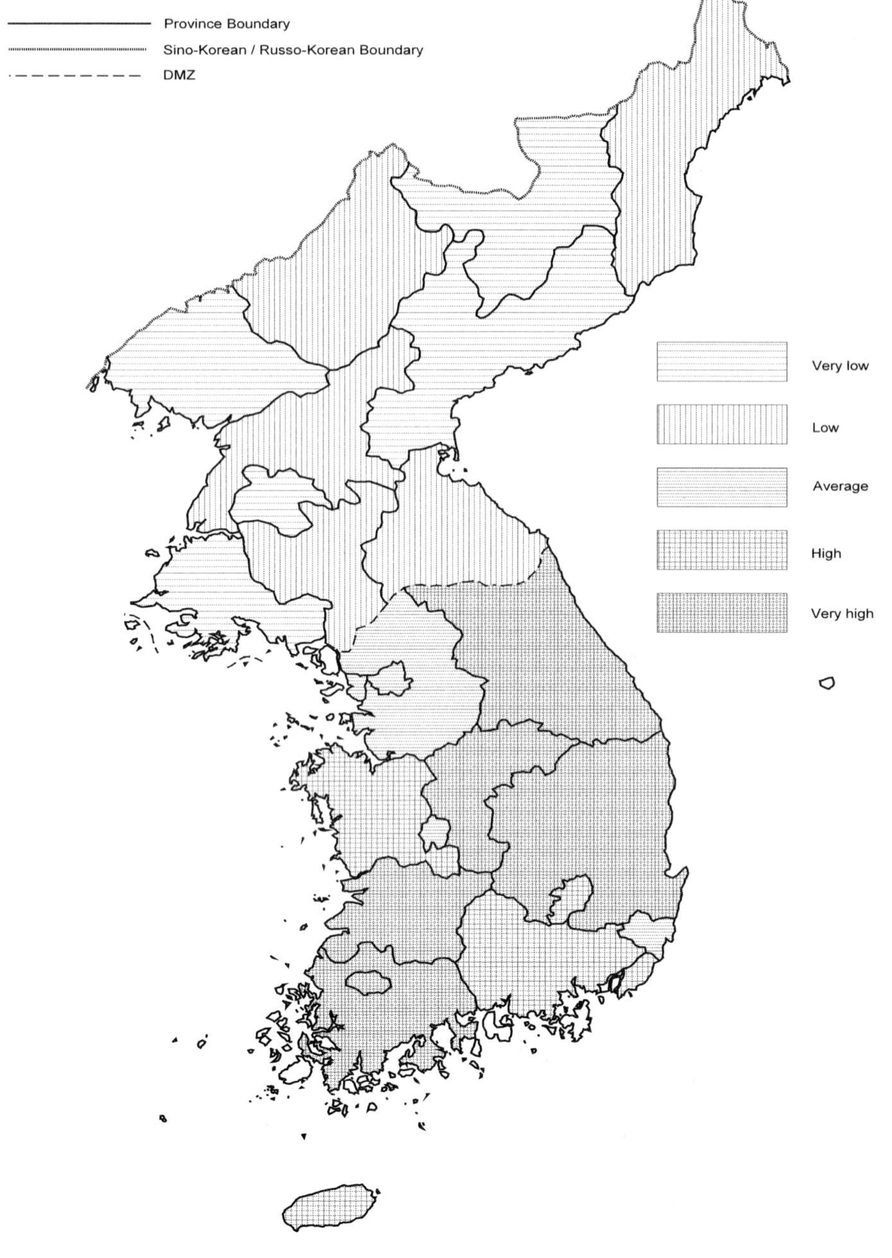

Notes: Unit = percent. South Korean data pertain to people with restrictions in activity aged 5 years and older, North Korean data to 'disabled' people aged 16 years and older. Cut-offs = below 0.878, 0.878 to below 4.983, 4.983 to below 7.057, 7.057 to below 9.157, 9.157 or above.

Map 9.8 Total population with restrictions in activity of South Korea (share)

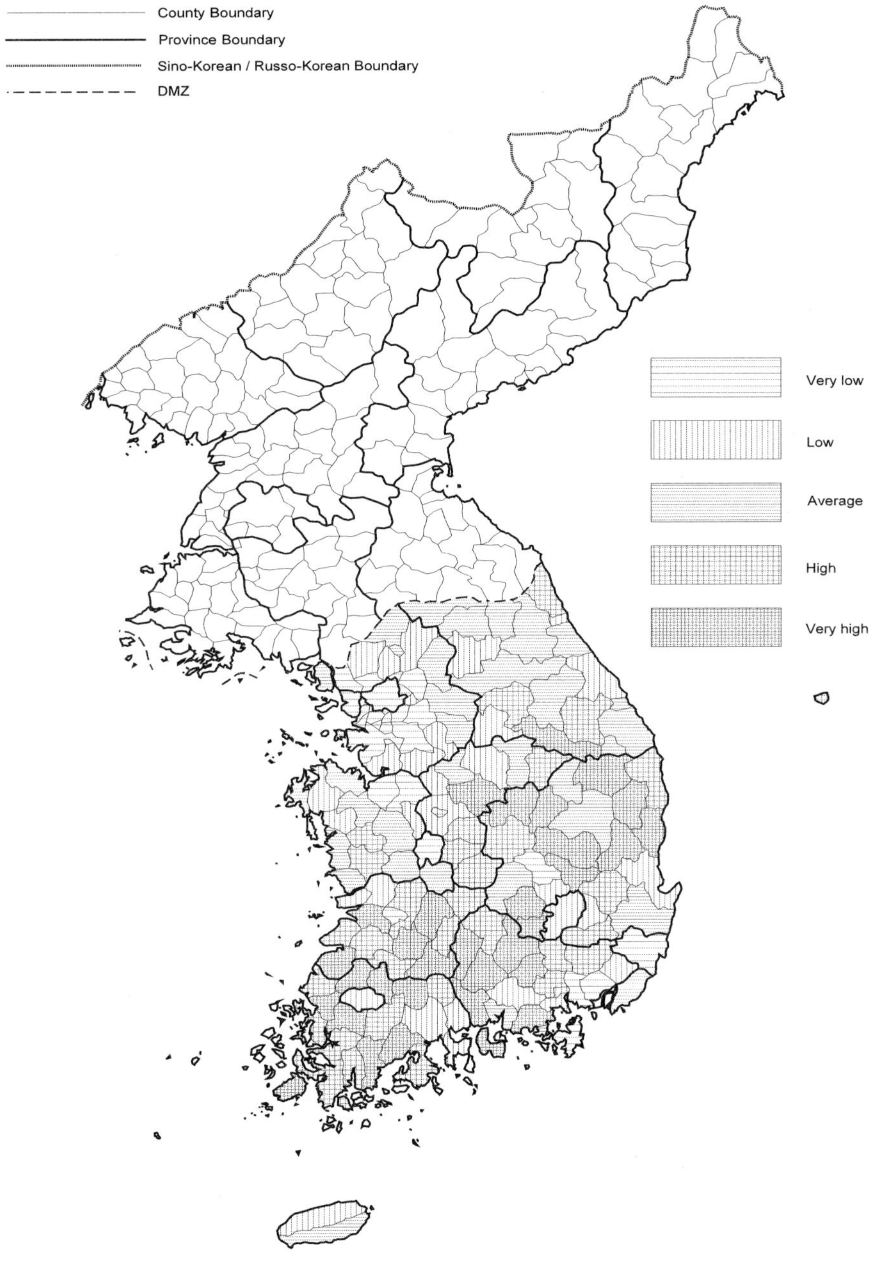

Notes: Unit = percent. Data pertain to people with restrictions in activity aged 5 years and older. Cut-offs = below 6.96, 6.96 to below 10.25, 10.25 to below 13.77, 13.77 to below 17.53, 17.53 or above.

10. Elderly Population

Map 10.1 Elderly population with no formal education of South Korea

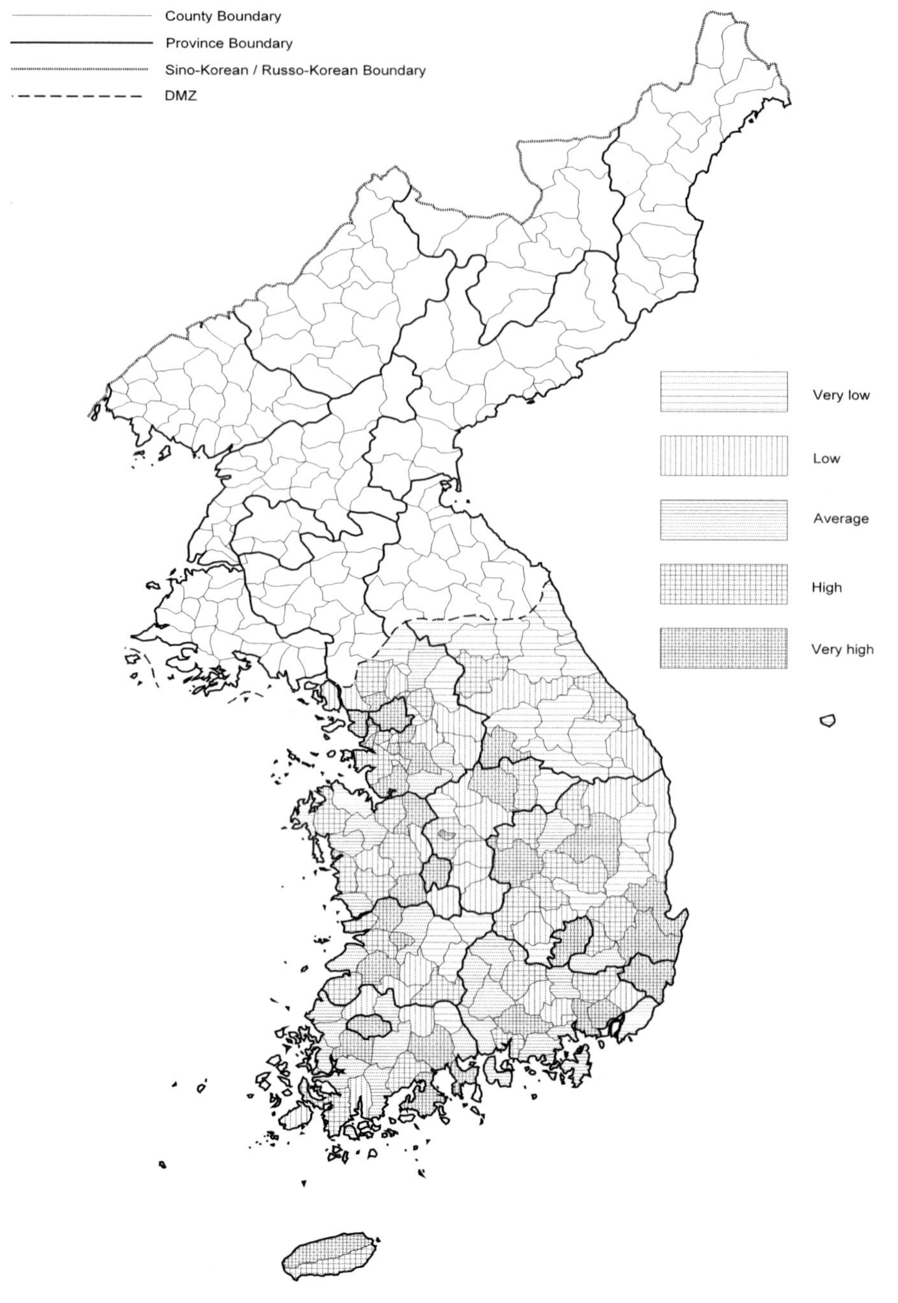

Notes: Unit = persons. Data pertain to persons aged 60 years and older. Cut-offs = below 3871.1, 3871.1 to below 5423.1, 5423.1 to below 7235.5, 7235.5 to below 9430.6, 9430.6 or above.

Map 10.2 Elderly university graduates of South Korea

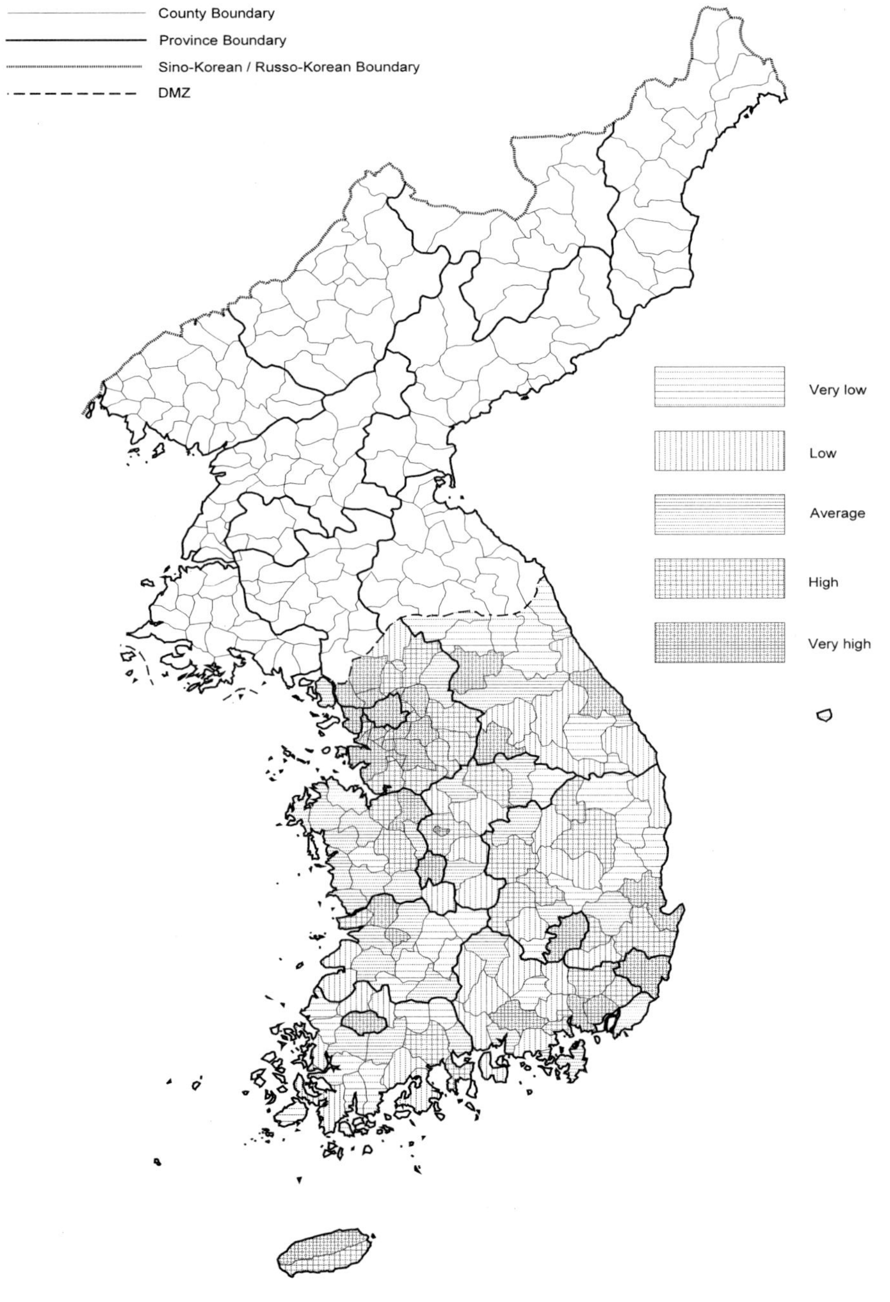

Notes: Unit = persons. Data pertain to persons aged 60 years and older. University degree refers to tertiary college education requiring 4 years and over. Cut-offs = below 182.2, 182.2 to below 364.7, 364.7 to below 727.0, 727.0 to below 1984.1, 1984.1 or above.

Map 10.3 Elderly never married population of South Korea

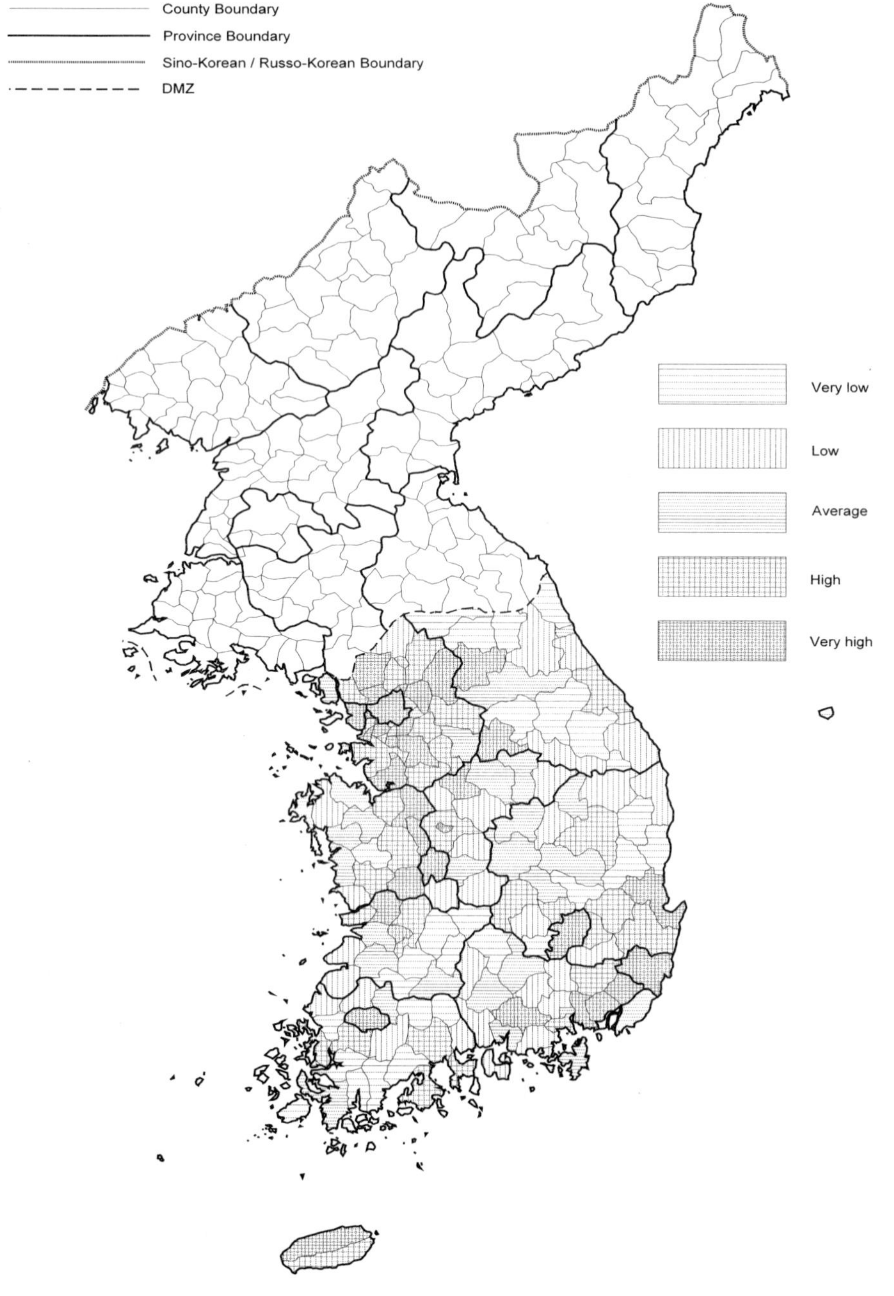

Notes: Unit = persons. Data pertain to persons aged 60 years and older. Cut-offs = below 66.0, 66.0 to below 112.5, 112.5 to below 190.0, 190.0 to below 340.7, 340.7 or above.

Map 10.4 Elderly married population of South Korea

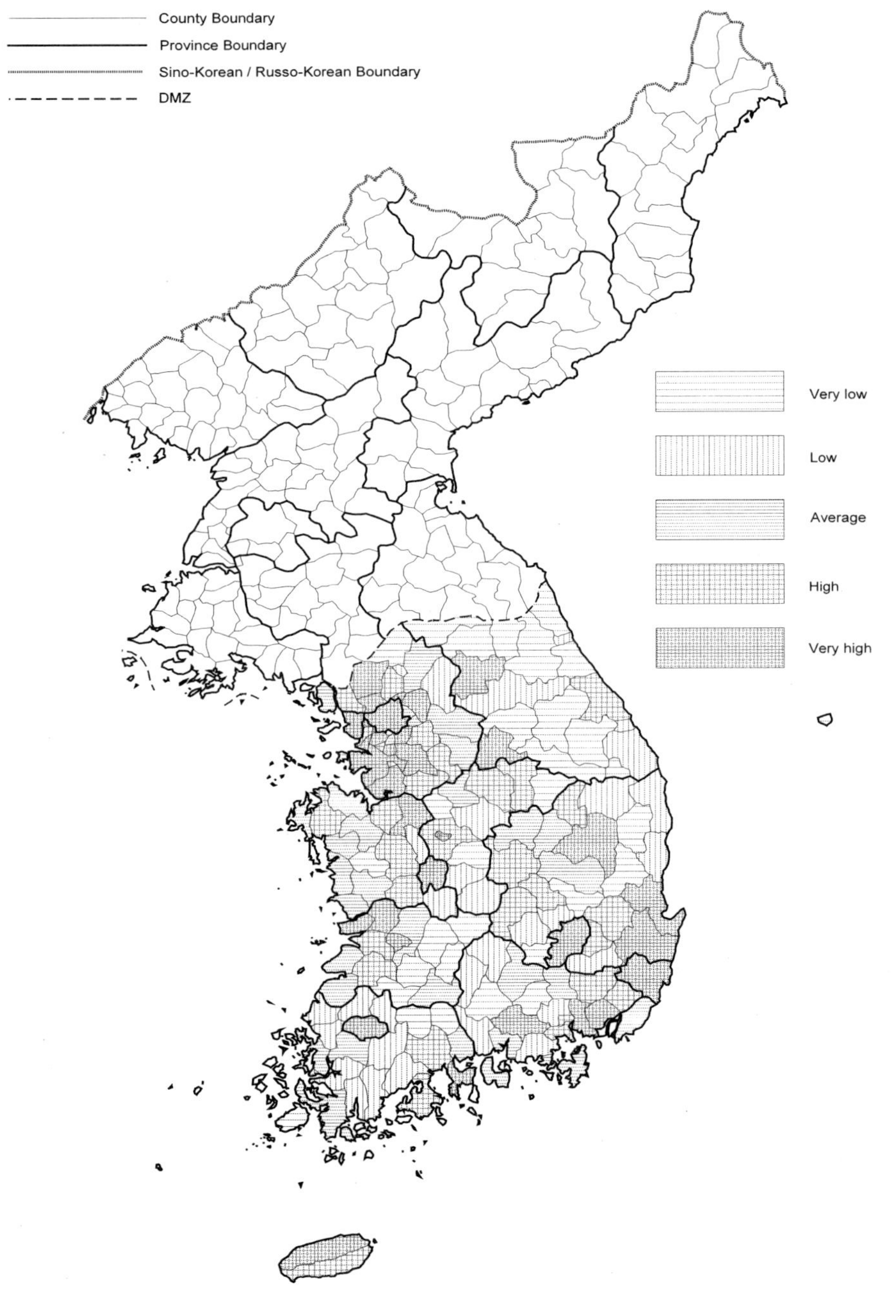

Notes: Unit = persons. Data pertain to persons aged 60 years and older. Cut-offs = below 7959.2, 7959.2 to below 10888.9, 10888.9 to below 16987.5, 16987.5 to below 26589.1, 26589.1 or above.

Map 10.5 Elderly widowed population of South Korea

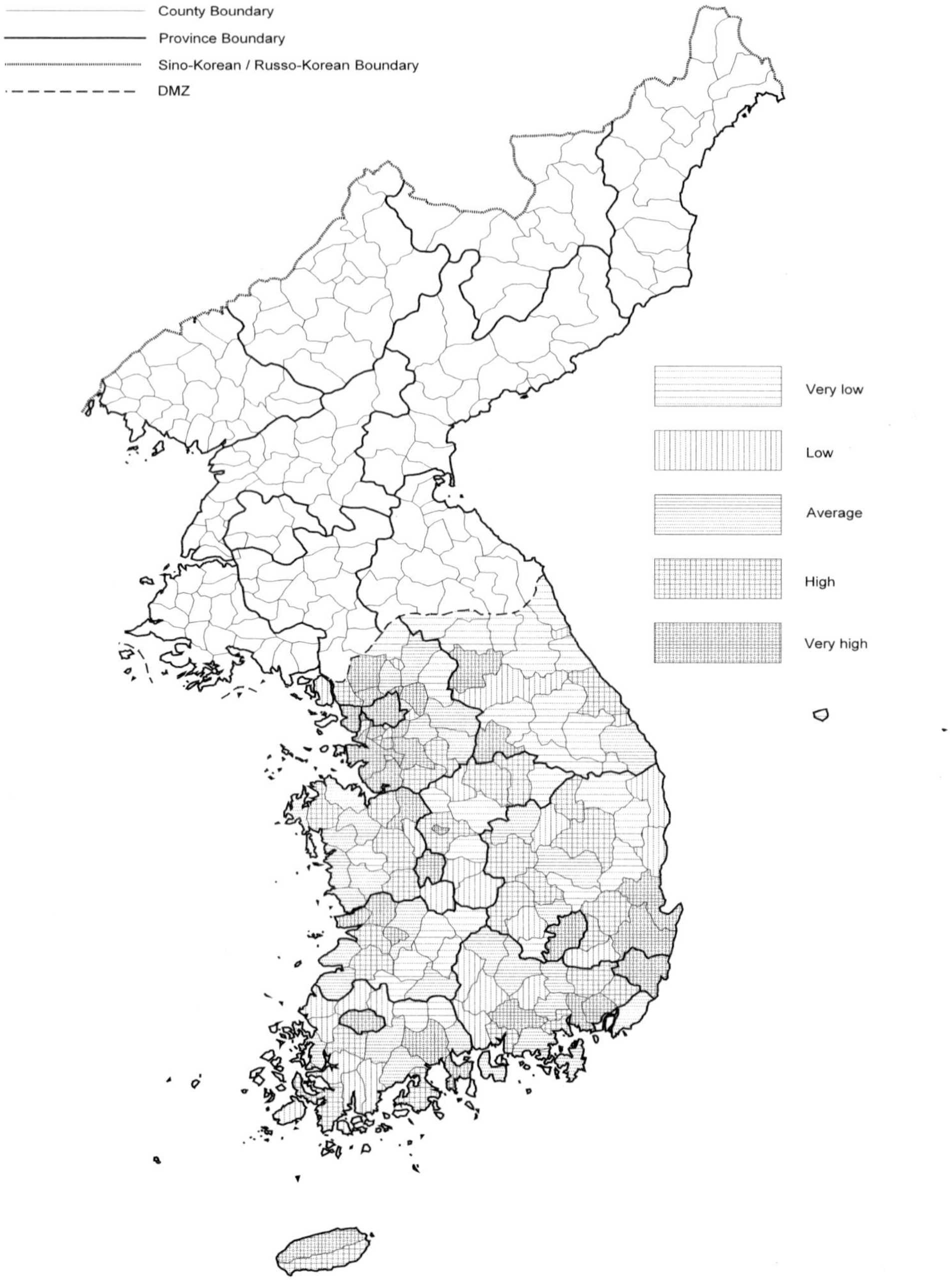

Notes: Unit = persons. Data pertain to persons aged 60 years and older. Cut-offs = below 4452.5, 4452.5 to below 6258.8, 6258.8 to below 9089.3, 9089.3 to below 15096.1, 15096.1 or above.

Map 10.6 Elderly divorced population of South Korea

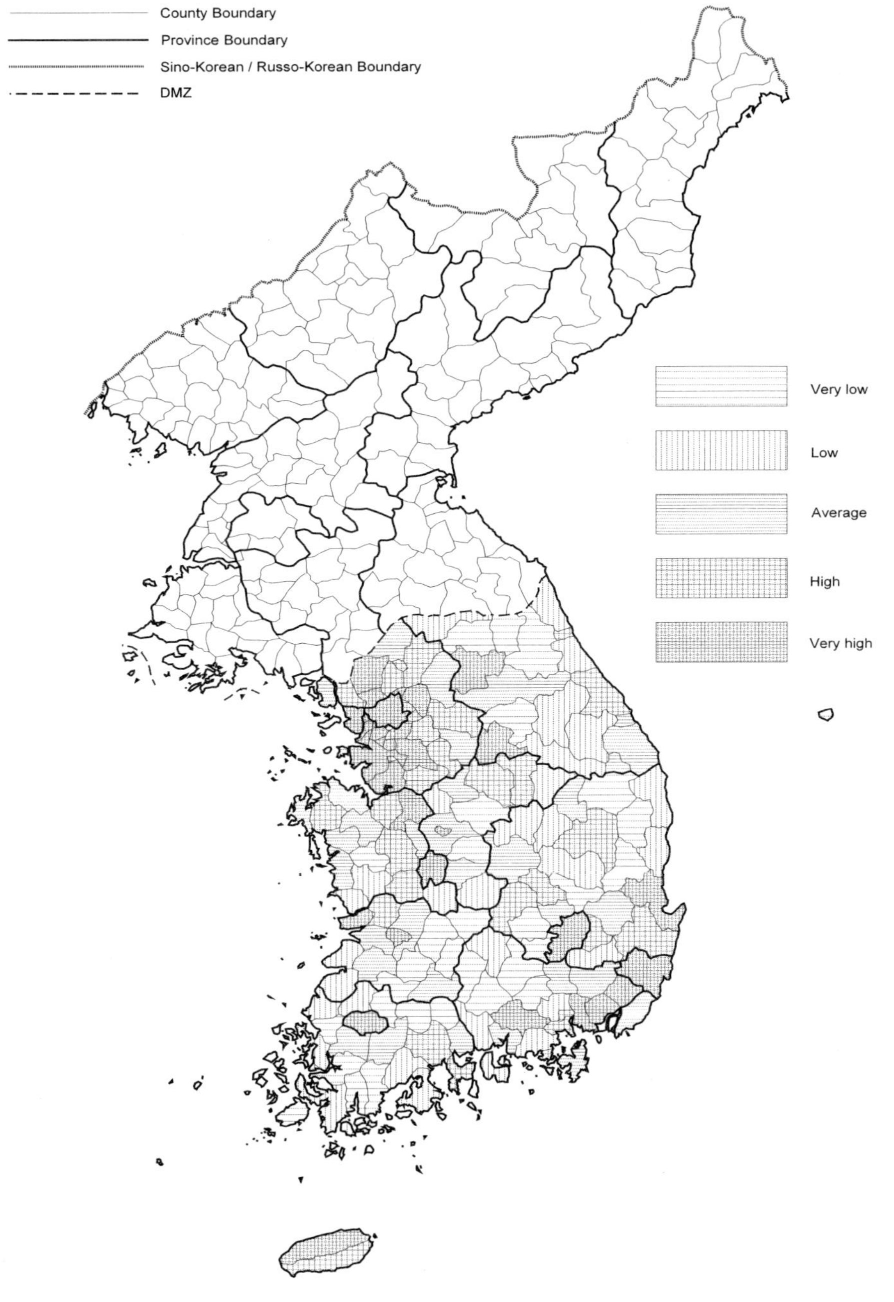

Notes: Unit = persons. Data pertain to persons aged 60 years and older. Cut-offs = below 116.0, 116.0 to below 233.3, 233.3 to below 451.1, 451.1 to below 1106.1, 1106.1 or above.

Map 10.7 Elderly working total population of South Korea

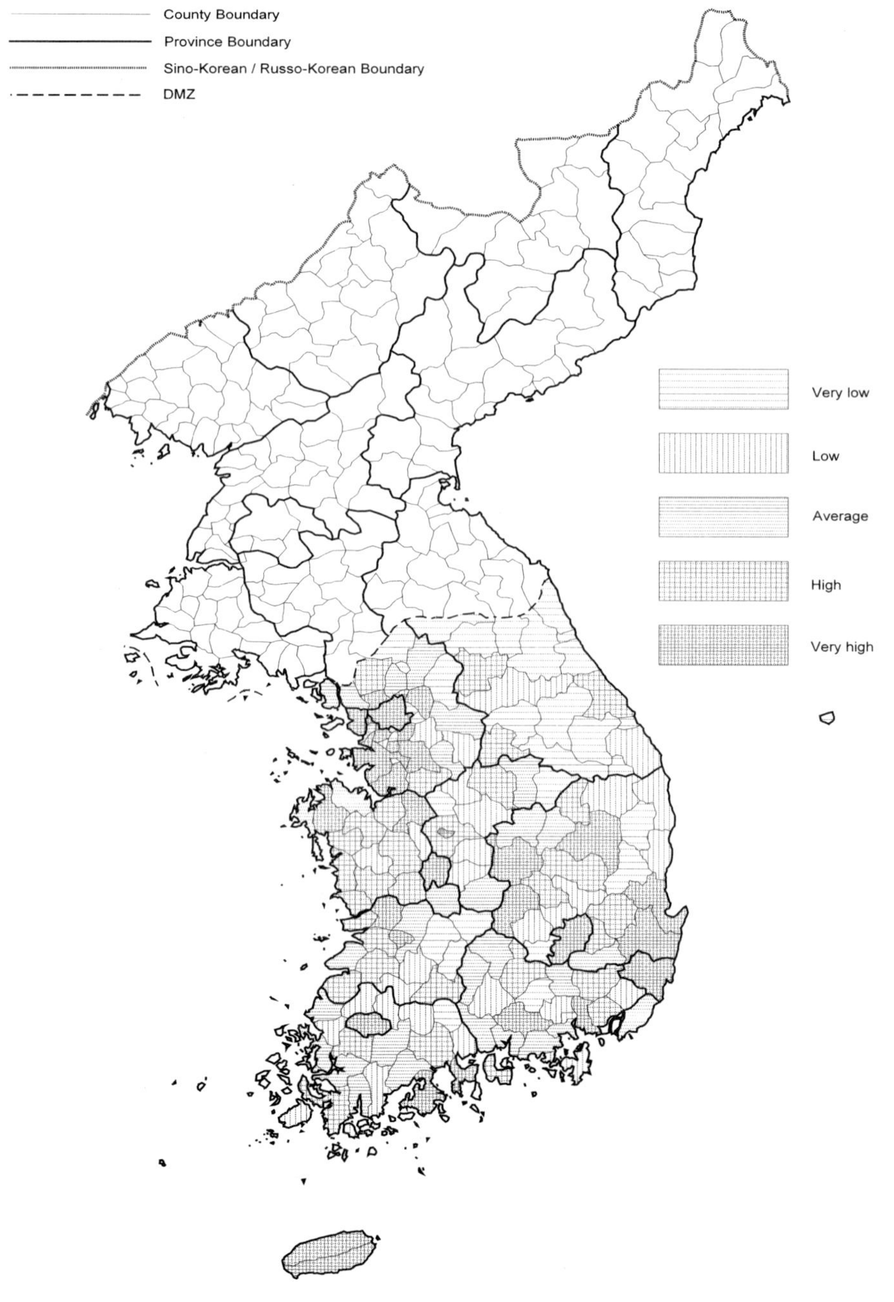

Notes: Unit = persons. Data pertain to persons aged 60 years and older. Cut-offs = below 5797.0, 5797.0 to below 8174.8, 8174.8 to below 10592.7, 10592.7 to below 15421.1, 15421.1 or above.

Map 10.8 Elderly non-working total population of South Korea

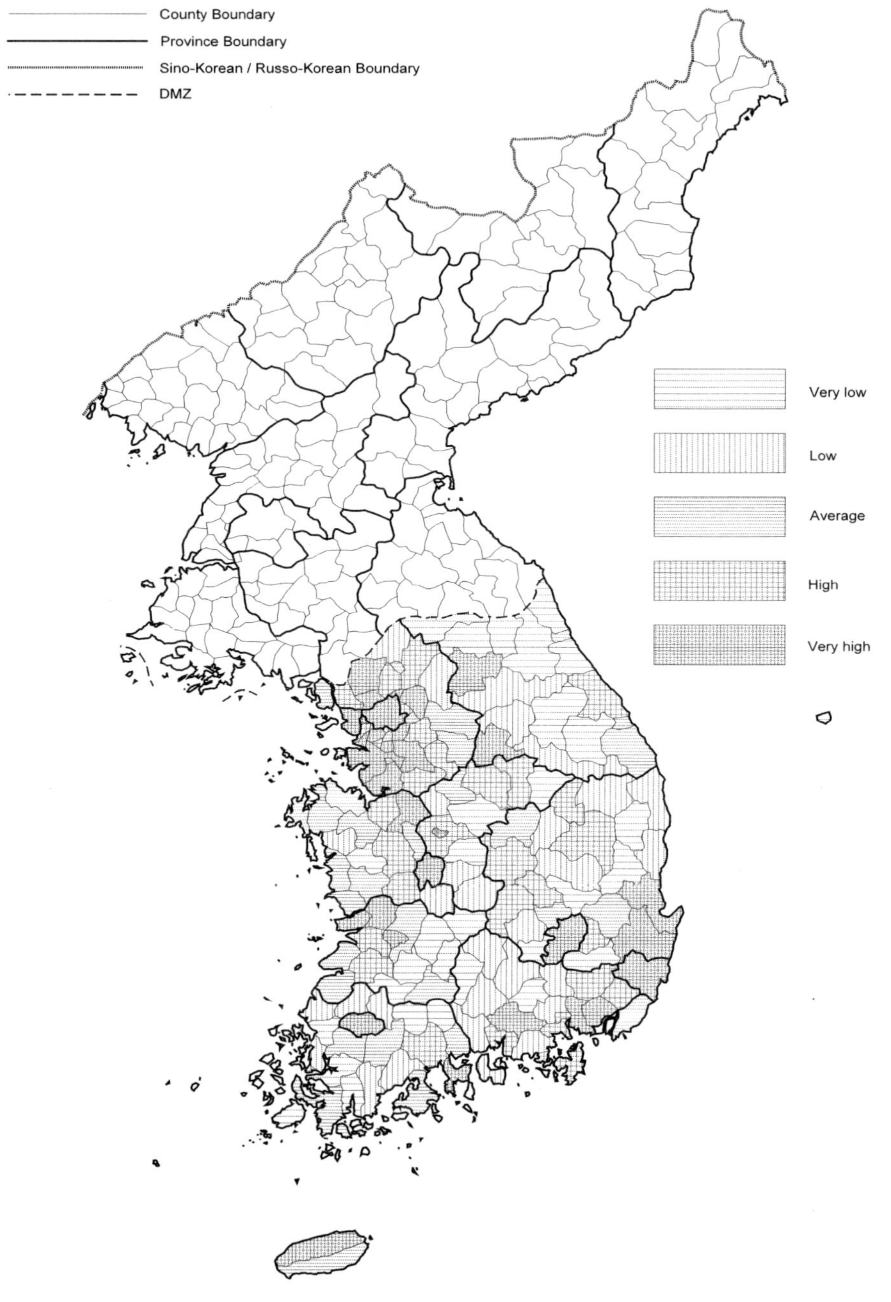

Notes: Unit = persons. Data pertain to persons aged 60 years and older. Cut-offs = below 6120.8, 6120.8 to below 9568.8, 9568.8 to below 15116.1, 15116.1 to below 29998.8, 29998.8 or above.

Map 10.9 Elderly working male population of South Korea

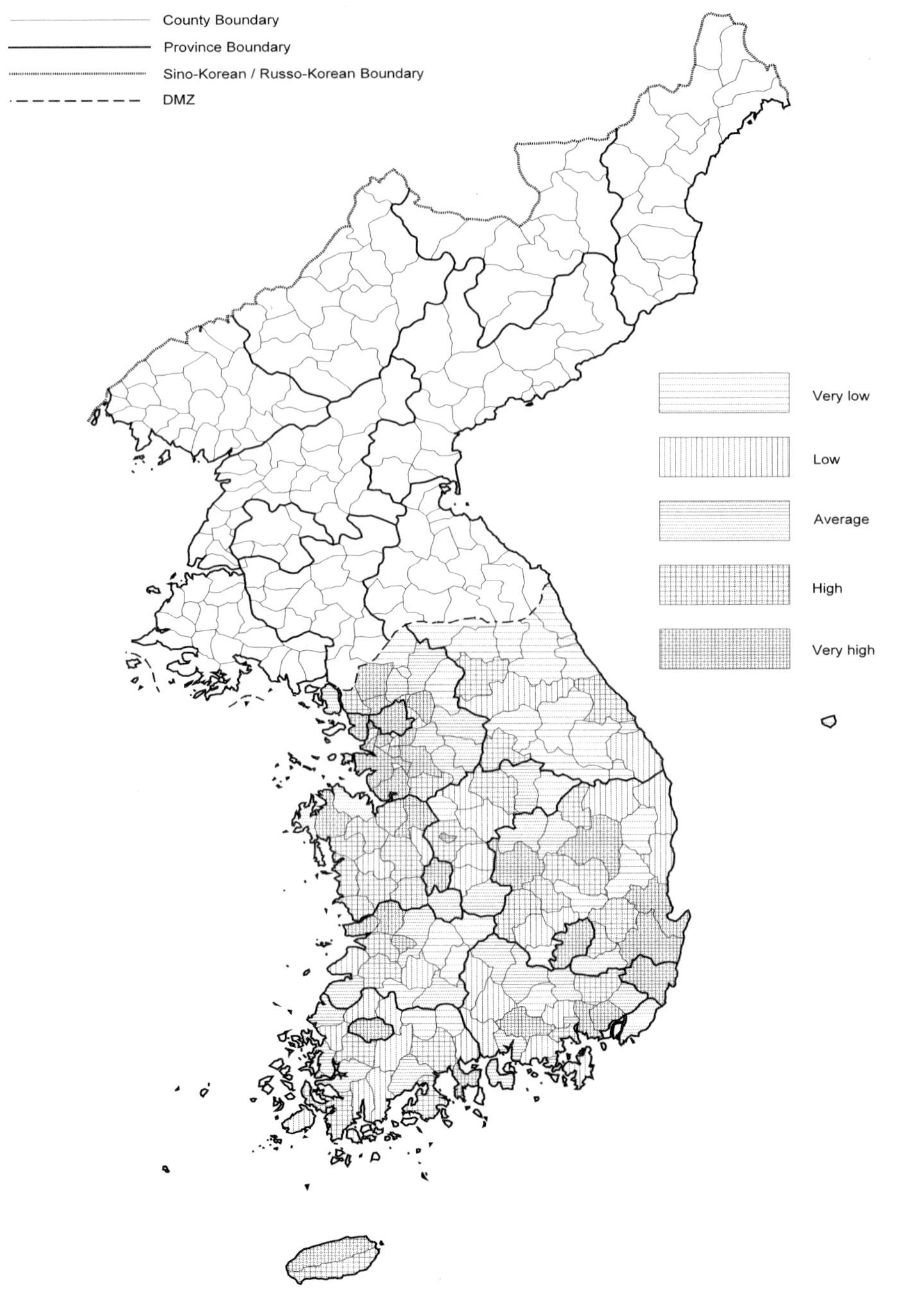

Notes: Unit = persons. Data pertain to persons aged 60 years and older. Cut-offs = below 2988.3, 2988.3 to below 4197.1, 4197.1 to below 5522.6, 5522.6 to below 8517.6, 8517.6 or above.

Map 10.10 Elderly non-working male population of South Korea

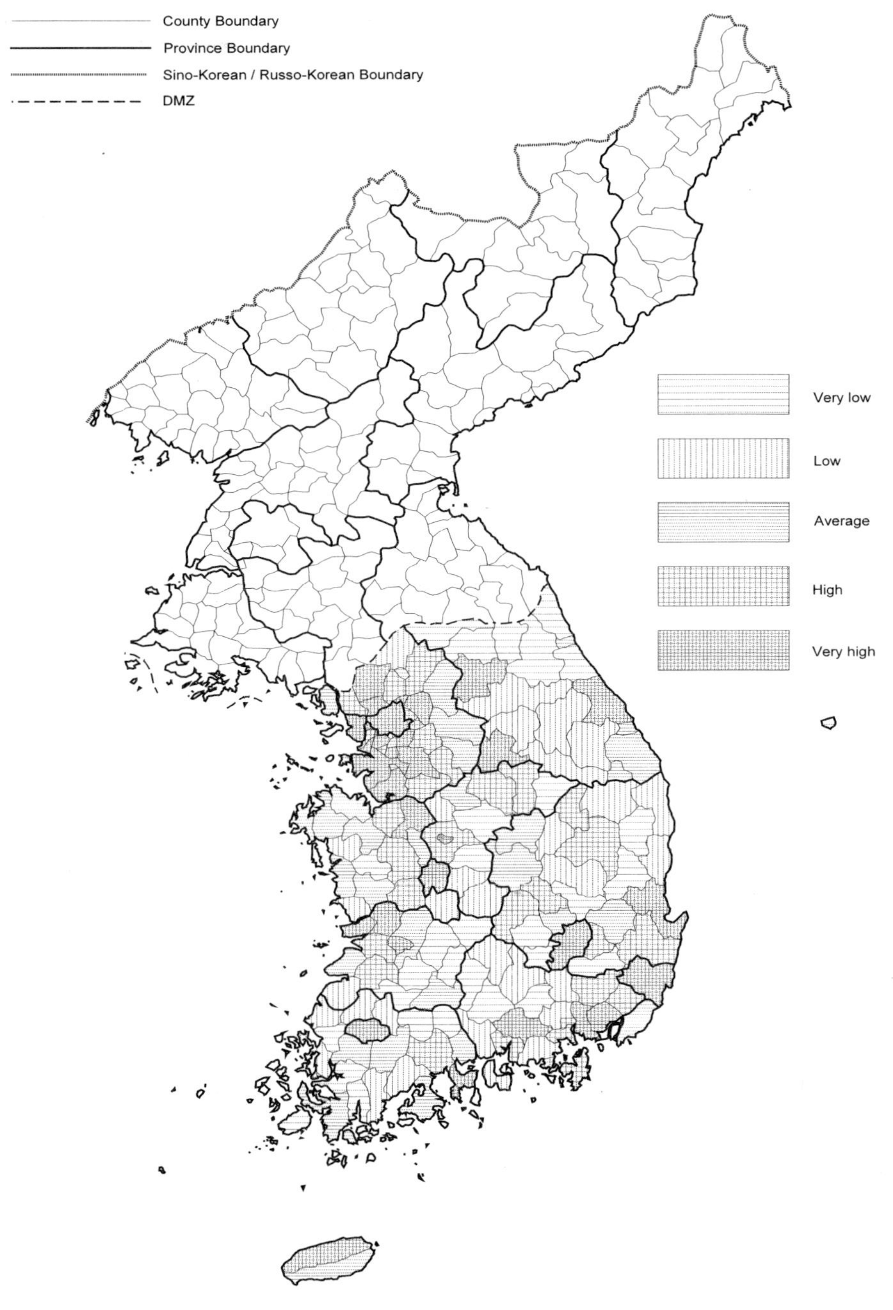

Notes: Unit = persons. Data pertain to persons aged 60 years and older. Cut-offs = below 1978.7, 1978.7 to below 3127.9, 3127.9 to below 5055.0, 5055.0 to below 10523.6, 10523.6 or above.

Map 10.11 Elderly working female population of South Korea

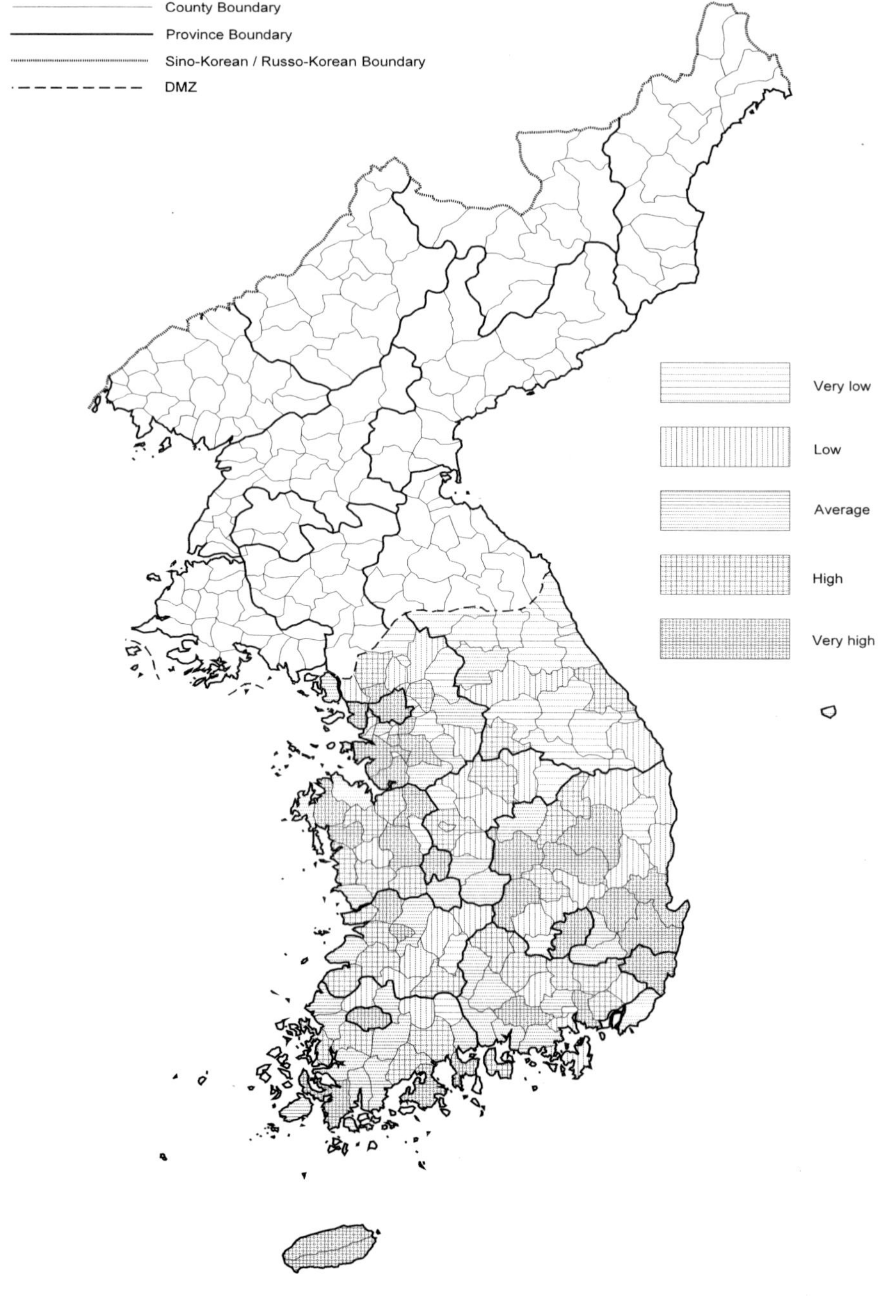

Notes: Unit = persons. Data pertain to persons aged 60 years and older. Cut-offs = below 2657.6, 2657.6 to below 3876.5, 3876.5 to below 5352.1, 5352.1 to below 7111.2, 7111.2 or above.

Map 10.12 Elderly non-working female population of South Korea

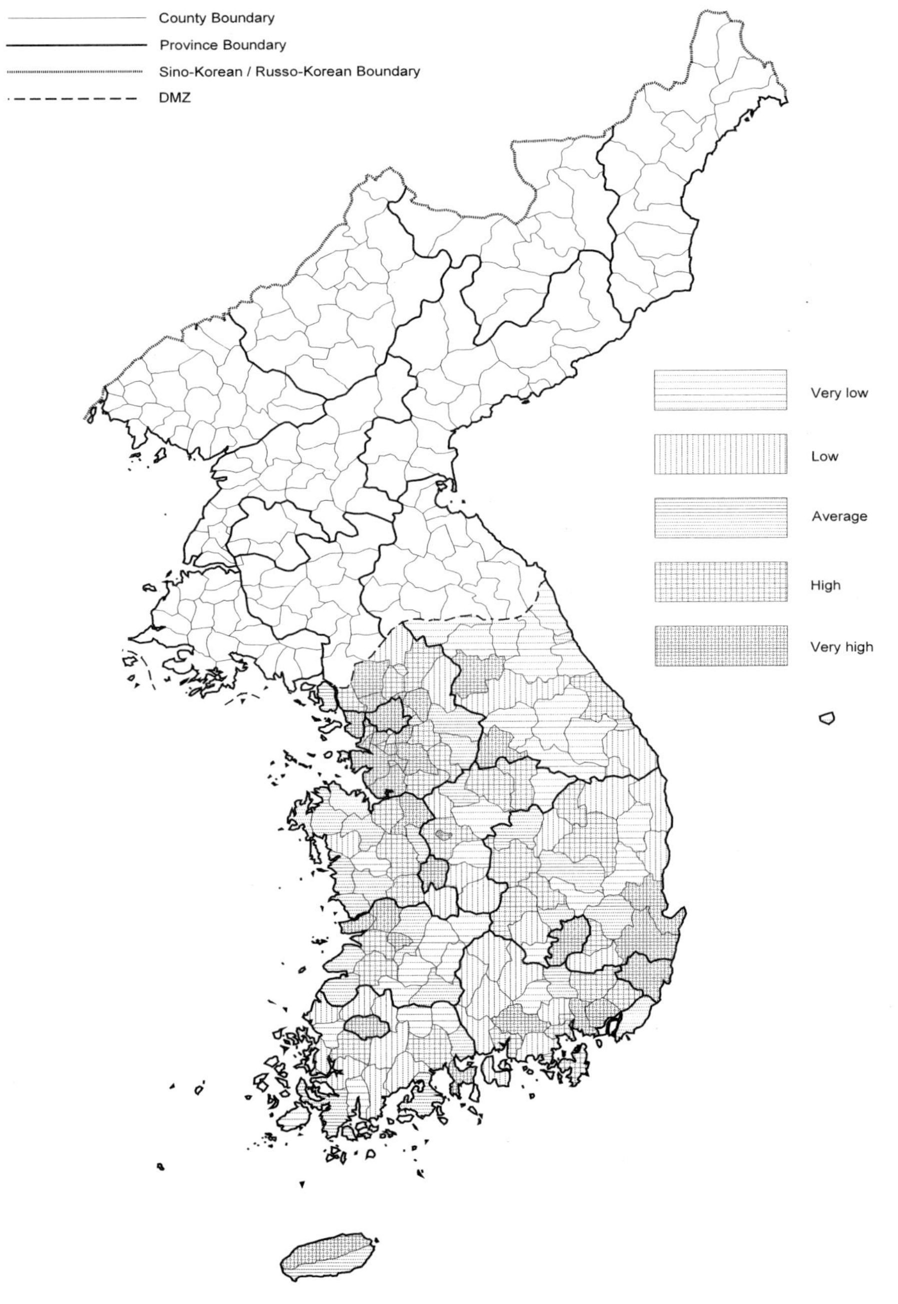

Notes: Unit = persons. Data pertain to persons aged 60 years and older. Cut-offs = below 4179.6, 4179.6 to below 6578.0, 6578.0 to below 9989.7, 9989.7 to below 19634.1, 19634.1 or above.

Map 10.13 Elderly population with no formal education of South Korea (share)

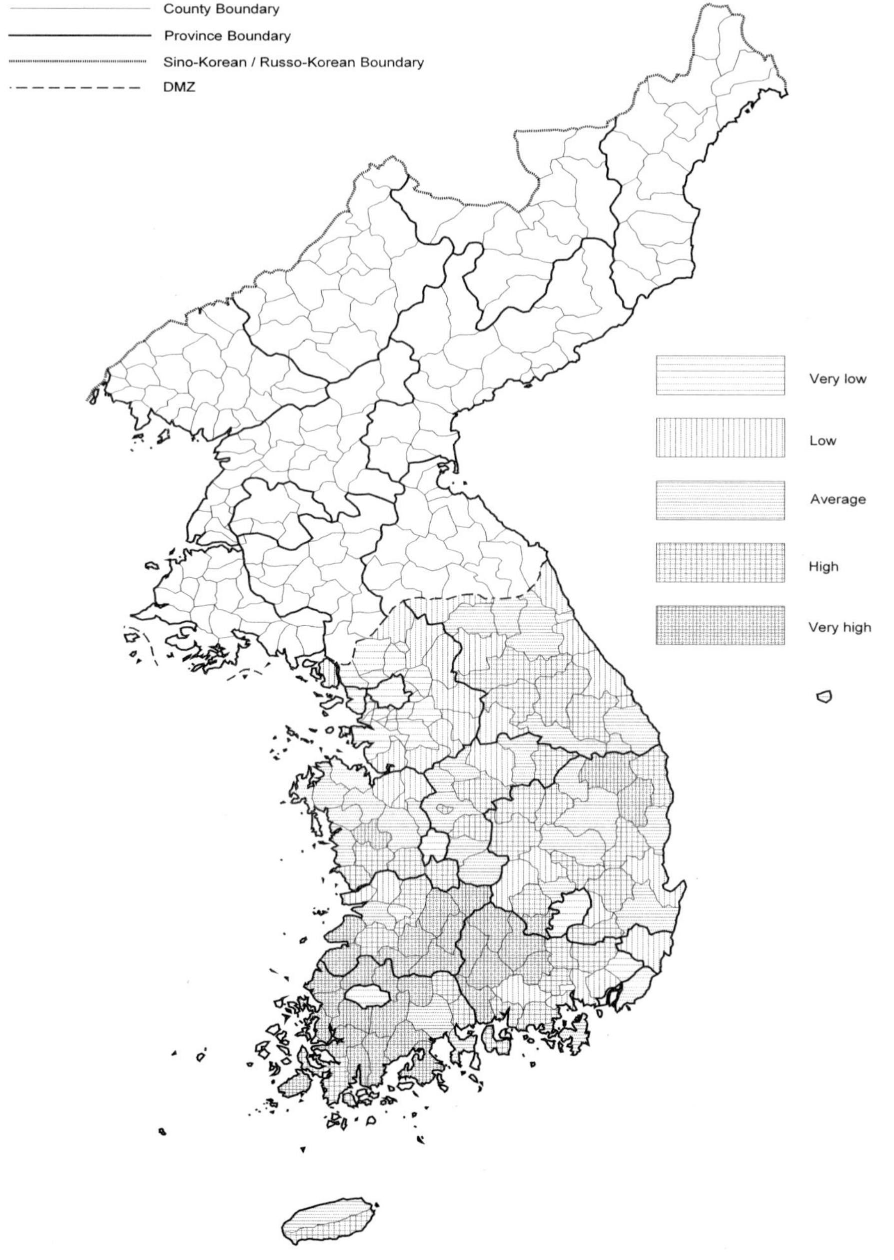

Notes: Unit = percent. Data pertain to persons aged 60 years and older. Cut-offs = below 17.68, 17.68 to below 25.39, 25.39 to below 30.50, 30.50 to below 35.22, 35.22 or above.

Map 10.14 Elderly working total population of South Korea (share)

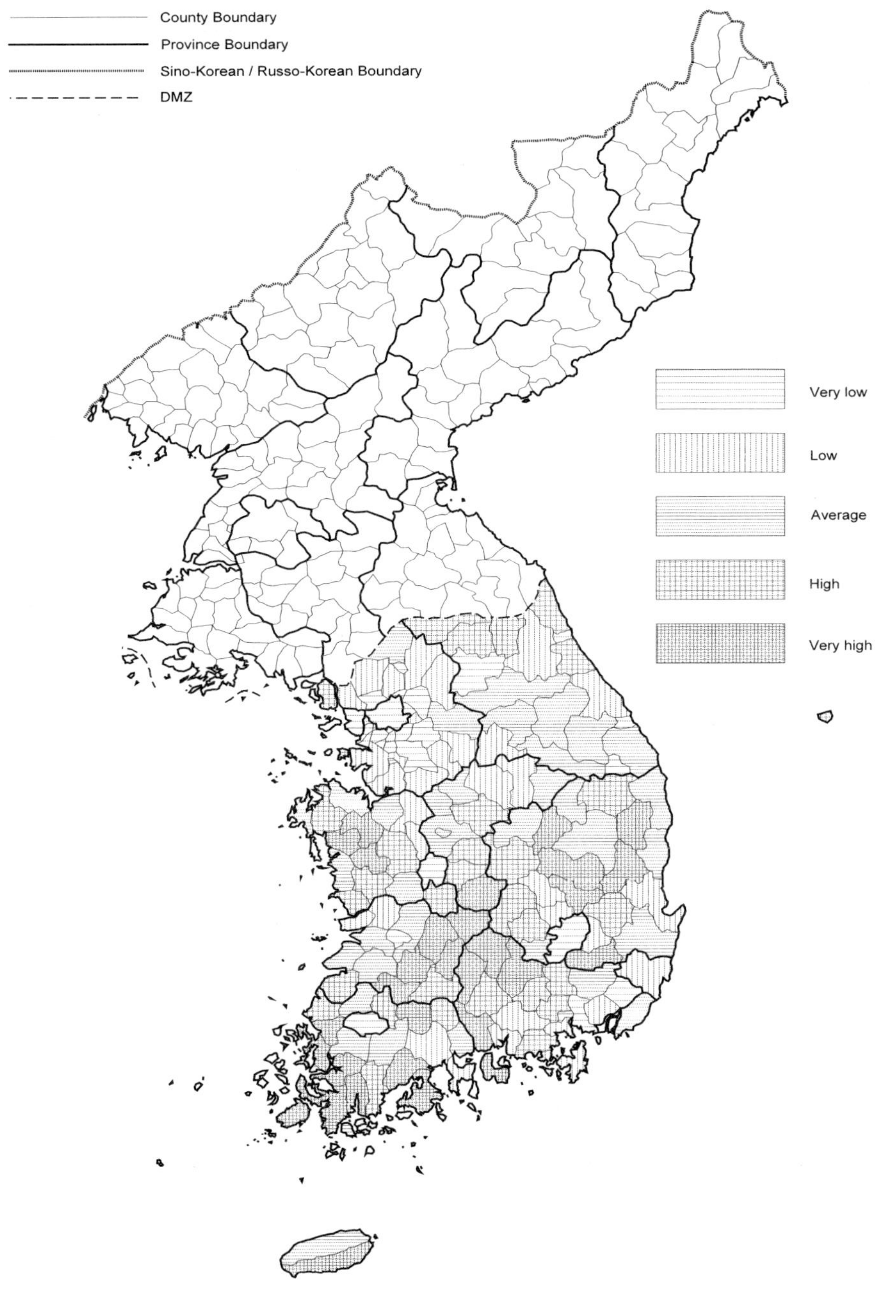

Notes: Unit = percent. Data pertain to persons aged 60 years and older. Cut-offs = below 26.80, 26.80 to below 38.60, 38.60 to below 46.50, 46.50 to below 55.10, 55.10 or above.

Map 10.15 Elderly non-working total population of South Korea (share)

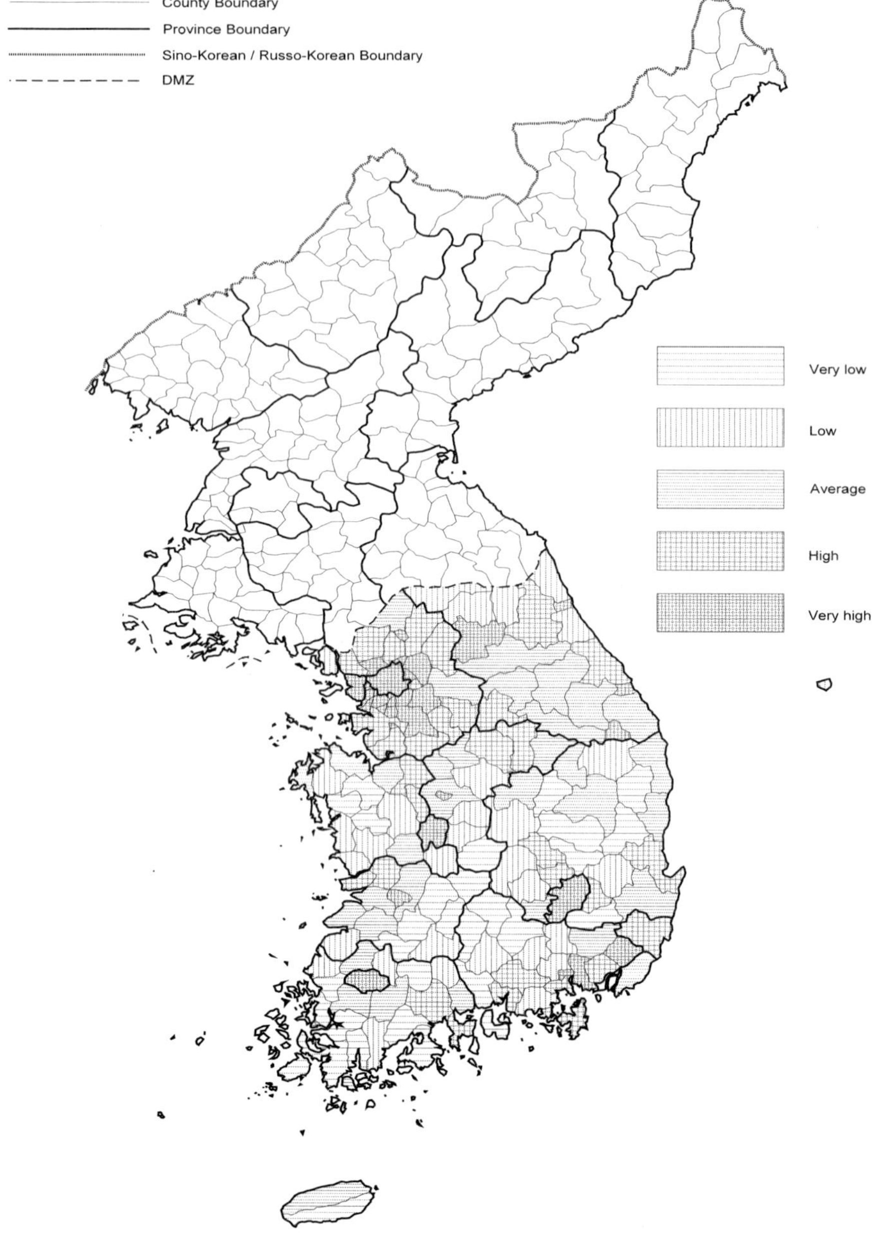

Notes: Unit = percent. Data pertain to persons aged 60 years and older. Cut-offs = below 44.90, 44.90 to below 53.53, 53.53 to below 61.49, 61.49 to below 73.19, 73.19 or above.

11. Social Activity

Map 11.1 Members of a social organization of South Korea

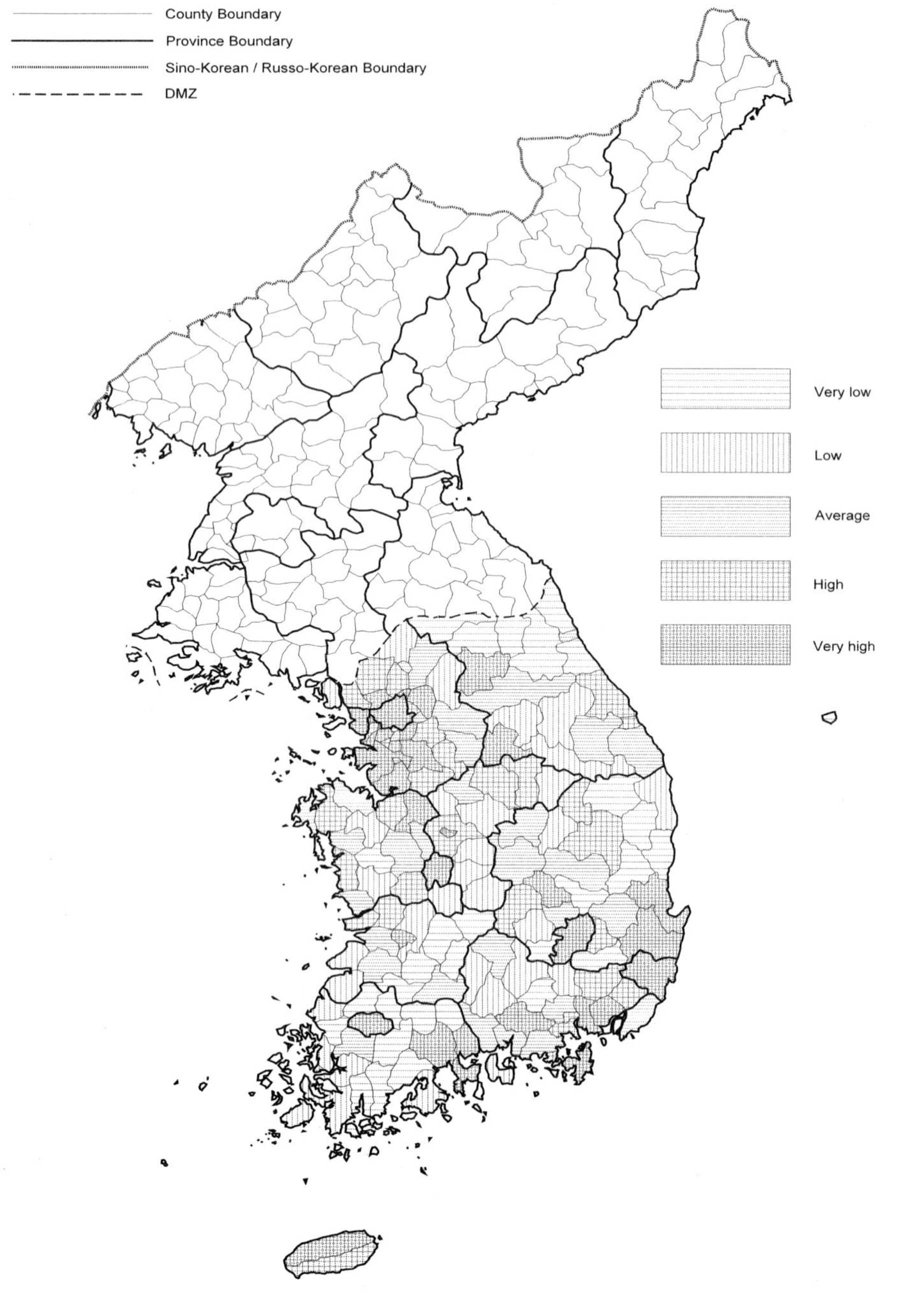

Notes: Unit = persons. Data pertain to people aged 15 years and older. Cut-offs = below 1305.3, 1305.3 to below 1890.1, 1890.1 to below 2951.8, 2951.8 to below 6018.2, 6018.2 or above.

Map 11.2 Members of an economic organization of South Korea

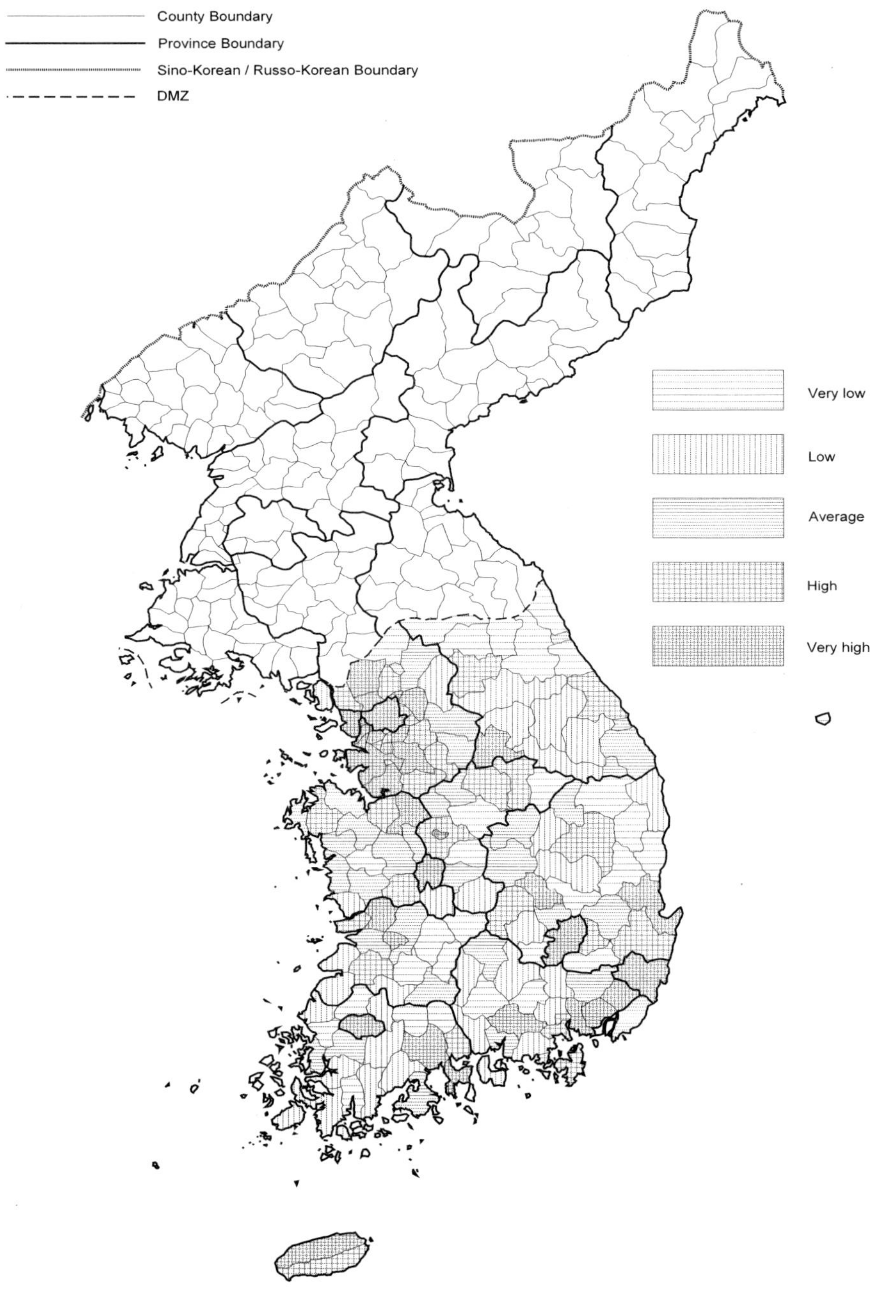

Notes: Unit = persons. Data pertain to people aged 15 years and older. Cut-offs = below 423.0, 423.0 to below 931.7, 931.7 to below 2054.5, 2054.5 to below 4749.0, 4749.0 or above.

Map 11.3 Members of a cultural organization of South Korea

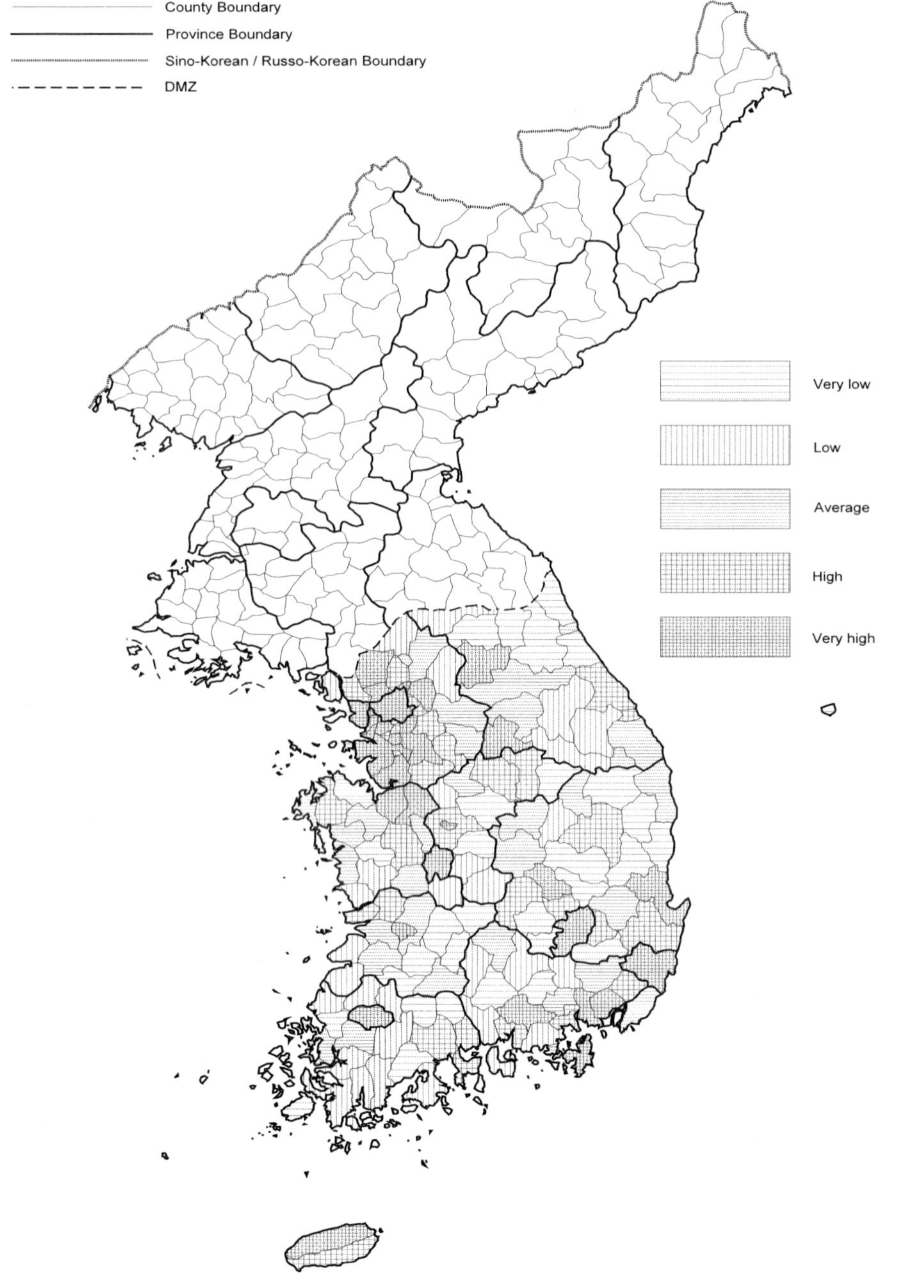

Notes: Unit = persons. Data pertain to people aged 15 years and older. Cut-offs = below 1283.1, 1283.1 to below 2302.7, 2302.7 to below 5079.7, 5079.7 to below 12310.6, 12310.6 or above.

Map 11.4 Members of a political organization of South Korea

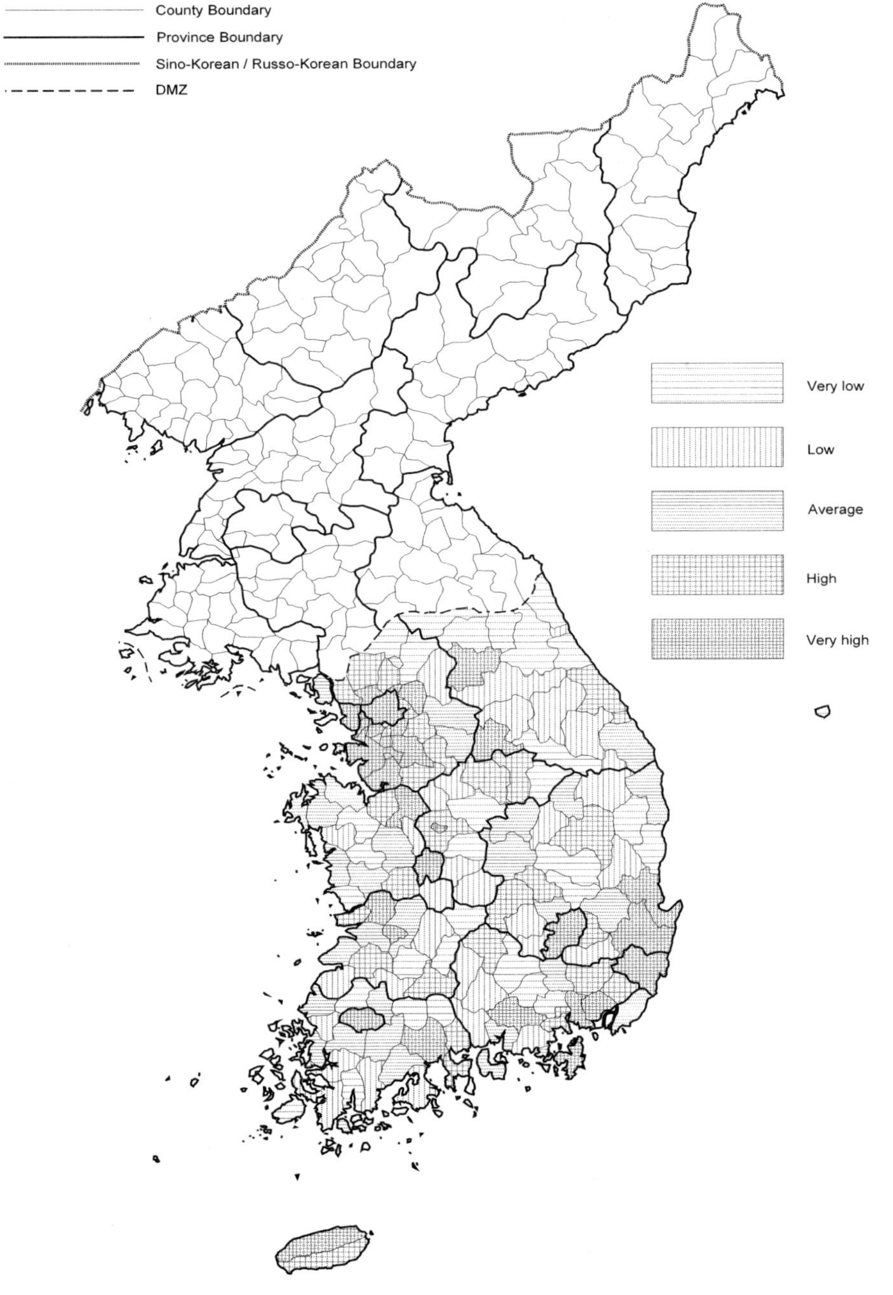

Notes: Unit = persons. Data pertain to people aged 15 years and older. Cut-offs = below 112.3, 112.3 to below 184.2, 184.2 to below 327.2, 327.2 to below 680.2, 680.2 or above.

Map 11.5 Members of a religious organization of South Korea

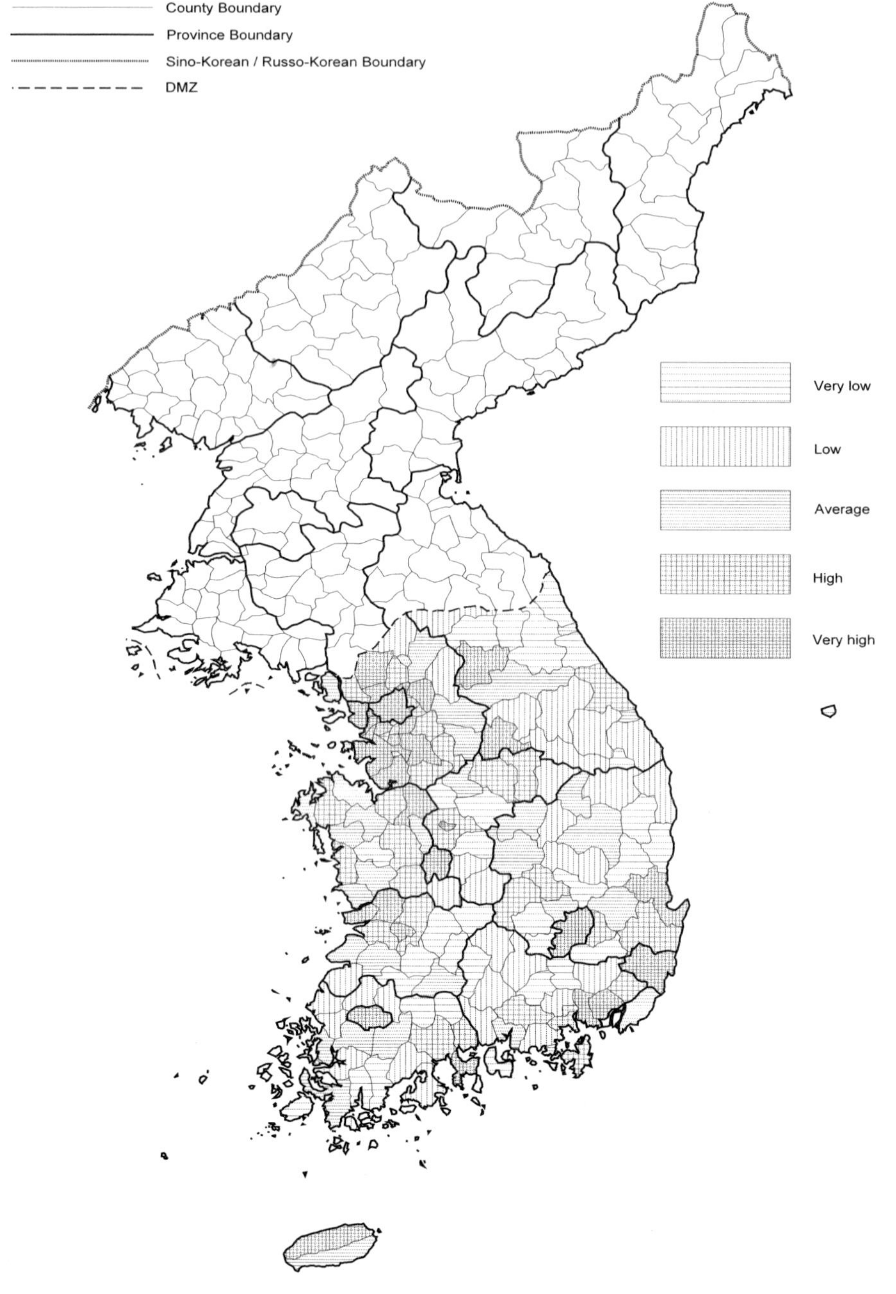

Notes: Unit = persons. Data pertain to people aged 15 years and older. Cut-offs = below 2354.4, 2354.4 to below 4680.5, 4680.5 to below 9456.3, 9456.3 to below 22936.9, 22936.9 or above.

Map 11.6 Members of a local group of South Korea

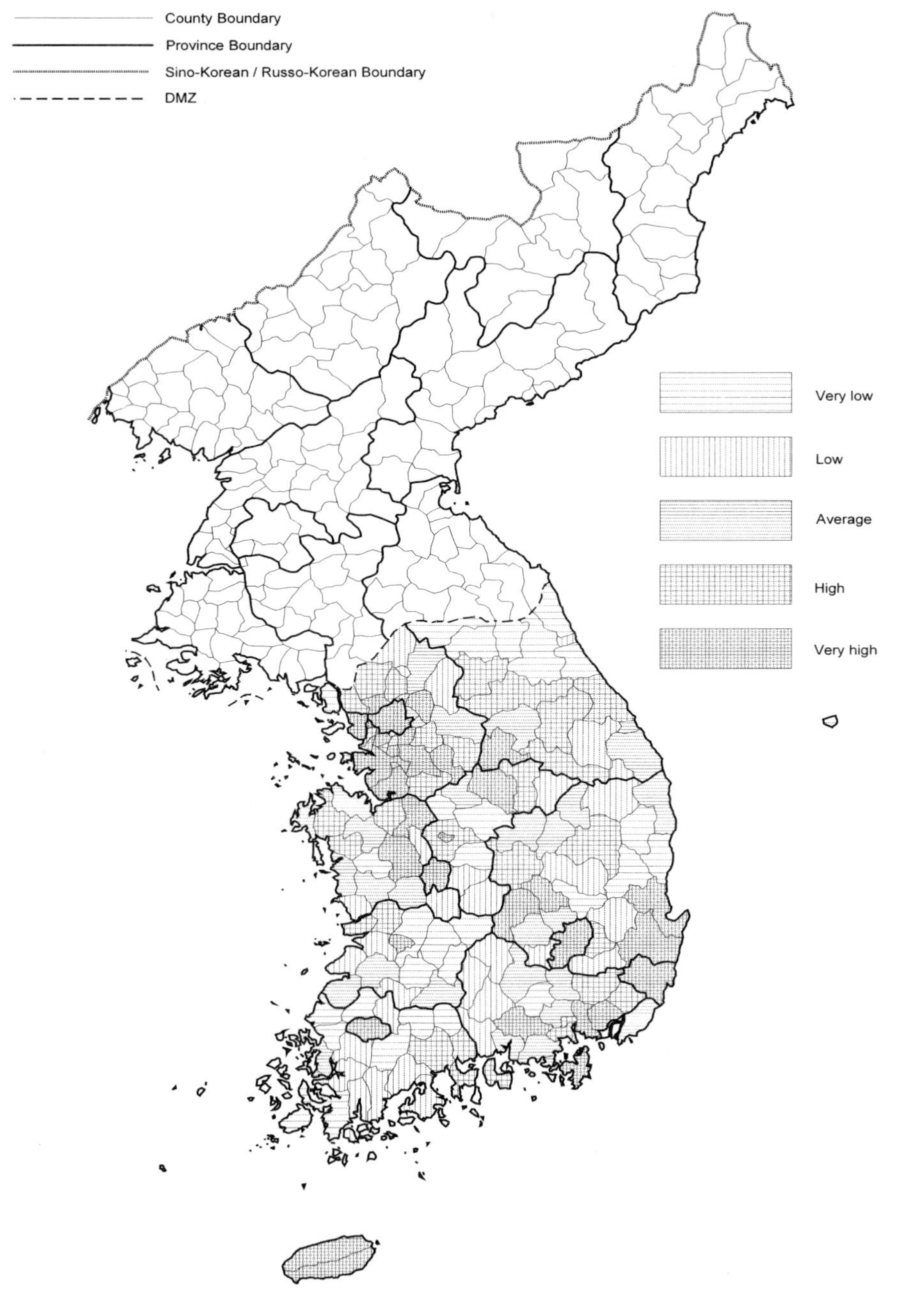

Notes: Unit = persons. Data pertain to people aged 15 years and older. Cut-offs = below 1034.3, 1034.3 to below 1616.5, 1616.5 to below 2440.0, 2440.0 to below 4205.2, 4205.2 or above.

Map 11.7 Members of a fraternal society of South Korea

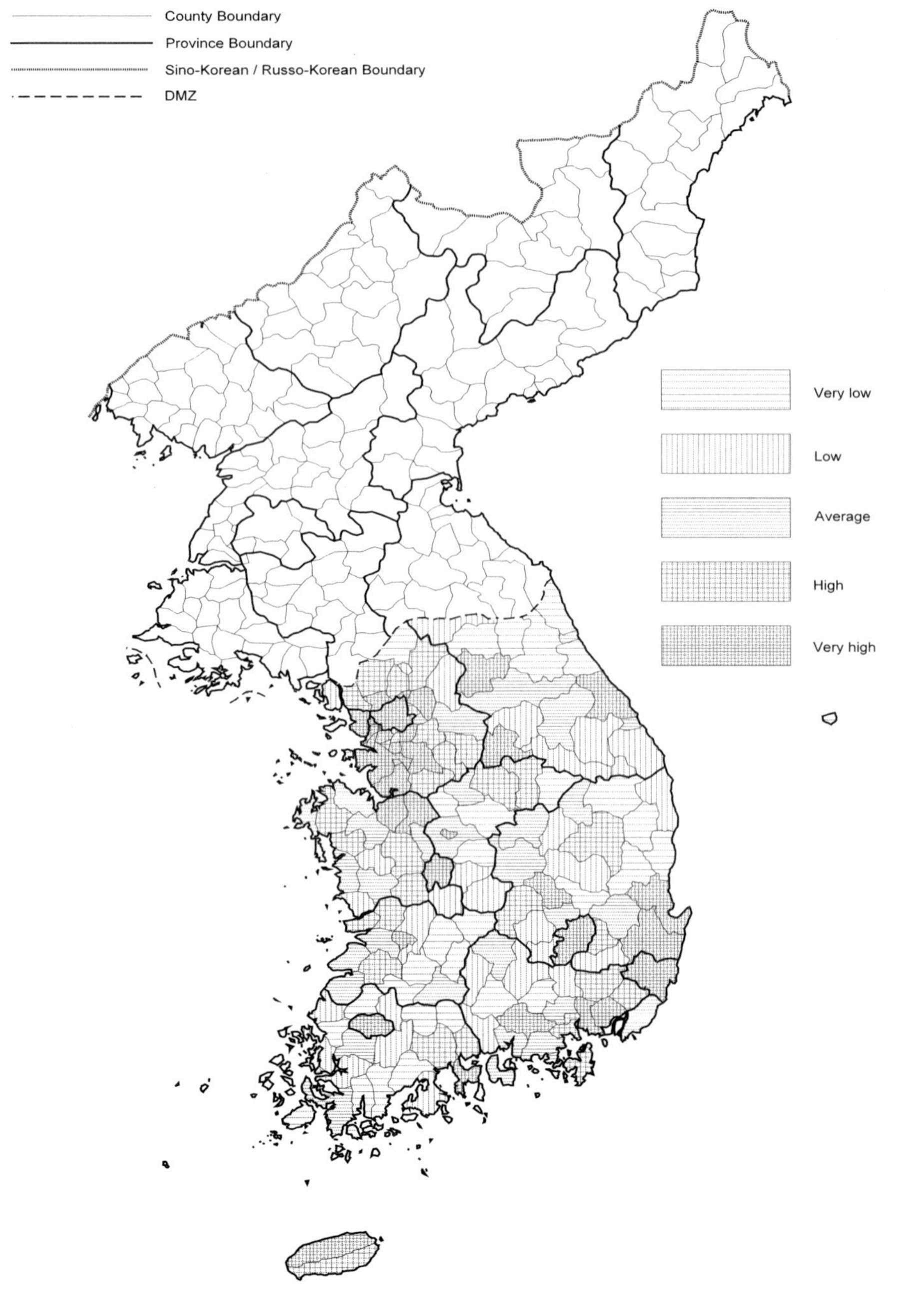

Notes: Unit = persons. Data pertain to people aged 15 years and older. Cut-offs = below 6693.2, 6693.2 to below 10582.9, 10582.9 to below 19235.8, 19235.8 to below 34986.7, 34986.7 or above.

Map 11.8 Members of an educational group of South Korea

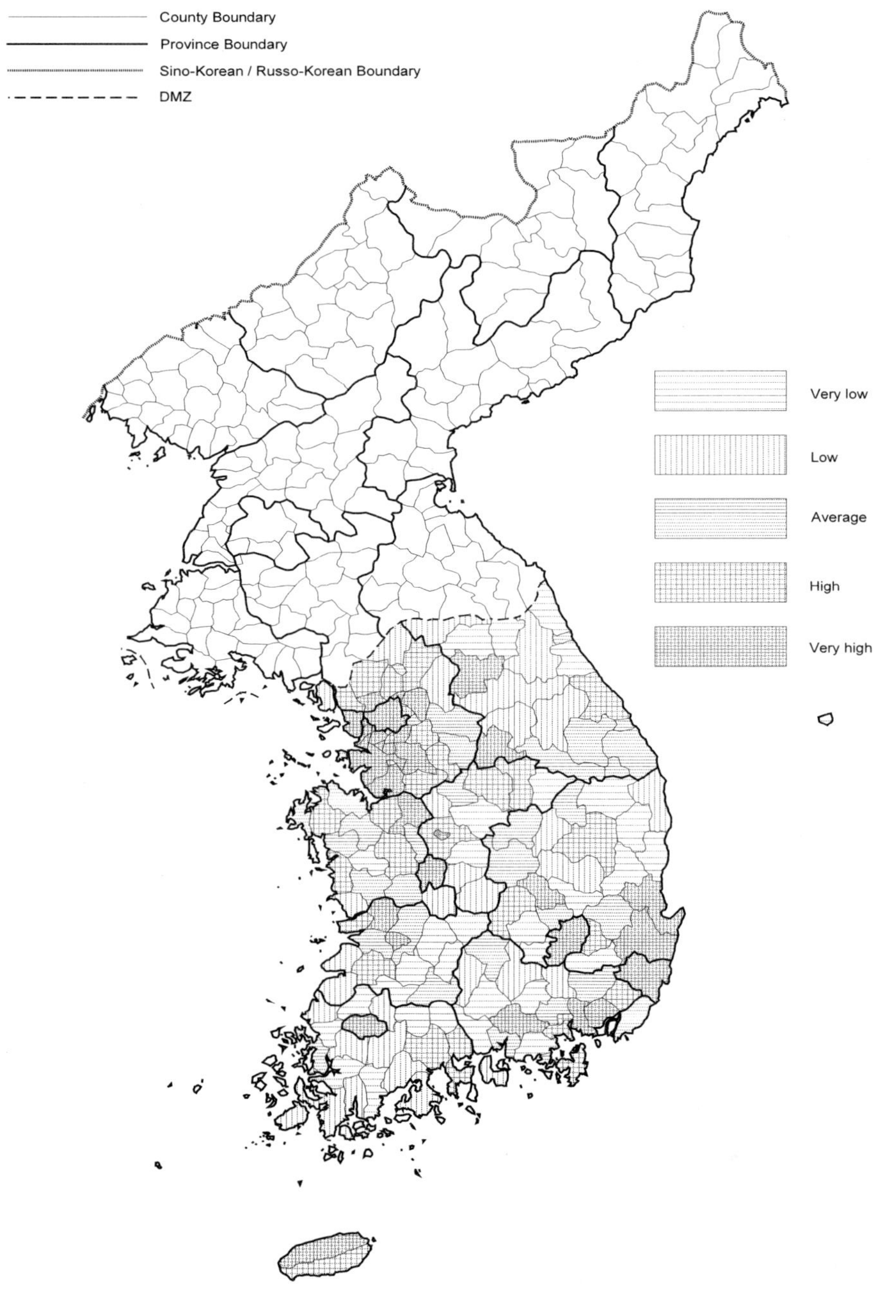

Notes: Unit = persons. Data pertain to people aged 15 years and older. Cut-offs = below 473.8, 473.8 to below 821.7, 821.7 to below 1882.1, 1882.1 to below 4614.7, 4614.7 or above.

12. Working Population

Map 12.1 Working population of the Korean peninsula

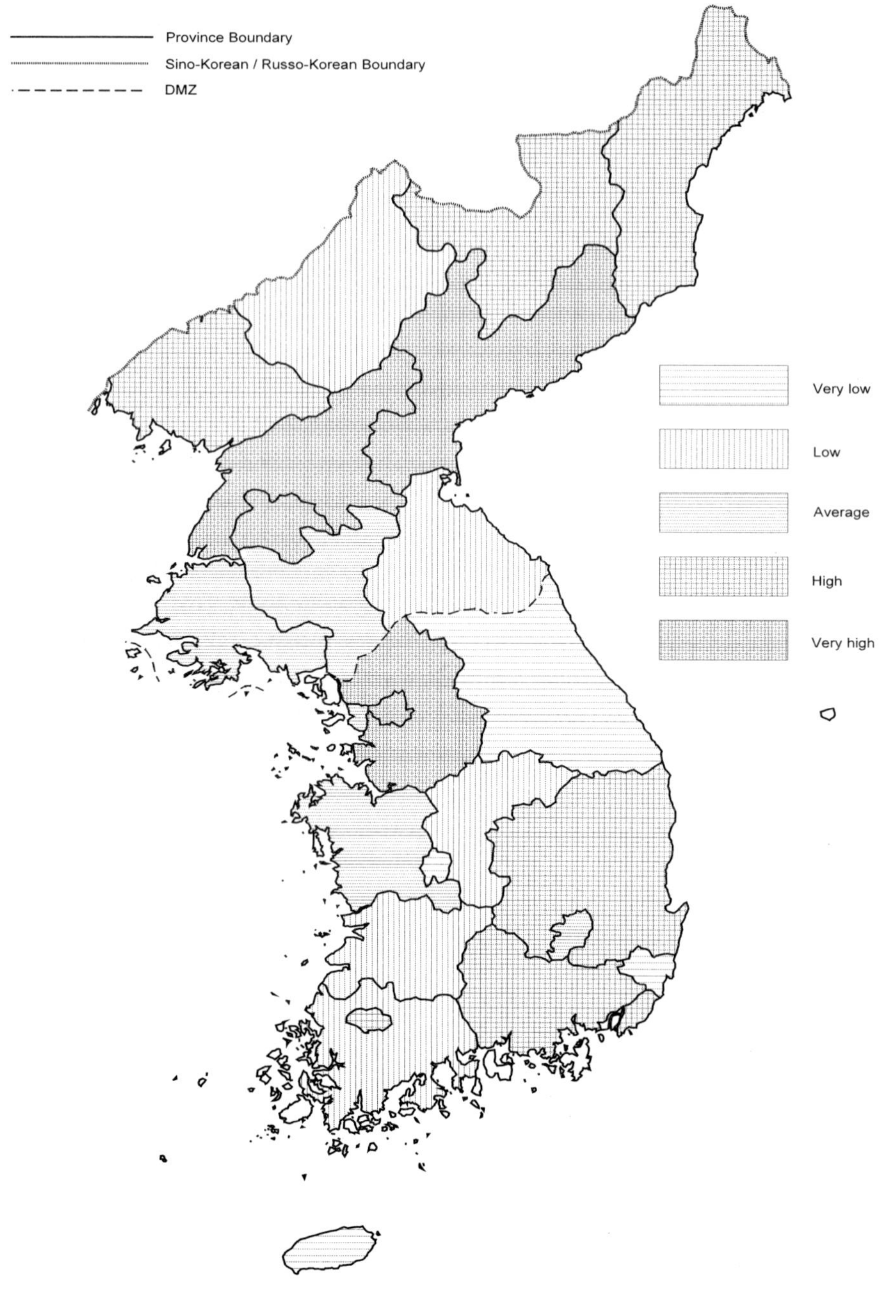

Notes: Unit = persons. Data pertain to people aged 15 years and older in South Korea and 16 years and older in North Korea. Cut-offs = below 682894.9, 682894.9 to 982743.1, 982743.1 to 1226316.0, 1226316.0 to 1503737.1, 1503737.1 or above.

Map 12.2 Working population of South Korea

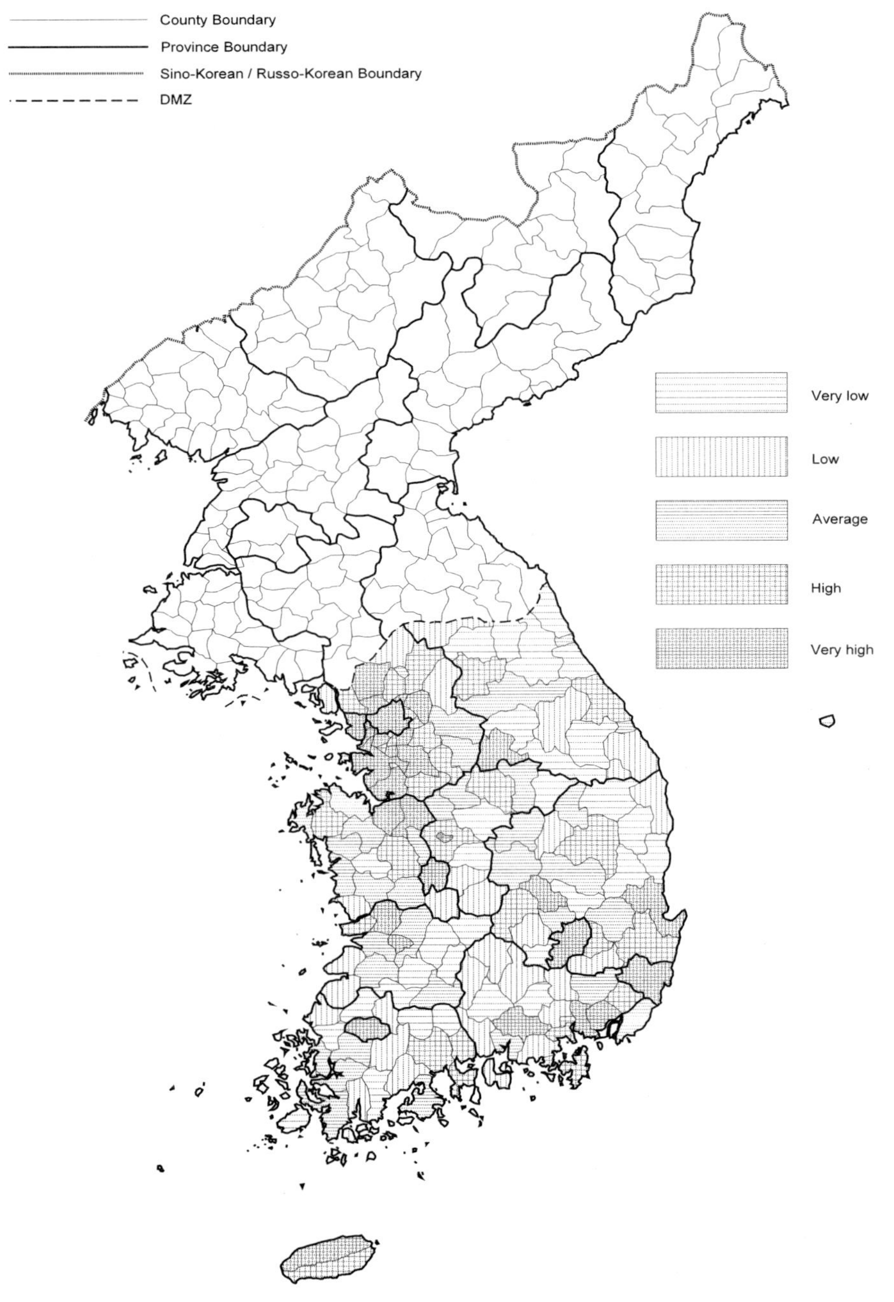

Notes: Unit = persons. Data pertain to people aged 15 years and older. Cut-offs = below 9300.5, 9300.5 to below 31059.0, 31059.0 to below 58517.5, 58517.5 to below 125012.0, 125012.0 or above.

Map 12.3 Mainly working population of South Korea

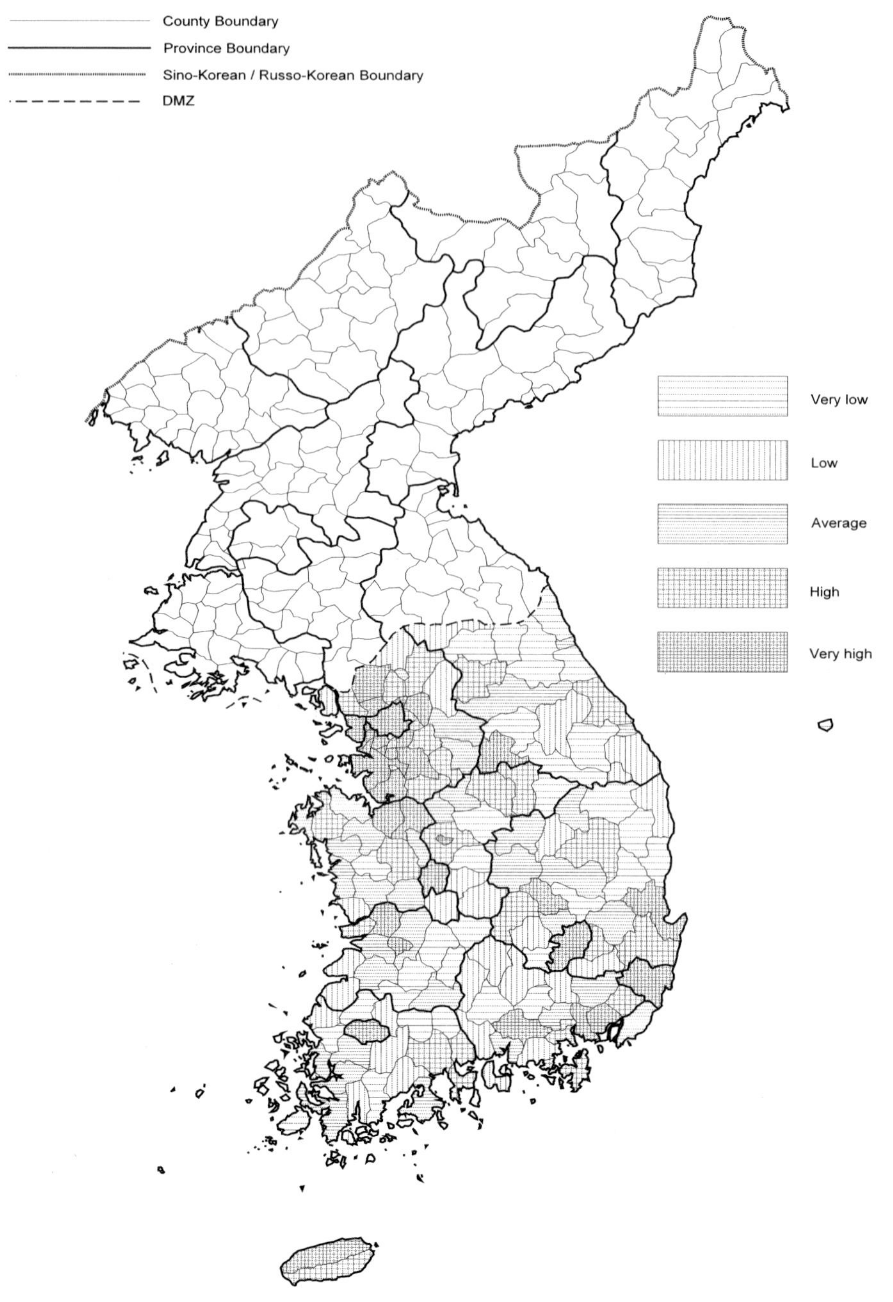

Notes: Unit = persons. Data pertain to people aged 15 years and older. Cut-offs = below 17443.3, 17443.3 to below 27520.3, 27520.3 to below 52071.0, 52071.0 to below 112790.4, 112790.4 or above.

Map 12.4 Partially working population of South Korea

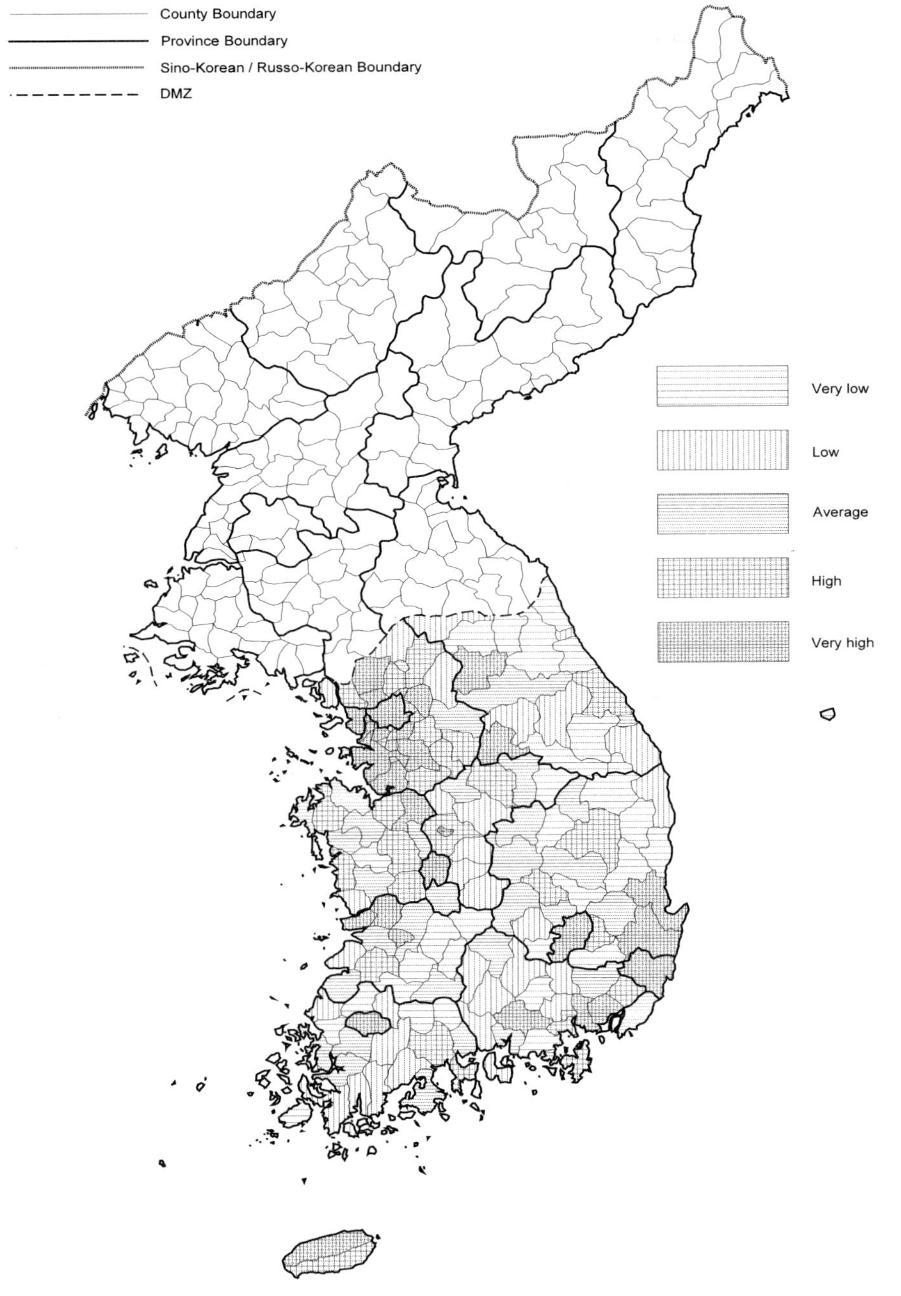

Notes: Unit = persons. Data pertain to people aged 15 years and older. Cut-offs = below 1249.0, 1249.0 to below 2172.4, 2172.4 to below 3661.9, 3661.9 to below 7861.0, 7861.0 or above.

Map 12.5 Temporarily laid off population of South Korea

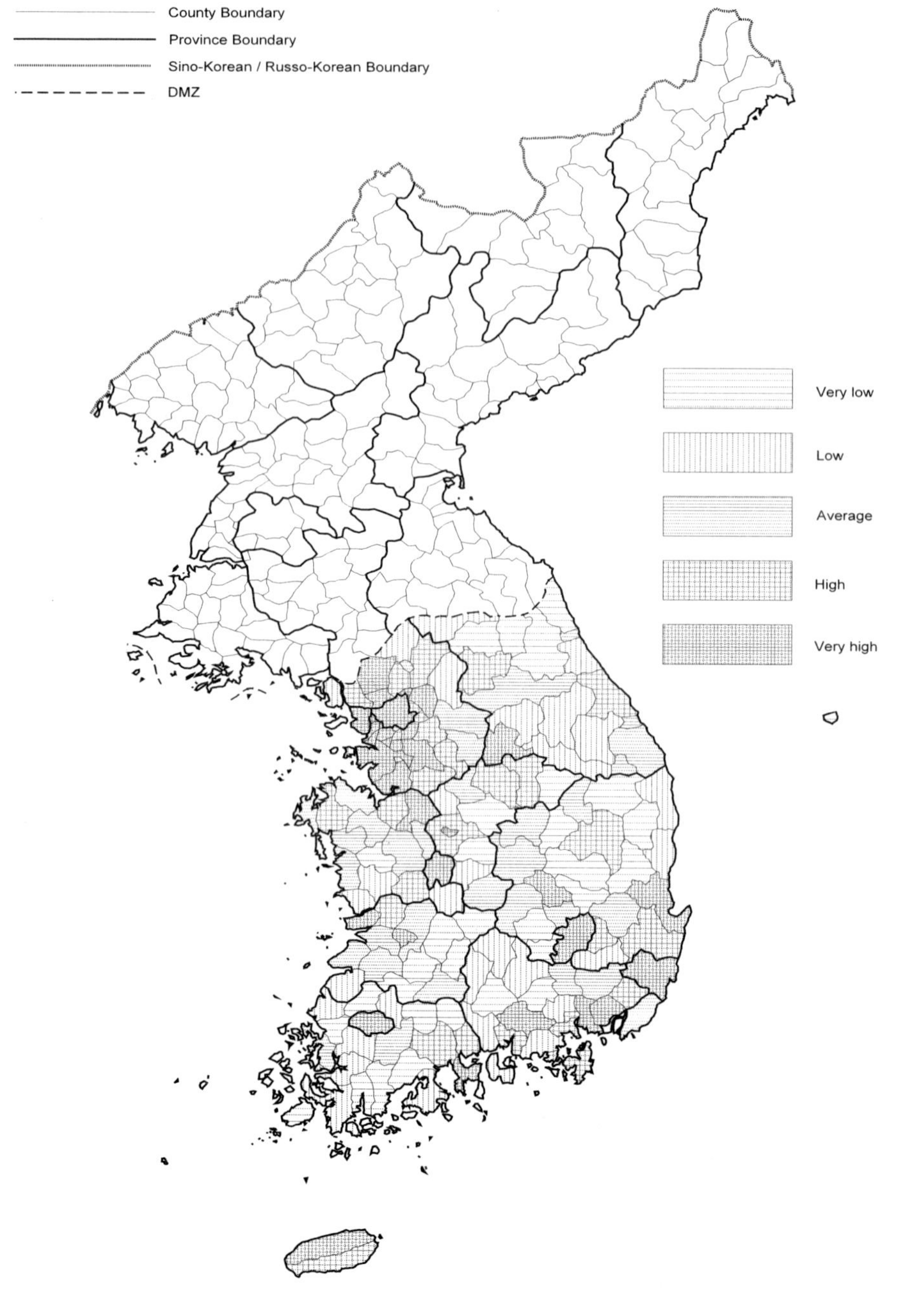

Notes: Unit = persons. Data pertain to people aged 15 years and older. Cut-offs = below 400.2, 400.2 to below 777.0, 777.0 to below 1443.9, 1443.9 to below 3648.9, 3648.9.

Map 12.6 Non-working population of the Korean peninsula

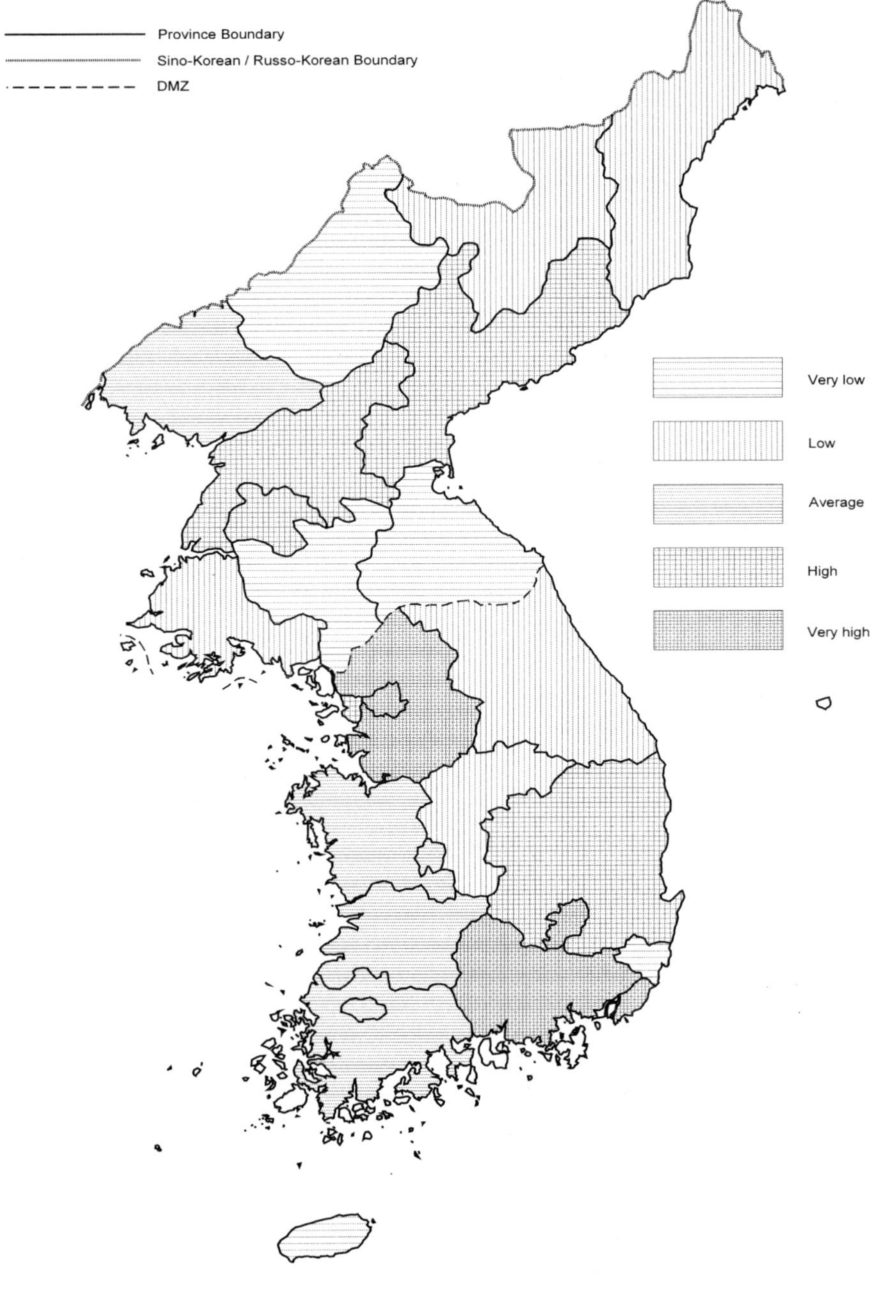

Notes: Unit = persons. Data pertain to people aged 15 years and older in South Korea and 16 years and older in North Korea. Non-working population of North Korea was not reported but calculated from the population 16 years and older less the working population 16 years and older. Cut-offs = below 483799.5, 483799.5 tobelow 555212.8, 555212.8 to below 666547.3, 666547.3 to below 961060.9, 961060.9 or above.

Map 12.7 Non-working population of South Korea

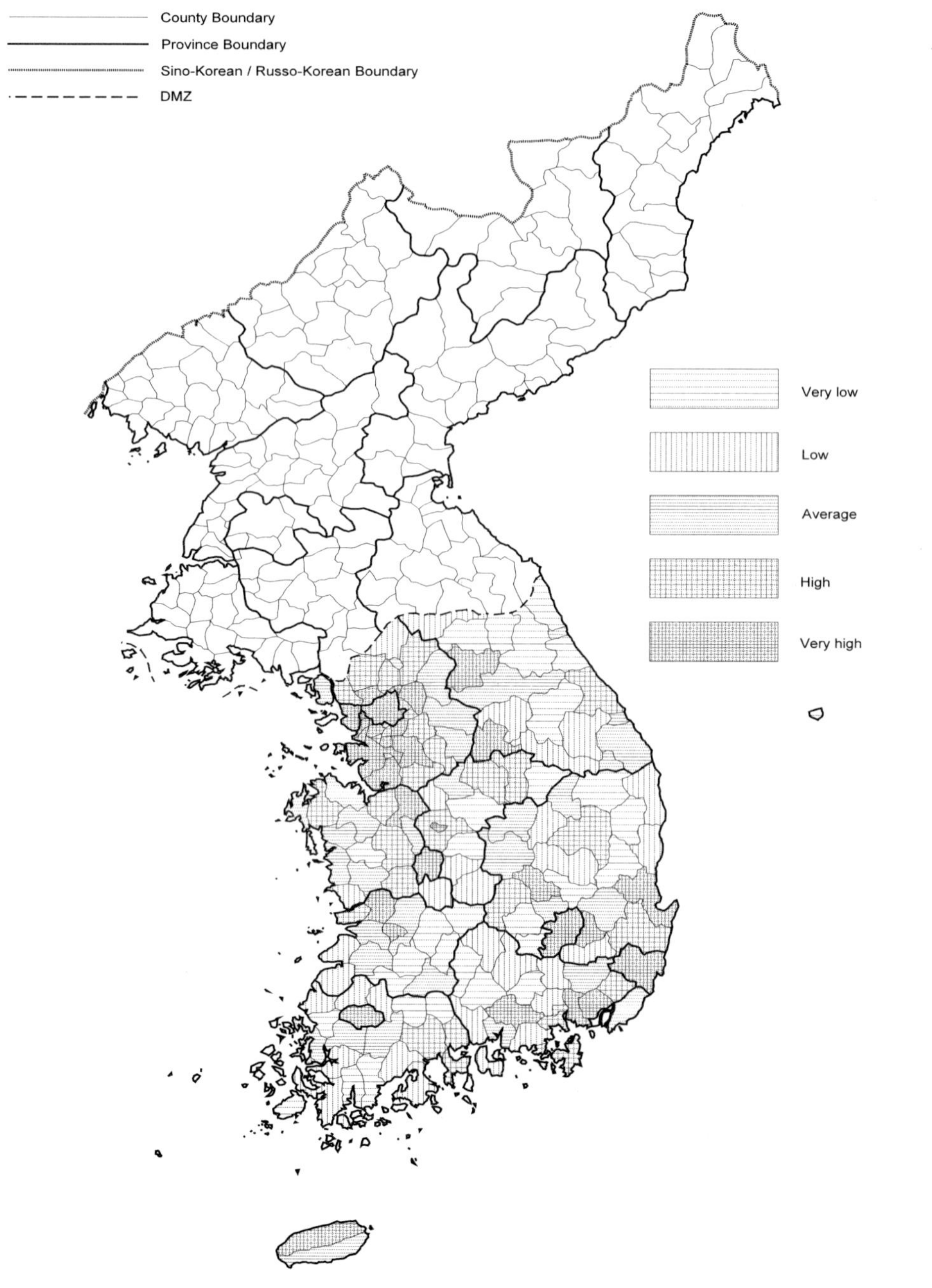

Notes: Unit = persons. Data pertain to people aged 15 years and older. Cut-offs = below 11643.0, 11643.0 to below 19108.5, 19108.5 to below 42254.0, 42254.0 to below 107966.0, 107966.0 or above.

Map 12.8 Working population of the Korean peninsula (share)

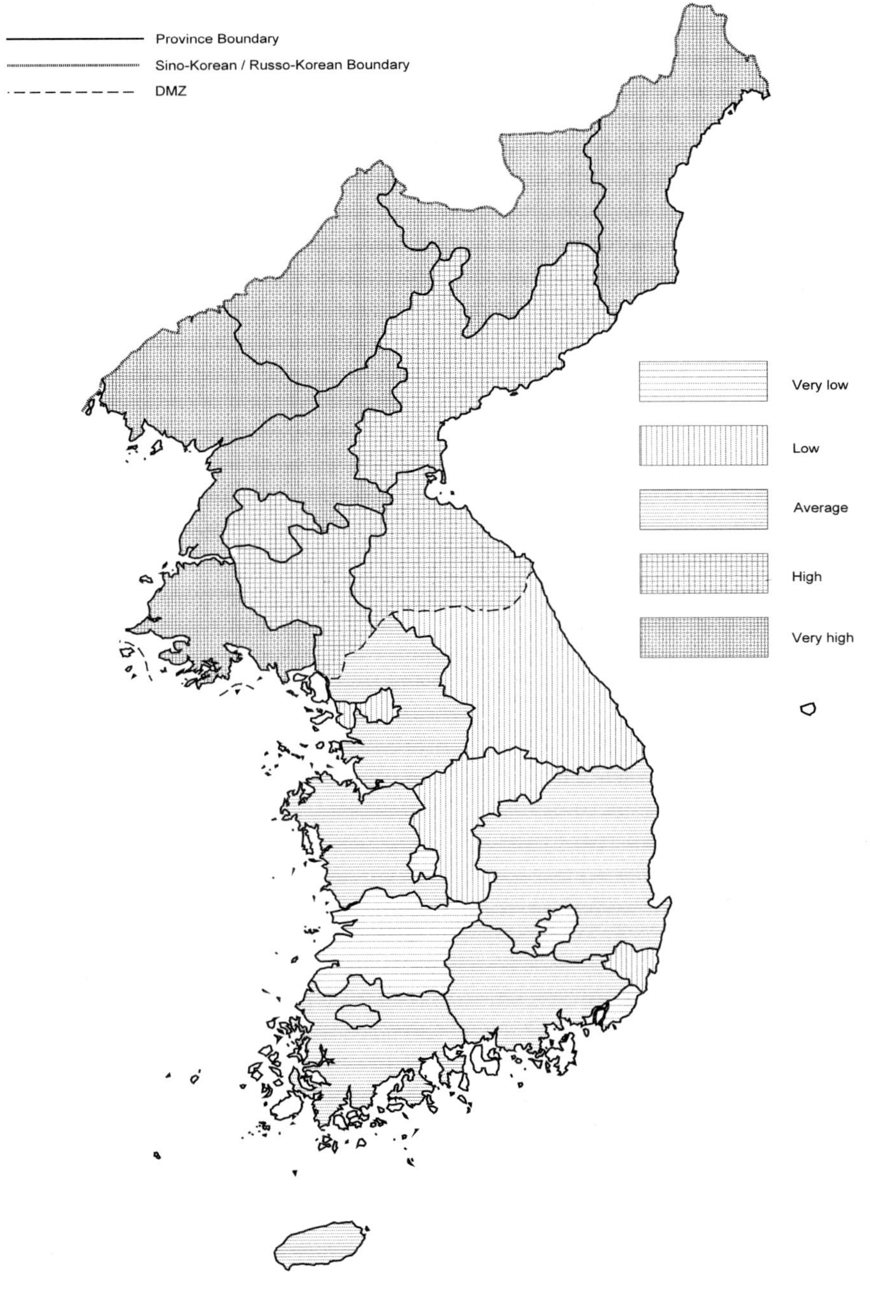

Notes: Unit = percent. Data pertain to people aged 15 years and older in South Korea and 16 years and older in North Korea. Non-working population of North Korea was not reported but calculated from the population 16 years and older less the working population 16 years and older. Cut-offs = below 54.74, 54.74 to below 56.98, 56.98 to below 63.67, 63.67 to below 70.74, 70.74 or above.

Map 12.9 Non-working population of the Korean peninsula (share)

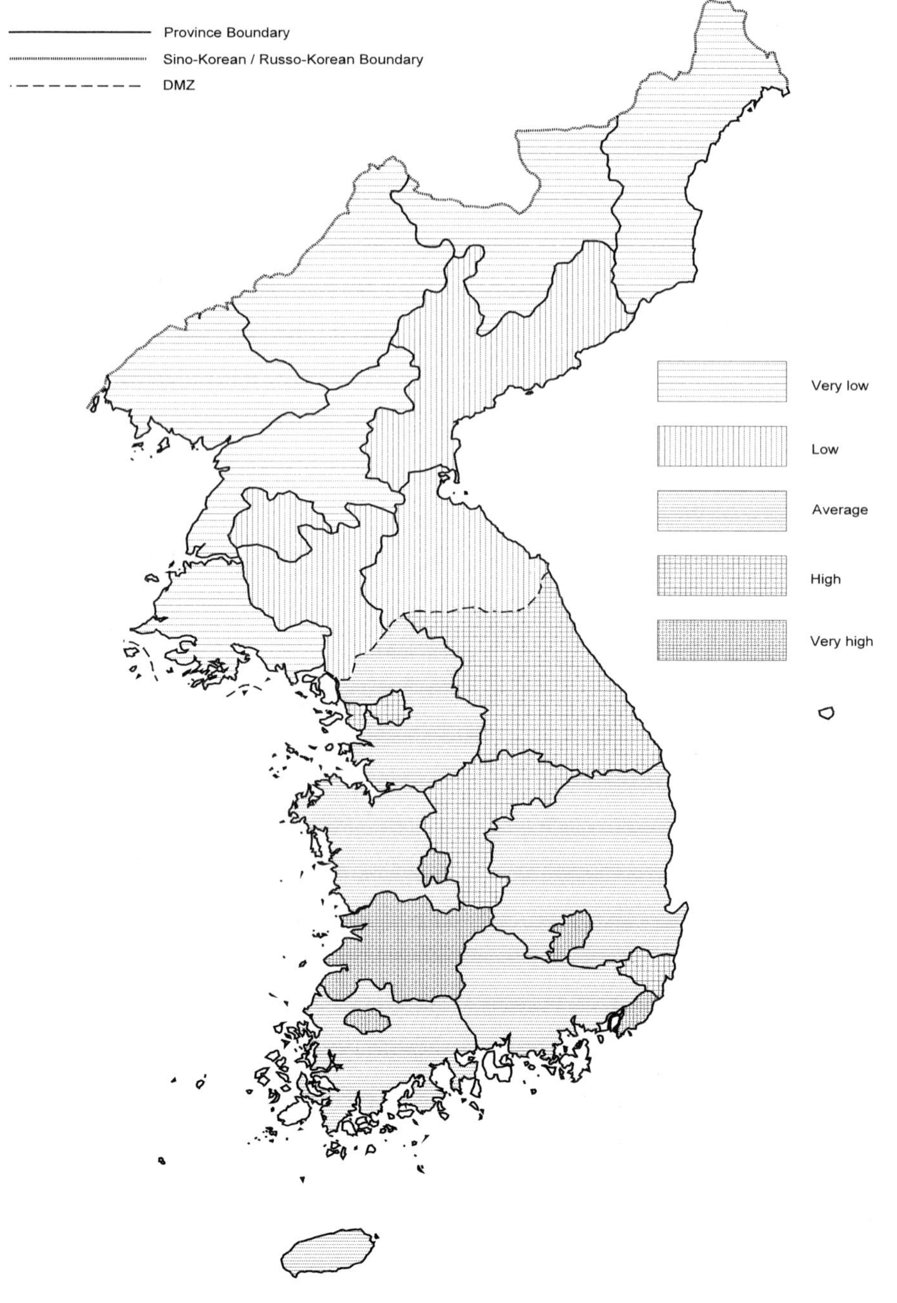

Notes: Unit = percent. Data pertain to people aged 15 years and older. Cut-offs = below 29.26, 29.26 to below 36.33, 36.33 to below 43.02, 43.02 to below 45.26, 45.26 or above.

Map 12.10 Working population of South Korea (share)

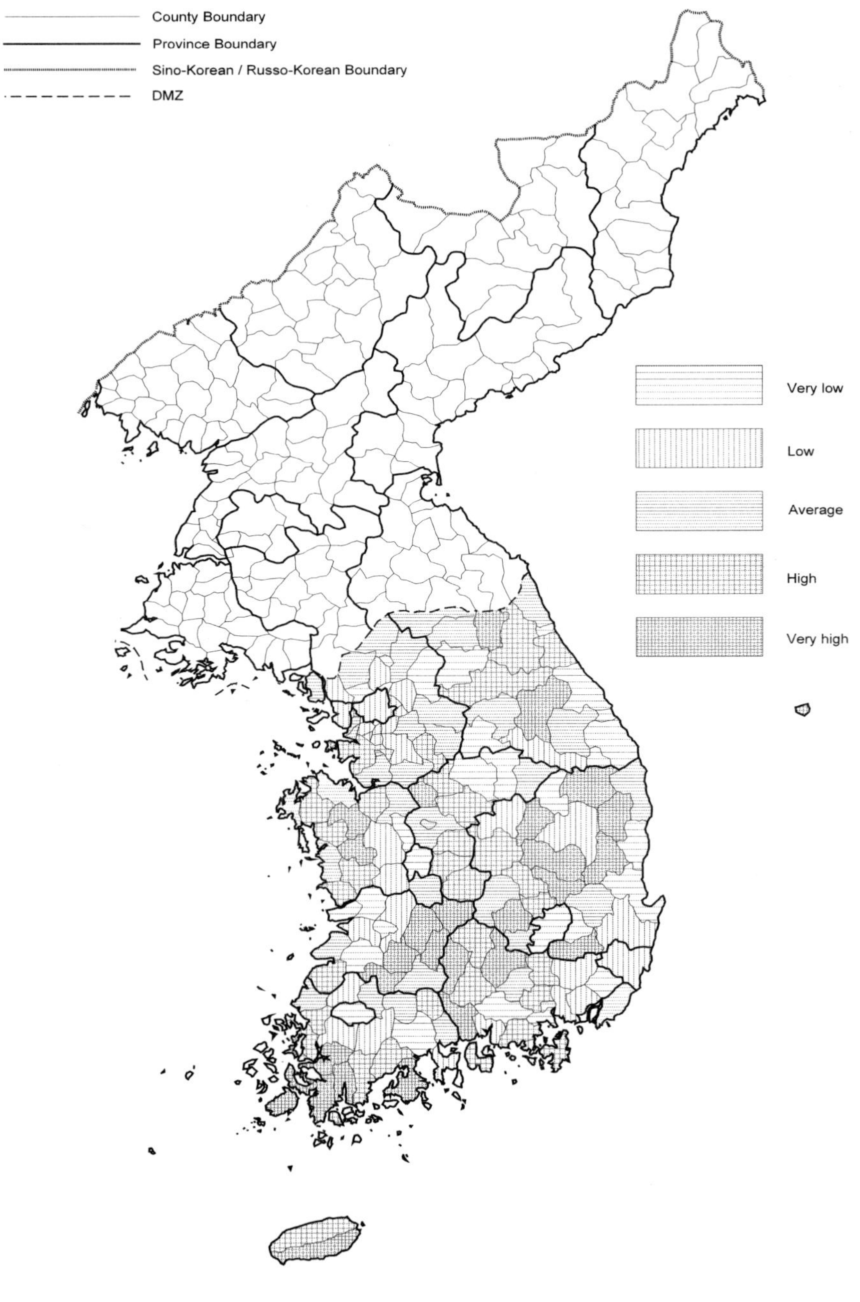

Notes: Unit = percent. Data pertain to people aged 15 years and older in South Korea and 16 years and older in North Korea. Non-working population of North Korea was not reported but calculated from the population 16 years and older less the working population 16 years and older. Cut-offs = below 55.22, 55.22 to below 57.62, 57.62 to below 60.95, 60.95 to below 63.54, 63.54 or above.

Map 12.11 Non-working population of South Korea (share)

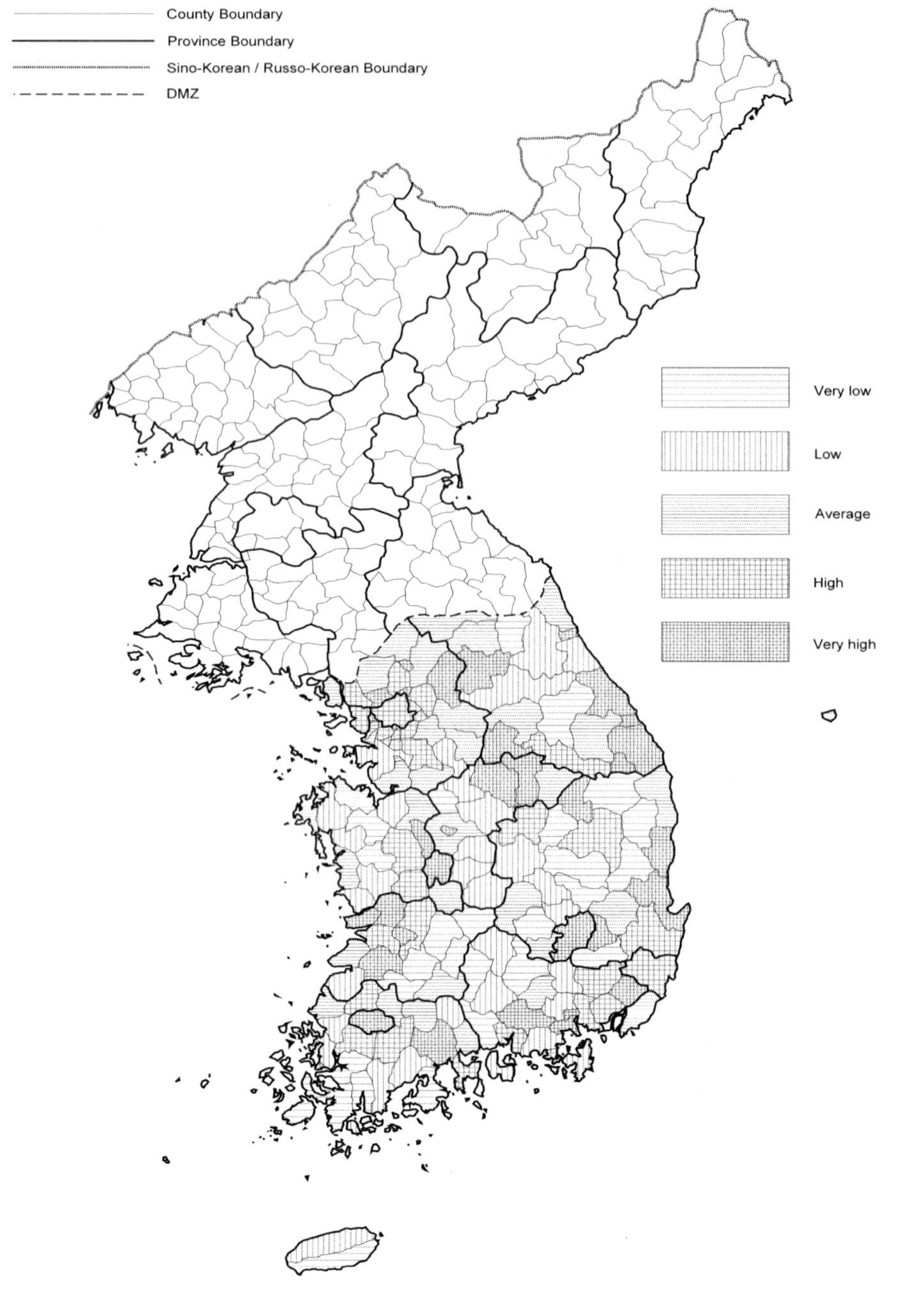

Notes: Unit = percent. Data pertain to people aged 15 years and older. Cut-offs = below 36.46, 36.46 to below 39.05, 39.05 to below 42.38, 42.38 to below 44.78, 44.78 or above.

13. Employment Status

Map 13.1 Total employed population of South Korea

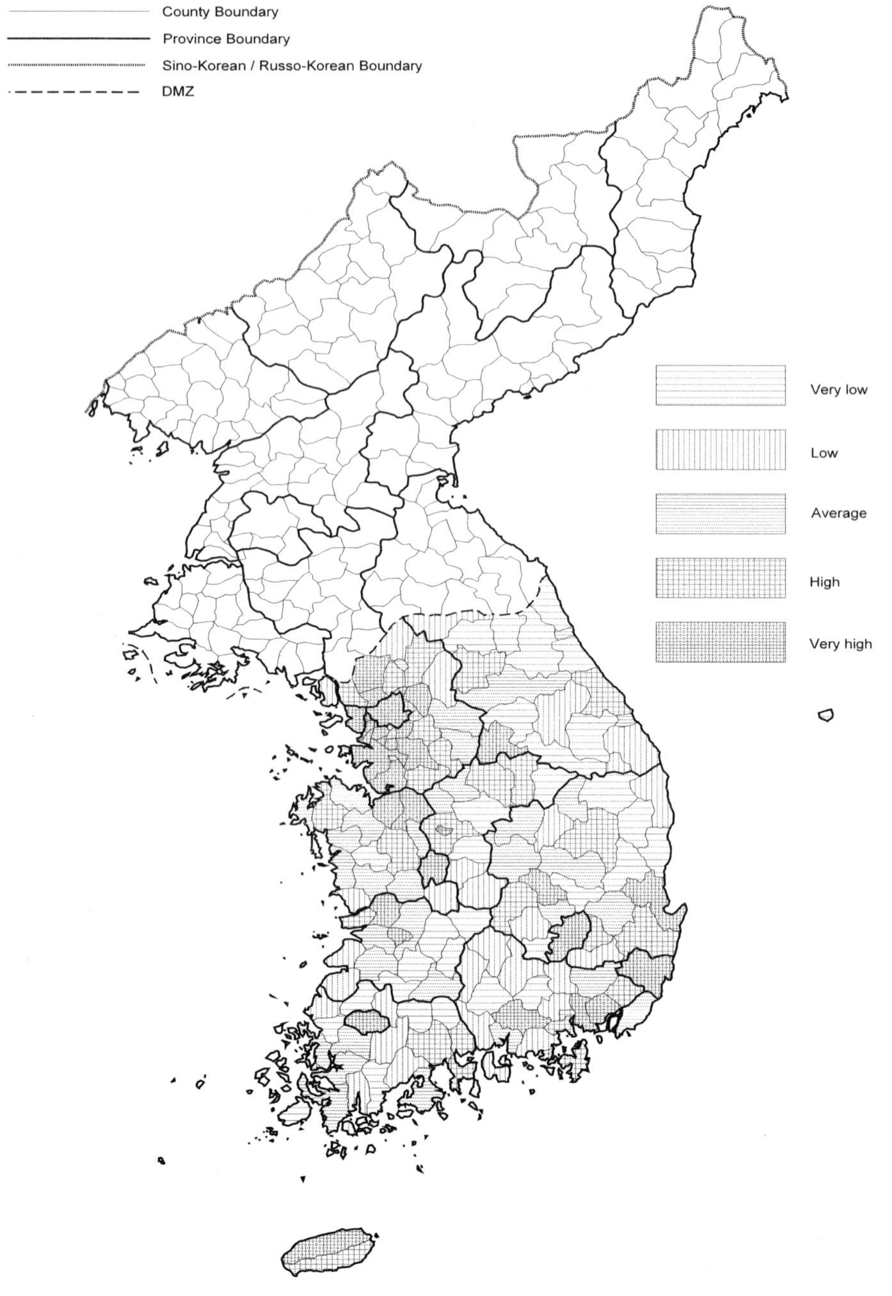

Notes: Unit = persons. Data pertain to people aged 15 years and older. Cut-offs = below 19294.7, 19294.7 to below 30653.4, 30653.4 to below 58228.0, 58228.0 to below 123555.9, 123555.9 or above.

Map 13.2 Total employee population of South Korea

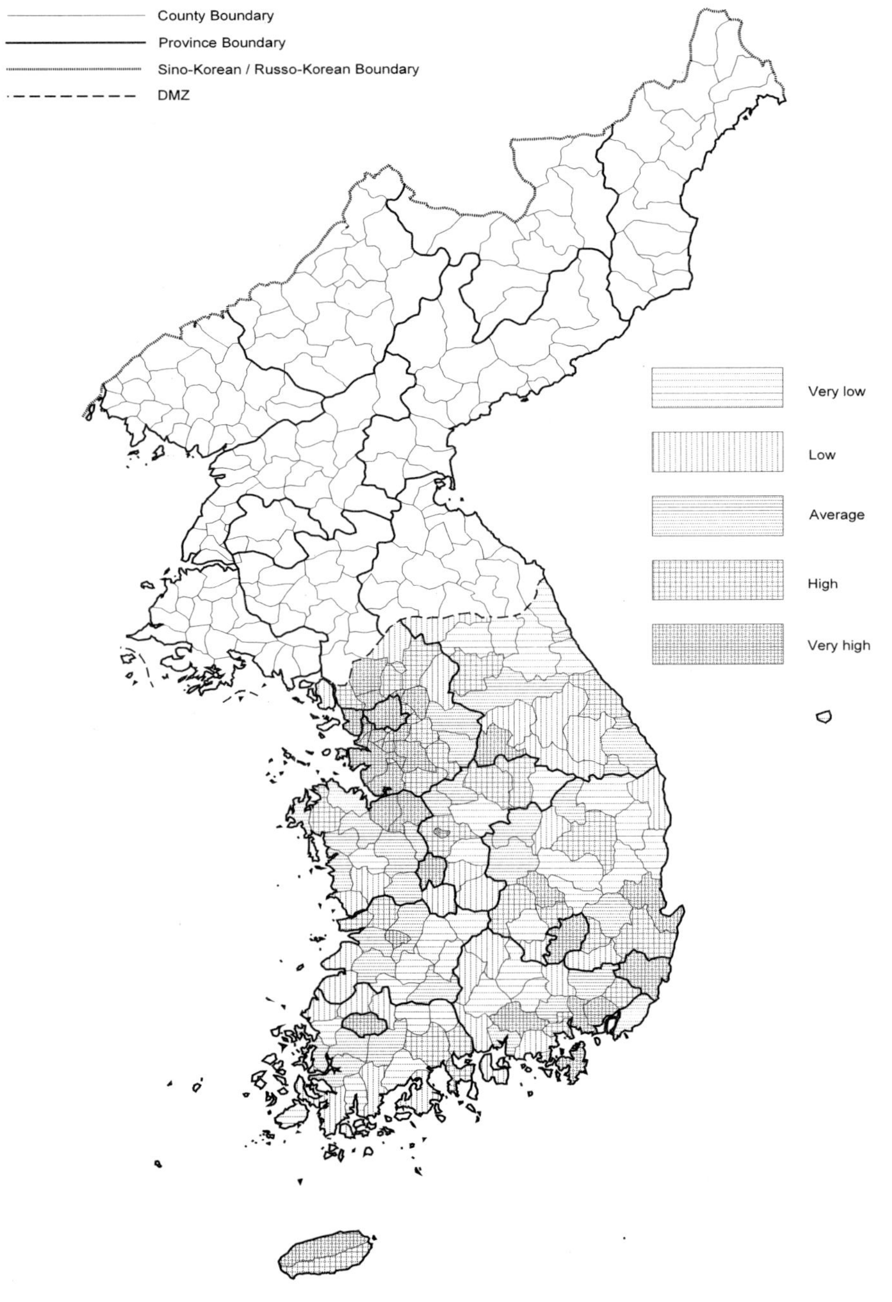

Notes: Unit = persons. Data pertain to people aged 15 years and older. Cut-offs = below 6898.6, 6898.6 to below 12800.2, 12800.2 to below 31228.3, 31228.3 to below 86488.2, 86488.2 or above.

Map 13.3 Total self-employed with no employee population of South Korea

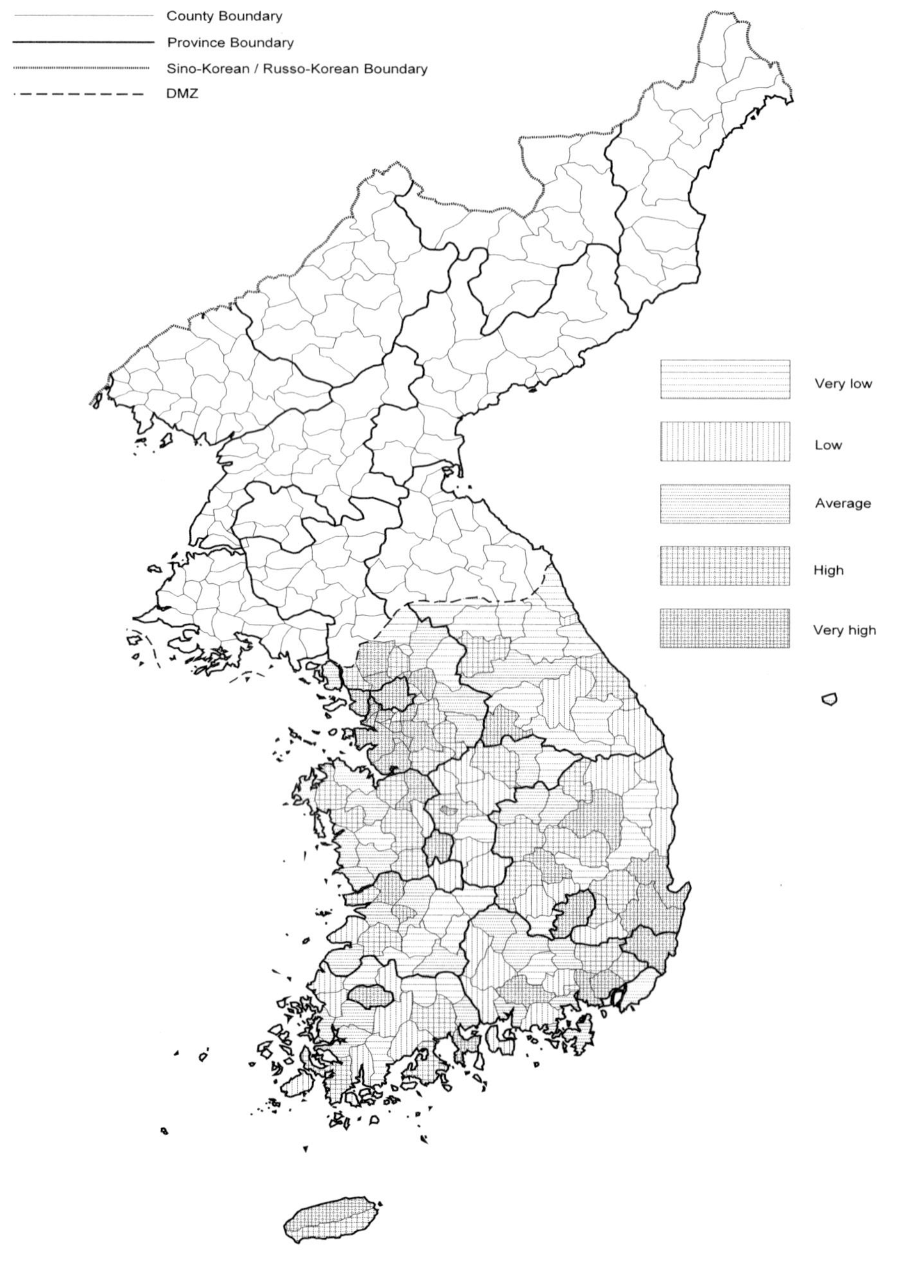

Notes: Unit = persons. Data pertain to people aged 15 years and older. Cut-offs = below 6289.8, 6289.8 to below 9434.1, 9434.1 to below 14016.0, 14016.0 to below 14016.0, 14016.0 to below 21696.8, 21696.8 or above.

Map 13.4 Total self-employed with employee population of South Korea

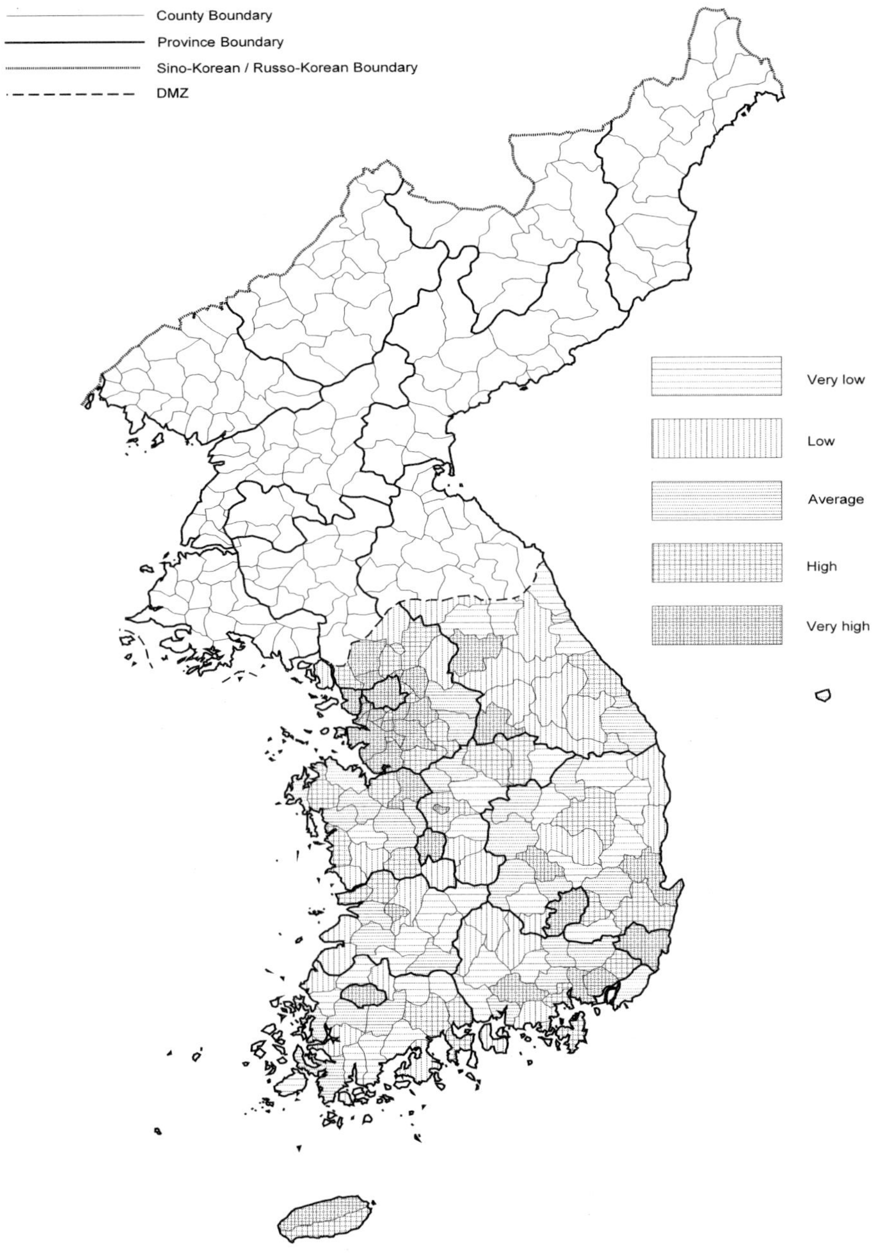

Notes: Unit = persons. Data pertain to people aged 15 years and older. Cut-offs = below 735.3, 735.3 to below 1398.0, 1398.0 to below 3233.6, 3233.6 to below 9587.5, 9587.5 or above.

Map 13.5 Total unpaid family worker population of South Korea

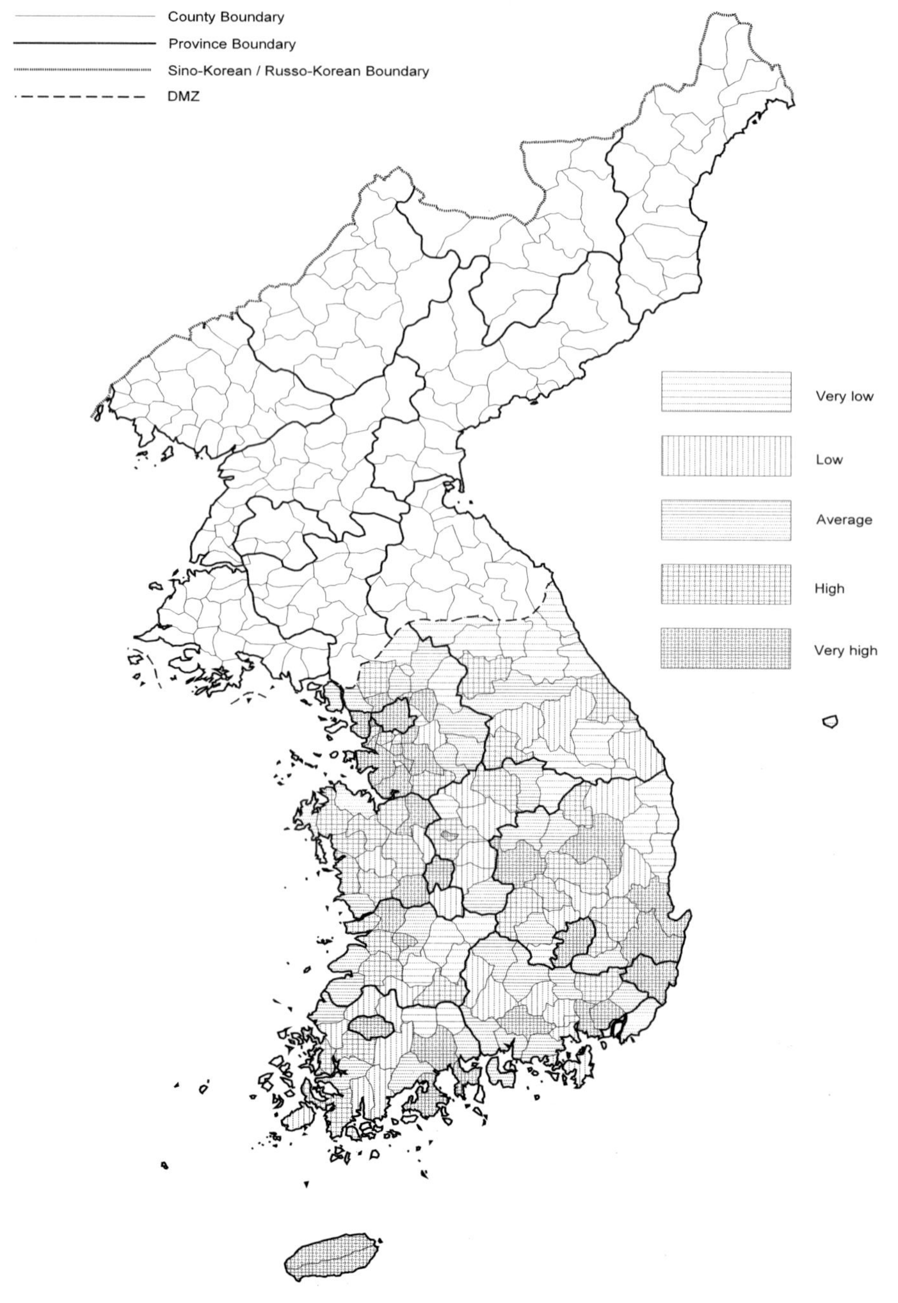

Notes: Unit = persons. Data pertain to people aged 15 years and older. Cut-offs = below 3718.6, 3718.6 to below 5767.3, 5767.3 to below 7592.9, 7592.9 to below 11158.7, 11158.7 or above.

Map 13.6 Male employed population of South Korea

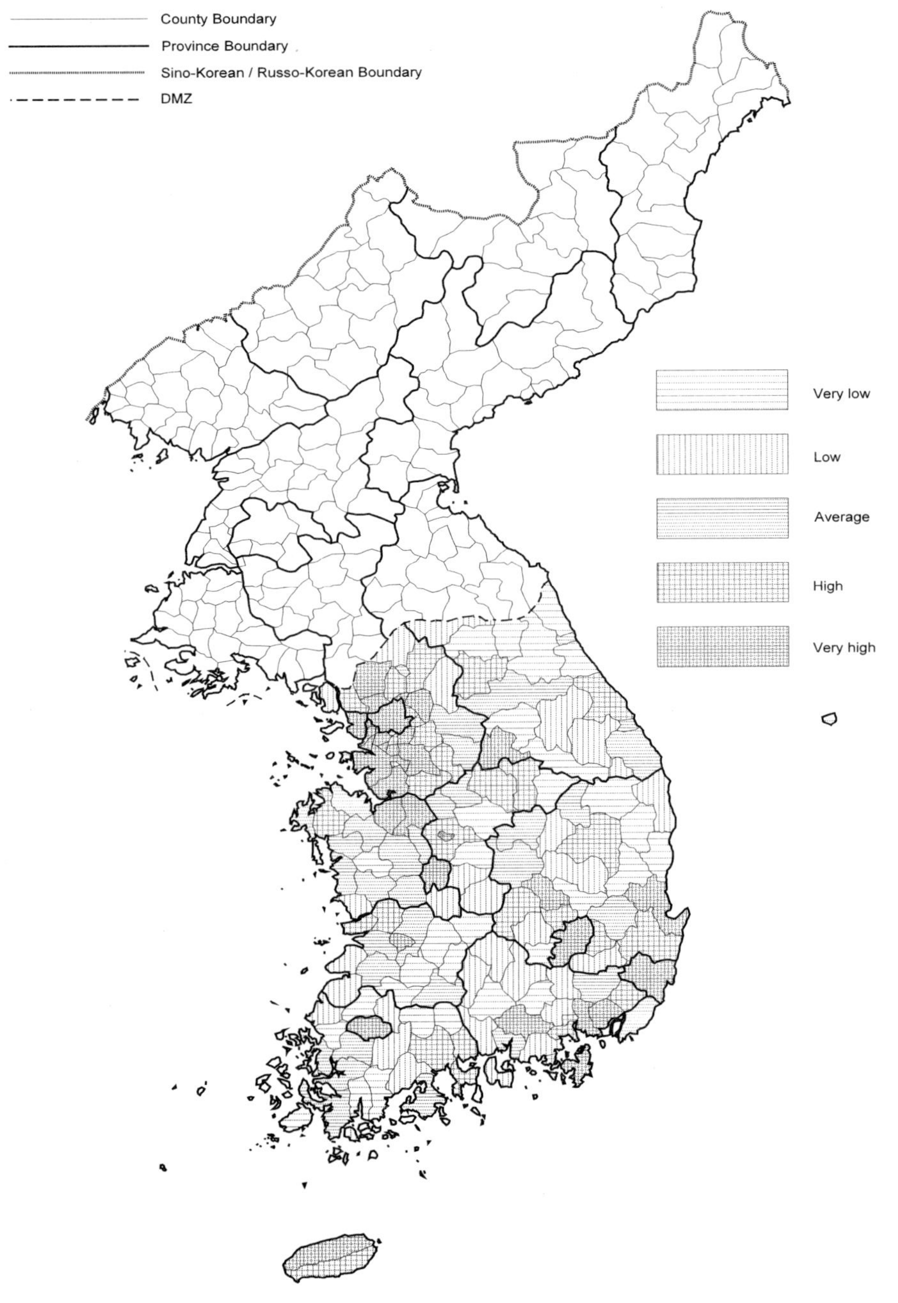

Notes: Unit = persons. Data pertain to people aged 15 years and older. Cut-offs = below 10340.2, 10340.2 to below 16969.7, 16969.7 to below 33438.7, 33438.7 to below 73870.0, 73870.0 or above.

Map 13.7 Male employee population of South Korea

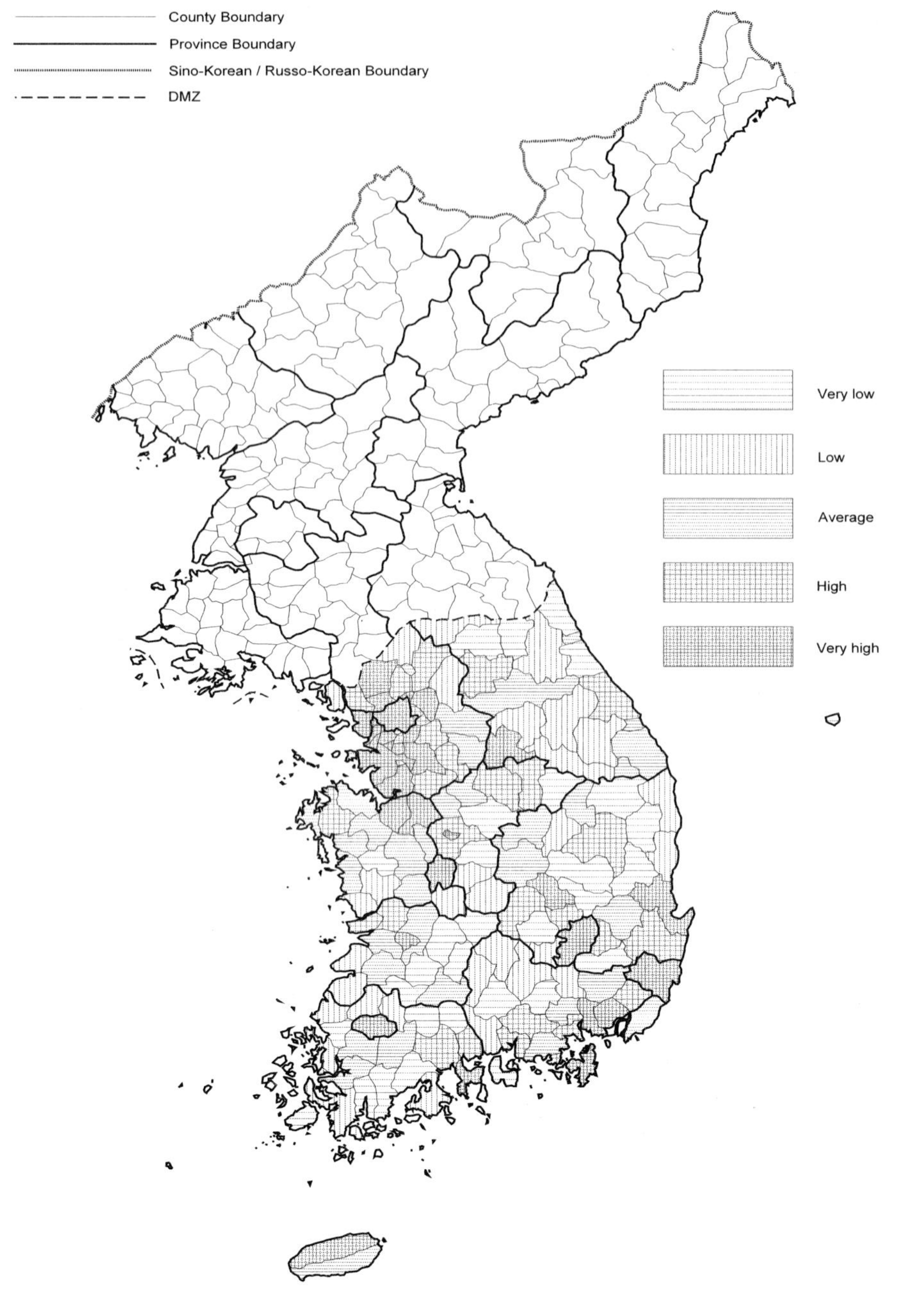

Notes: Unit = persons. Data pertain to people aged 15 years and older. Cut-offs = below 3712.7, 3712.7 to below 7650.4, 7650.4 to below 17998.2, 17998.2 to below 50148.1, 50148.1 or above.

Map 13.8 Male self-employed with no employee population of South Korea

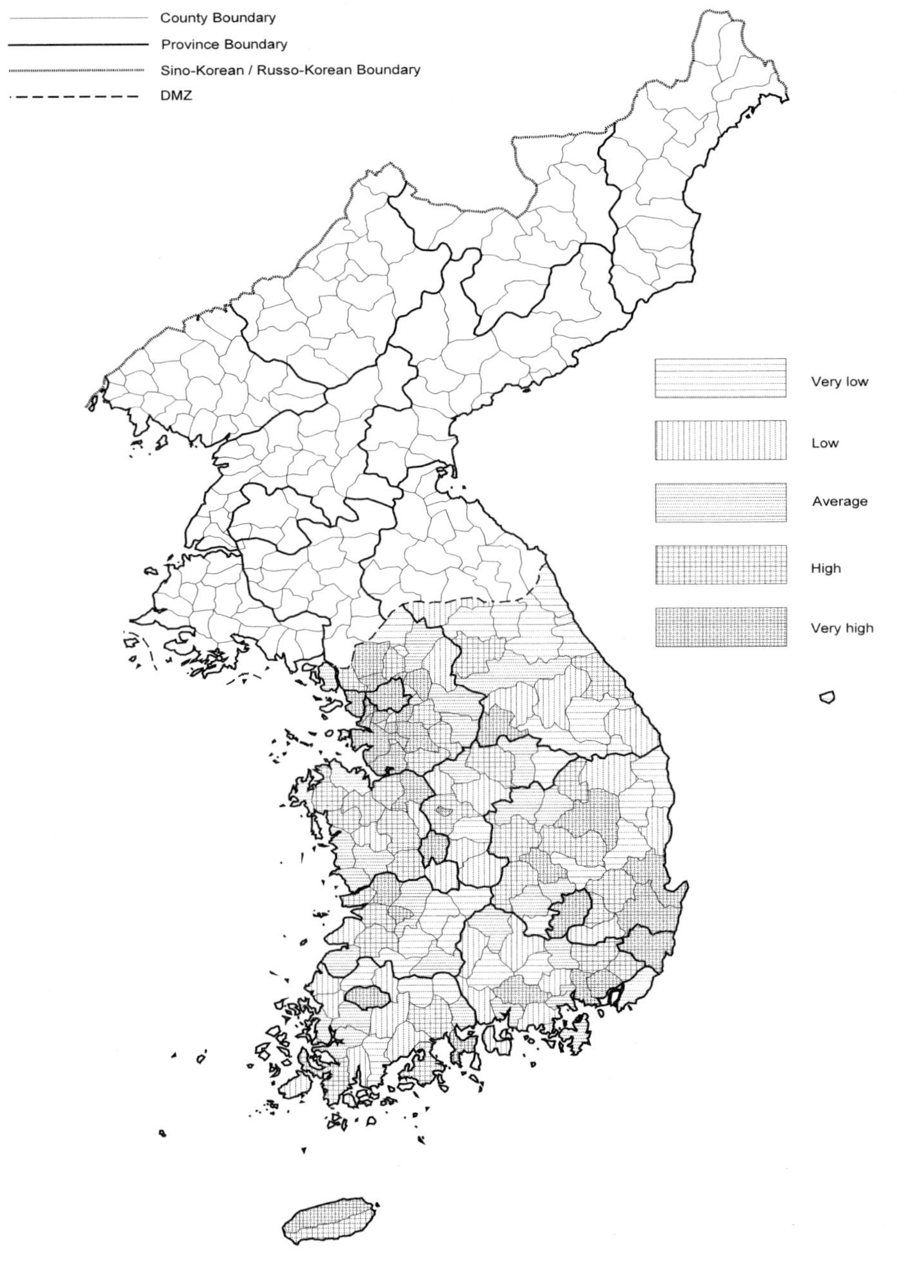

Notes: Unit = persons. Data pertain to people aged 15 years and older. Cut-offs = below 4579.4, 4579.4 to below 6948.8, 6948.8 to below 10166.6, 10166.6 to below 15782.9, 15782.9 or above.

Map 13.9 Male self-employed with employee population of South Korea

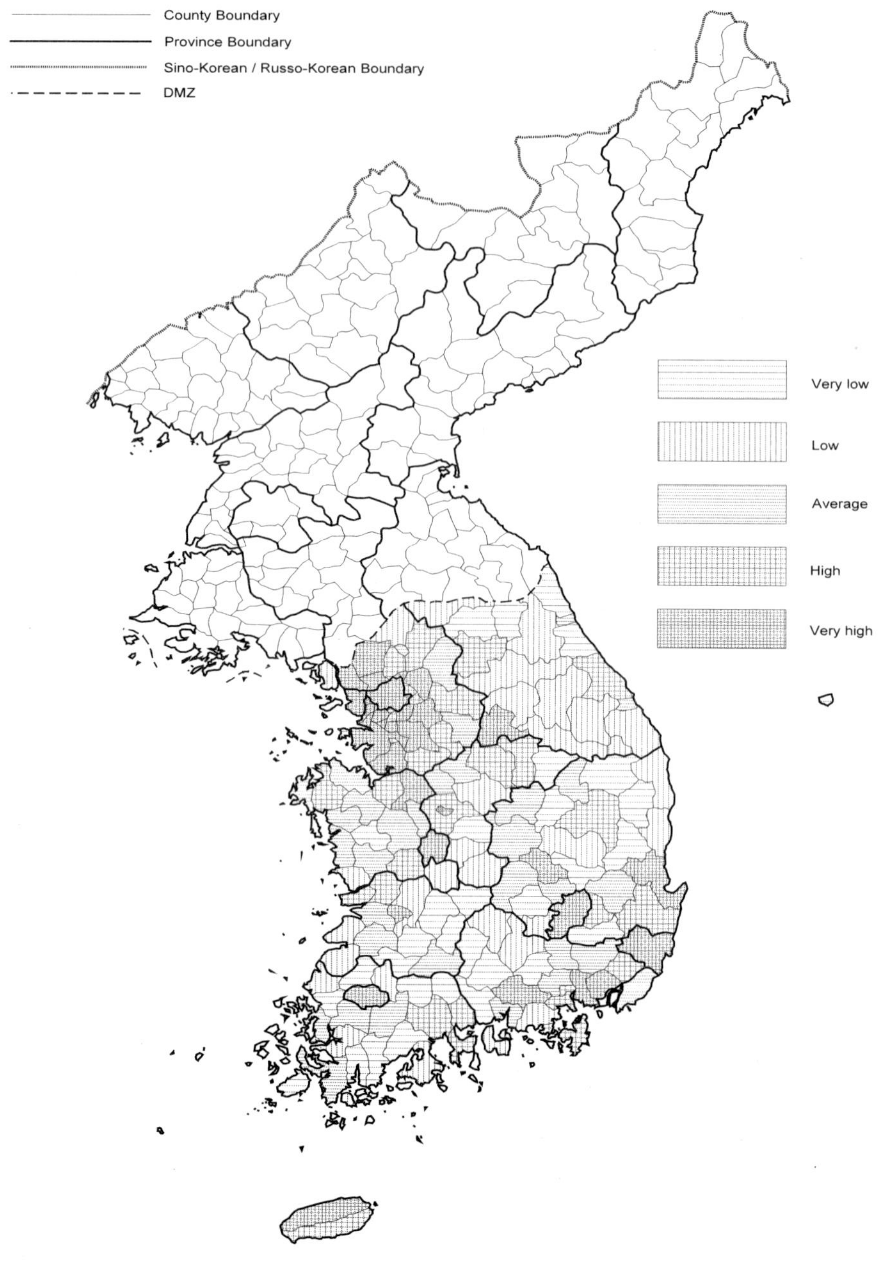

Notes: Unit = persons. Data pertain to people aged 15 years and older. Cut-offs = below 499.8, 499.8 to below 969.3, 969.3 to below 2202.8, 2202.8 to below 6808.8, 6808.8 or above.

Map 13.10 Male unpaid family worker population of South Korea

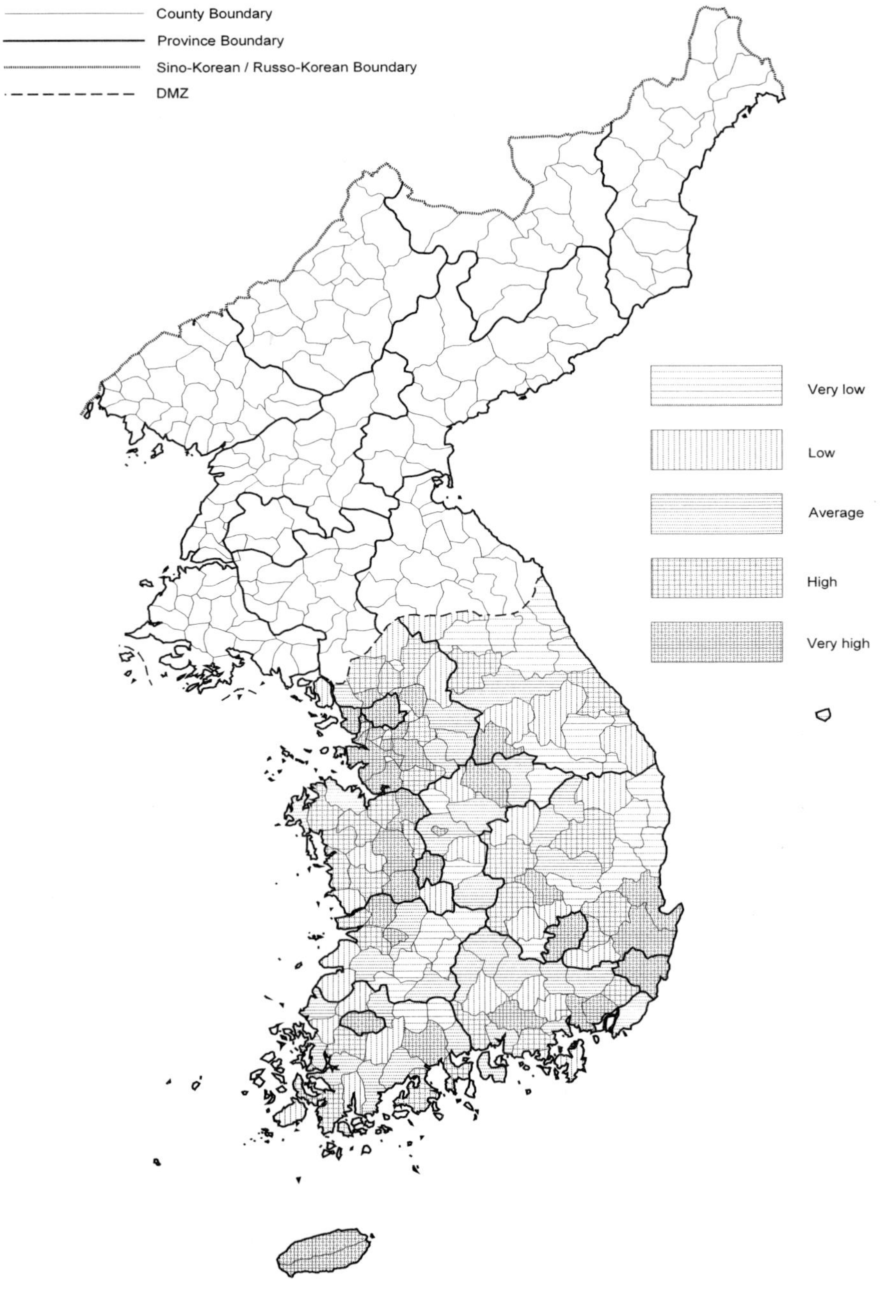

Notes: Unit = persons. Data pertain to people aged 15 years and older. Cut-offs = below 660.0, 660.0 to below 1059.7, 1059.7 to below 1431.1, 1431.1 to below 2205.7, 2205.7 or above.

Map 13.11 Female employed population of South Korea

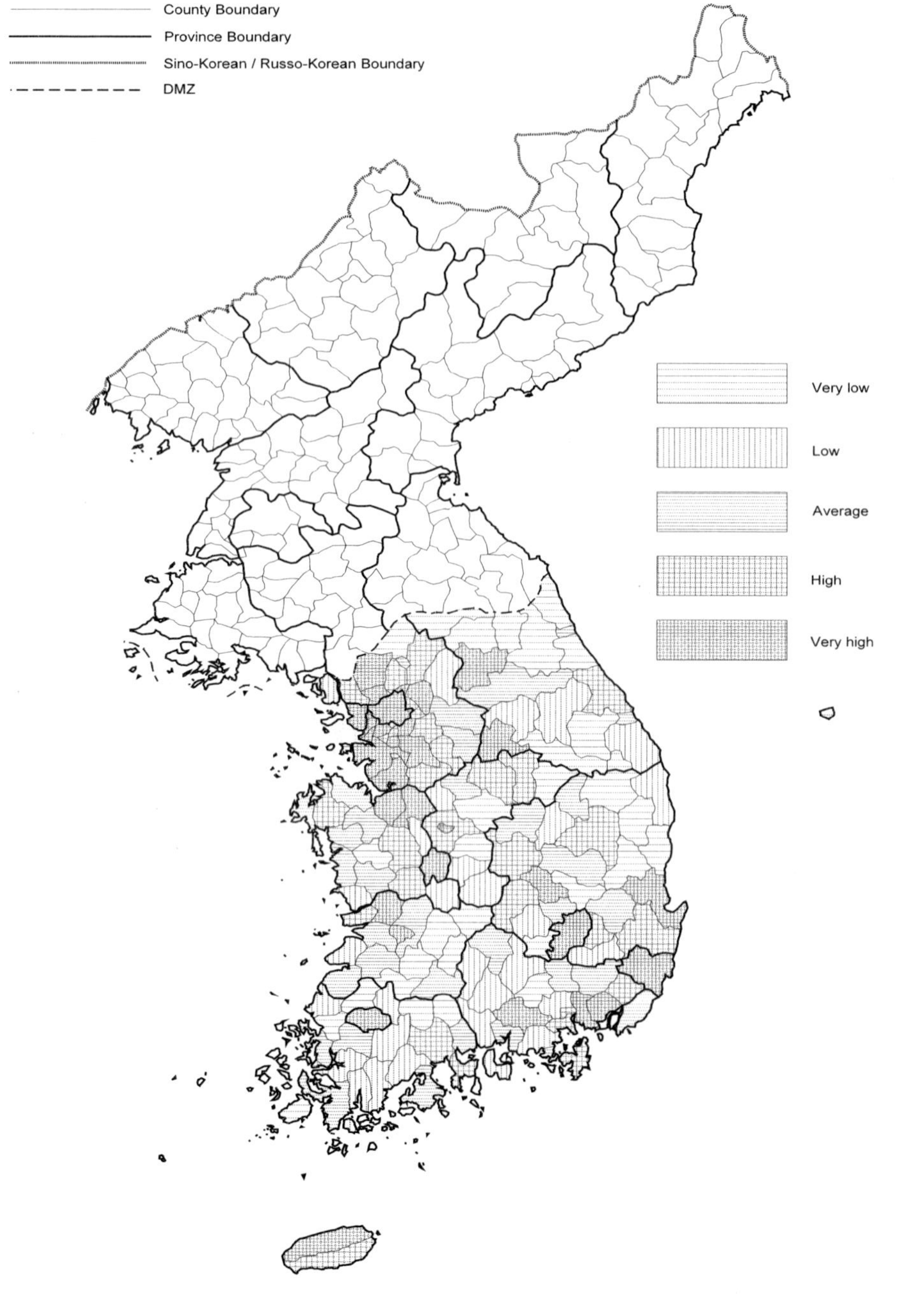

Notes: Unit = persons. Data pertain to people aged 15 years and older. Cut-offs = below 8744.7, 8744.7 to below 14211.1, 14211.1 to below 23843.1, 23843.1 to below 50932.9, 50932.9 or above.

Map 13.12 Female employee population of South Korea

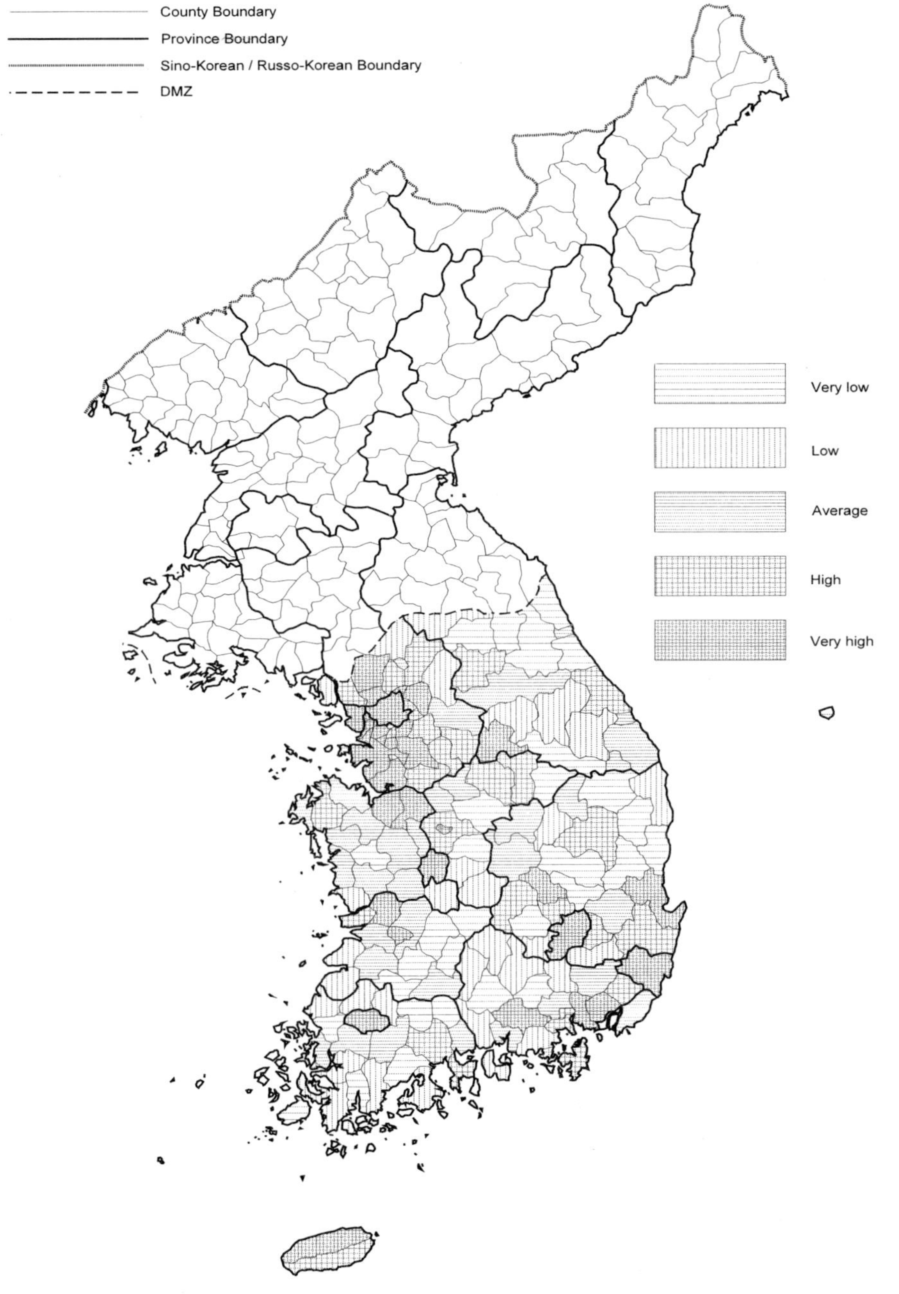

Notes: Unit = persons. Data pertain to people aged 15 years and older. Cut-offs = below 3090.2, 3090.2 to below 5699.6, 5699.6 to below 13309.6, 13309.6 to below 34284.3, 34284.3 or above.

Map 13.13 Female self-employed with no employee population of South Korea

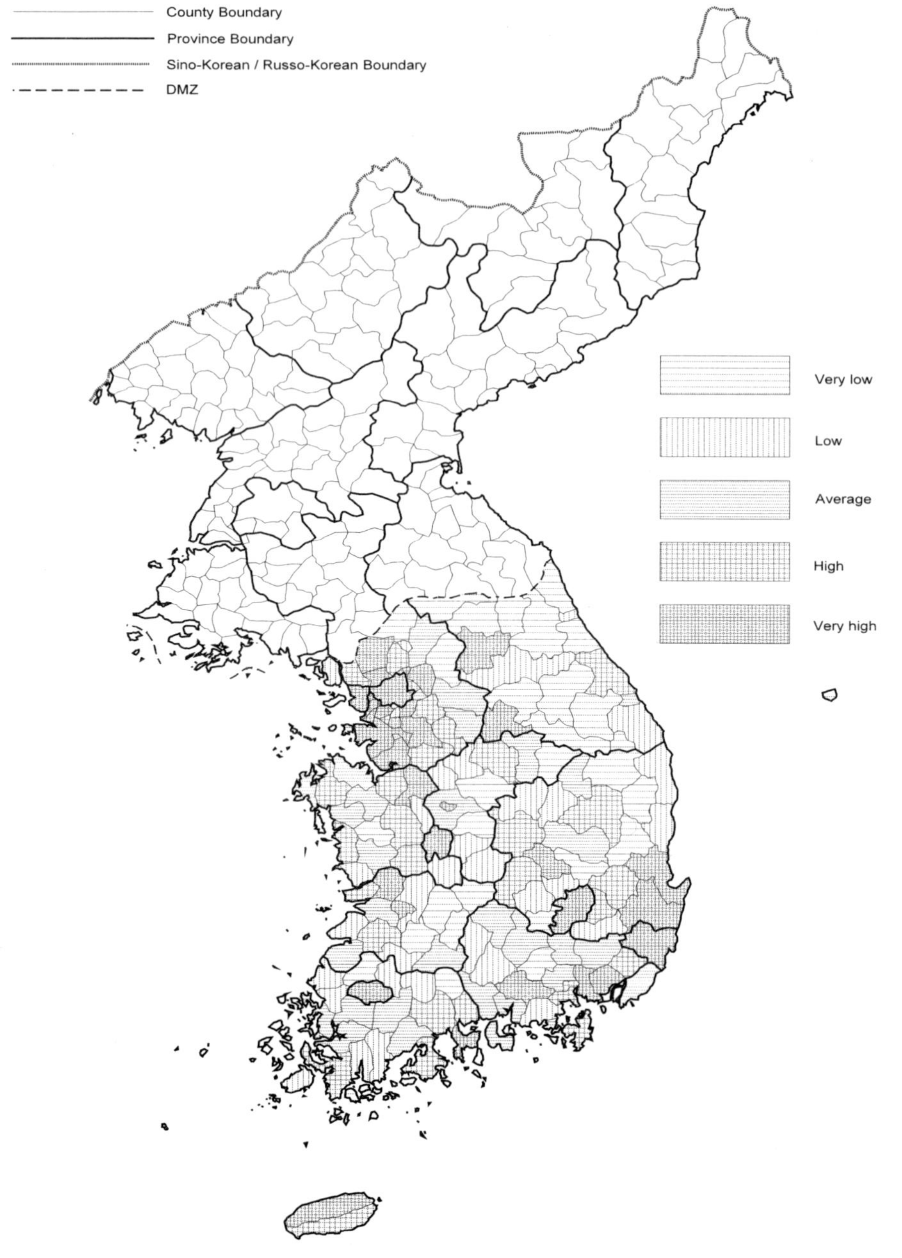

Notes: Unit = persons. Data pertain to people aged 15 years and older. Cut-offs = below 1632.3, 1632.3 to below 2628.5, 2628.5 to below 3841.7, 3841.7 to below 6658.8, 6658.8 or above.

Map 13.14 Female self-employed with employee population of South Korea

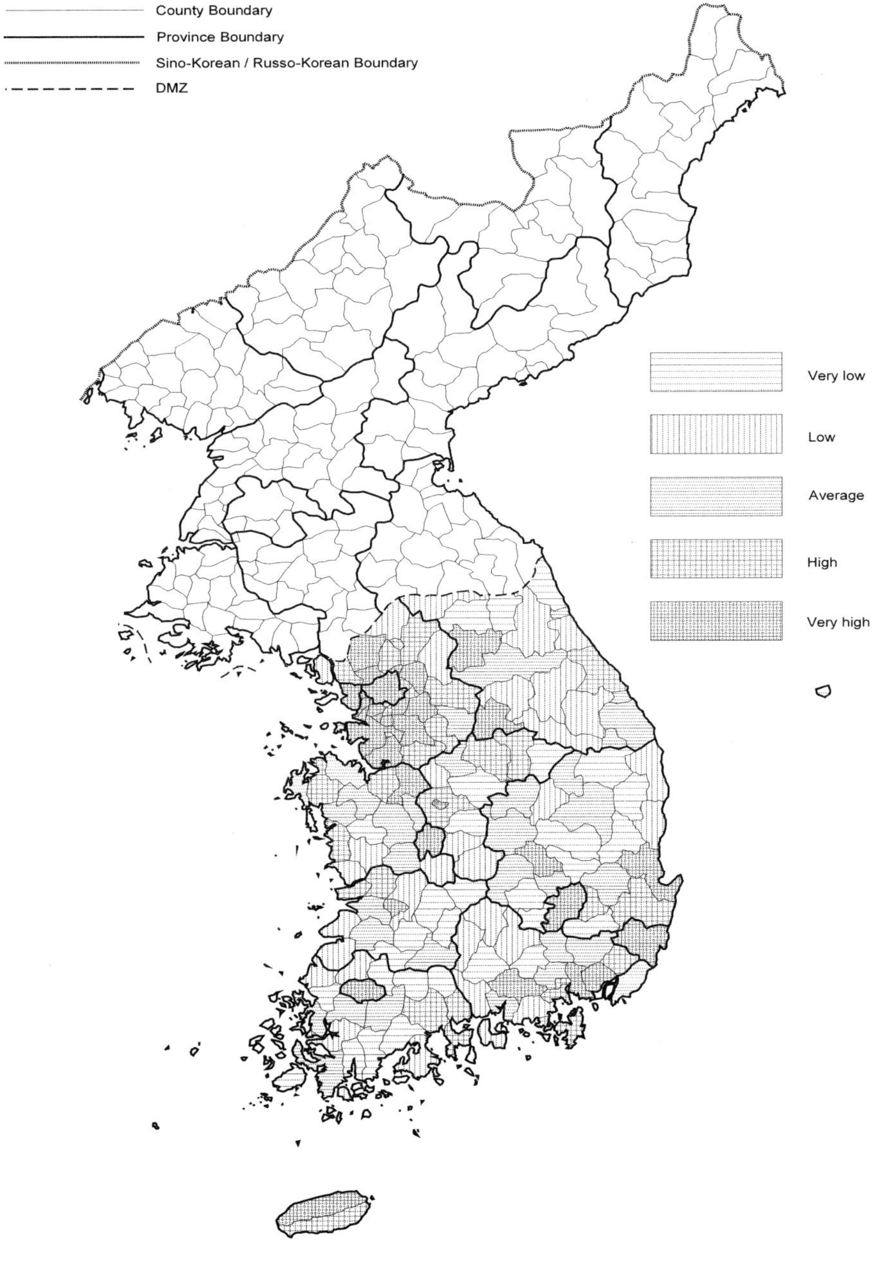

Notes: Unit = persons. Data pertain to people aged 15 years and older. Cut-offs = below 237.6, 237.6 to below 447.0, 447.0 to below 1005.7, 1005.7 to below 2547.7, 2547.7 or above.

Map 13.15 Female unpaid family worker population of South Korea

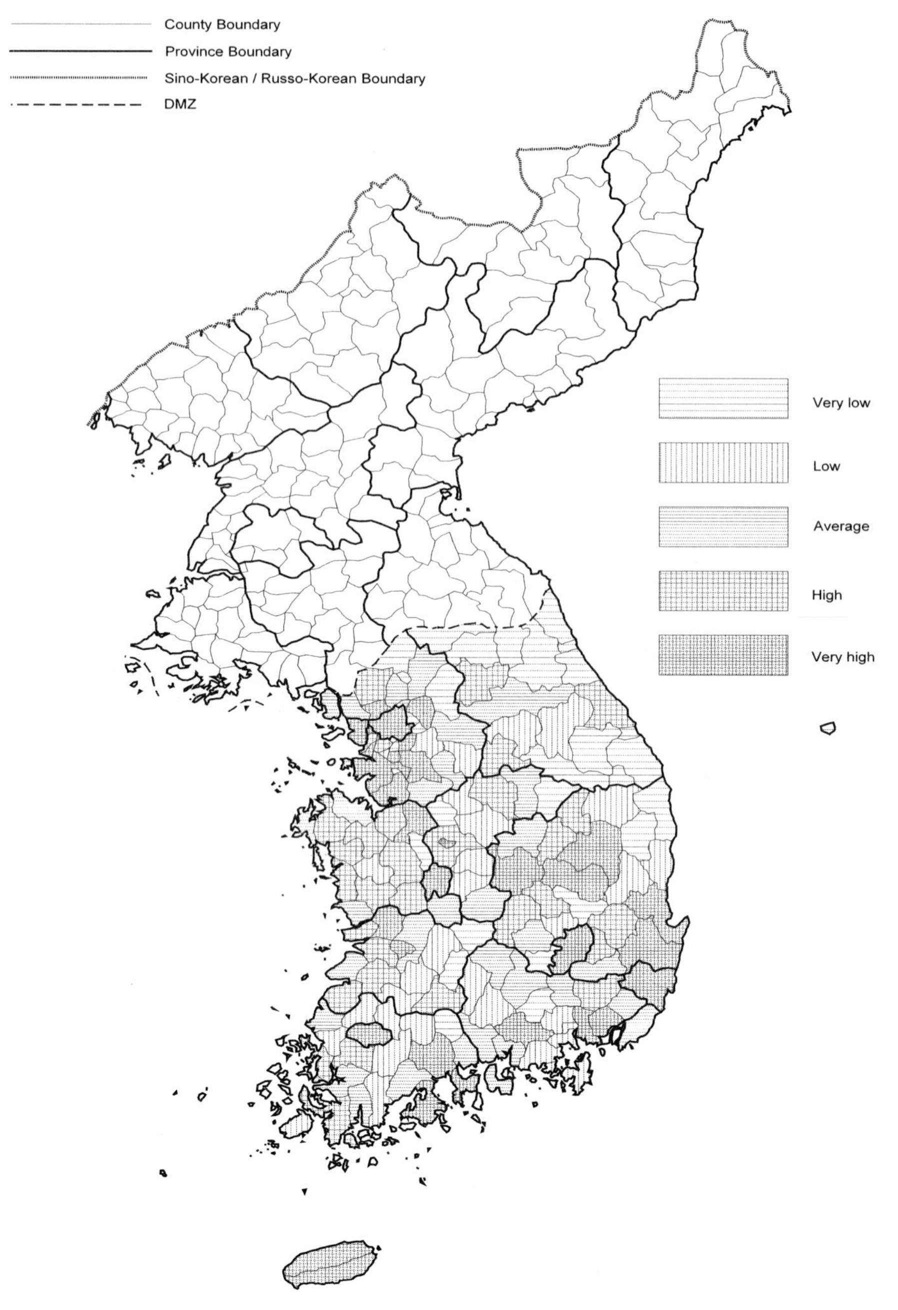

Notes: Unit = persons. Data pertain to people aged 15 years and older. Cut-offs = below 3096.8, 3096.8 to below 4644.2, 4644.2 to below 5948.8, 5948.8 to below 9131.8, 9131.8 or above.

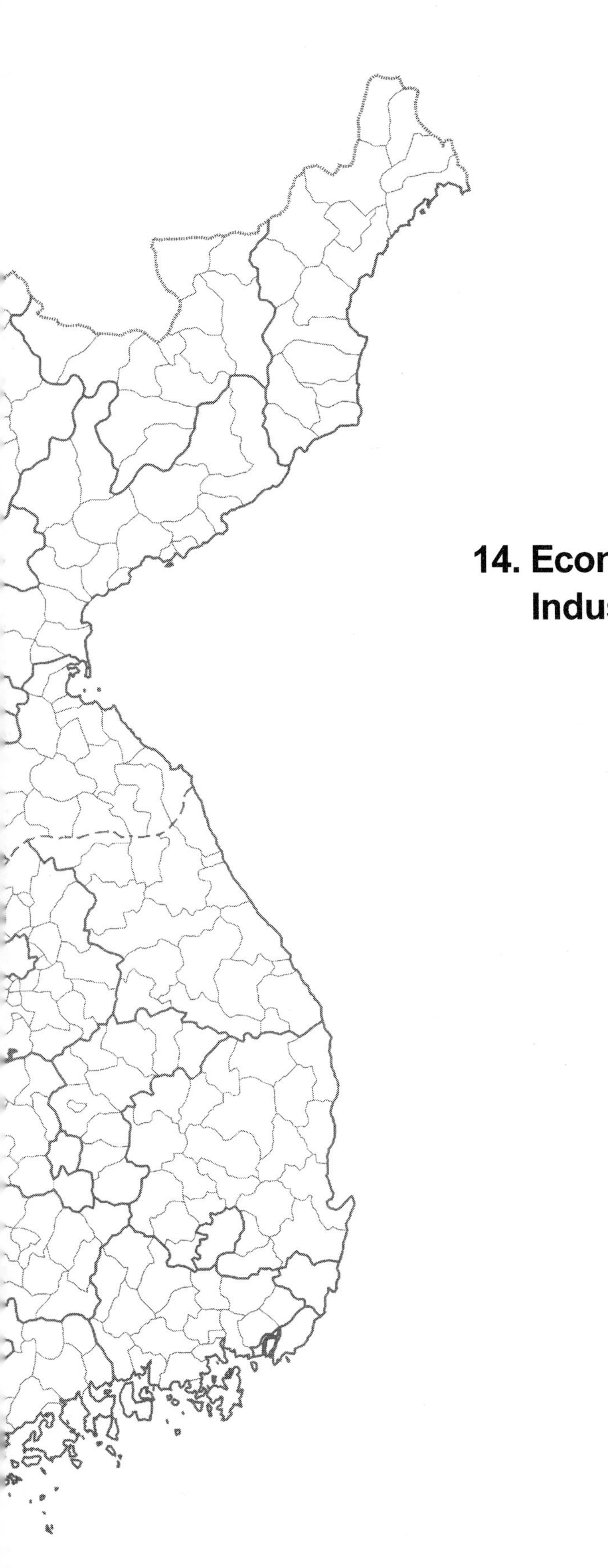

14. Economic Activity by Specific Industry

Map 14.1 Population employed in agriculture forestry & fishing of the Korean peninsula

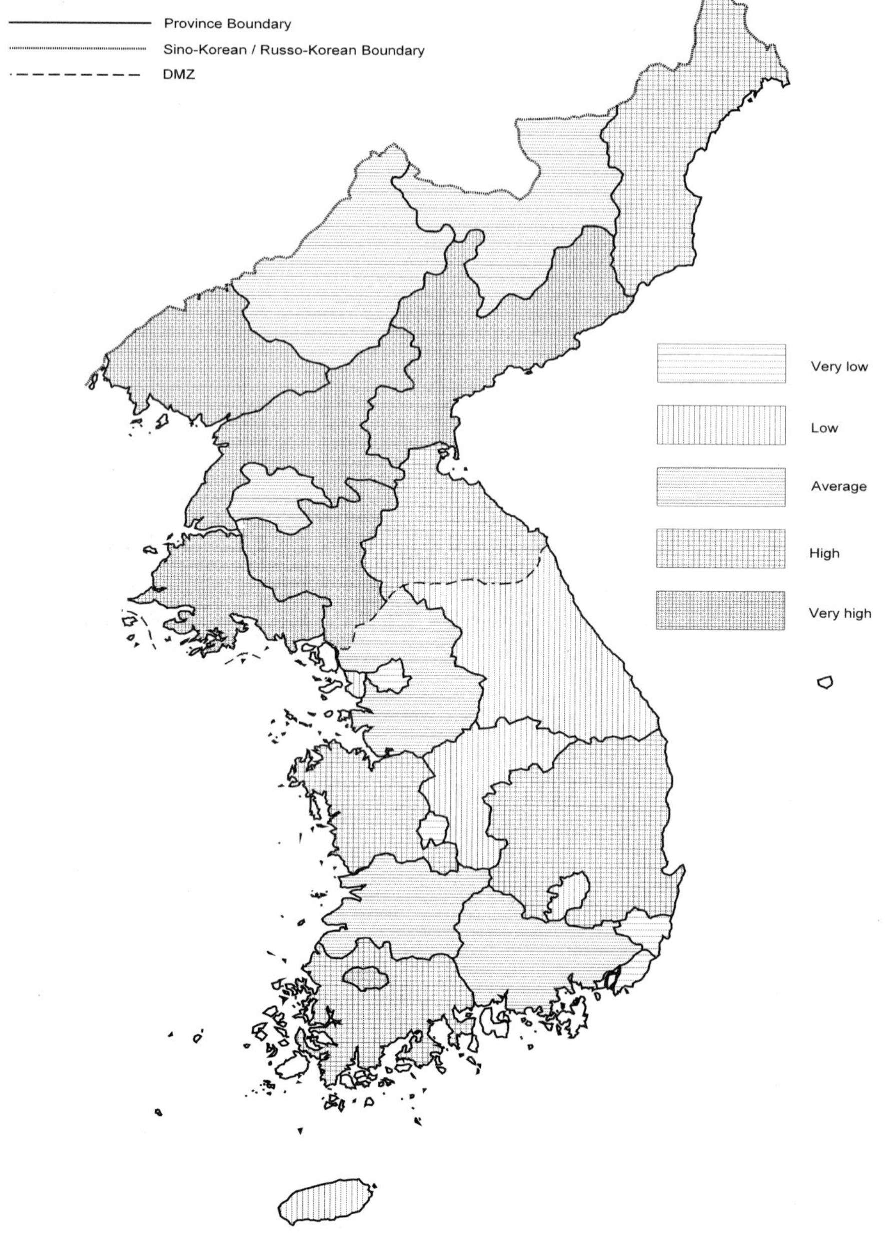

Notes: Unit = persons. Data pertain to people aged 15 years and older. Cut-offs = below 16451.3, 16451.3 to below 125226.5, 125226.5 to below 229373.4, 229373.4 to below 412990.9, 412990.9 or above.

Map 14.2 Population employed in agriculture forestry & fishing of South Korea

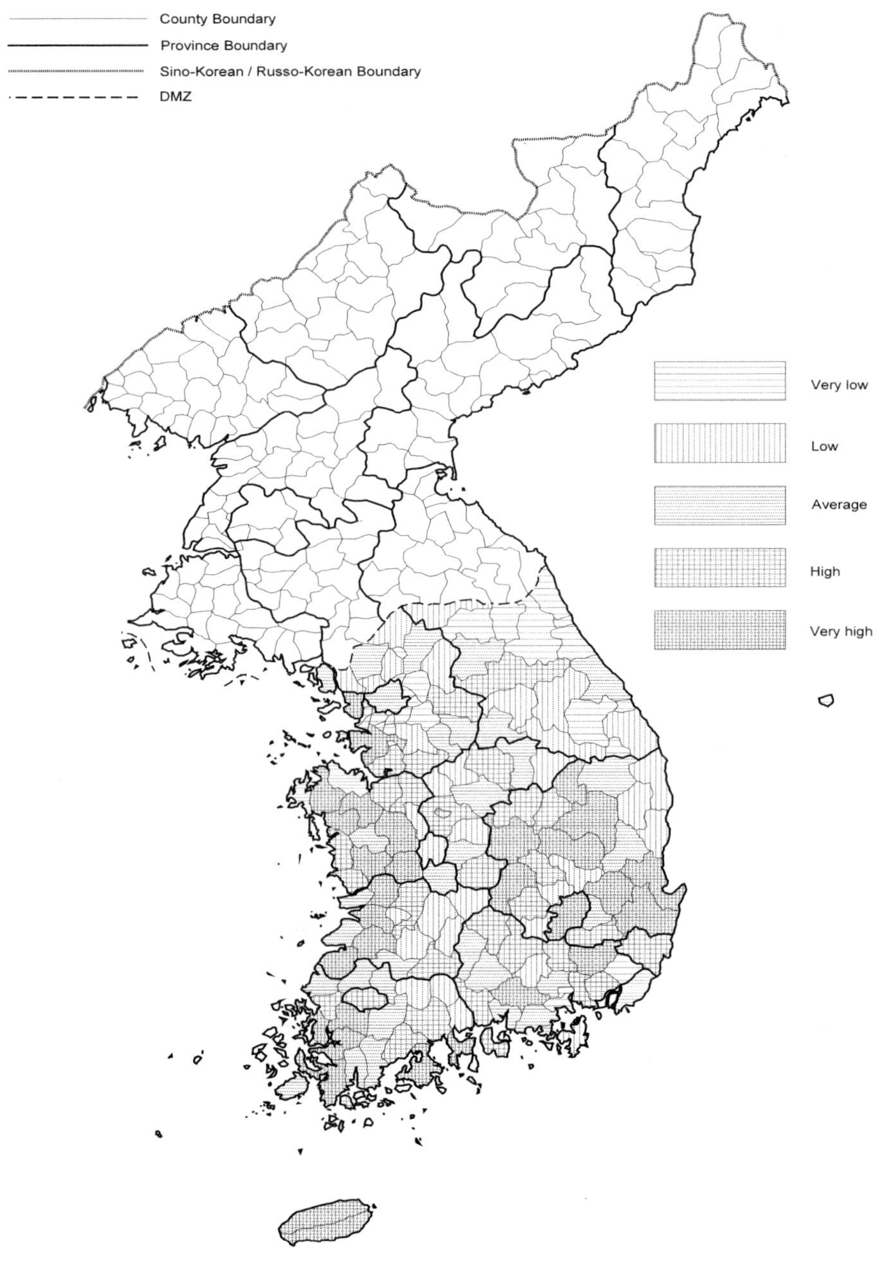

Notes: Unit = persons. Data pertain to people aged 15 years and older. Cut-offs = below 4944.5, 4944.5 to below 8454.5, 8454.5 to below 11651.5, 11651.5 to below 15817.5, 15817.5 or above.

Map 14.3 Population employed in mining & quarrying of the Korean peninsula

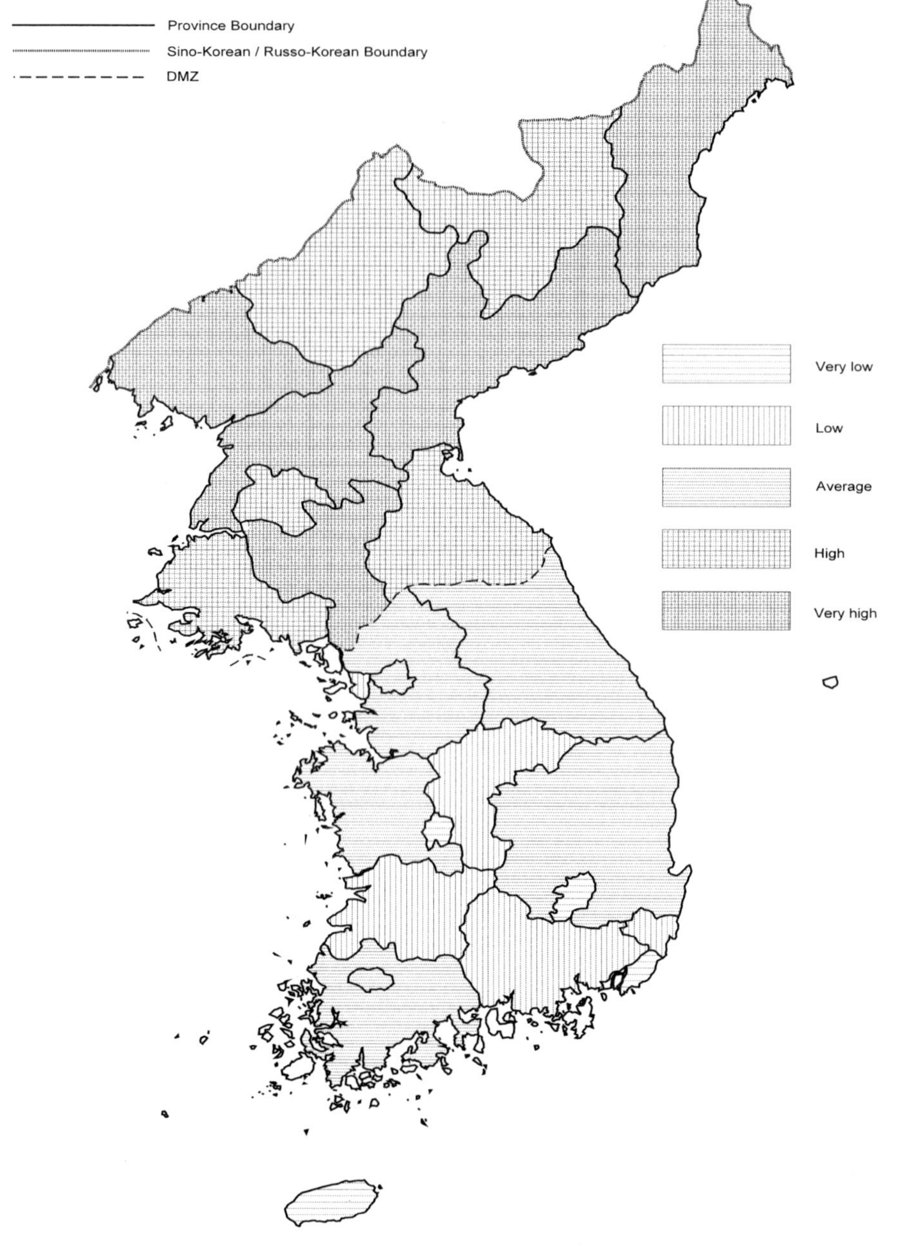

Notes: Unit = persons. Data pertain to people aged 15 years and older. Cut-offs = below 411.1, 411.1 to below 1112.5, 1112.5 to below 7210.4, 7210.4 to below 41556.3, 41556.3 or above.

Map 14.4 Population employed in mining & quarrying of South Korea

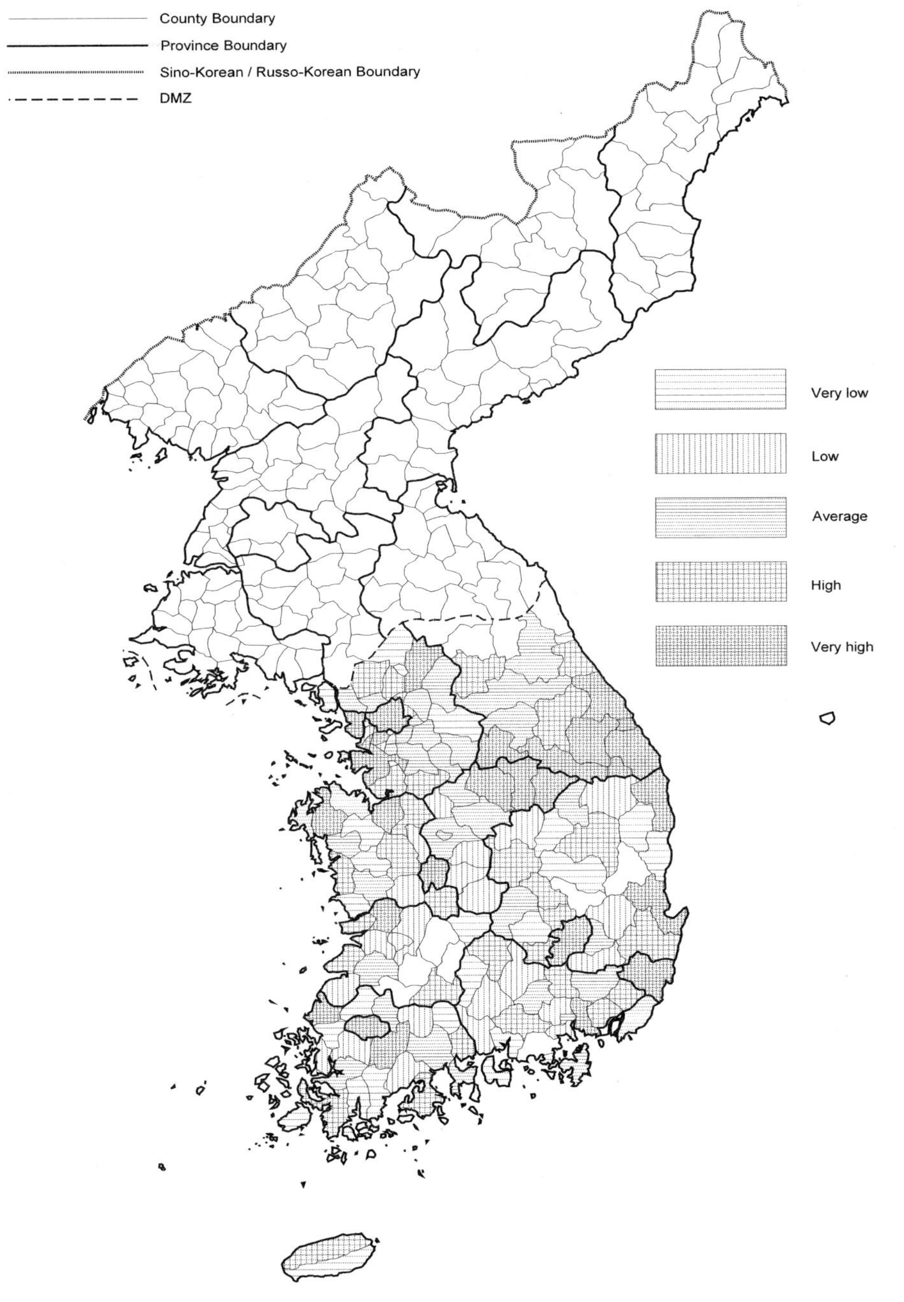

Notes: Unit = persons. Data pertain to people aged 15 years and older. Cut-offs = below 17.1, 17.1 to below 34.0, 34.0 to below 64.0, 64.0 to below 134.4, 134.4 or above.

Map 14.5 Population employed in manufacturing of the Korean peninsula

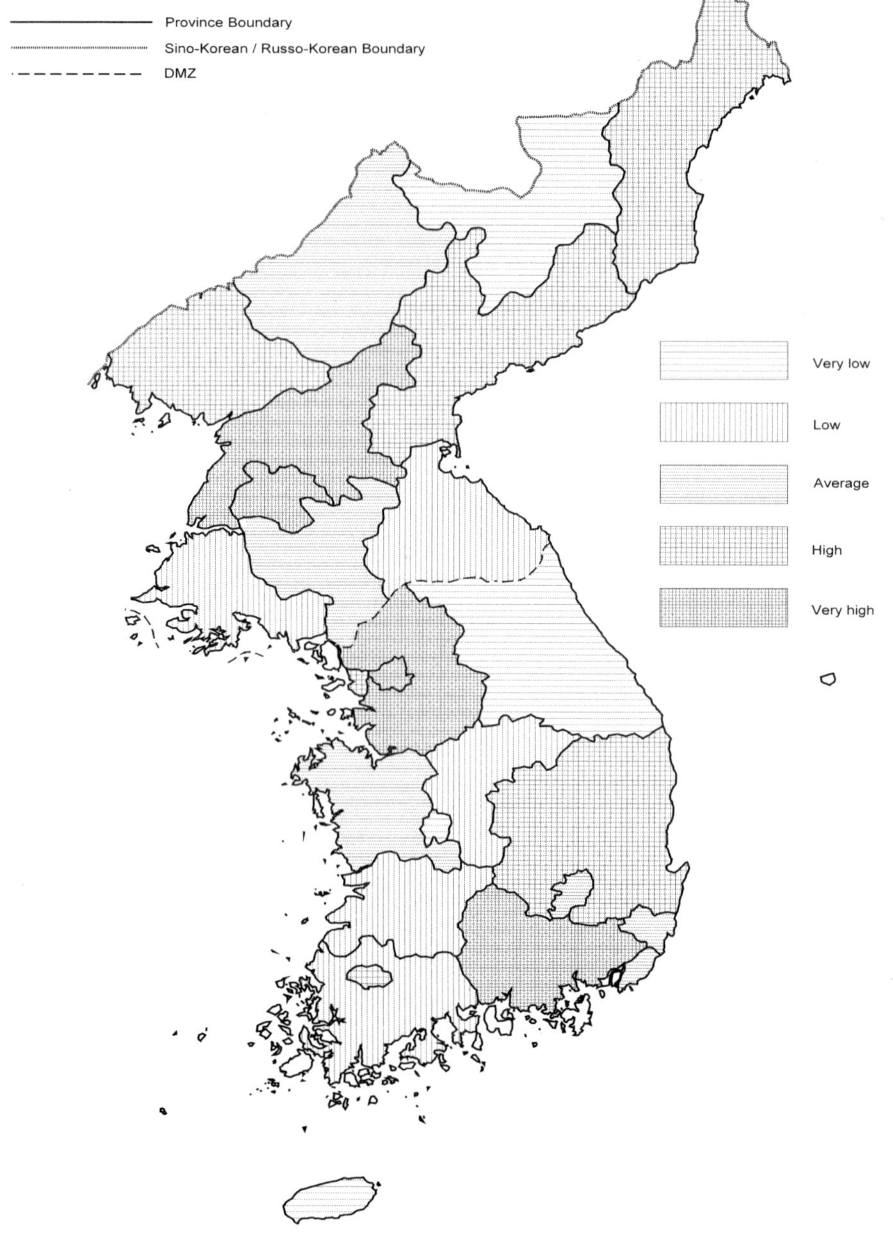

Notes: Unit = persons. Data pertain to people aged 15 years and older. Cut-offs = below 95172.9, 95172.9 to below 173942.9, 173942.9 to below 235073.5, 235073.5 to below 378200.1, 378200.1 or above.

Map 14.6 Population employed in manufacturing of South Korea

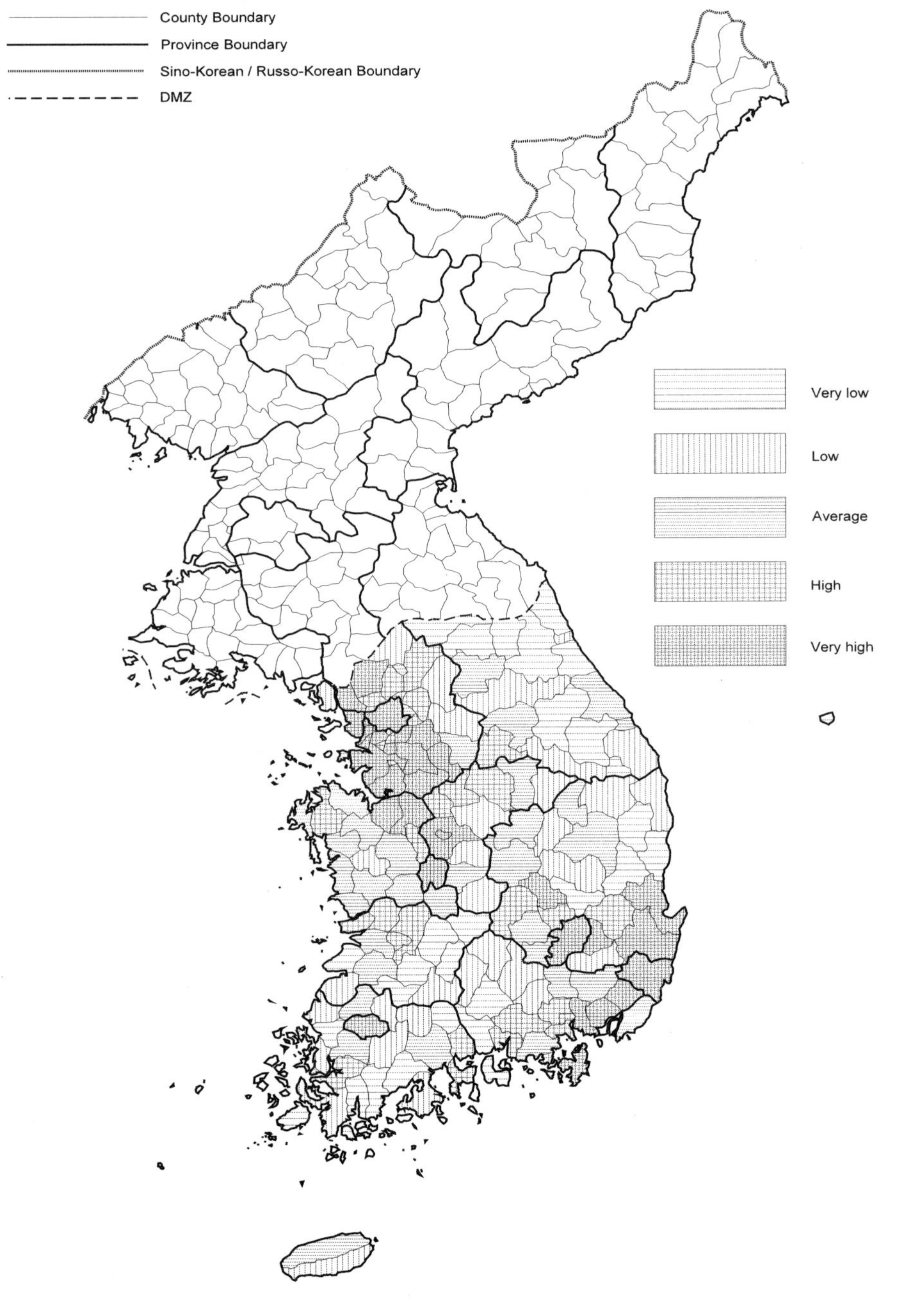

Notes: Unit = persons. Data pertain to people aged 15 years and older. Cut-offs = below 1182.5, 1182.5 to below 2786.5, 2786.5 to below 8182.0, 8182.0 to below 27587.5, 27587.5 or above.

Map 14.7 Population employed in electricity, gas & water supply of the Korean peninsula

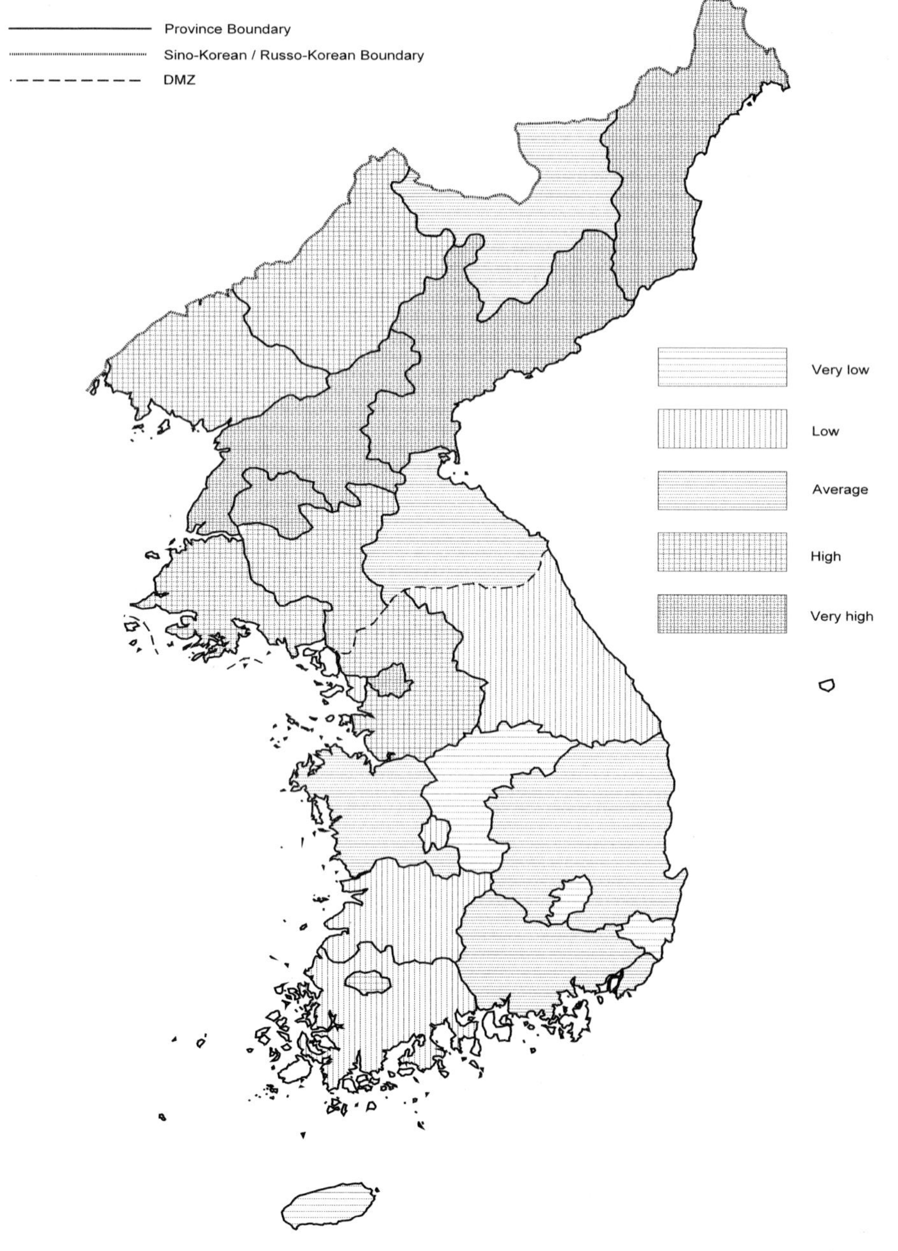

Notes: Unit = persons. Data pertain to people aged 15 years and older. Cut-offs = below 2925.9, 2925.9 to below 5679.9, 5679.9 to below 9641.5, 9641.5 to below 14141.3, 14141.3 or above.

Map 14.8 Population employed in electricity, gas & water utilities of South Korea

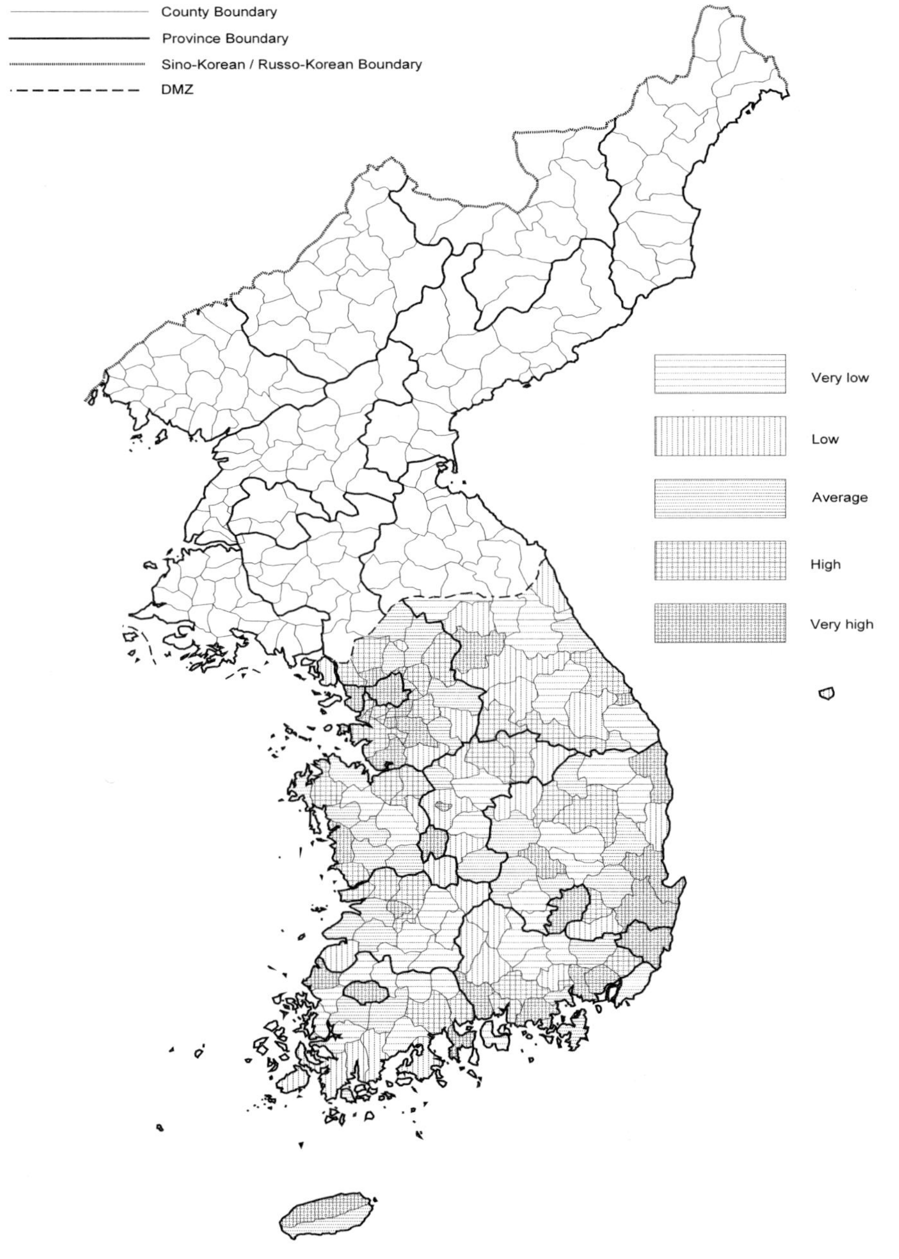

Notes: Unit = persons. Data pertain to people aged 15 years and older. Cut-offs = below 63.5, 63.5 to below 121.0, 121.0 to below 230.5, 230.5 to below 518.5, 518.5 or above.

Map 14.9 Population employed in sewerage, waste management materials, recovery & remediation activities of the Korean peninsula

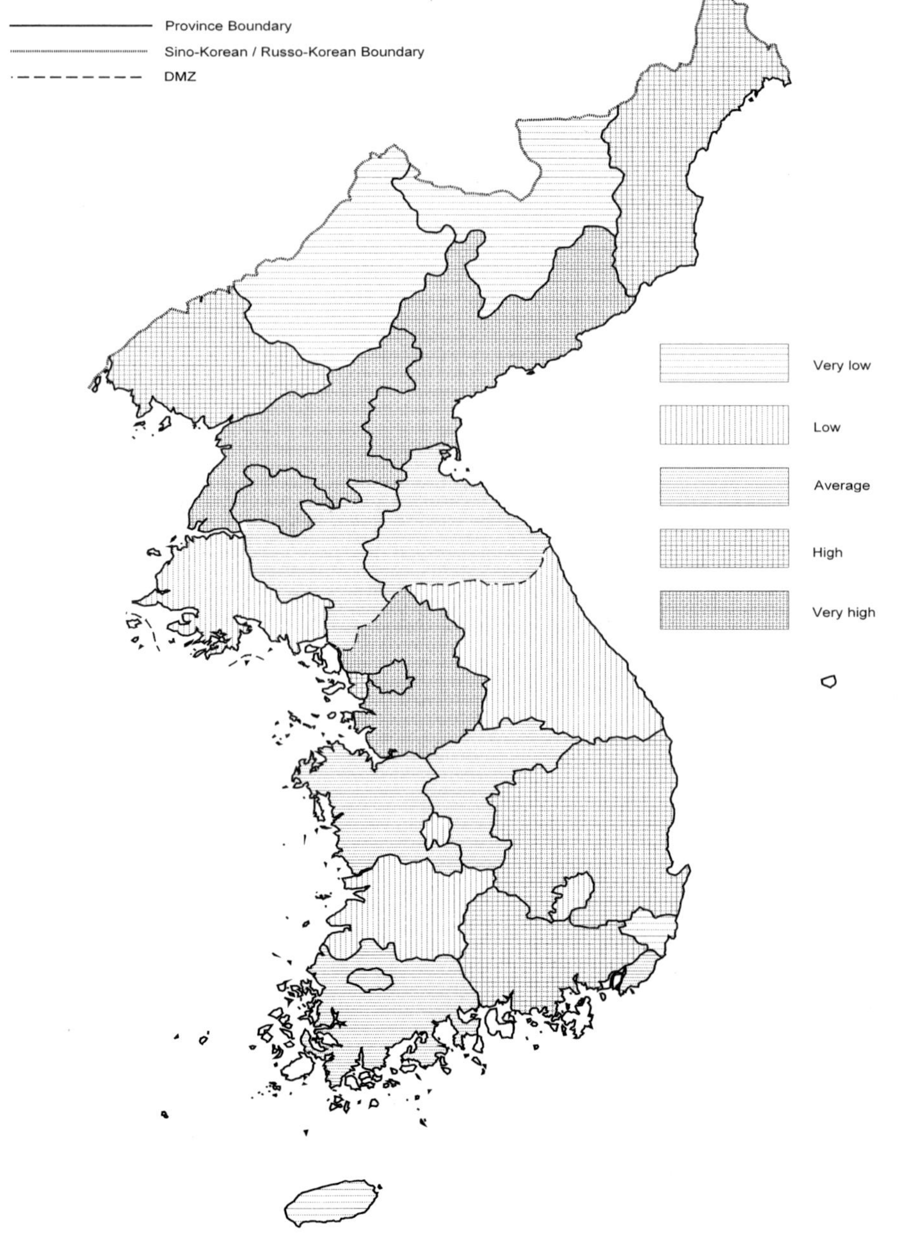

Notes: Unit = persons. Data pertain to people aged 15 years and older. Cut-offs = below 2016.6, 2016.6 to below 2648.4, 2648.4 to below 4488.3, 4488.3 to below 5754.2, 5754.2 or above.

Map 14.10 Population employed in sewerage, waste management materials, recovery & remediation activities of South Korea

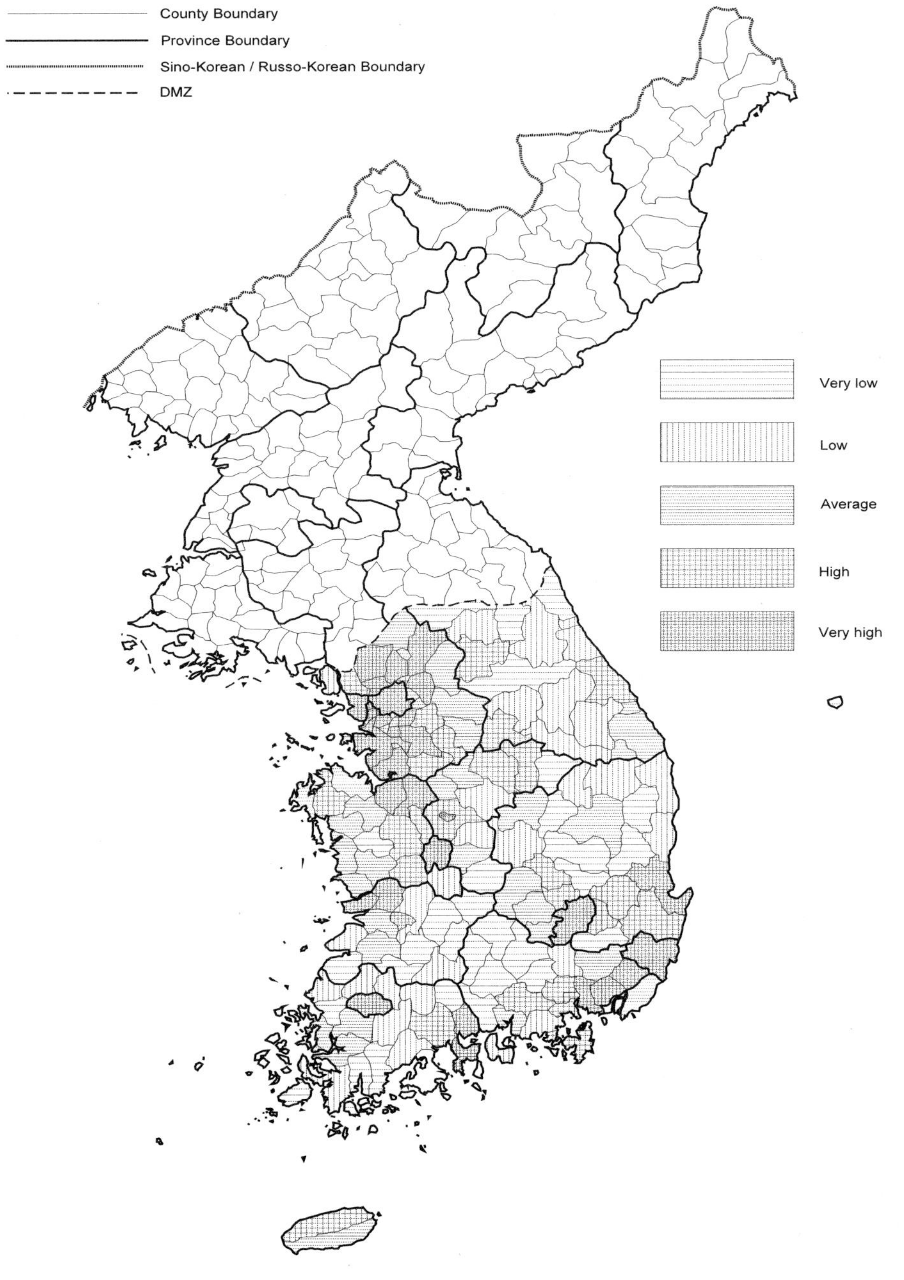

Notes: Unit = persons. Data pertain to people aged 15 years and older. Cut-offs = below 52.3, 52.3 to below 108.8,108.8 to below 230.1, 230.1 to below 555.3, 555.3 or above.

Map 14.11 Population employed in construction of the Korean peninsula

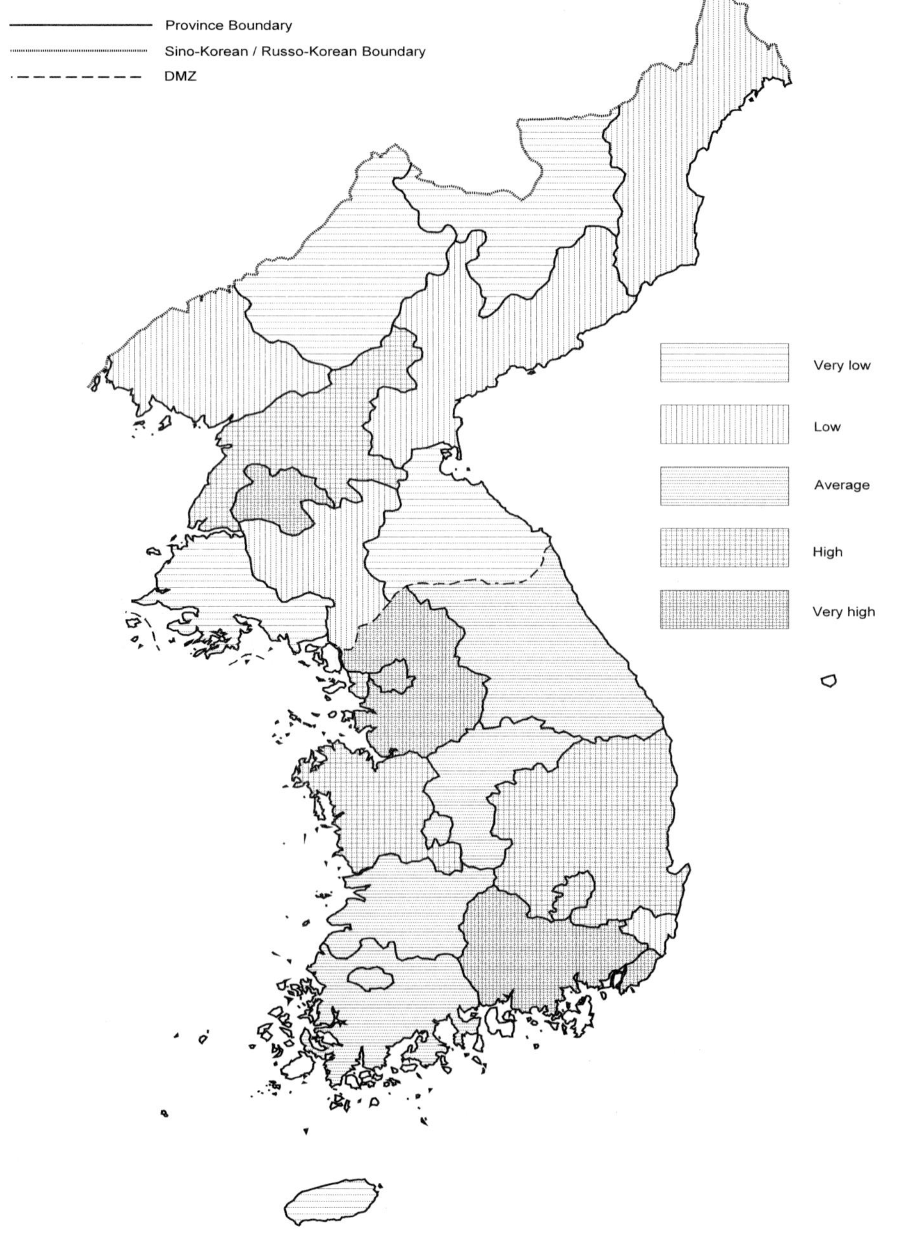

Notes: Unit = persons. Data pertain to people aged 15 years and older. Cut-offs = below 31234.1, 31234.1 to below 46430.6, 46430.6 to below 64864.0, 64864.0 to below 93412.5, 93412.5 or above.

Map 14.12 Population employed in construction of South Korea

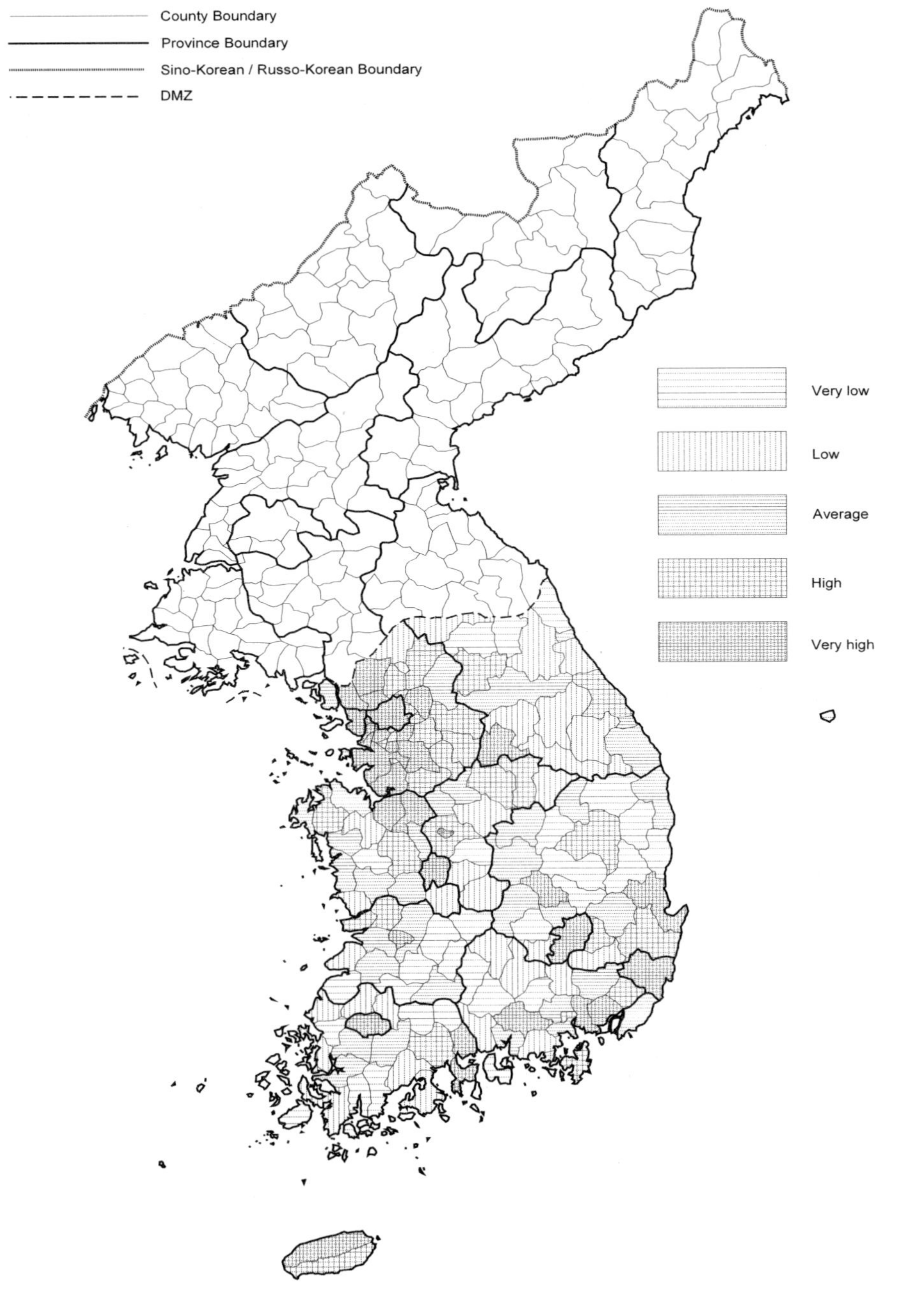

Notes: Unit = persons. Data pertain to people aged 15 years and older. Cut-offs = below 1134.5, 1134.5 to below 1960.5, 1960.5 to below 3720.0, 3720.0 to below 9754.5, 9754.5 or above.

Map 14.13 Population employed in wholesale & retail trades of the Korean peninsula

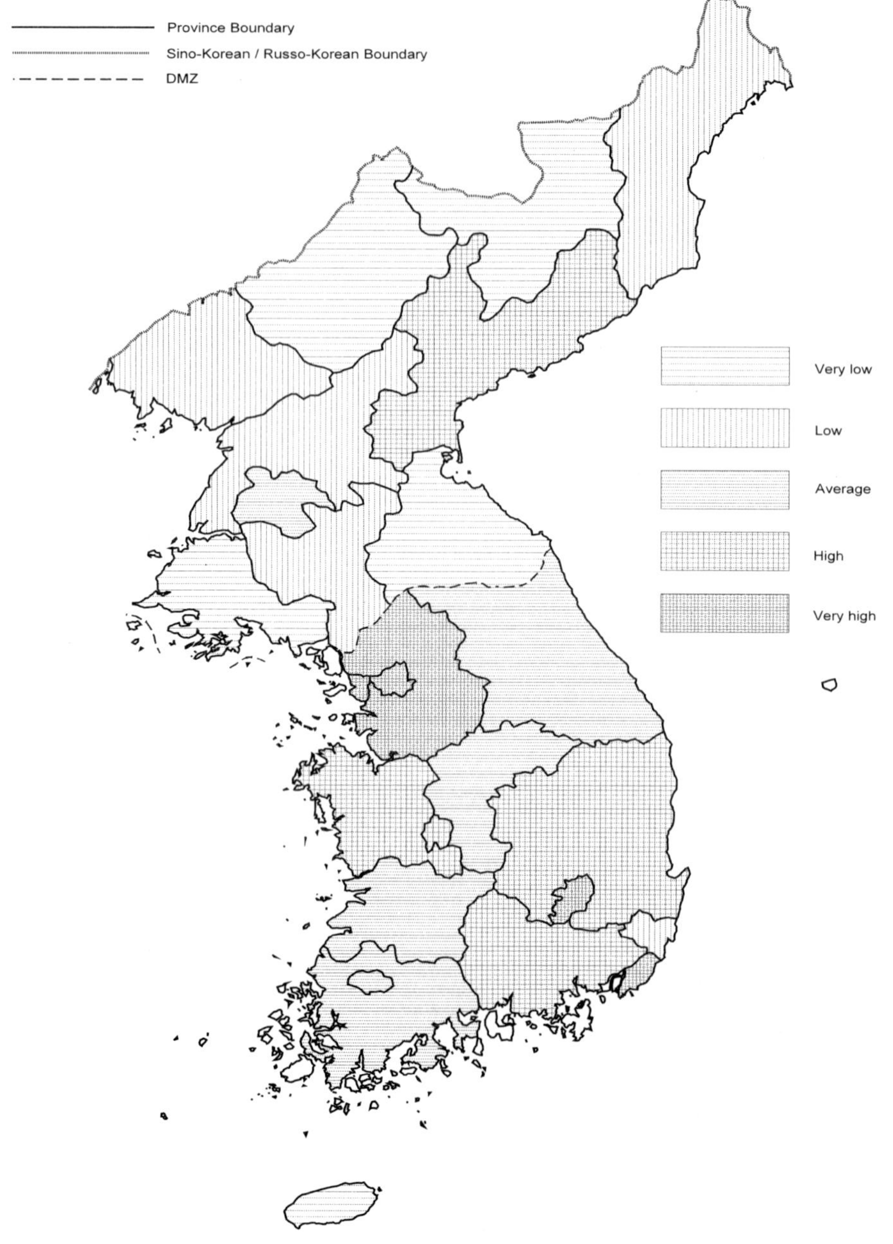

Notes: Unit = persons. Data pertain to people aged 15 years and older. Cut-offs = below 49813.3, 49813.3 to below 75337.6, 75337.6 to below 93955.8, 93955.8 to below 158988.0, 158988.0 or above.

Map 14.14 Population employed in wholesale & retail trades of South Korea

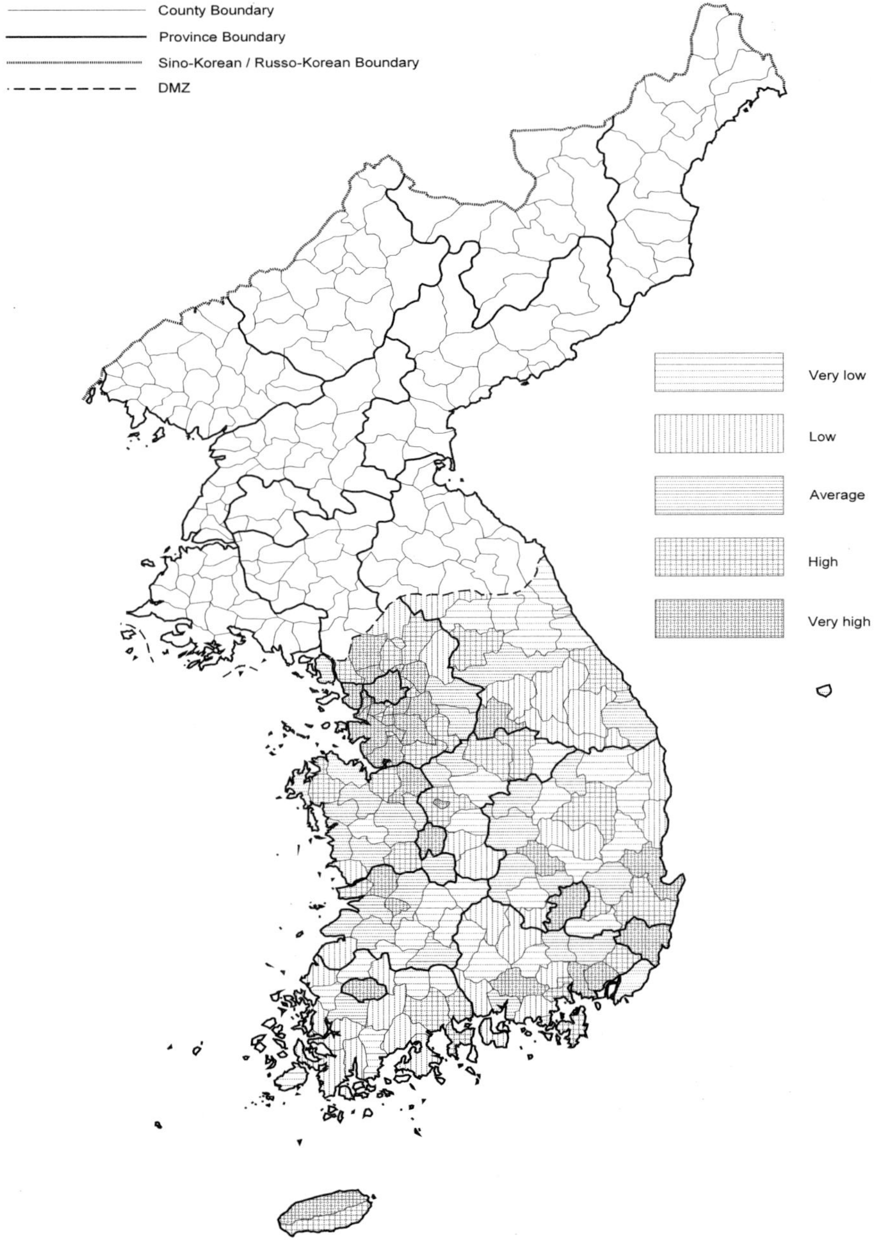

Notes: Unit = persons. Data pertain to people aged 15 years and older. Cut-offs = below 1502.0, 1502.0 to below 2598.5, 2598.5 to below 5701.0, 5701.0 to below 14796.5, 14796.5 or above.

Map 14.15 Population employed in transport of the Korean peninsula

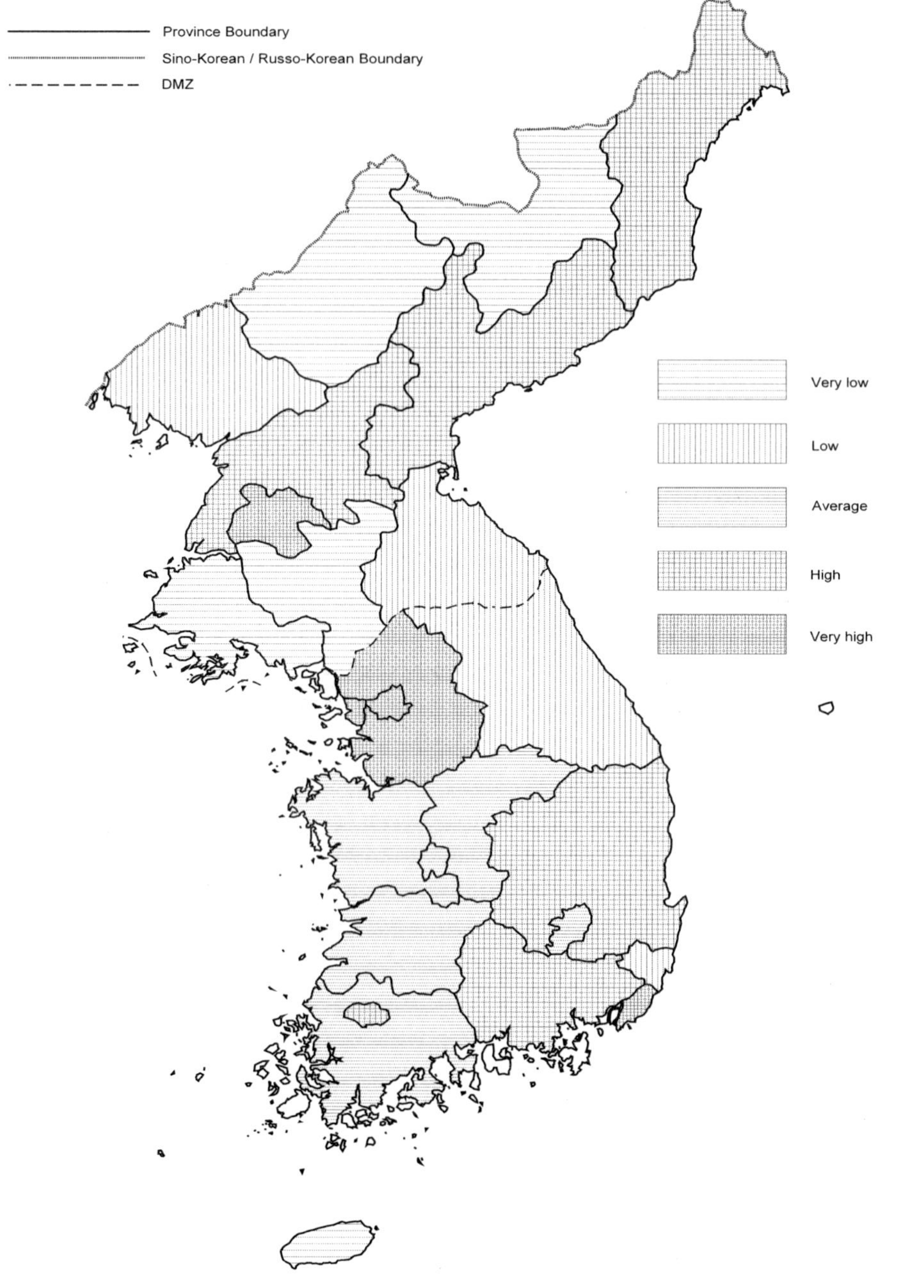

Notes: Unit = persons. Data pertain to people aged 15 years and older. Cut-offs = below 19601.9, 19601.9 to below 29183.4, 29183.4 to below, 44982.2, 44982.2 to below 64732.5, 64732.5 or above.

Map 14.16 Population employed in transport of South Korea

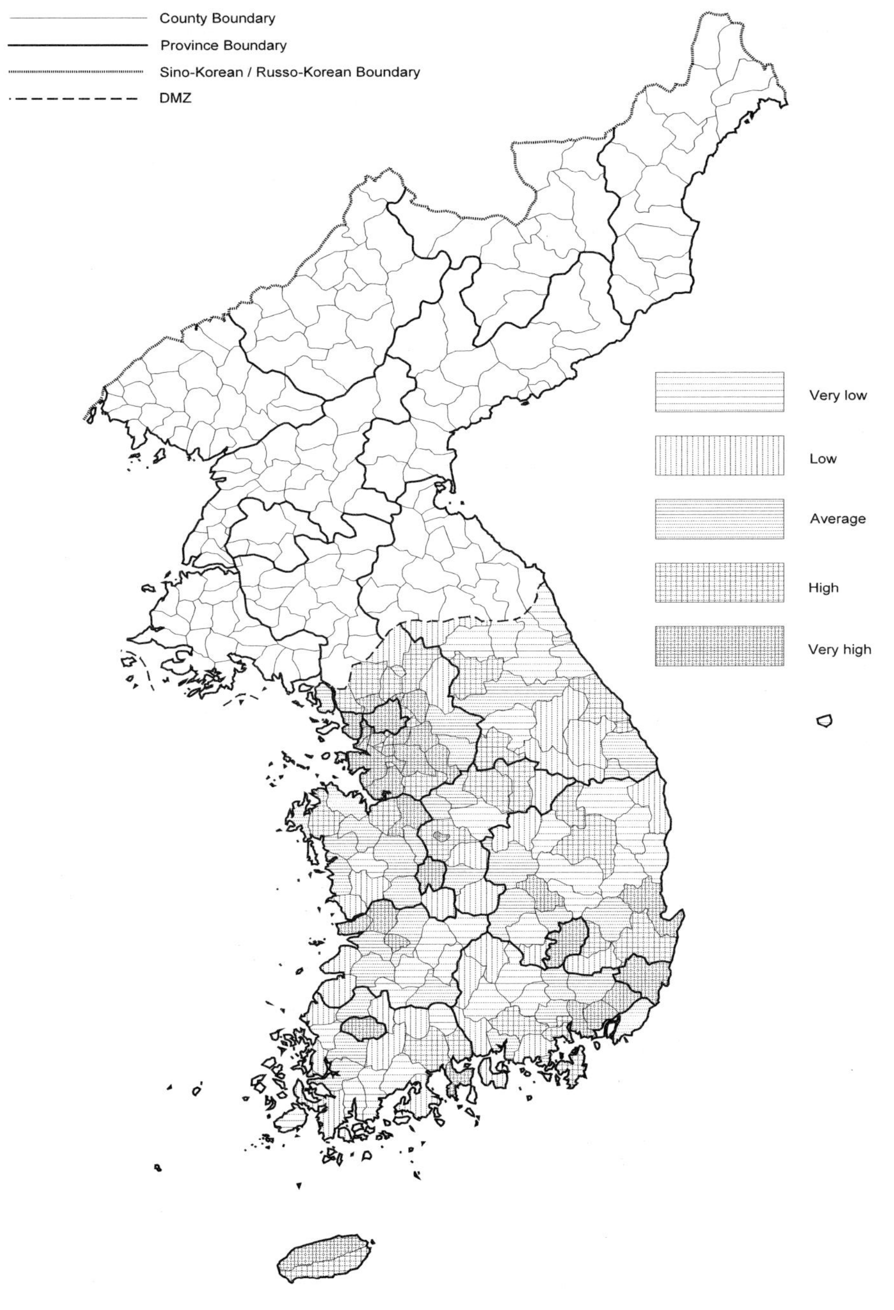

Notes: Unit = persons. Data pertain to people aged 15 years and older. Cut-offs = below 395.5, 395.5 to below 864.0, 864.0 to below 2151.5, 2151.5 to below 6412.0, 6412.0 or above.

Map 14.17 Population employed in hotels & restaurants of the Korean peninsula

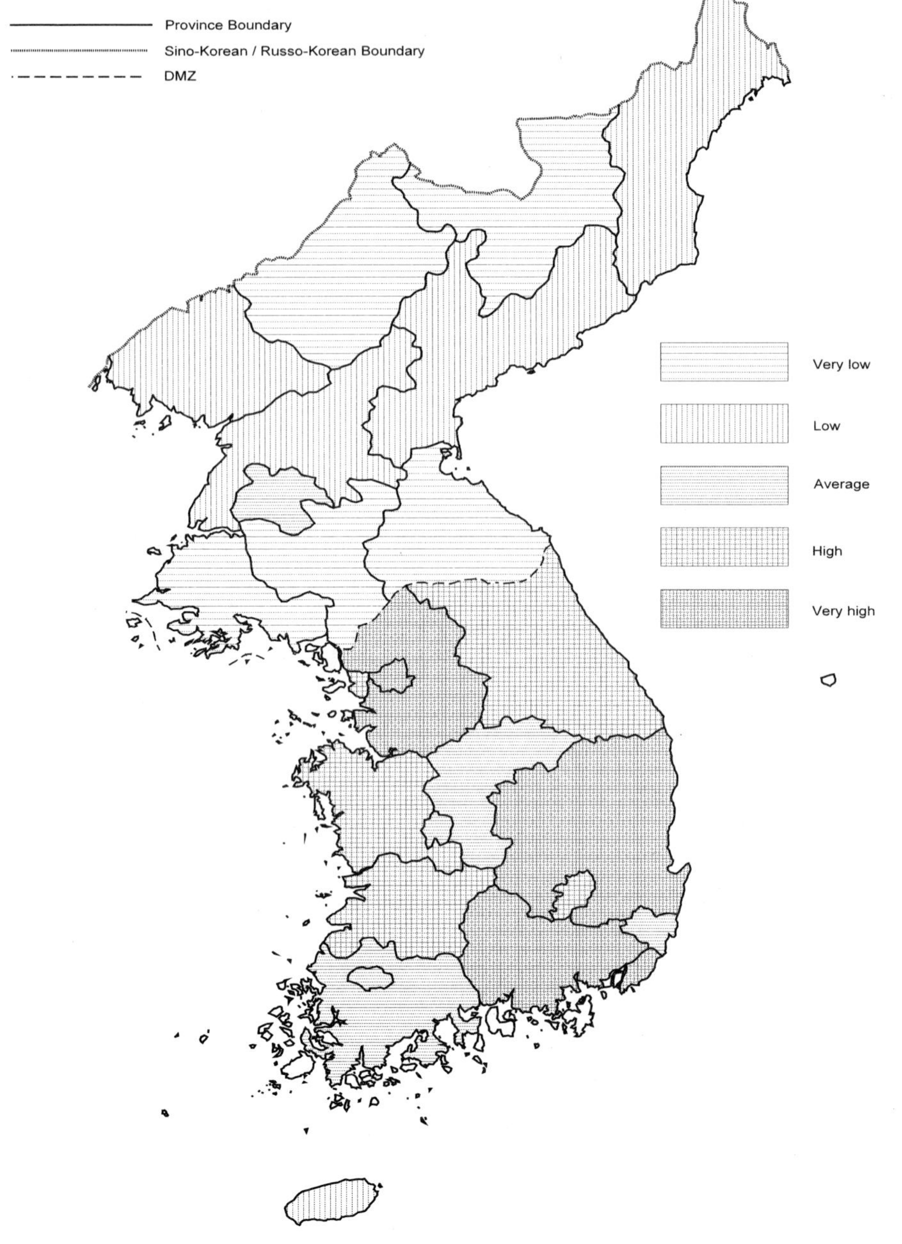

Notes: Unit = persons. Data pertain to people aged 15 years and older. Cut-offs = below 10828.2, 10828.2 to below 35222.3, 35222.3 to below 52218.7, 52218.7 to below 84800.2, 84800.2 or above.

Map 14.18 Population employed in hotels & restaurants of South Korea

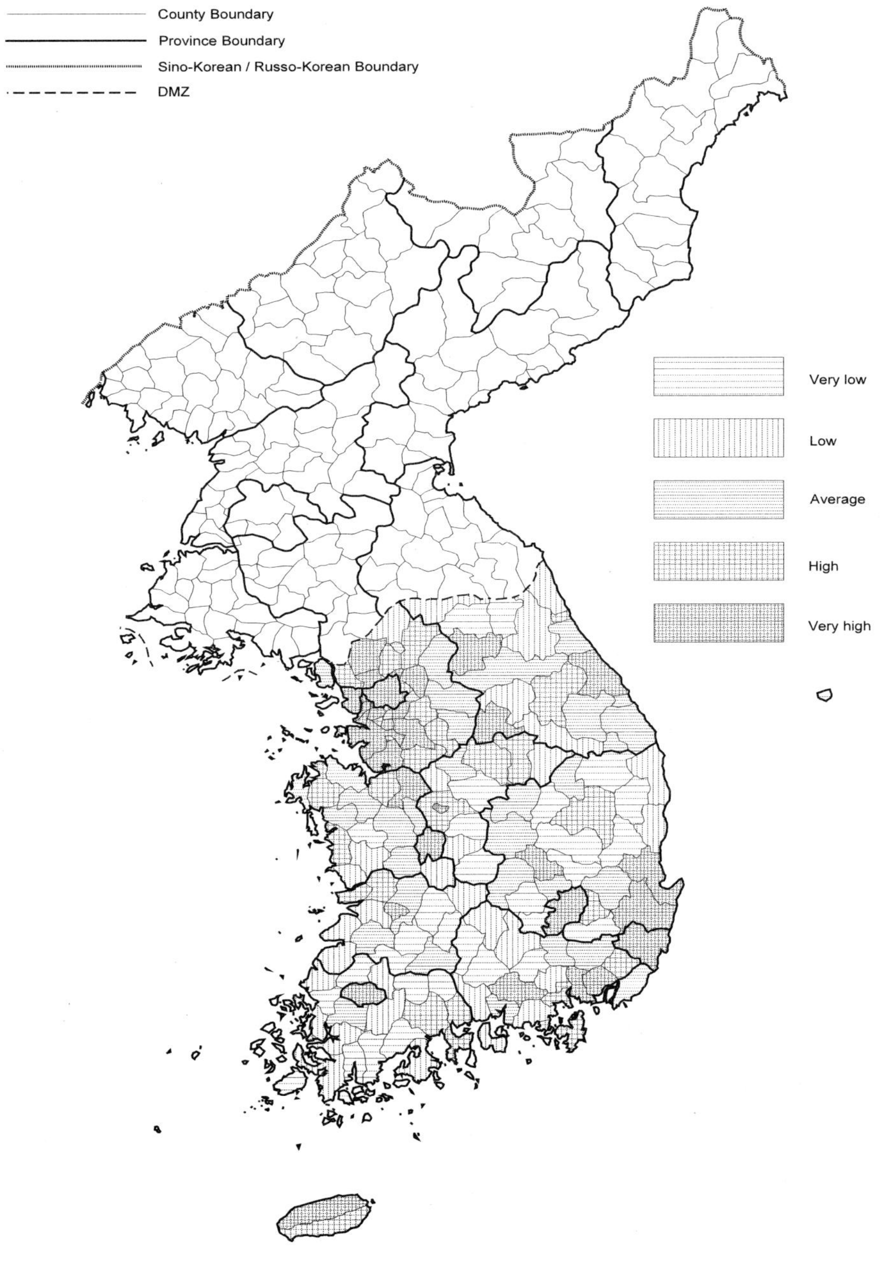

Notes: Unit = persons. Data pertain to people aged 15 years and older. Cut-offs = below 1114.5, 1114.5 to below 2105.0, 2105.0 to below 3992.5, 3992.5 to below 9104.0, 9104.0 or above.

Map 14.19 Population employed in information & communications of the Korean peninsula

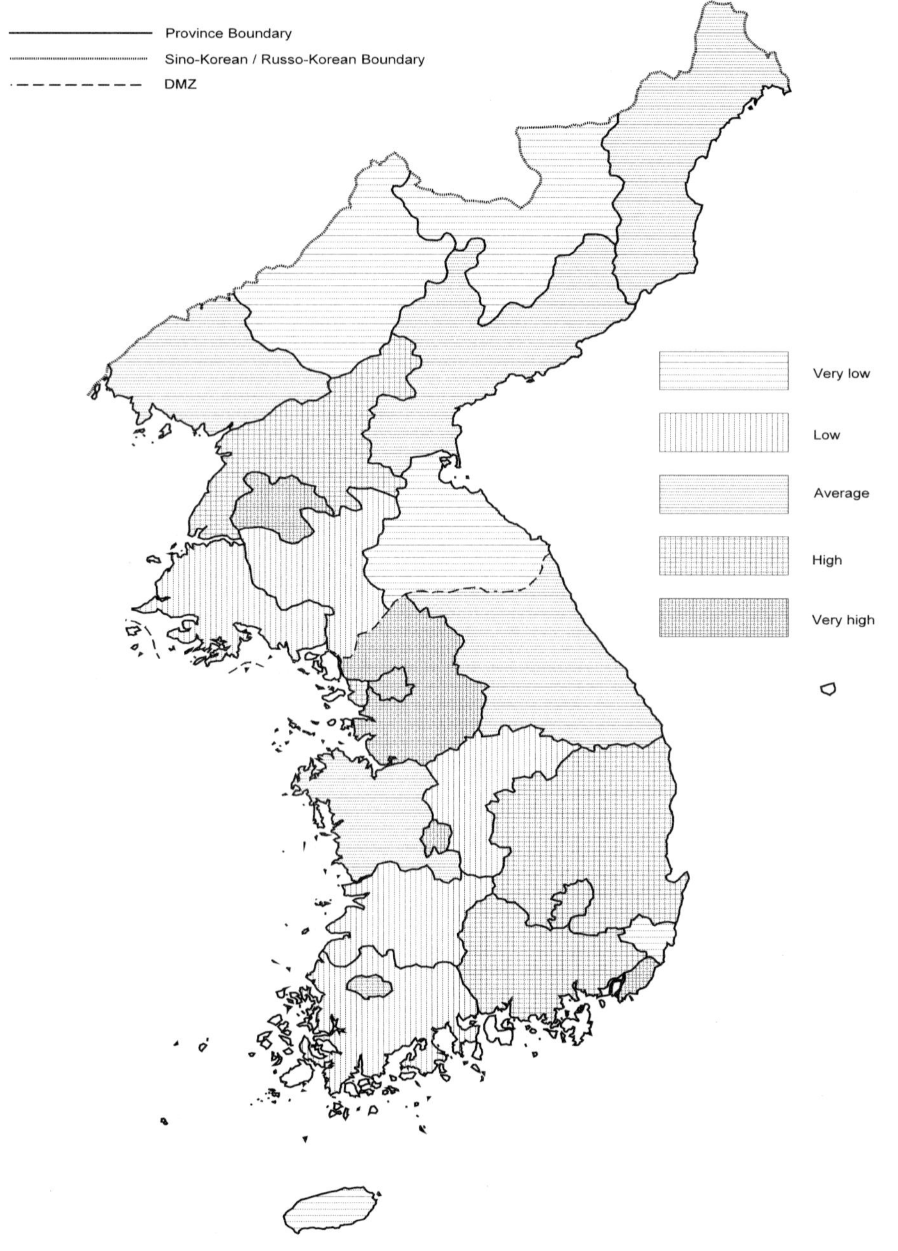

Notes: Unit = persons. Data pertain to people aged 15 years and older. Cut-offs = below 7853.9, 7853.9 to below 9569.5, 9569.5 to below 12637.5, 12637.5 to below 16758.8, 16758.8 or above.

Map 14.20 Population employed in information & communications of South Korea

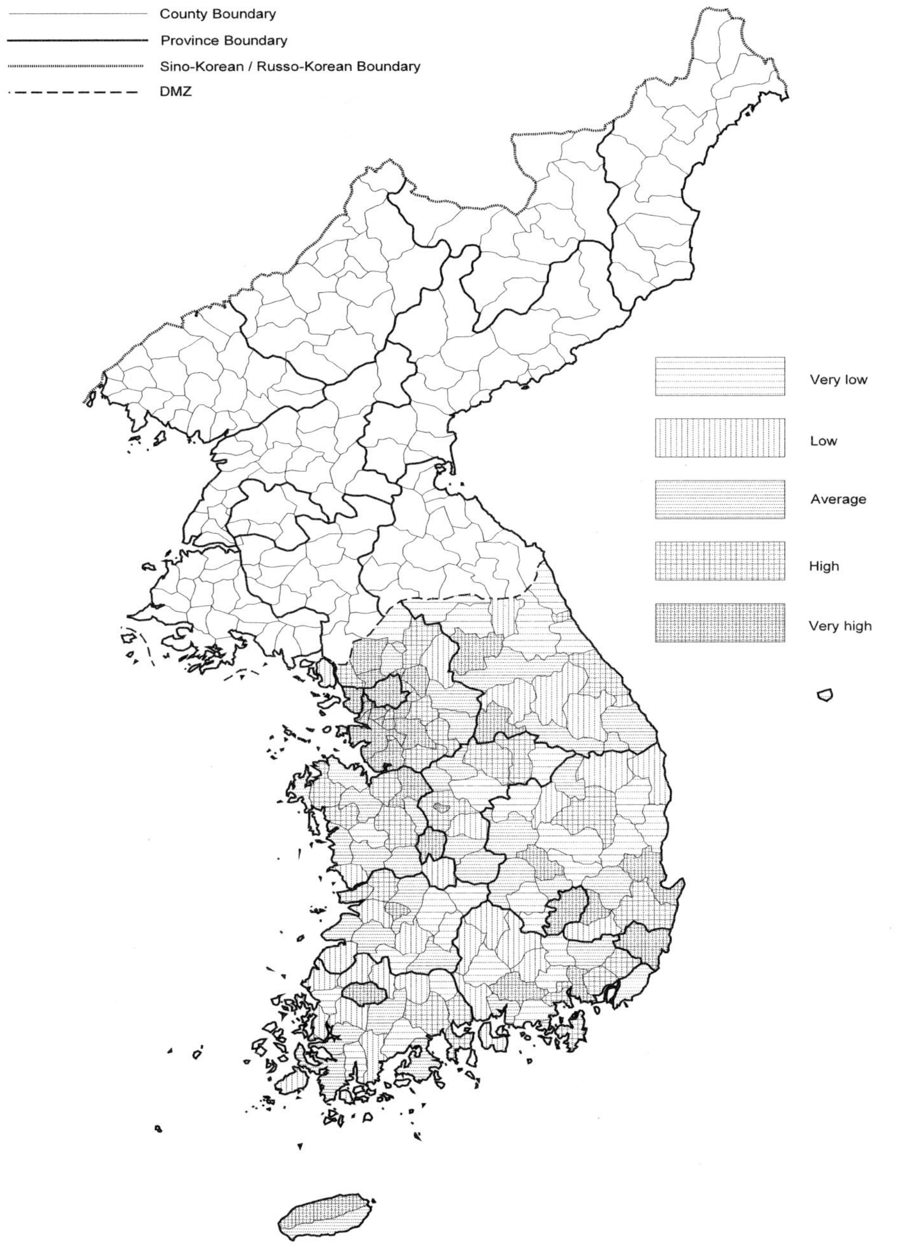

Notes: Unit = persons. Data pertain to people aged 15 years and older. Cut-offs = below 149.0, 149.0 to below 260.0, 260.0 to below 450.0, 450.0 to below 1623.5, 1623.5 or above.

Map 14.21 Population employed in financial institutions & insurance of the Korean peninsula

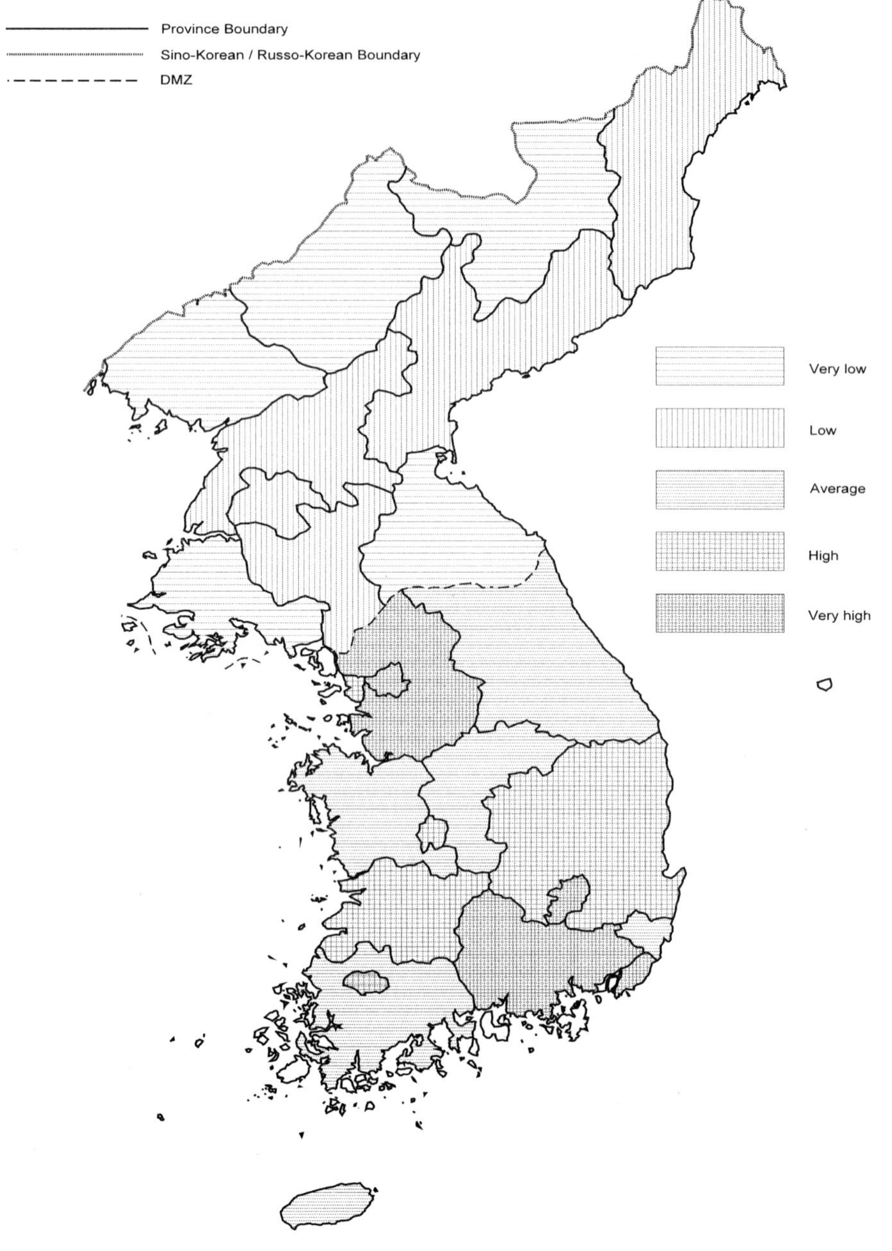

Notes: Unit = persons. Data pertain to people aged 15 years and older. Cut-offs = below 2556.4, 2556.4 to below 8363.5, 8363.5 to below 20893.4, 20893.4 to below 31951.2, 31951.2 or above.

Map 14.22 Population employed in financial institutions & insurance of South Korea

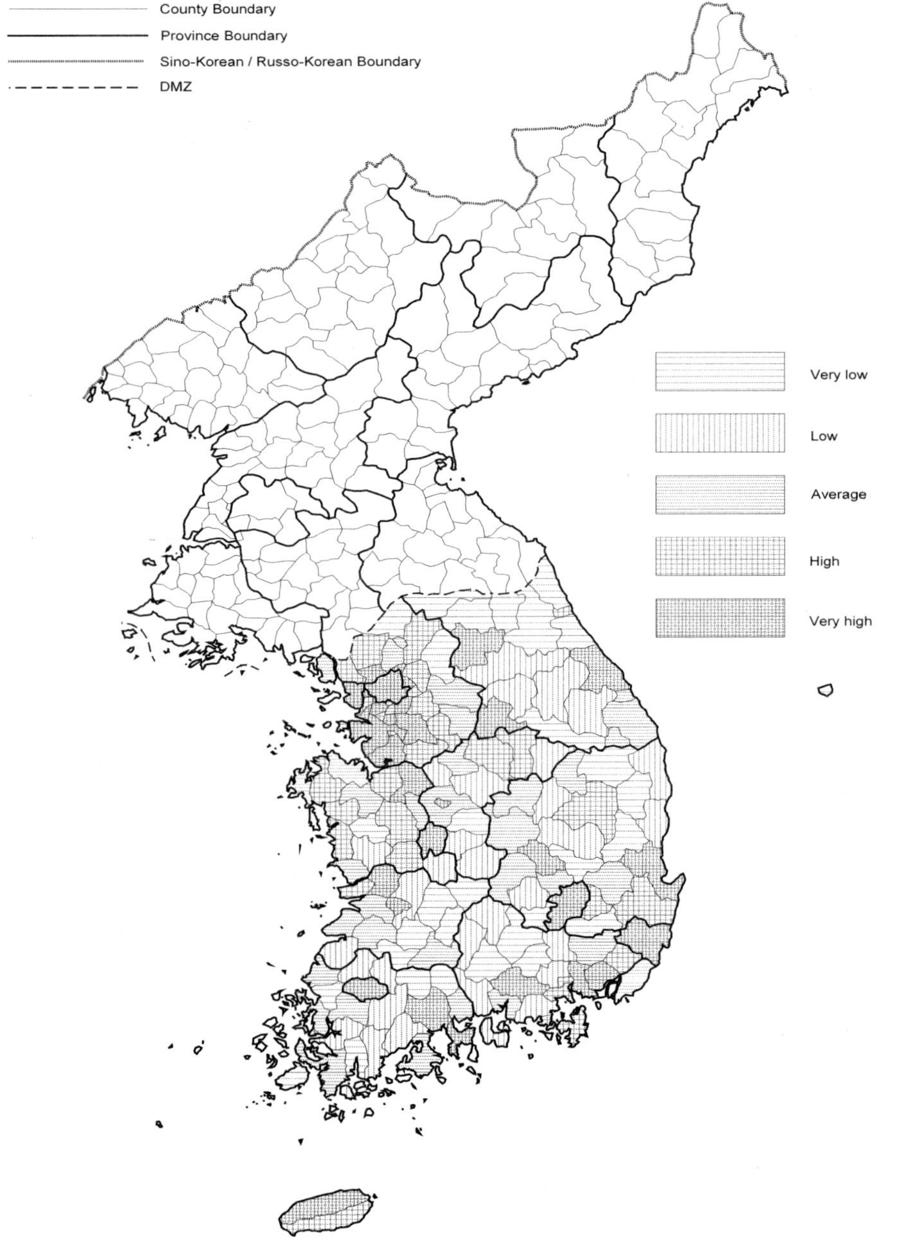

Notes: Unit = persons. Data pertain to people aged 15 years and older. Cut-offs = below 354.0, 354.0 to below 587.0, 587.0 to below 1150.5, 1150.5 to below 3097.5, 3097.5 or above.

Map 14.23 Population employed in real estate, renting & leasing of South Korea

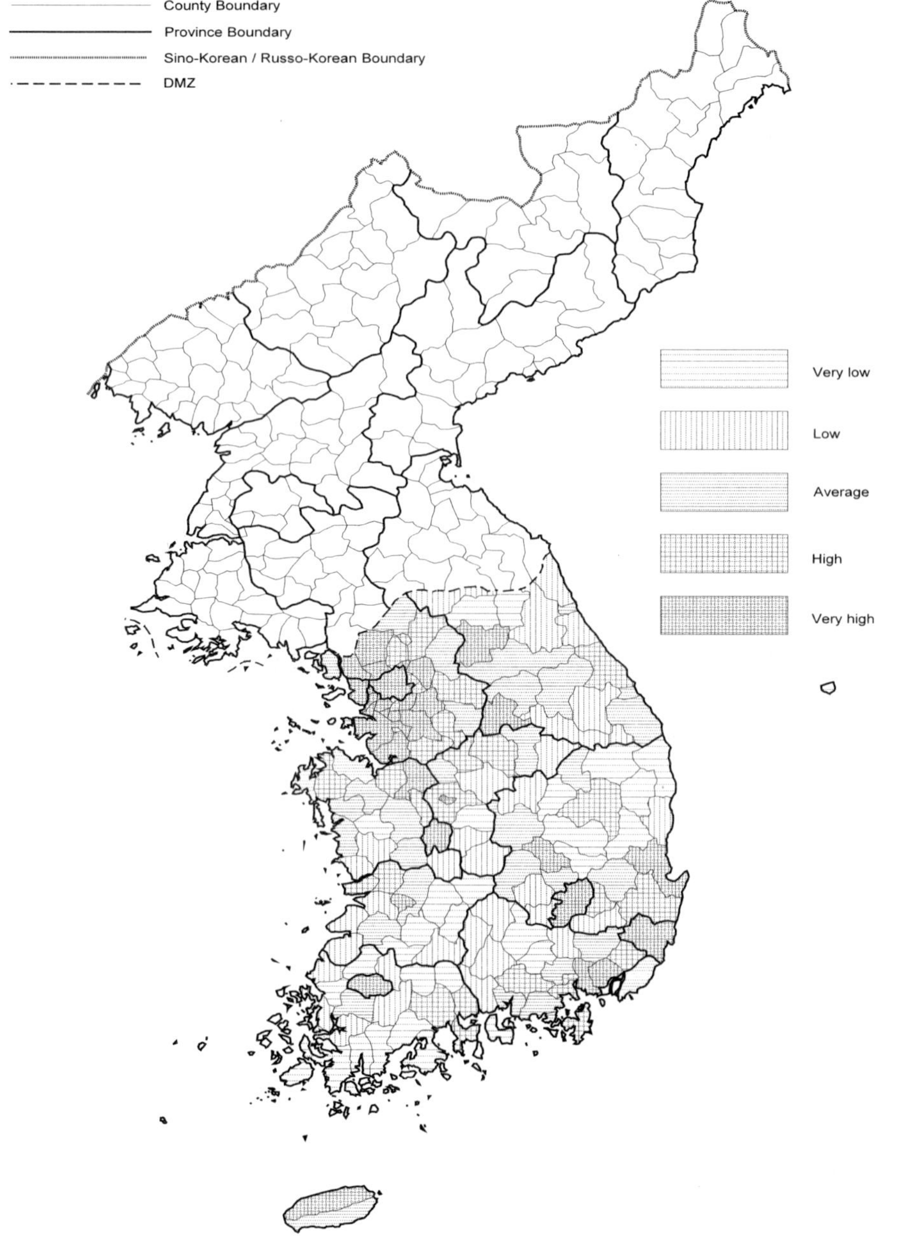

Notes: Unit = persons. Data pertain to people aged 15 years and older. Cut-offs = below 90.6, 90.6 to below 284.2, 284.2 to below 750.3, 750.3 to below 2376.1, 2376.1 or above.

Map 14.24 Population employed in professional scientific & technical activities of South Korea

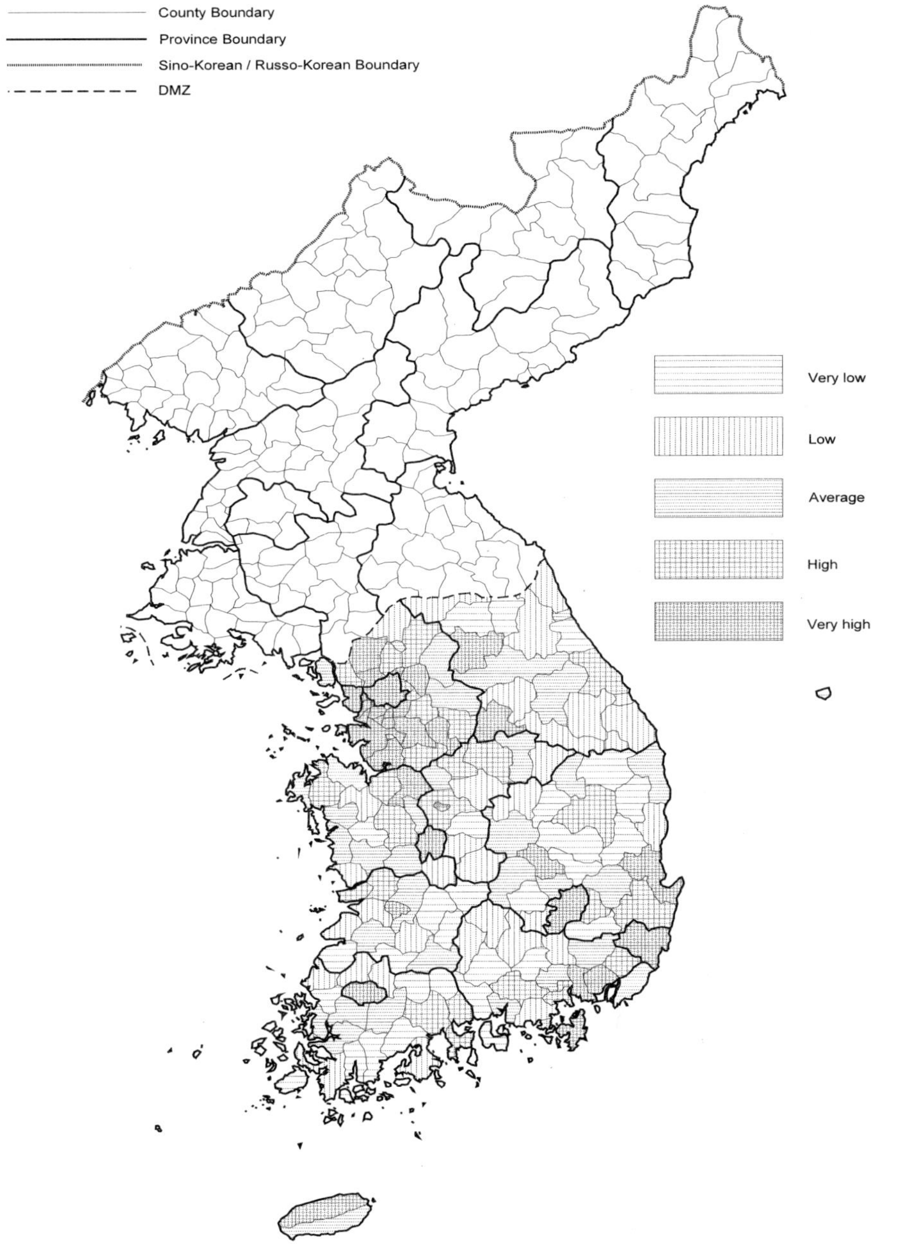

Notes: Unit = persons. Data pertain to people aged 15 years and older. Cut-offs = below 164.8, 164.8 to below 360.2, 360.2 to below 932.6, 932.6 to below 2827.1, 2827.1 or above.

Map 14.25 Population employed in business facilities, management & business support service of South Korea

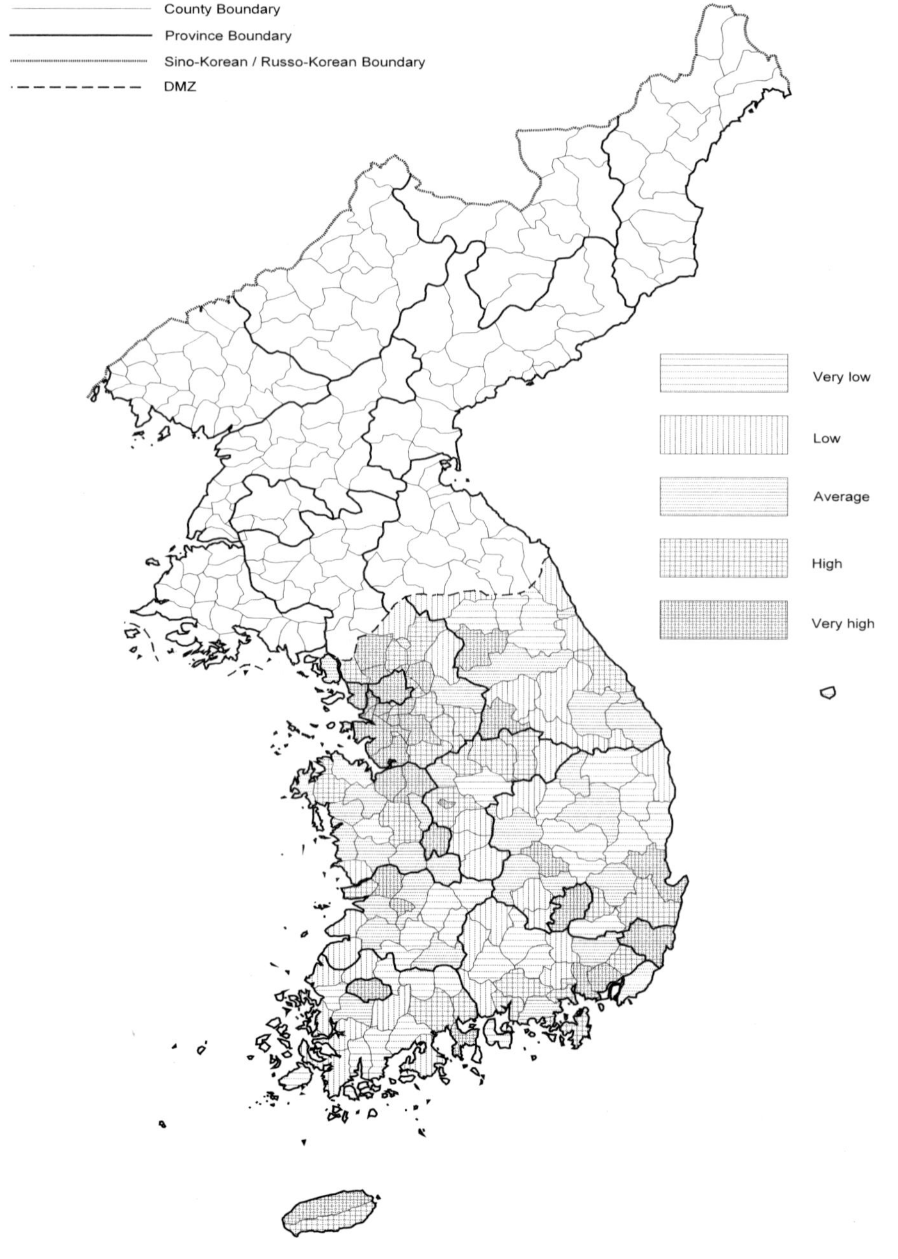

Notes: Unit = persons. Data pertain to people aged 15 years and older. Cut-offs = below 340.0, 340.0 to below 687.6, 687.6 to below 1531.9, 1531.9 to below 4024.0, 4024.0 or above.

Map 14.26 Population employed in public administration, defense & compulsory social security of South Korea

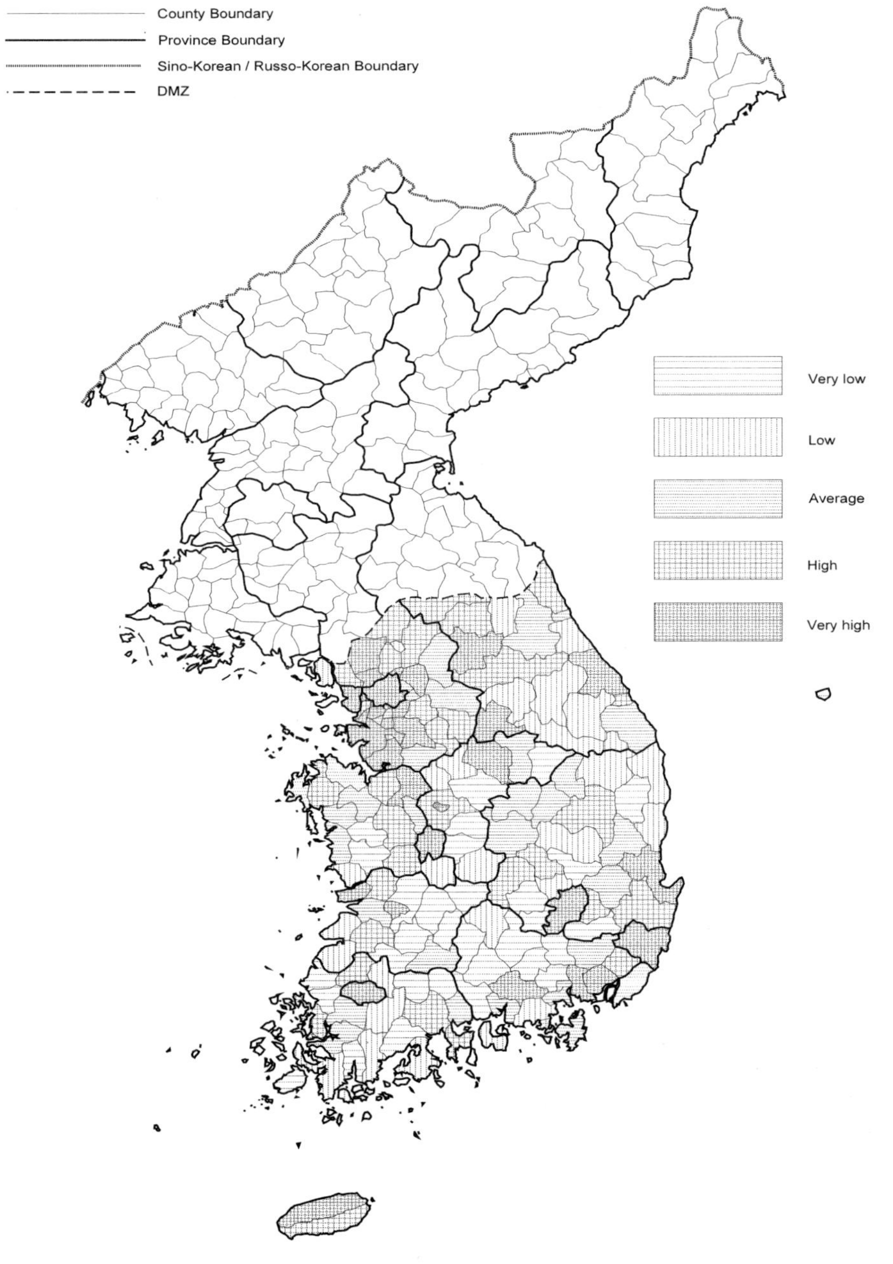

Notes: Unit = persons. Data pertain to people aged 15 years and older. Cut-offs = below 1432.2, 1432.2 to below 2044.1, 2044.1 to below 2813.5, 2813.5 to below 5212.3, 5212.3 or above.

Map 14.27 Population employed in education of the Korean peninsula

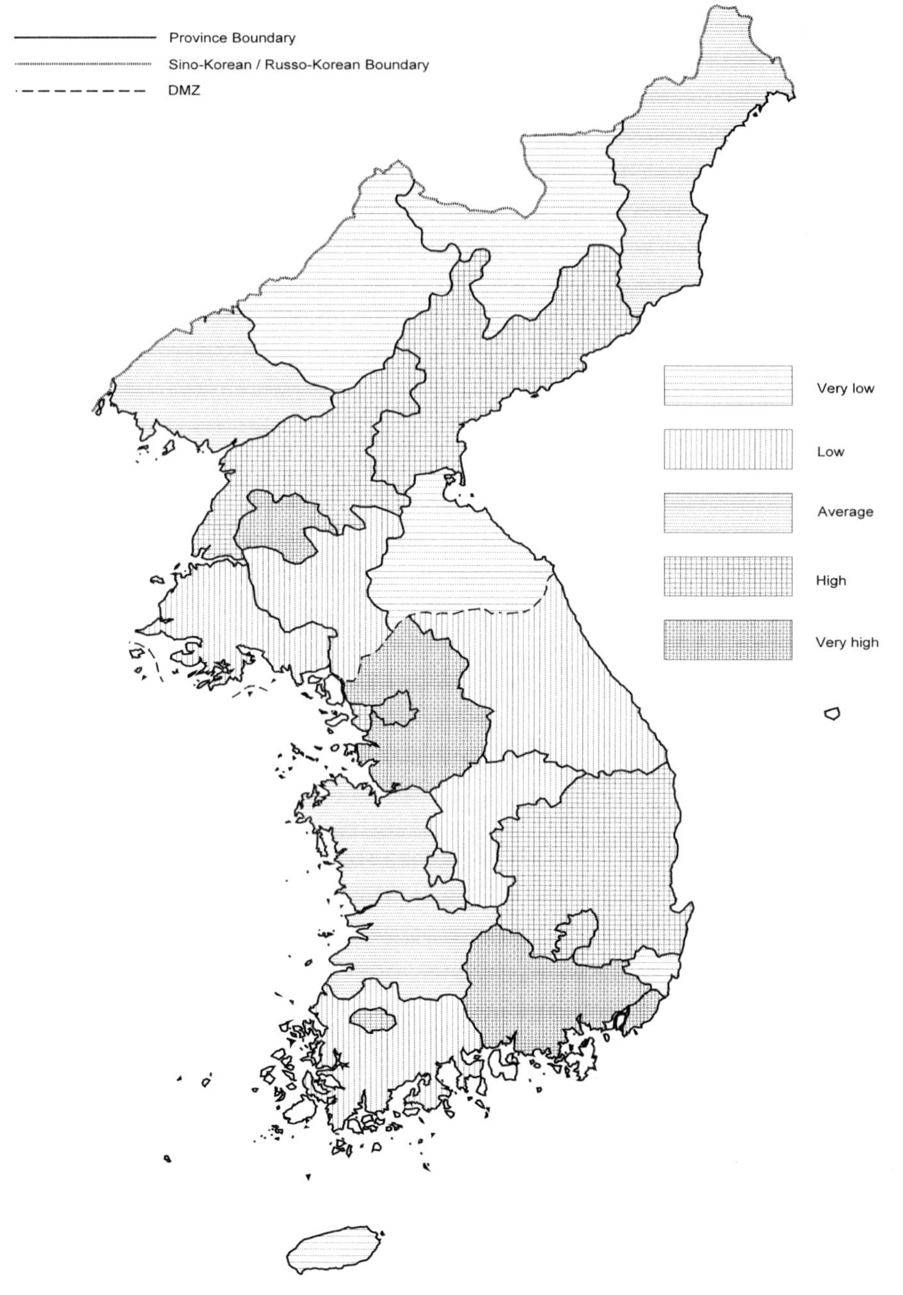

Notes: Unit = persons. Data pertain to people aged 15 years and older. Cut-offs = below 44469.4, 44469.4 to below 54429.6, 54429.6 to below 64837.1, 64837.1 to below 84661.4, 84661.4 or above.

Map 14.28 Population employed in education of South Korea

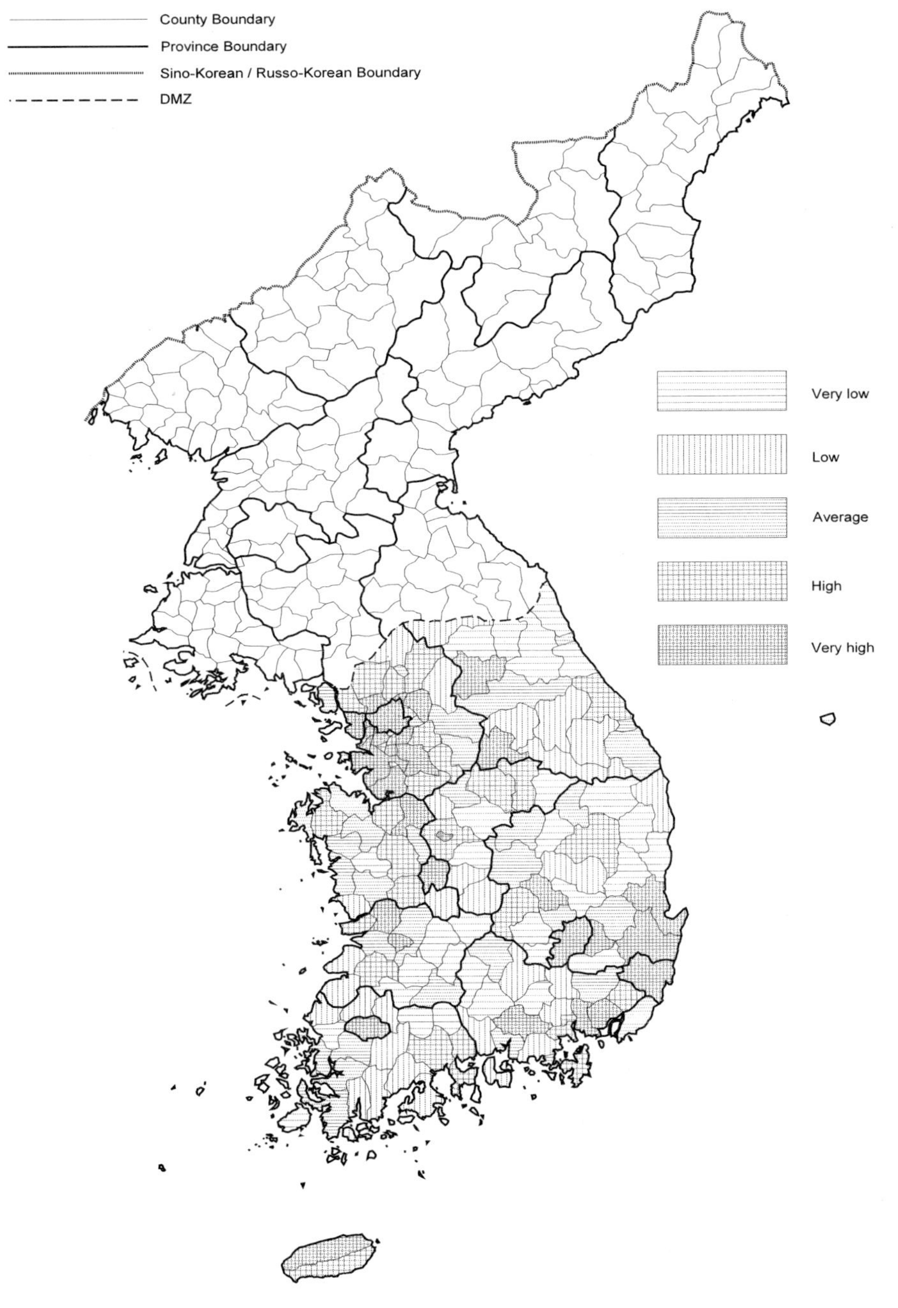

Notes: Unit = persons. Data pertain to people aged 15 years and older. Cut-offs = below 982.0, 982.0 to below 1592.5, 1592.5 to below 3340.0, 3340.0 to below 8864.0, 8864.0 or above.

Map 14.29 Population employed in health & social work of South Korea

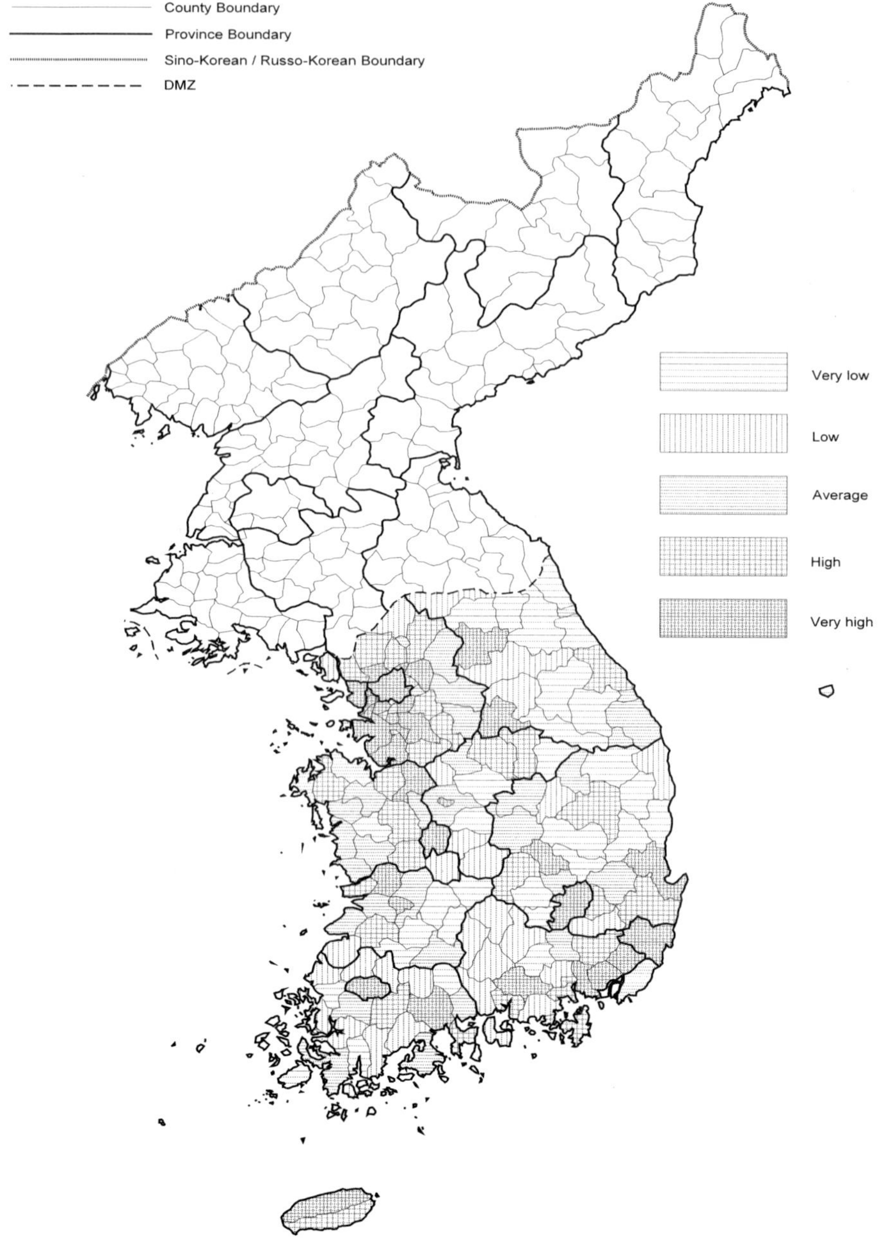

Notes: Unit = persons. Data pertain to people aged 15 years and older. Cut-offs = below 777.6, 777.6 to below 1313.0, 1313.0 to below 2646.6, 2646.6 to below 6594.3, 6594.3 or above.

Map 14.30 Population employed in arts, sports & recreation services of South Korea

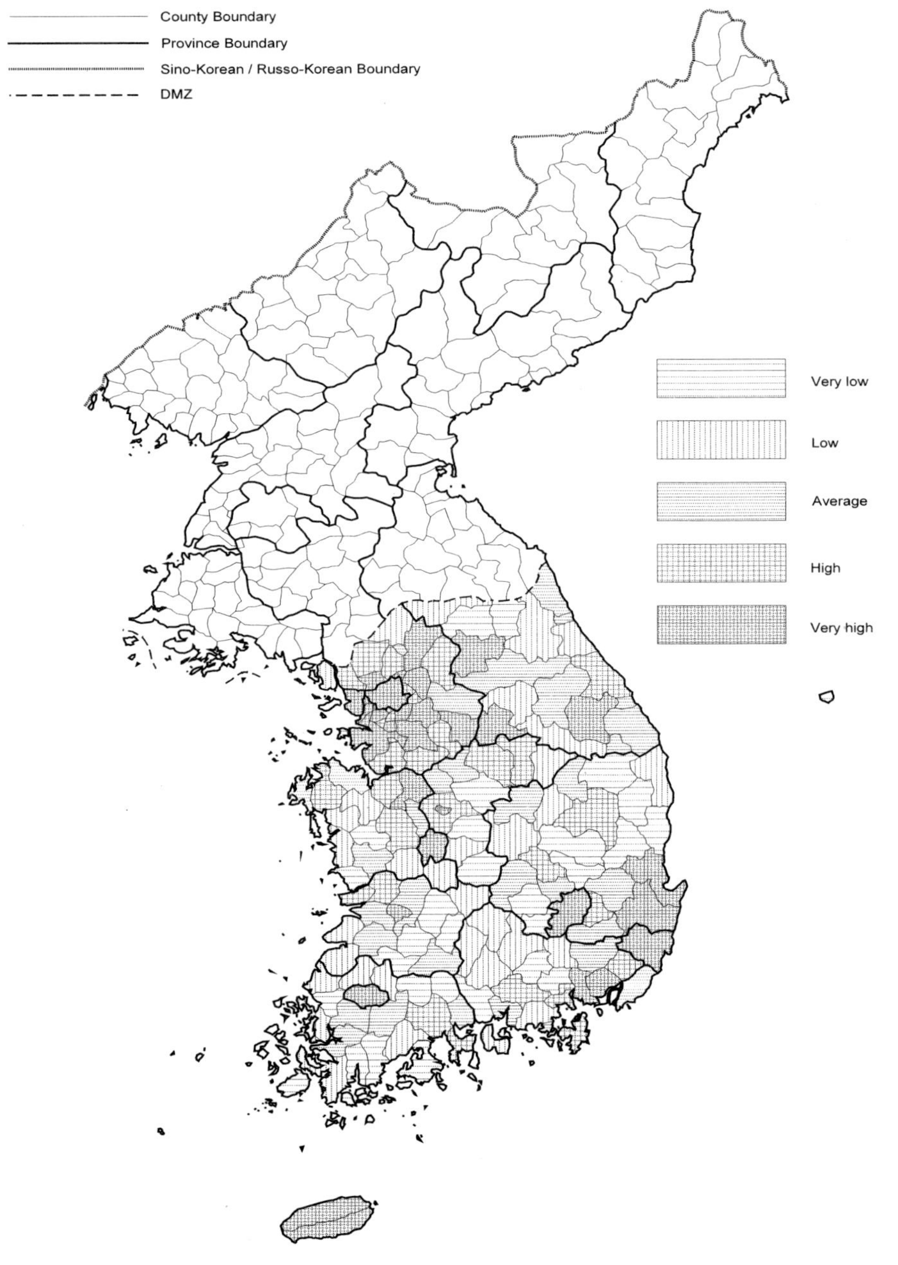

Notes: Unit = persons. Data pertain to people aged 15 years and older. Cut-offs = below 177.6, 177.6 to below 366.6, 366.6 to below 783.4, 783.4 to below 2015.3, 2015.3 or above.

Map 14.31 Population employed in membership organizations, repair & other personal services of South Korea

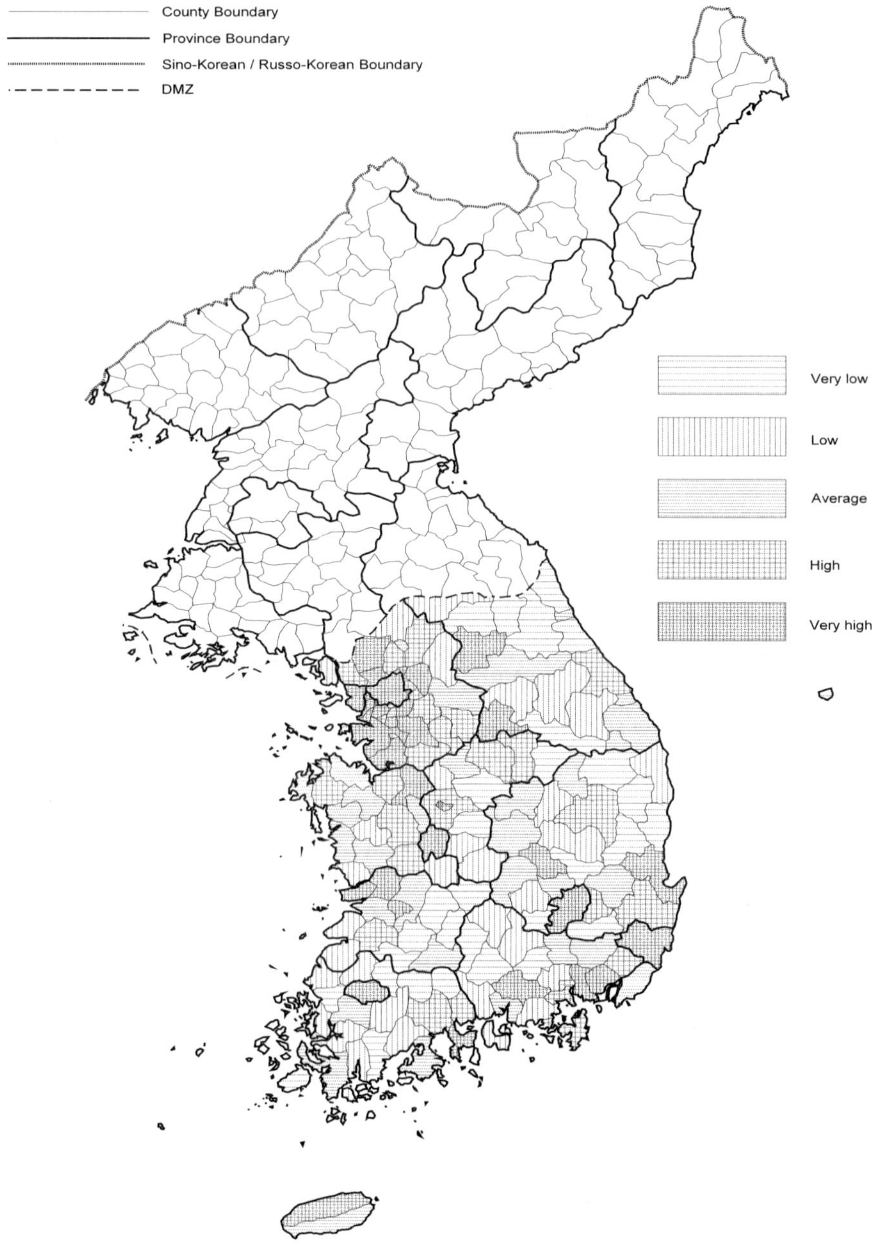

Notes: Unit = persons. Data pertain to people aged 15 years and older. Cut-offs = below 644.4, 644.4 to below 1147.6, 1147.6 to below 2304.5, 2304.5 to below 5662.1, 5662.1 or above.

Map 14.32 Population employed in household activities of South Korea

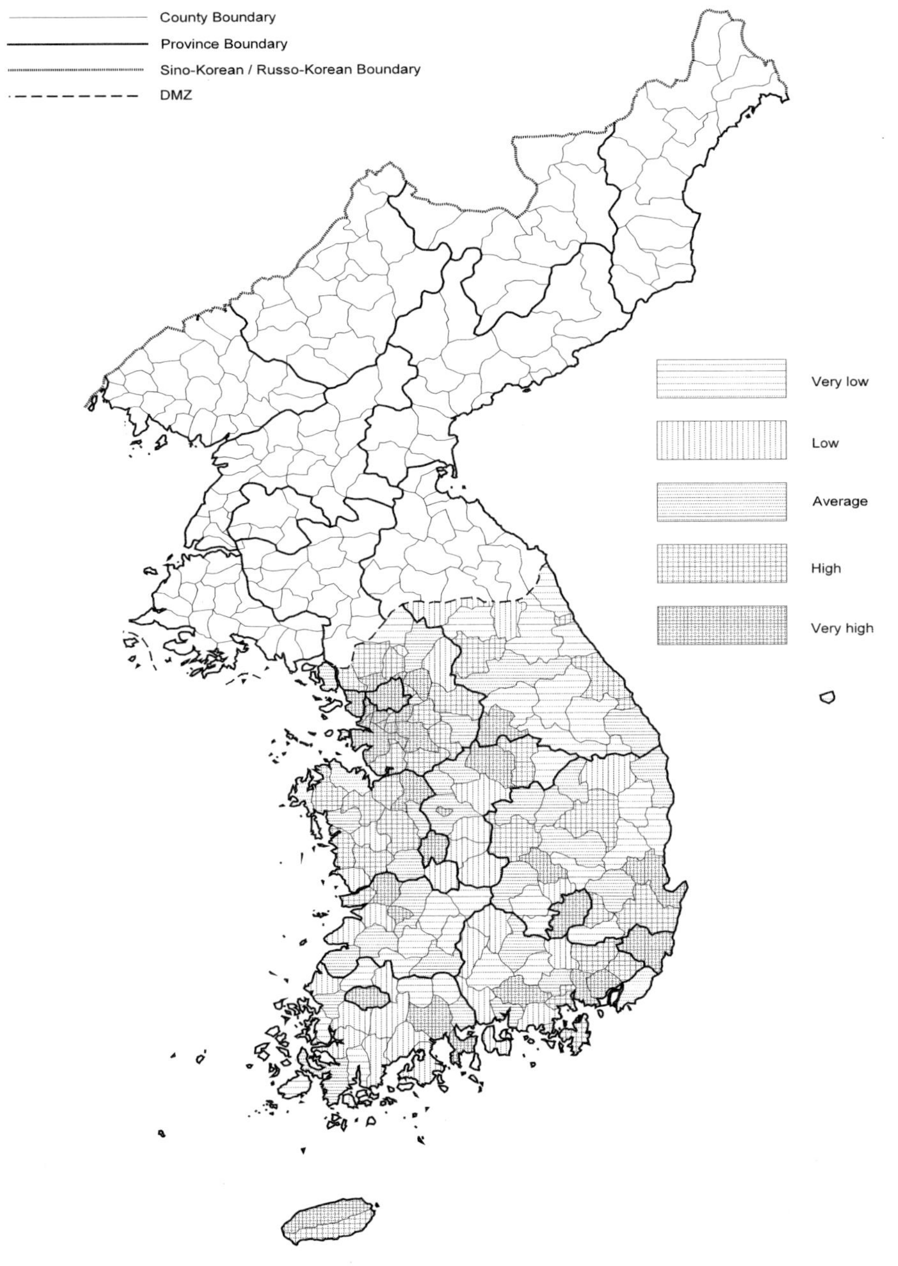

Notes: Unit = persons. Data pertain to people aged 15 years and older. Cut-offs = below 64.3, 64.3 to below 104.1, 104.1 to below 221.0, 221.0 to below 506.8, 506.8 or above.

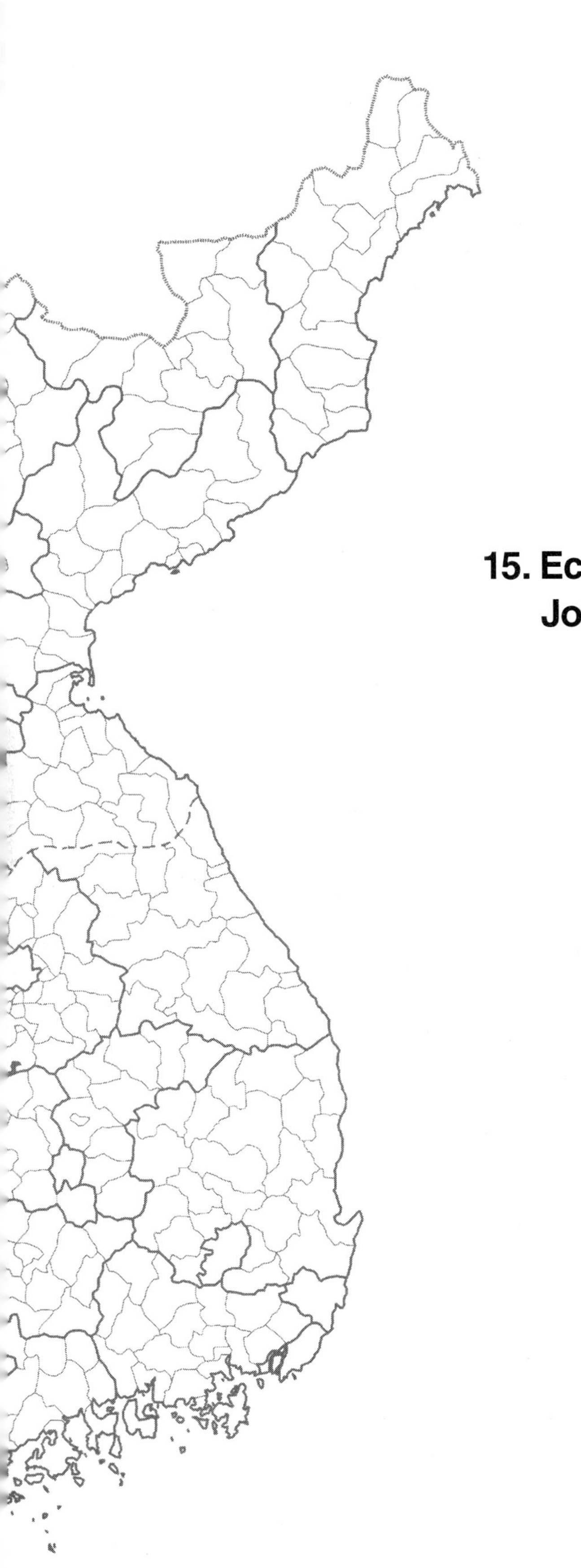

15. Economic Activity by Specific Job Status

Map 15.1 Population employed as managers of the Korean peninsula

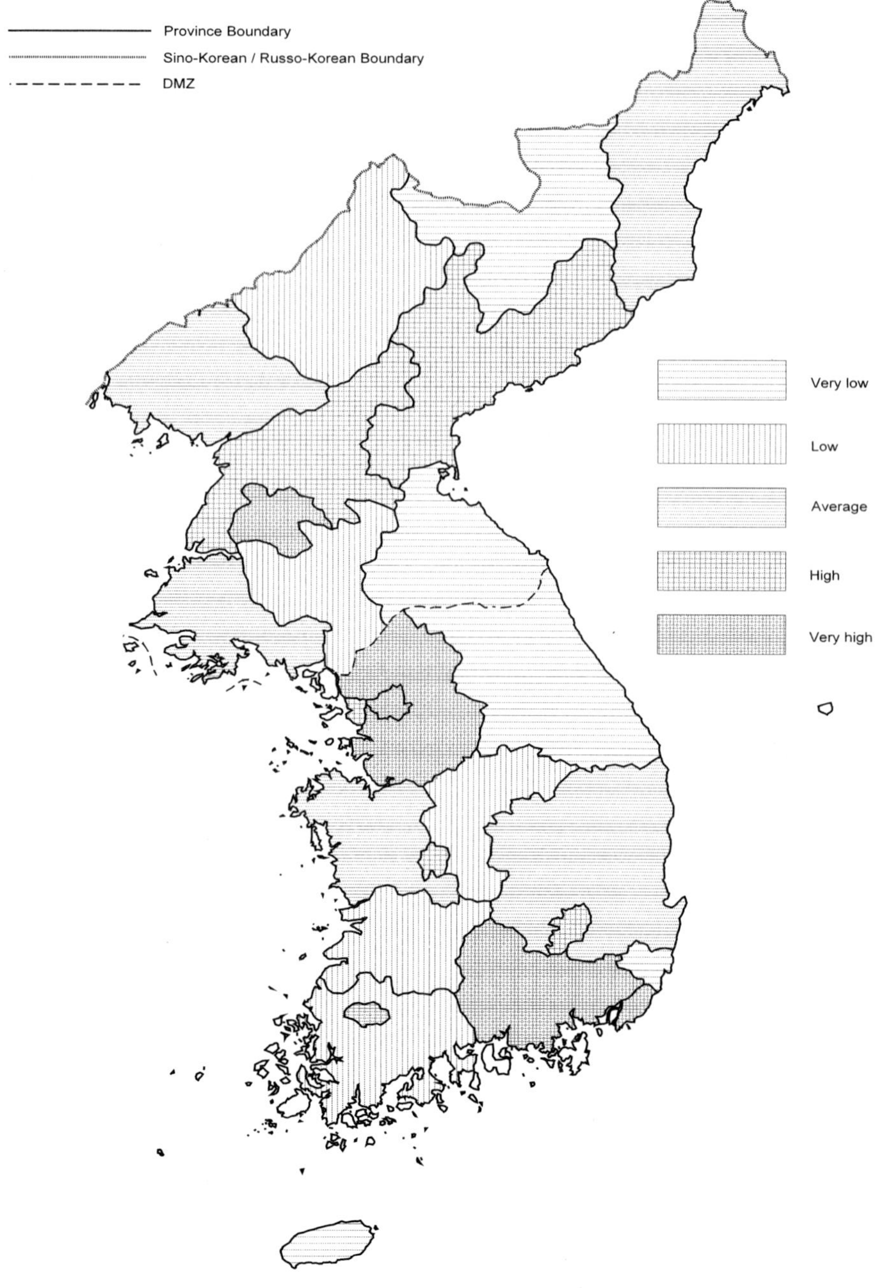

Notes: Unit = persons. Data pertain to people aged 15 years and older. Cut-offs = below 12574.3, 12574.3 to below 15766.6, 15766.6 to below 20942.1, 20942.1 to below 29696.3, 29696.3 or above.

Map 15.2 Population employed as managers of South Korea

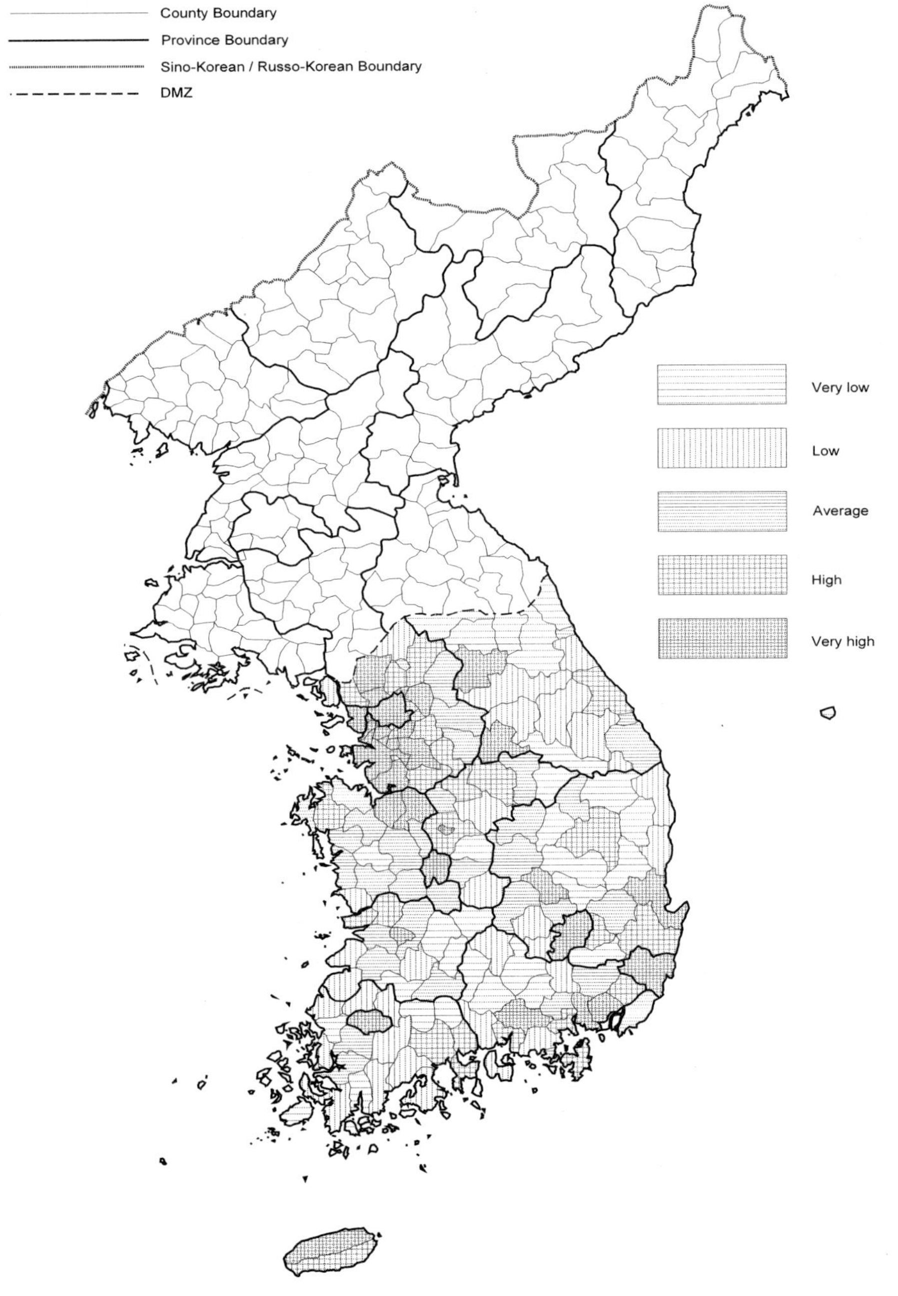

Notes: Unit = persons. Data pertain to people aged 15 years and older. Cut-offs = below 250.5, 250.5 to below 431.0, 431.0 to below 1025.5, 1025.5 to below 2676.0, 2676.0 or above.

Map 15.3 Population employed as professionals & related workers of the Korean peninsula

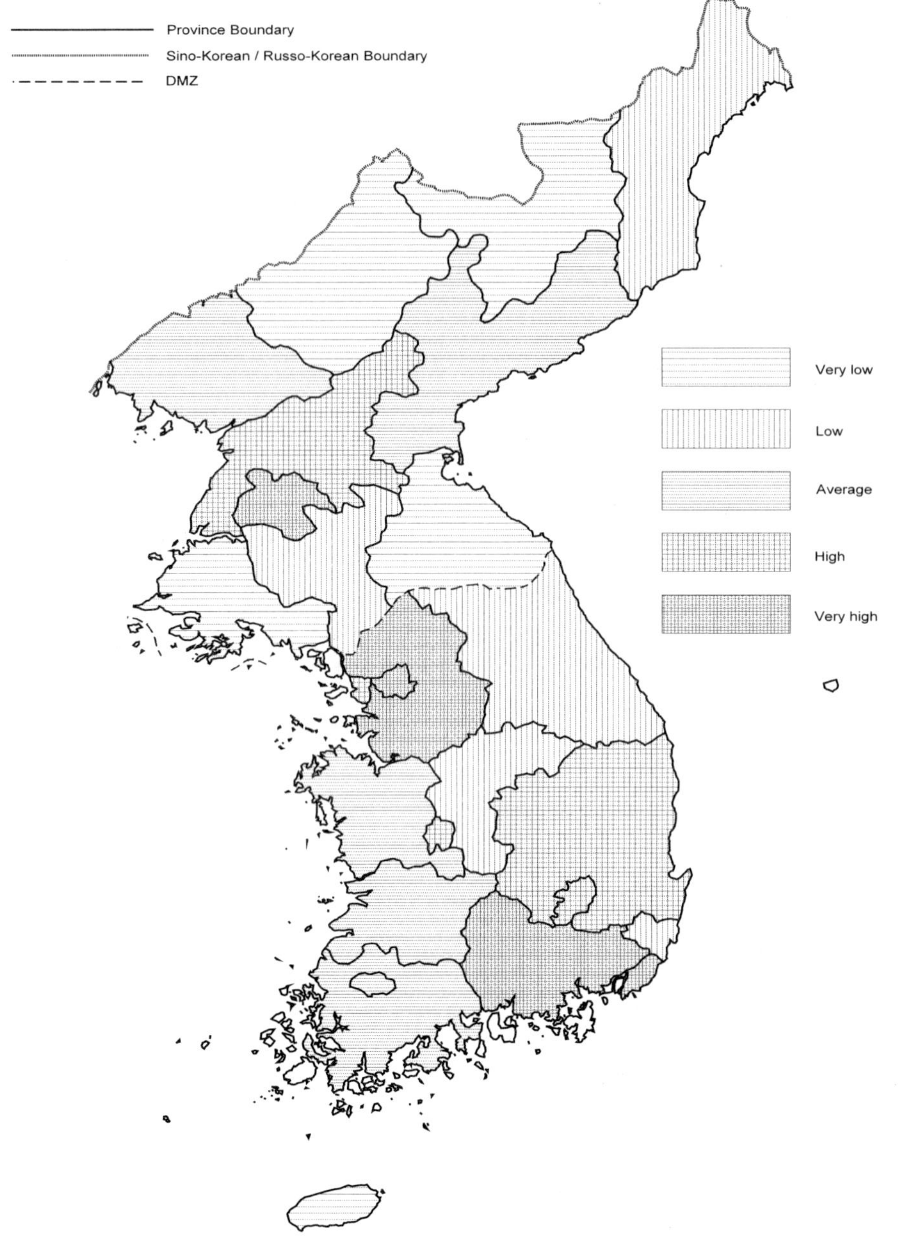

Notes: Unit = persons. Data pertain to people aged 15 years and older. Cut-offs = below 76502.5, 76502.5 to below 110051.4, 110051.4 to below 142483.9, 142483.9 to below 207040.0, 207040. or above.

Map 15.4 Population employed as professionals & related workers of South Korea

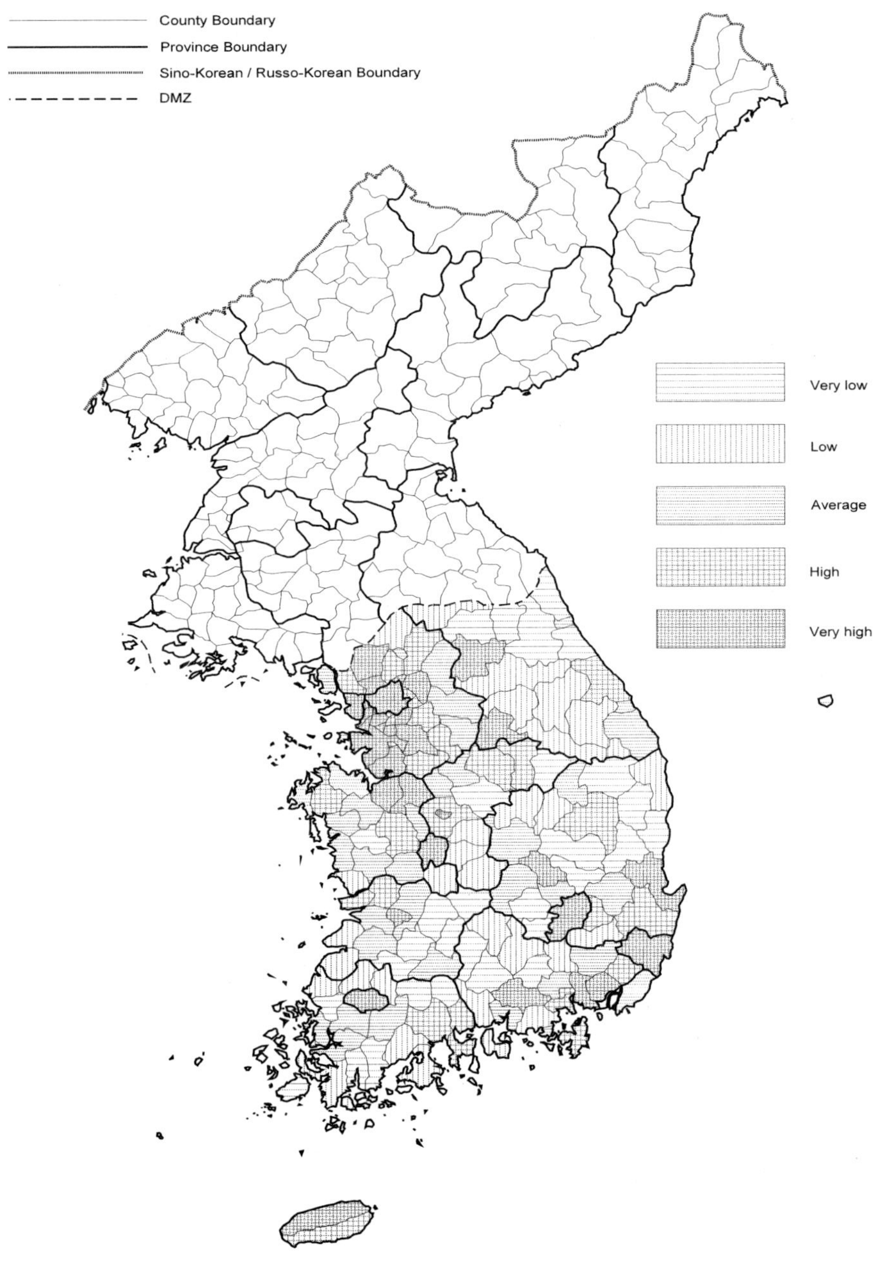

Notes: Unit = persons. Data pertain to people aged 15 years and older. Cut-offs = below 1858.0, 1858.0 to below 3506.5, 3506.5 to below 8005.0, 8005.0 to below 20619.5, 20619.5 or above.

Map 15.5 Population employed as clerks of the Korean peninsula

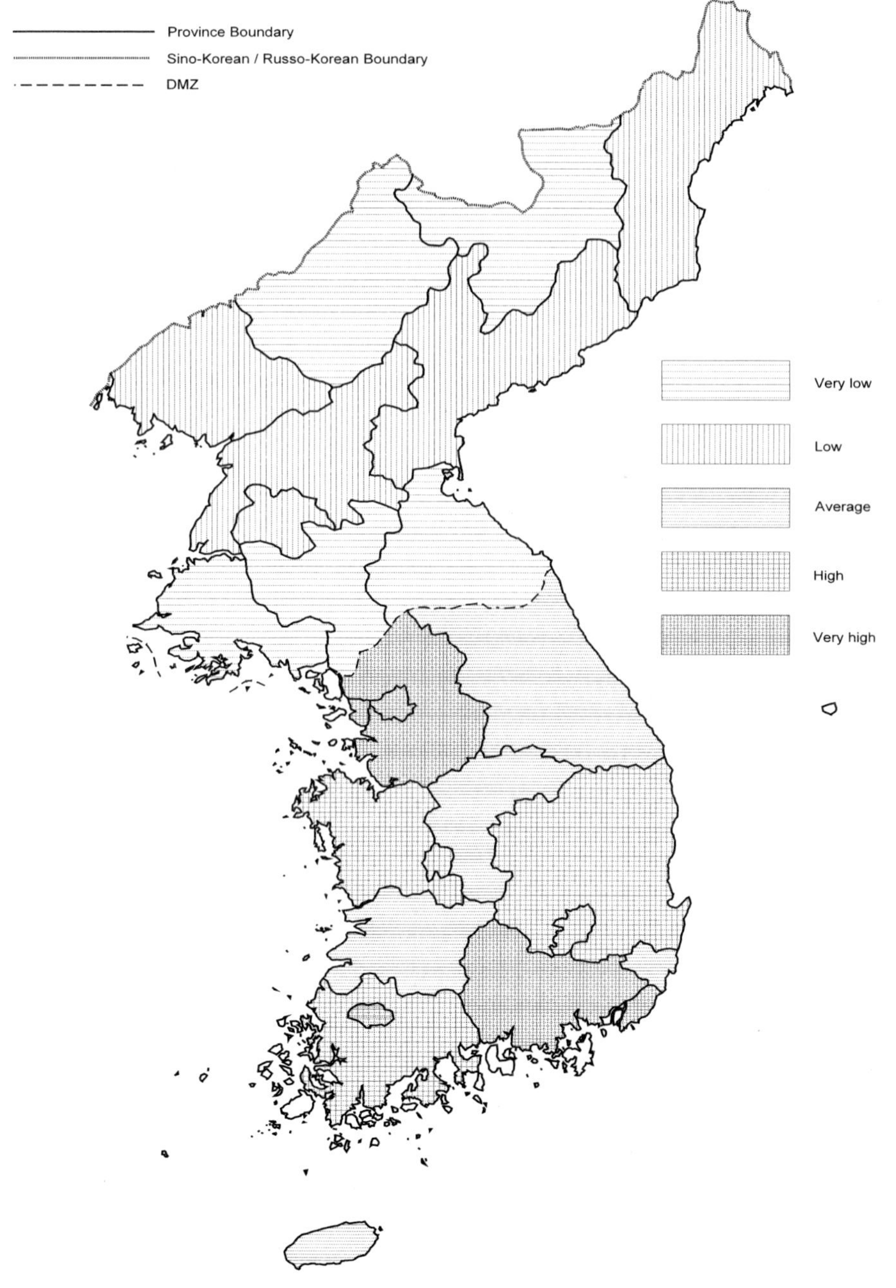

Notes: Unit = persons. Data pertain to people aged 15 years and older. Cut-offs = below 9623.5, 9623.5 to below 33317.2, 33317.2 to below 97956.0, 97956.0 to below 167687.9, 167687.9 or above.

Map 15.6 Population employed as clerks of South Korea

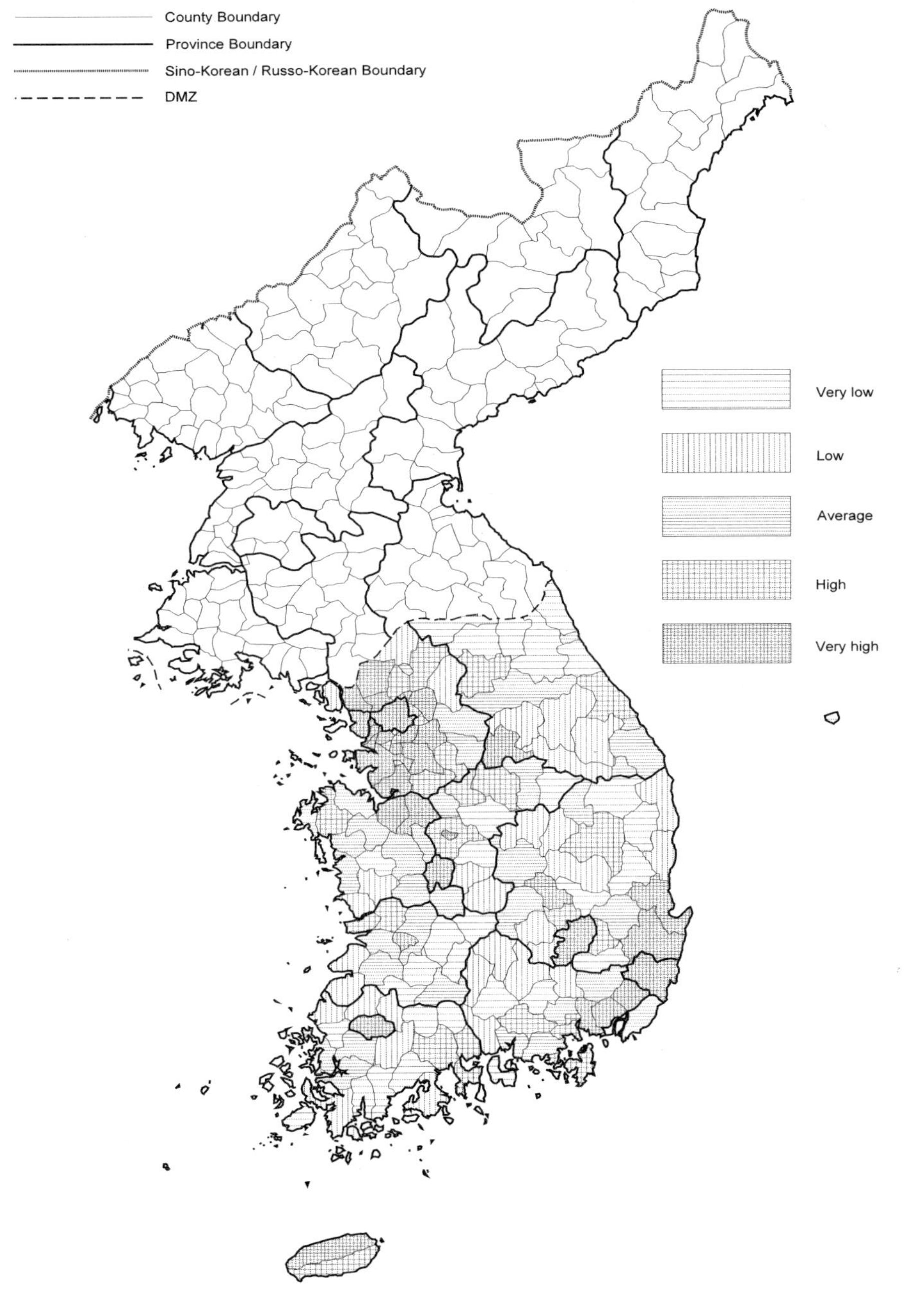

Notes: Unit = persons. Data pertain to people aged 15 years and older. Cut-offs = below 1963.5, 1963.5 to below 3202.5, 3202.5 to below 7308.0, 7308.0 to below 16649.5, 16649.5 or above.

Map 15.7 Population employed as service workers of South Korea

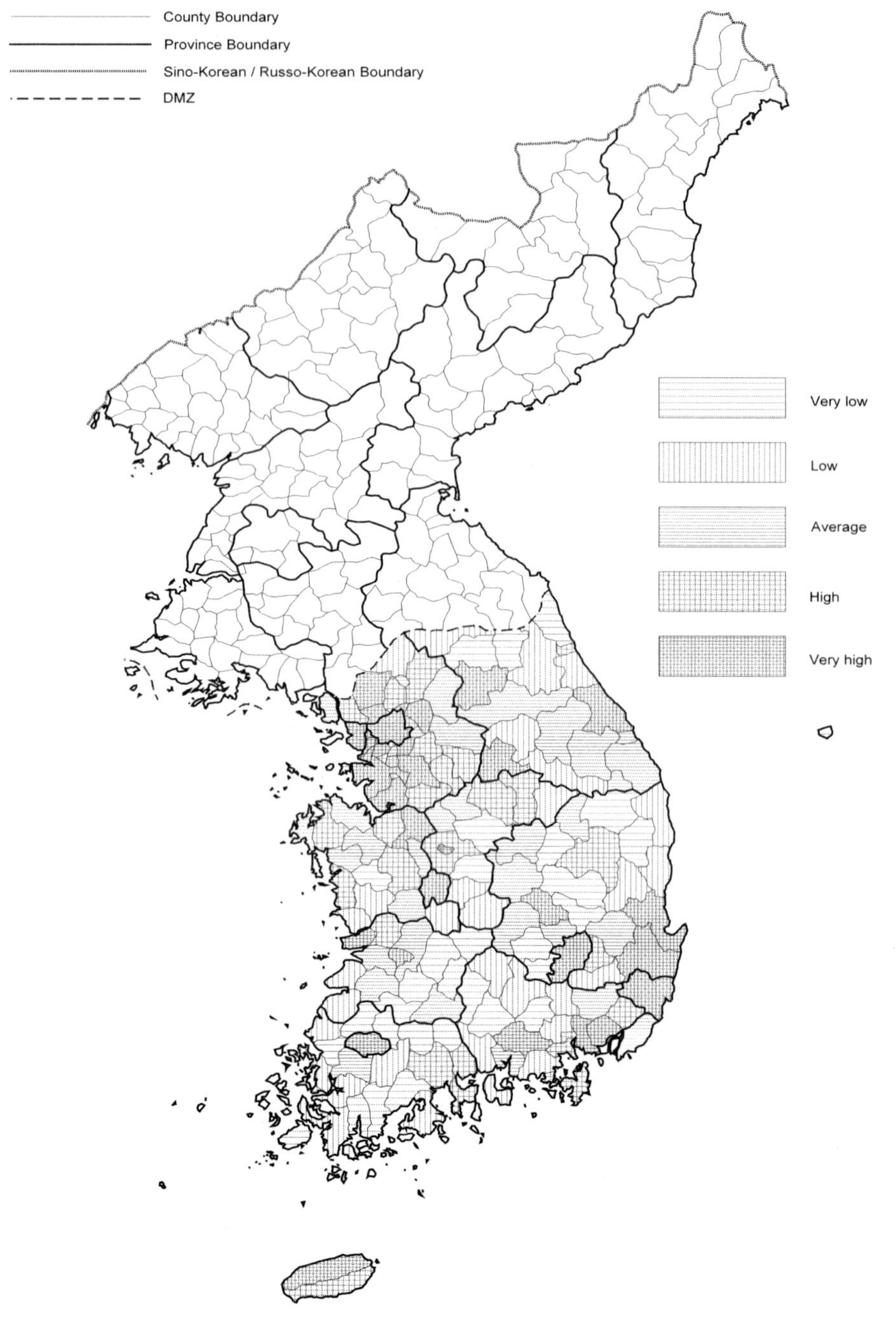

Notes: Unit = persons. Data pertain to people aged 15 years and older. Cut-offs = below 1727.0, 1727.0 to below 2788.1, 2788.1 to below 5462.6, 5462.6 to below 11689.3, 11689.3 or above.

Map 15.8 Population employed as sales workers of South Korea

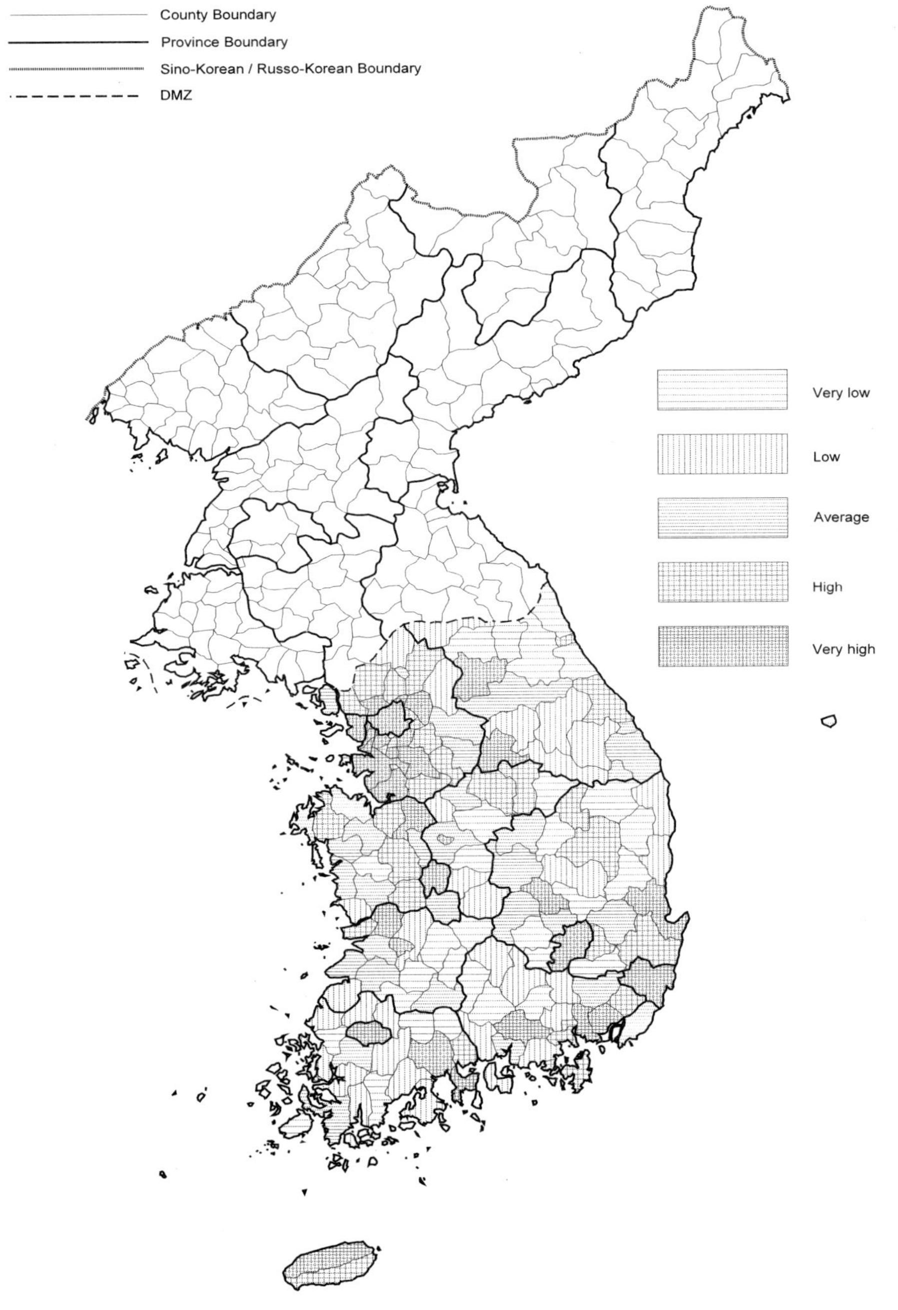

Notes: Unit = persons. Data pertain to people aged 15 years and older. Cut-offs = below 1313.6, 1313.6 to below 2369.6, 2369.6 to below 5163.6, 5163.6 to below 13329.8, 13329.8 or above.

Map 15.9 Population employed as skilled agricultural, forestry & fishery workers of the Korean peninsula

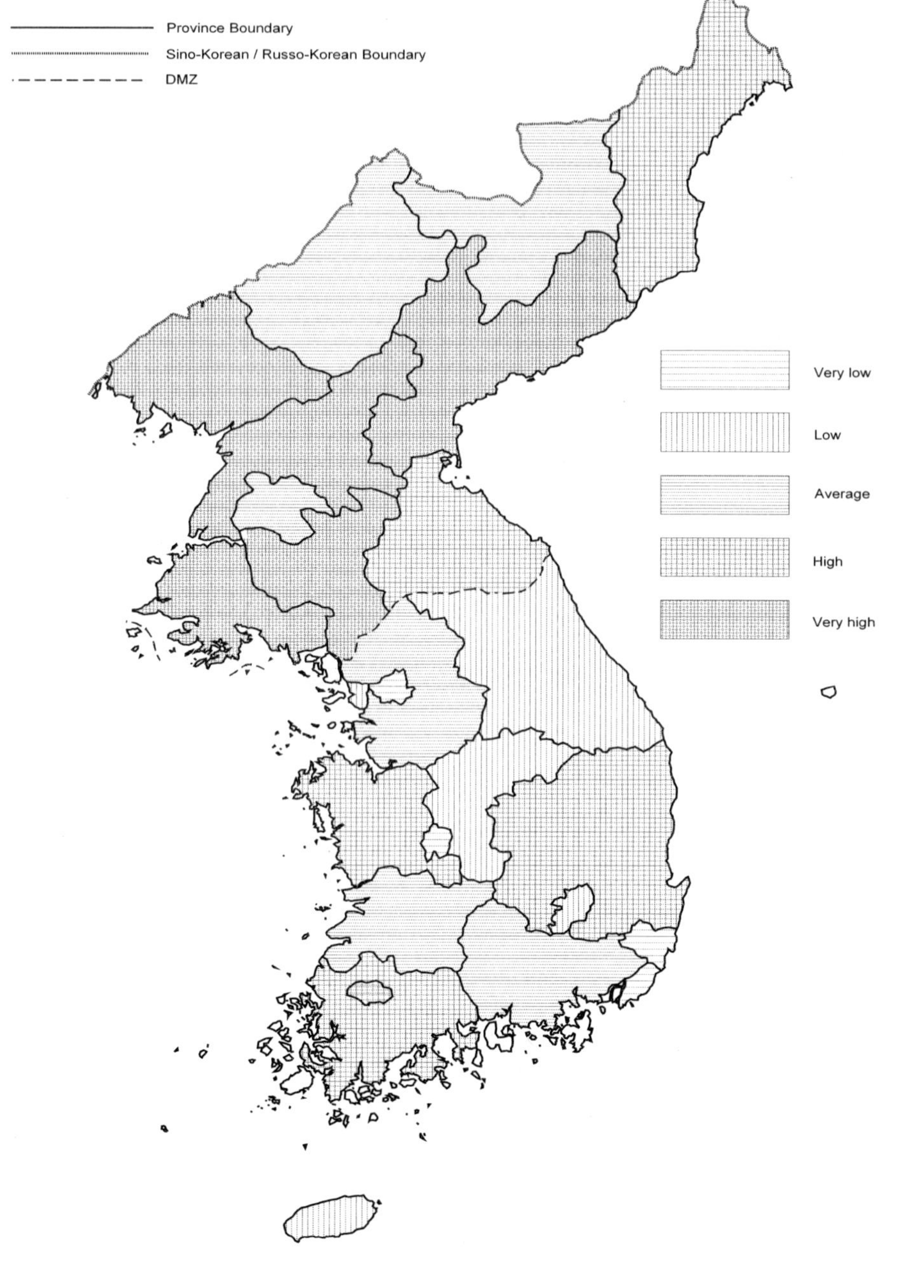

Notes: Unit = persons. Data pertain to people aged 15 years and older. Cut-offs = below 15886.1, 15886.1 to below 119846.0, 119846.0 to below 227170.0, 227170.0 to below 410106.5, 410106.5 or above.

Map 15.10 Population employed as skilled agricultural, forestry & fishery workers of South Korea

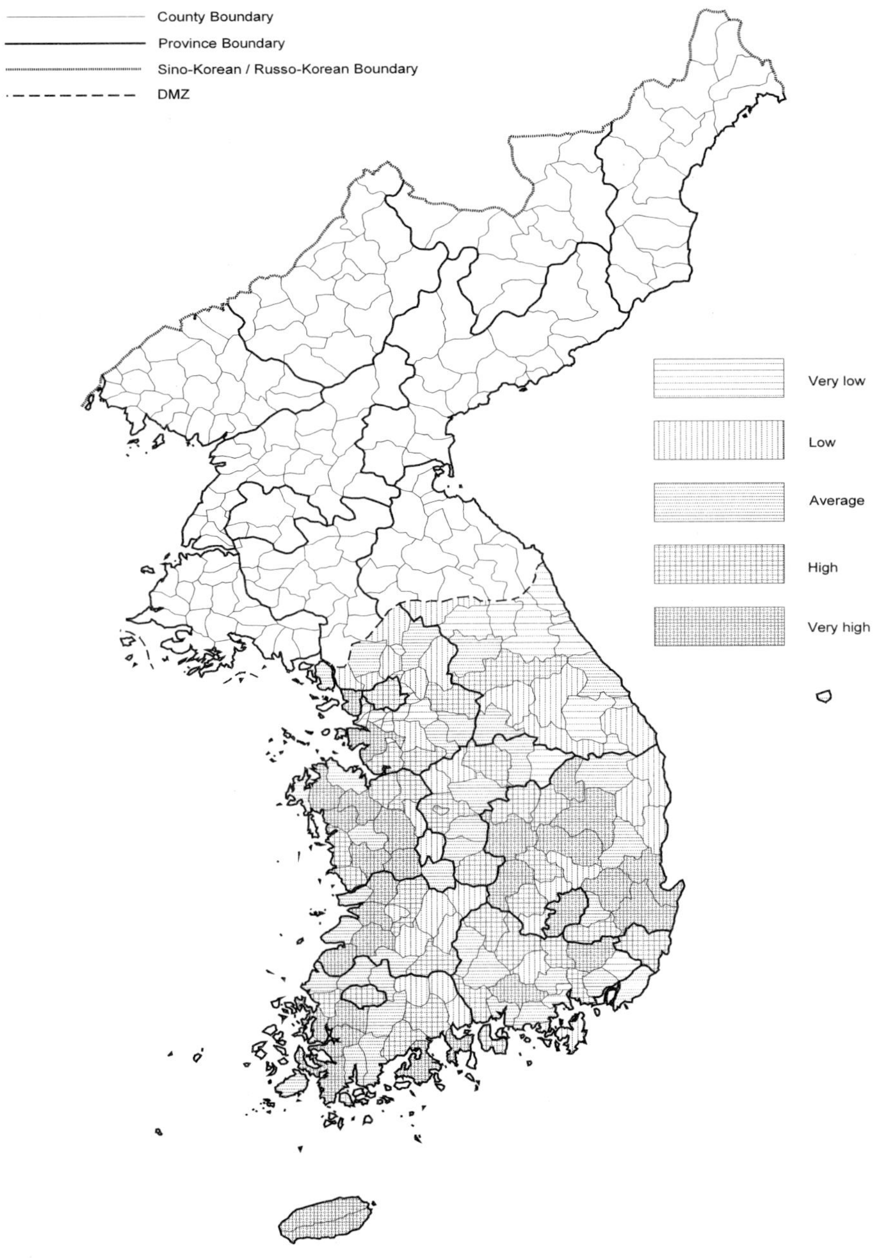

Notes: Unit = persons. Data pertain to people aged 15 years and older. Cut-offs = below 4904.0, 4904.0 to below 8076.0, 8076.0 to below 11373.0, 11373.0 to below 15257.5, 15257.5 or above.

Map 15.11 Population employed as crafts & related trades workers of the Korean peninsula

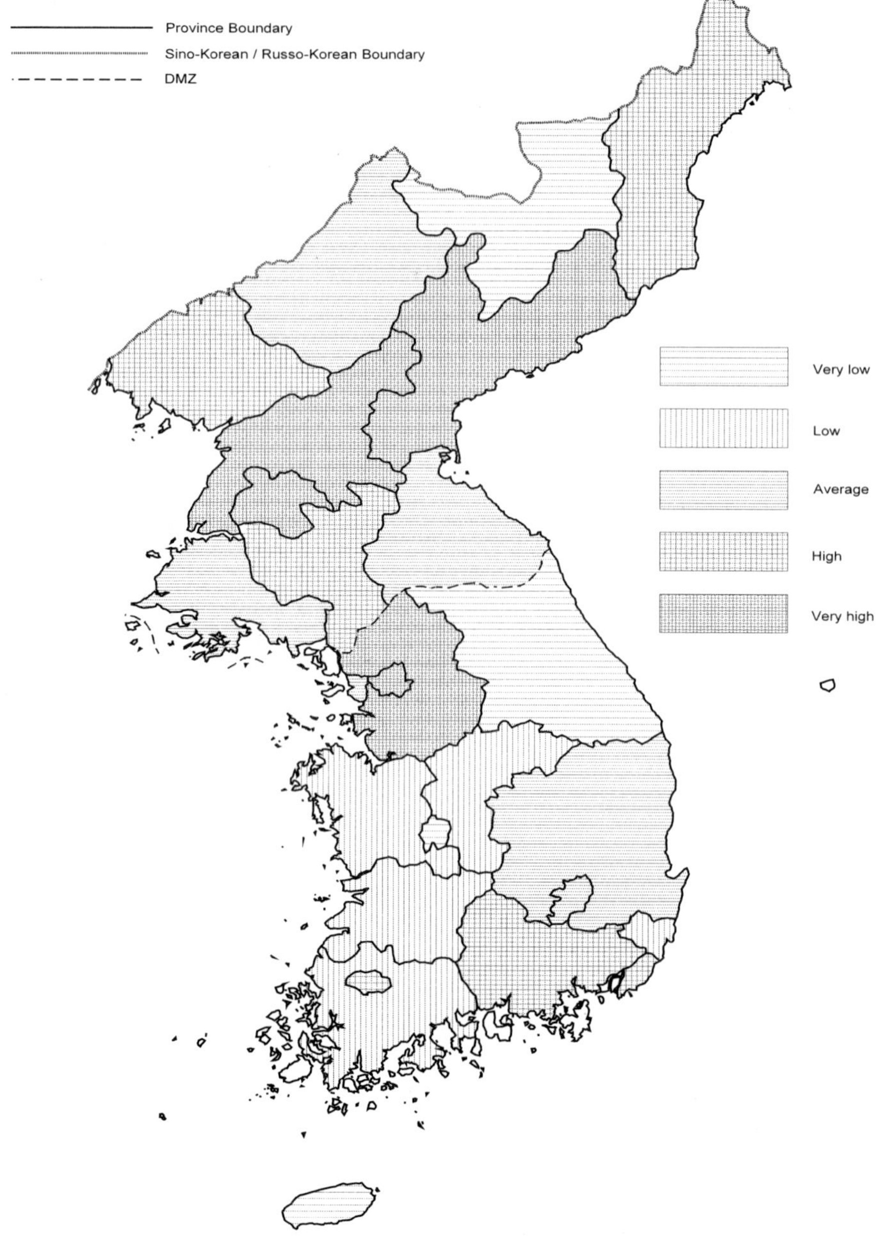

Notes: Unit = persons. Data pertain to people aged 15 years and older. Cut-offs = below 56929.7, 56929.7 to below 90664.5, 90664.5 to below 129025.0, 129025.0 to below 248979.5, 248979.5 or above.

Map 15.12 Population employed as crafts & related trades workers of South Korea

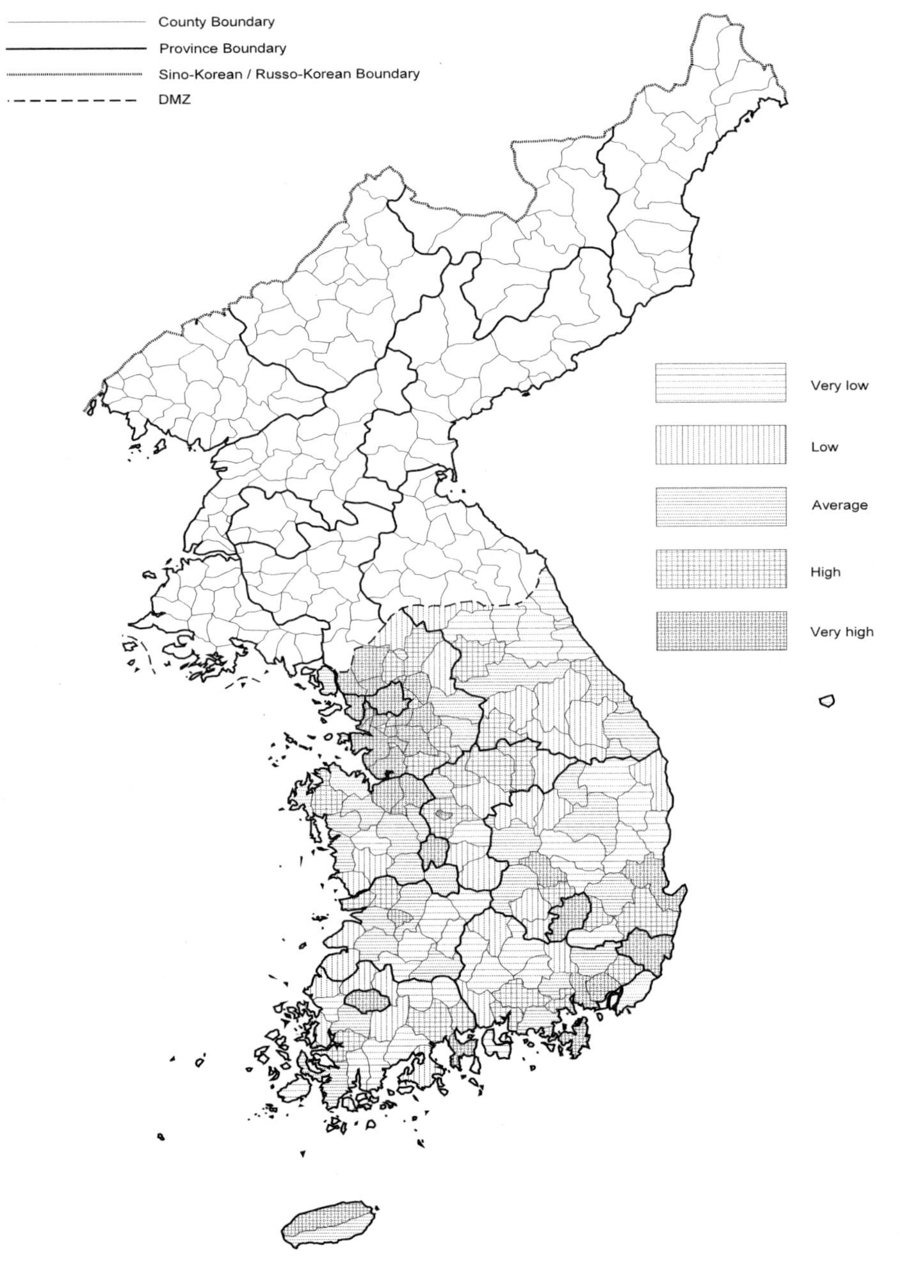

Notes: Unit = persons. Data pertain to people aged 15 years and older. Cut-offs = below 1146.5, 1146.5 to below 2227.0, 2227.0 to below 4833.5, 4833.5 to below 12134.5, 12134.5 or above.

Map 15.13 Population employed as plant machine operators & assembly workers of the Korean peninsula

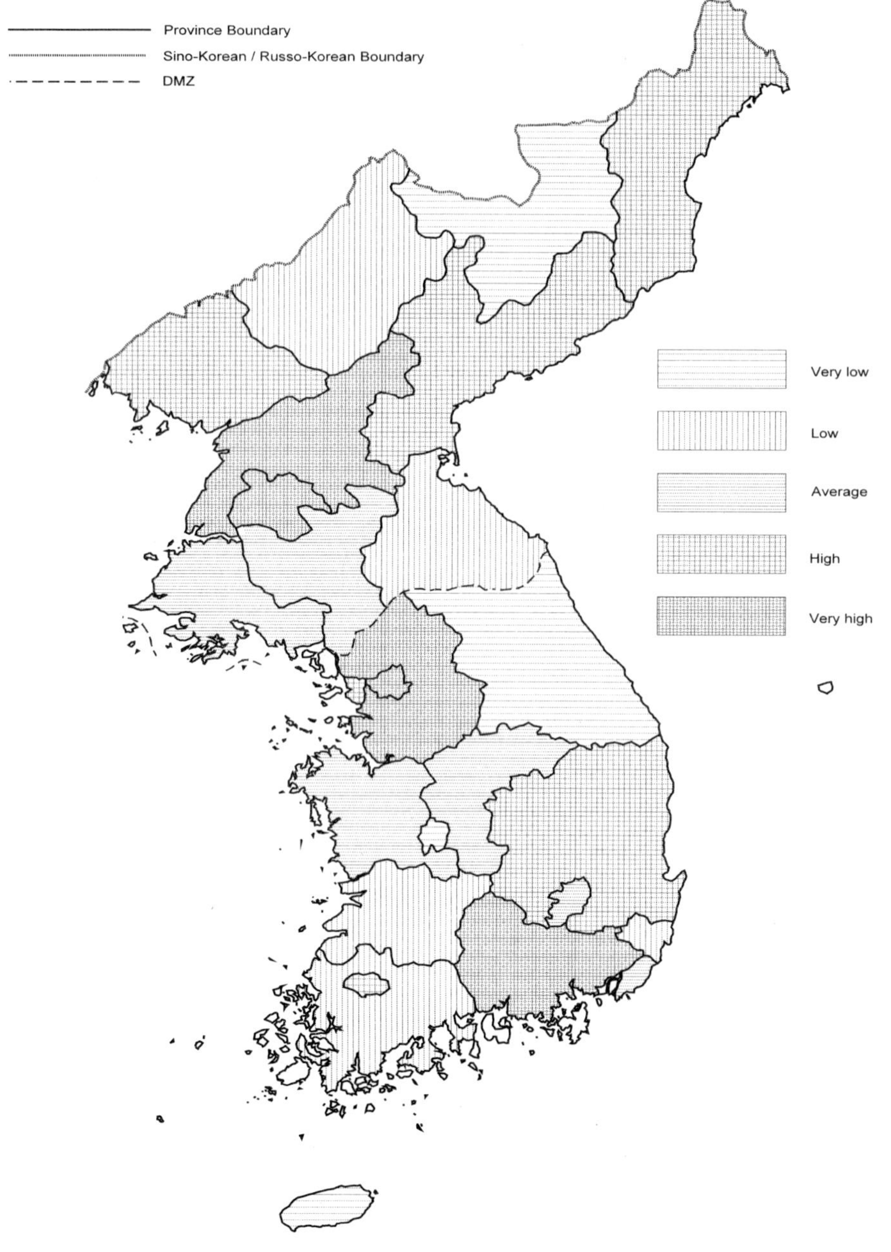

Notes: Unit = persons. Data pertain to people aged 15 years and older. Cut-offs = below 77763.1, 77763.1 to below 110671.6, 110671.6 to below 179725.4, 179725.4 to below 238708.2, 238708.2 or above.

Map 15.14 Population employed as plant machine operators & assembly workers of South Korea

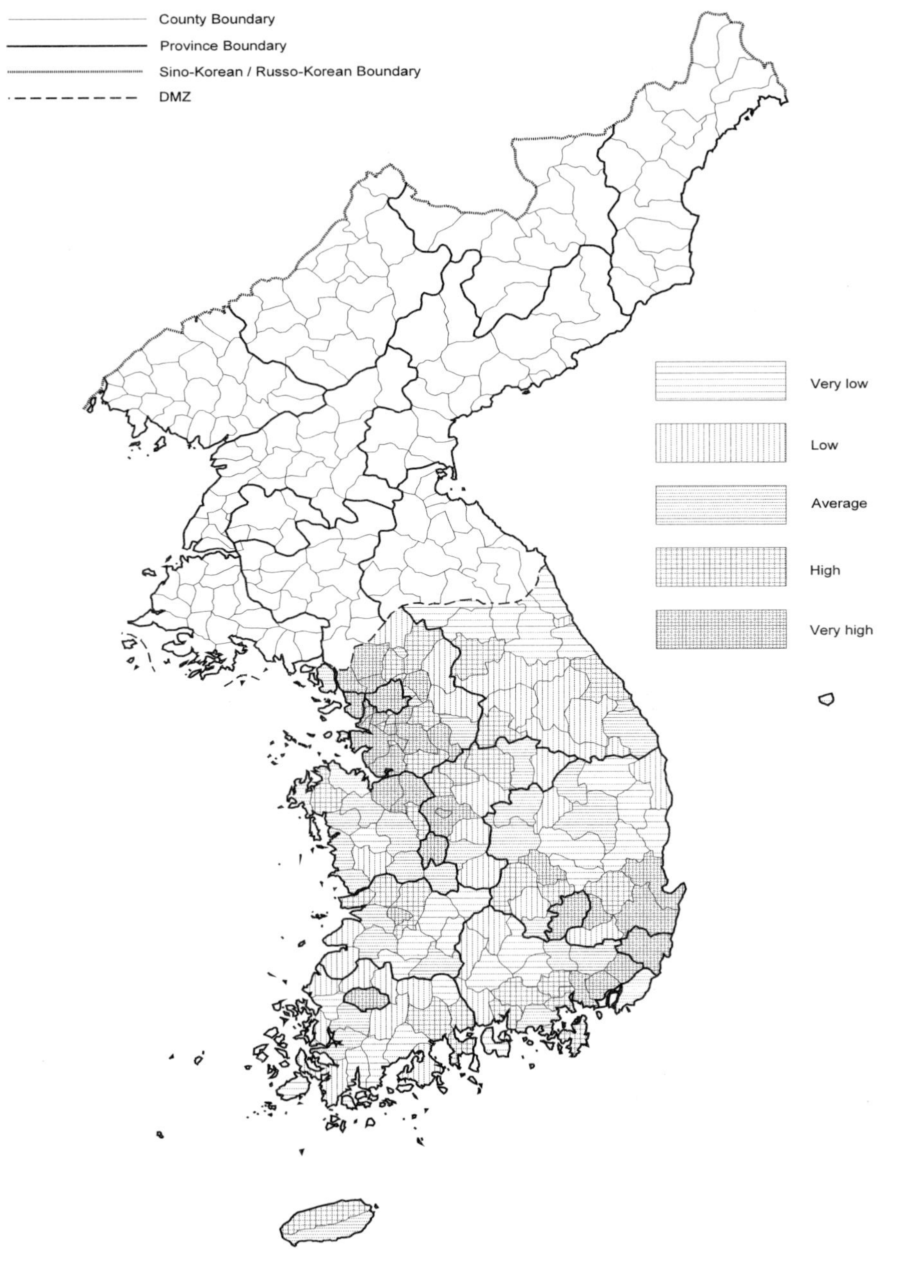

Notes: Unit = persons. Data pertain to people aged 15 years and older. Cut-offs = below 1322.5, 1322.5 to below 2637.0, 2637.0 to below 7254.0, 7254.0 to below 19914.0, 19914.0 or above.

Map 15.15 Population employed in elementary occupations of the Korean peninsula

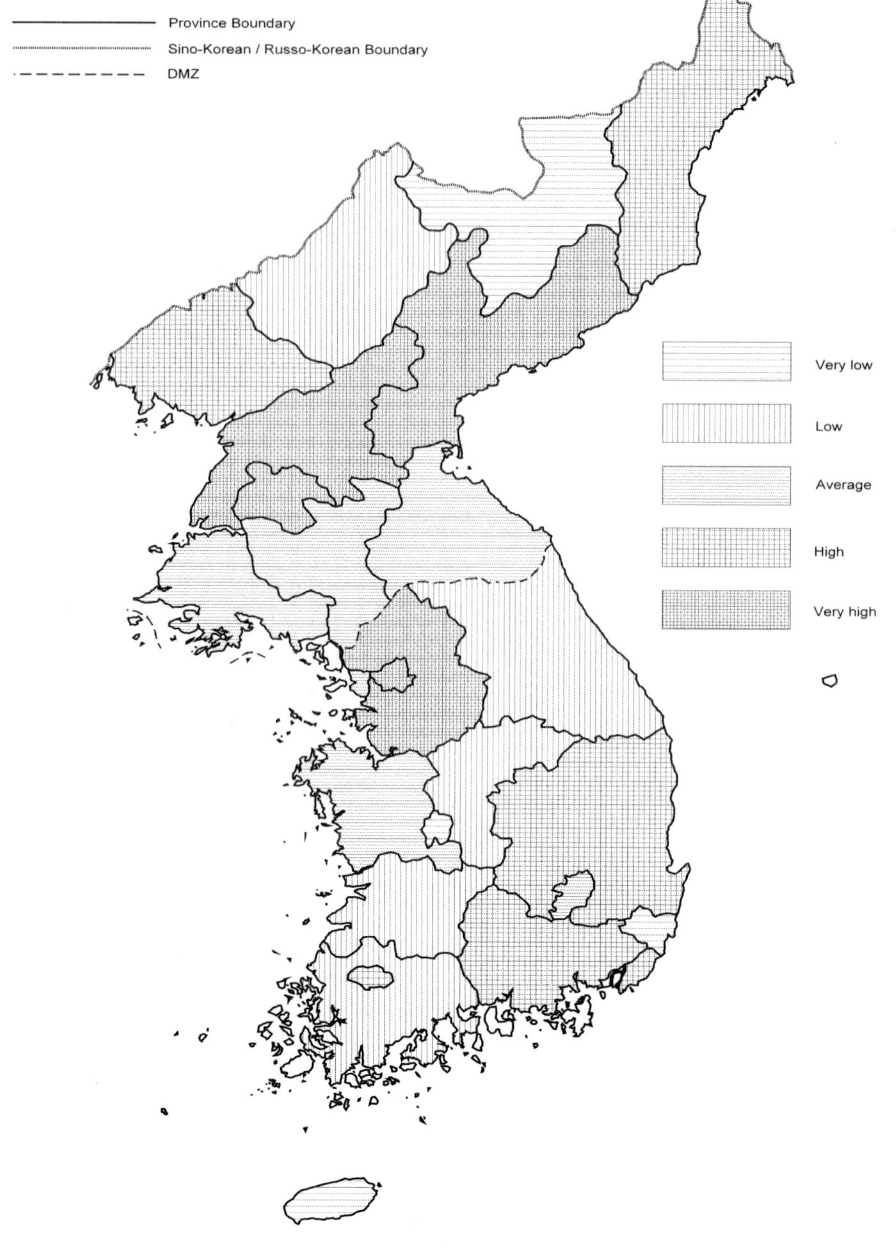

Notes: Unit = persons. Data pertain to people aged 15 years and older. Cut-offs = below 69763.6, 69763.6 to below 102823.3, 102823.3 to below 124231.5, 124231.5 to below 161992.8, 161992.8 or above.

Map 15.16 Population employed in elementary occupations of South Korea

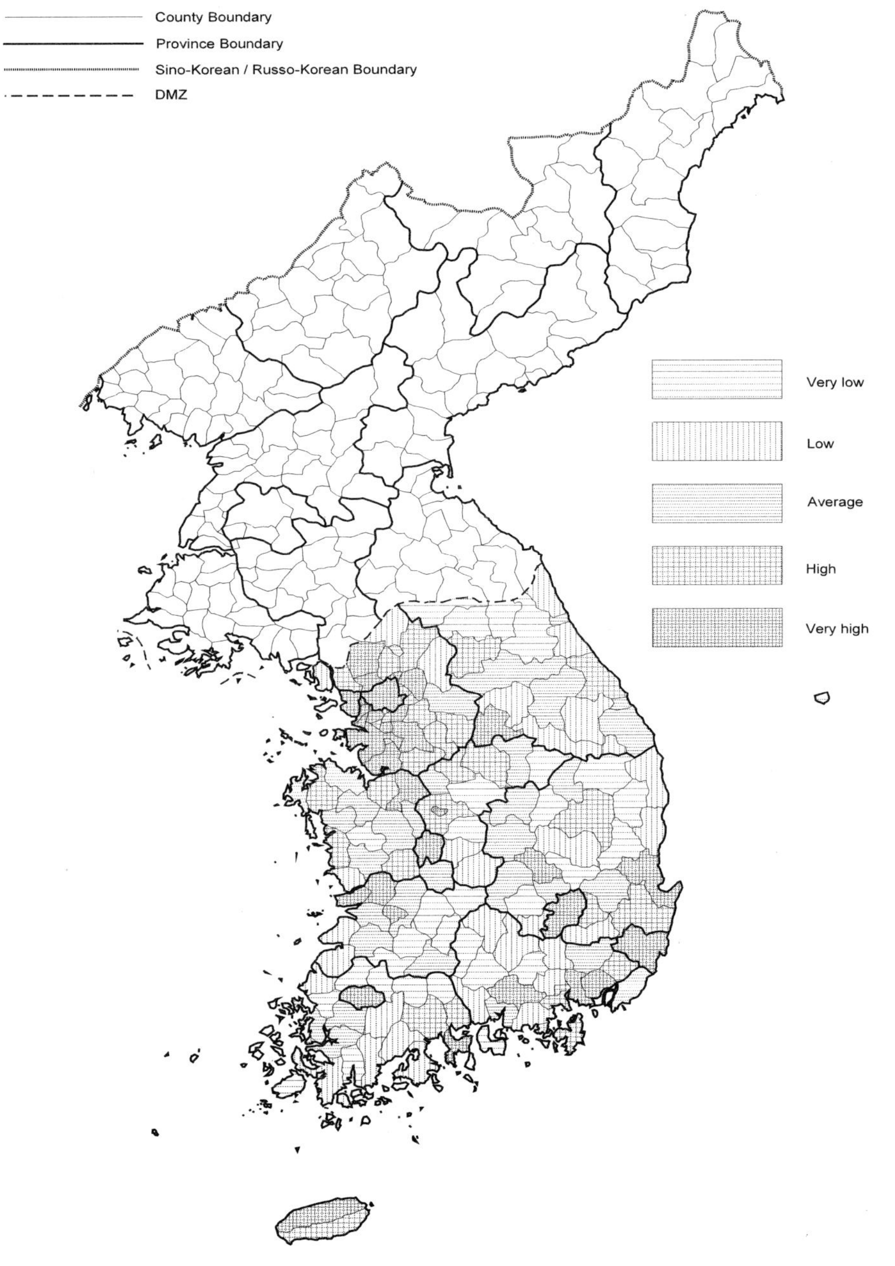

Notes: Unit = persons. Data pertain to people aged 15 years and older. Cut-offs = below 2043.5, 2043.5 to below 3369.5, 3369.5 to below 6099.5, 6099.5 to below 13505.5,13505.5 or above.

16. Work Experience

Map 16.1 Population with work experience of less than 6 months of South Korea

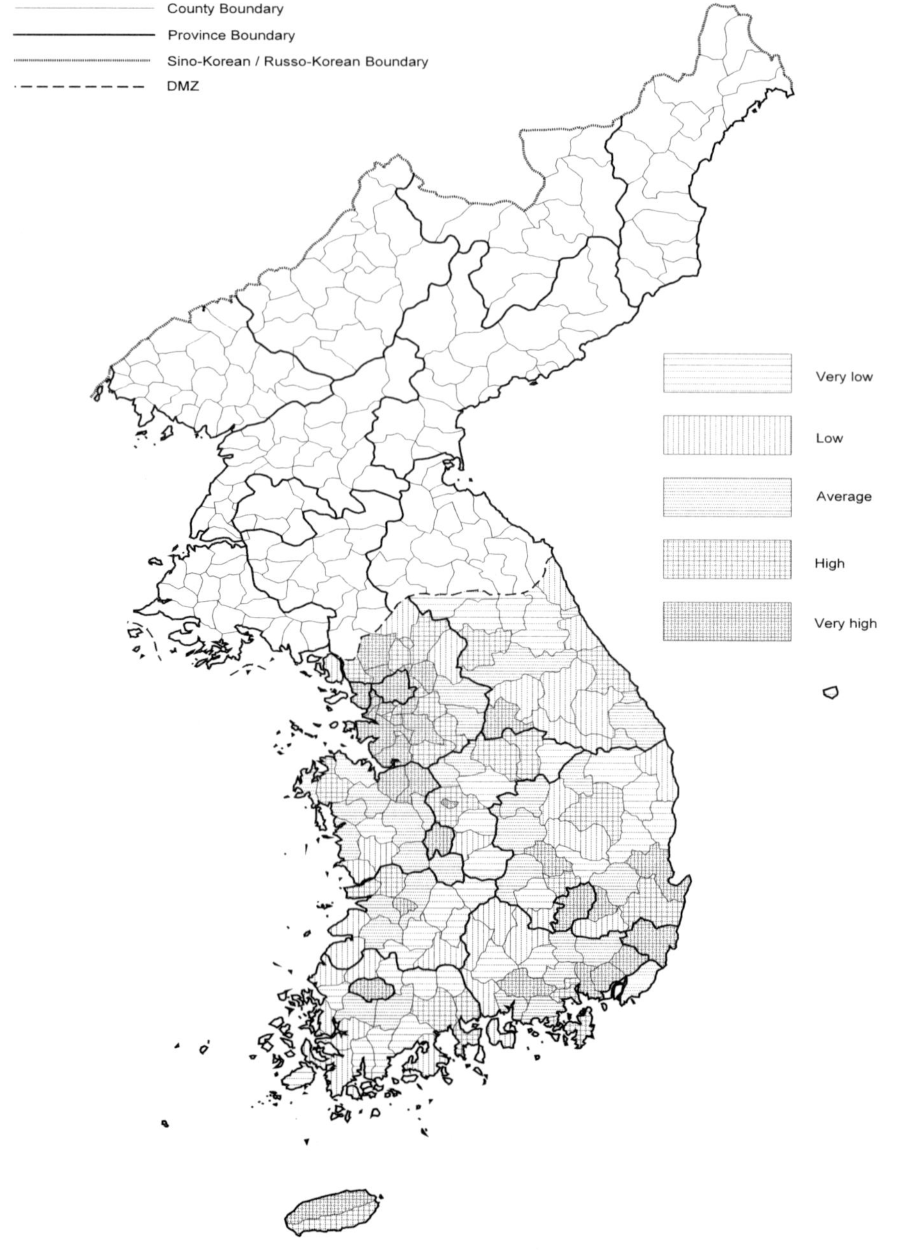

Notes: Unit = persons. Data pertain to people aged 15 years and older. Cut-offs = below 898.0, 898.0 to below 1968.4, 1968.4 to below 4615.1, 4615.1 to below 12804.0,12804.0 or above.

Map 16.2 Population with work experience of 6 to less than 12 months of South Korea

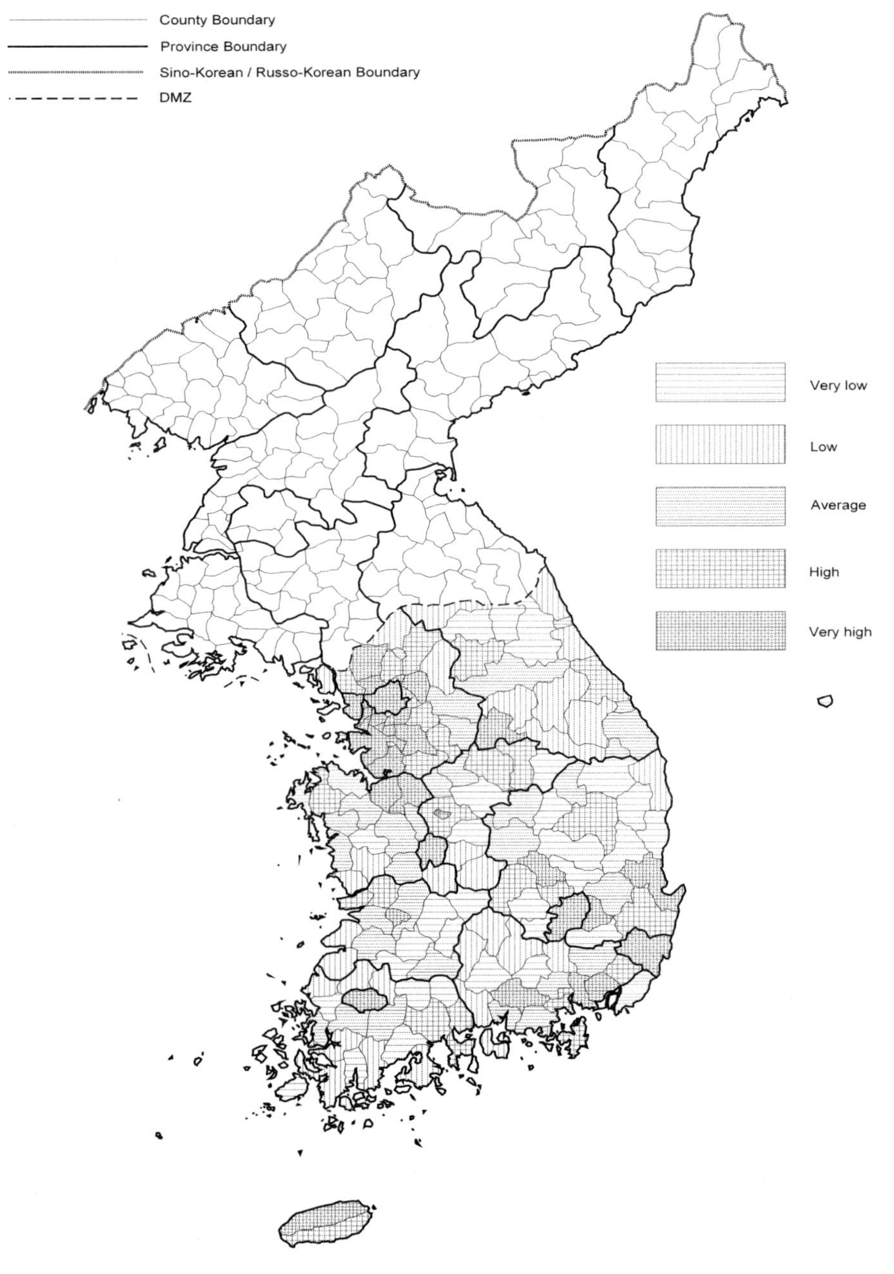

Notes: Unit = persons. Data pertain to people aged 15 years and older. Cut-offs = below 888.4, 888.4 to below 1614.7, 1614.7 to below 4038.4, 4038.4 to below 9965.7, 9965.7 or above.

Map 16.3 Population with work experience of 1 year to less than 3 years of South Korea

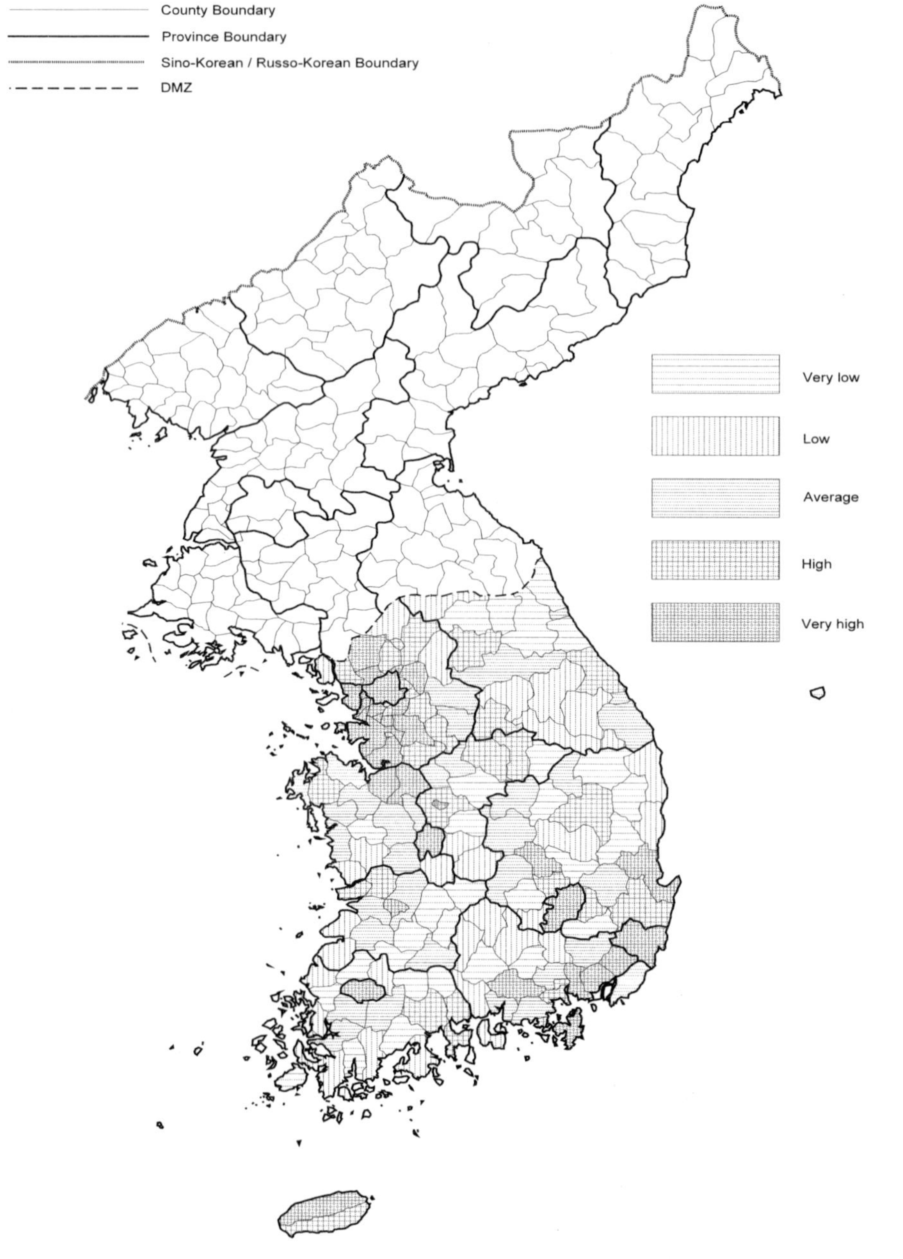

Notes: Unit = persons. Data pertain to people aged 15 years and older. Cut-offs = below 1790.6, 1790.6 to below 3402.0, 3402.0 to below 7827.0, 7827.0 to below 20915.2, 20915.2 or above.

Map 16.4 Population with work experience of 3 to less than 5 years of South Korea

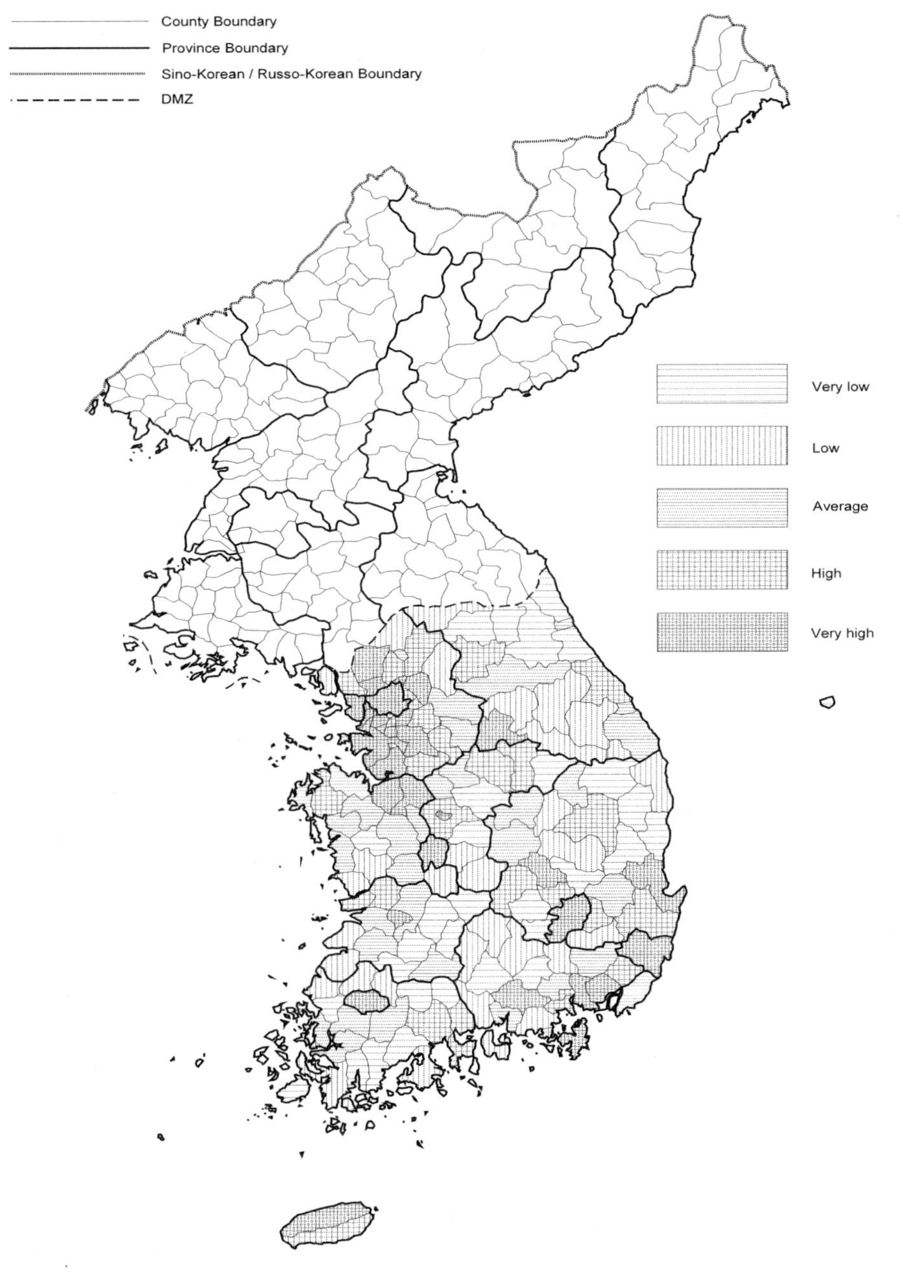

Notes: Unit = persons. Data pertain to people aged 15 years and older. Cut-offs = below 1534.6, 1534.6 to below 2870.0, 2870.0 to below 6008.0, 6008.0 to below 15976.2, 15976.2 or above.

Map 16.5 Population with work experience of 5 to less than 10 years of South Korea

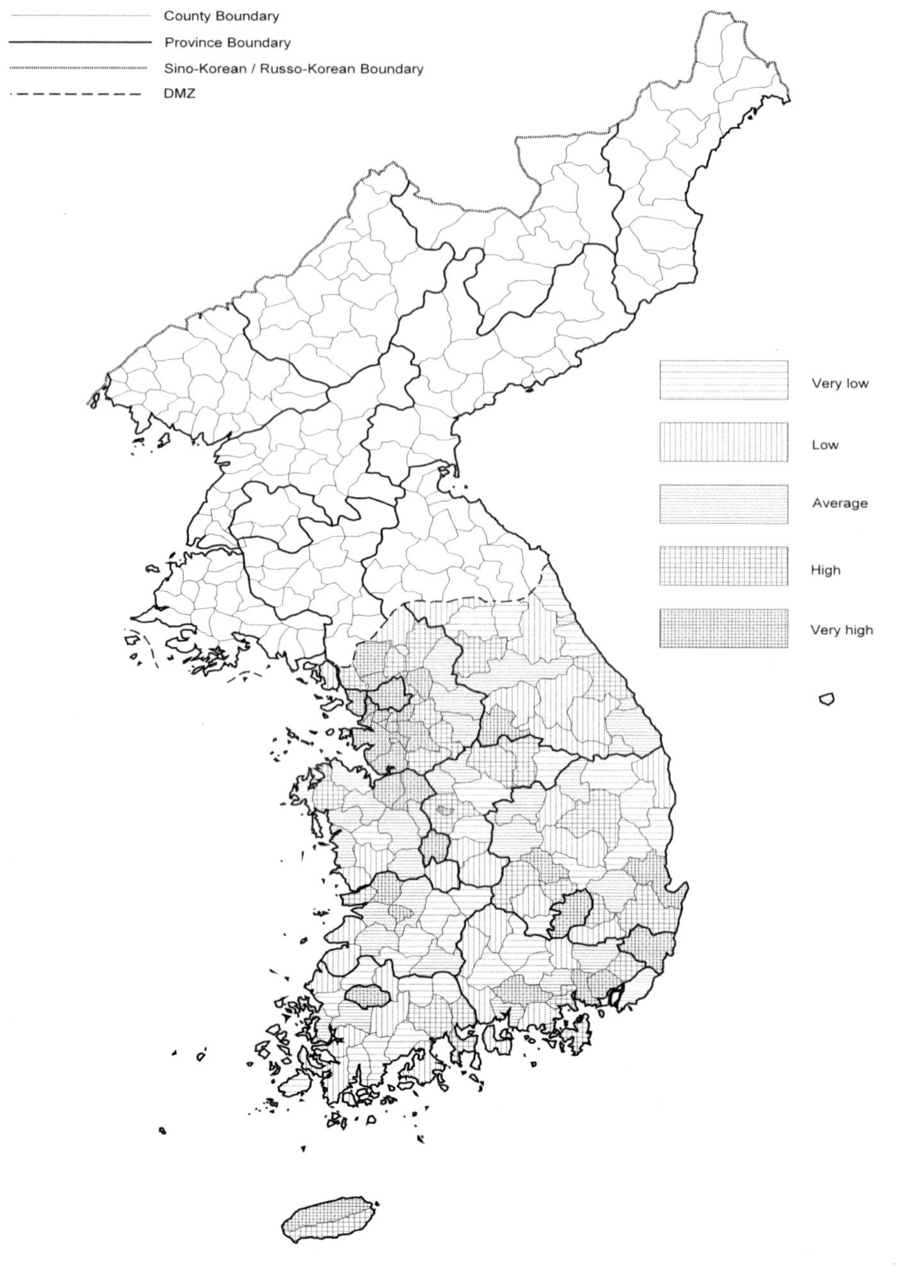

Notes: Unit = persons. Data pertain to people aged 15 years and older. Cut-offs = below 2226.8, 2226.8 to below 3998.2, 3998.2 to below 8442.2, 8442.2 to below 20871.3, 20871.3 or above.

Map 16.6 Population with work experience of 10 to less than 15 years of South Korea

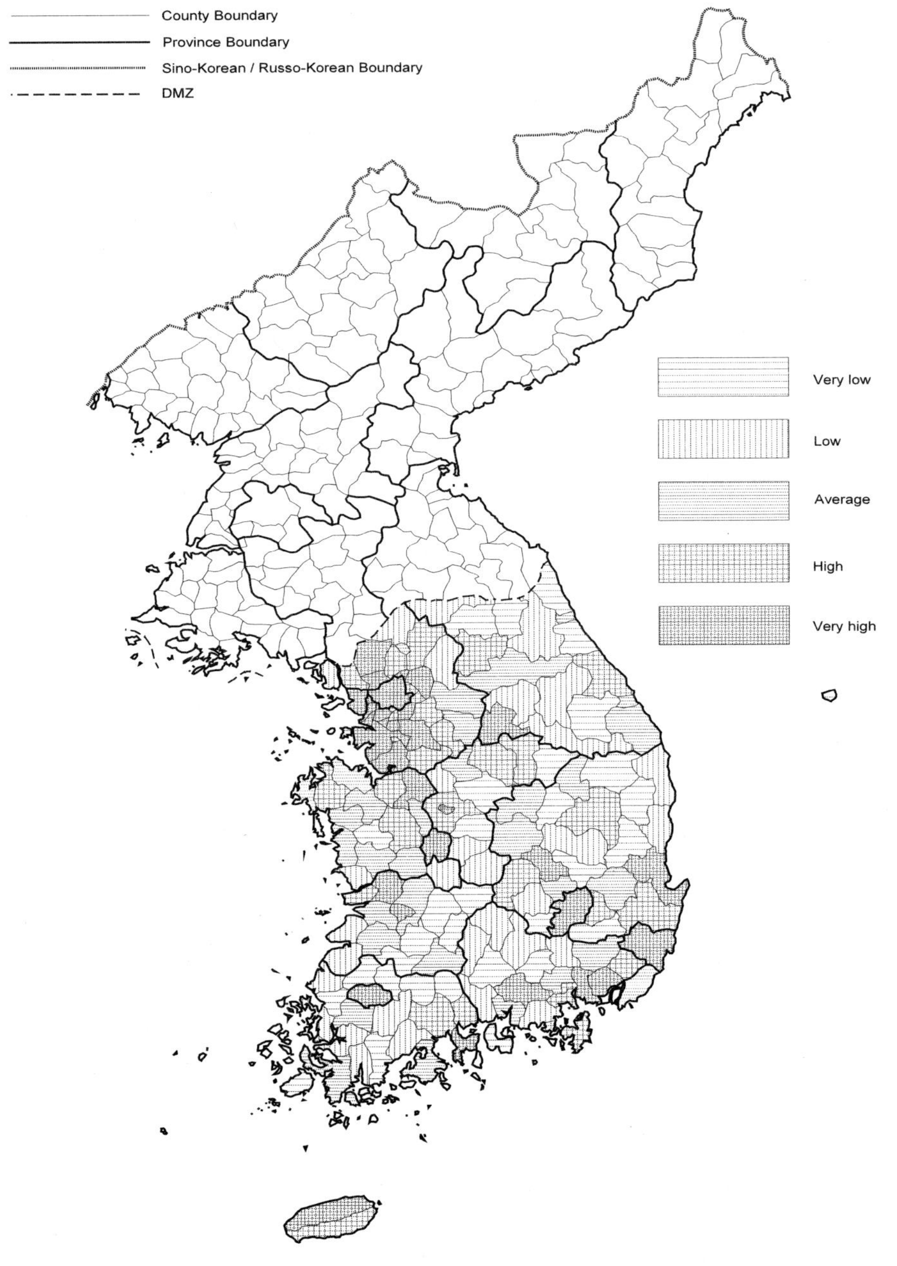

Notes: Unit = persons. Data pertain to people aged 15 years and older. Cut-offs = below 1963.5. 1963.5 to below 3290.4, 3290.4 to below 6299.8, 6299.8 to below 14067.1, 14067.1 or above.

Map 16.7 Population with work experience of 15 to less than 20 years of South Korea

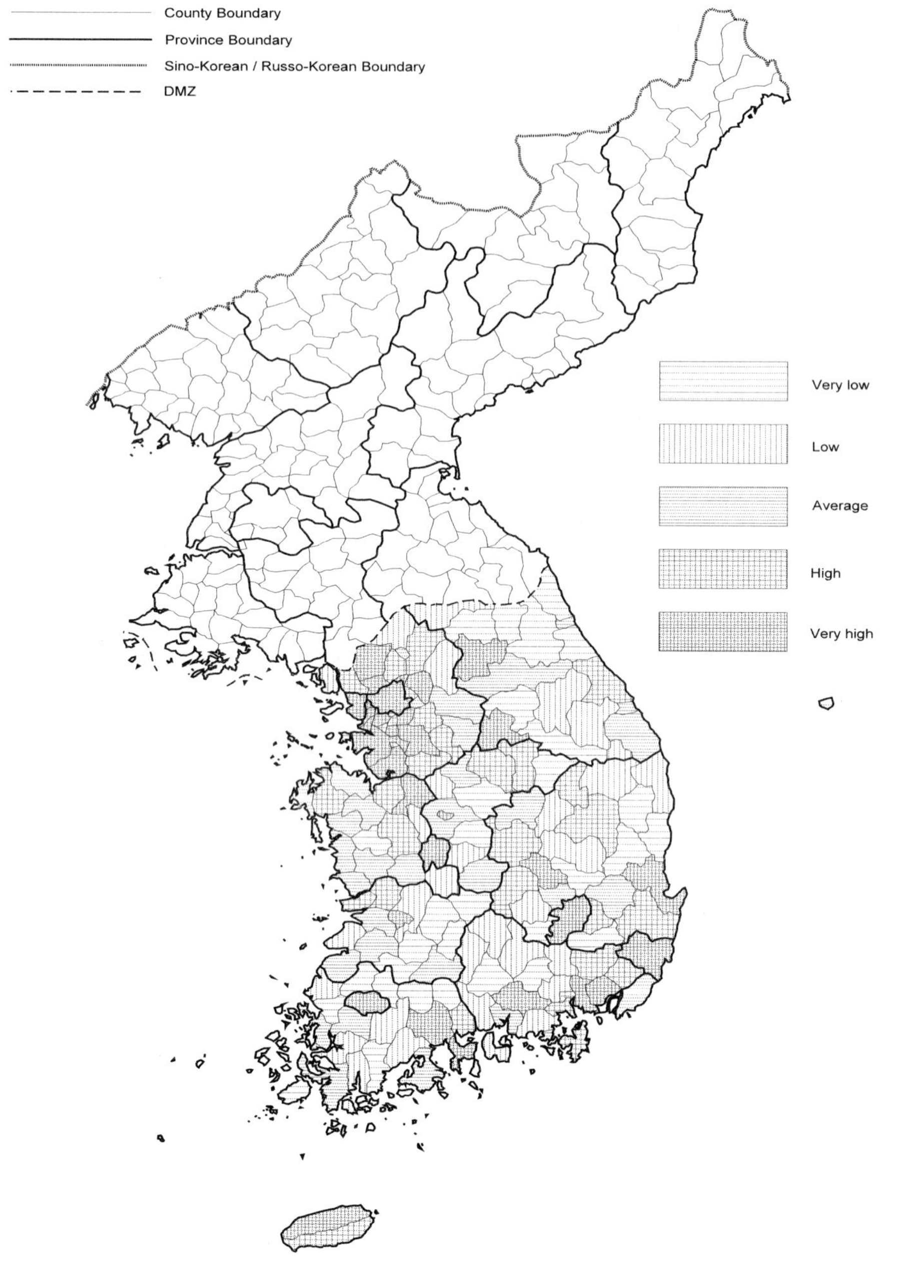

Notes: Unit = persons. Data pertain to people aged 15 years and older. Cut-offs = below 1389.8, 1389.8 to below 2252.5, 2252.5 to below 4308.0, 4308.0 to below 9493.6, 9493.6 or above.

Map 16.8 Population with work experience of 20 years and over of South Korea

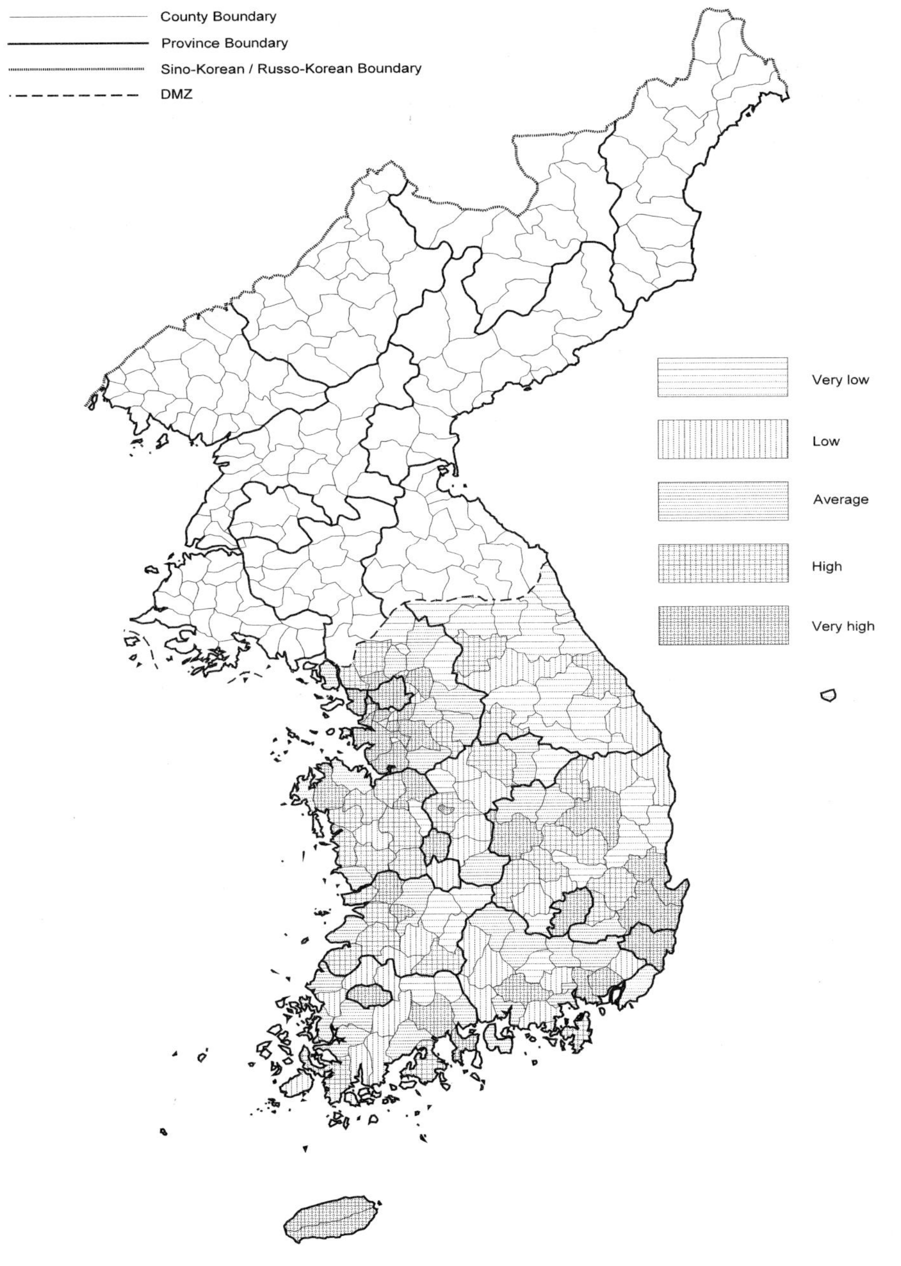

Notes: Unit = persons. Data pertain to people aged 15 years and older. Cut-offs = below 7368.0, 7368.0 to below 10538.5, 10538.5 to below 14553.2, 14553.2 to below 22189.7, 22189.7 or above.

References

Central Bureau of Statistics. 2009. DPR Korea: 2008 Population Census. Pyongyang.

Choi J-Y. 2011. Korea Atlas: Complete Guide. Paju: Sung Ji Mun Hwa.

Cho C-G. 2000. General Review of Administrative Districts of Korea (in Korean). Seoul: Cheil Kaje Pomnyong.

Park Y-H, Lee K-S, Lee H-Y, Son I, Lee J-R. 2003. Atlas of Korea. Paju: Sung Ji Mun Hwa.

Schwekendiek D. 2009. The Data Atlas of North Korea: Demography, Economy, Society. Seoul: Institute for Peace and Unification Studies - Seoul National University.

Statistics Korea. 2013. 2010 Population Census of the Republic of Korea. Under: http://kosis.kr (accessed from June to September 2013).

Appendix

List of administrative divisions of the Korean peninsula

Province		County		
Name	Classification	Name	Classification	Alternative Name
Seoul	Special Administrative City	n/a	n/a	
Busan	Wider City Area	n/a	n/a	
Daegu	Wider City Area	n/a	n/a	
Incheon	Wider City Area	n/a	n/a	
Gwangju	Wider City Area	n/a	n/a	
Daejeon	Wider City Area	n/a	n/a	
Ulsan	Wider City Area	n/a	n/a	
Gyeonggi	Province	n/a	n/a	
———	———	Suwon	City	
———	———	Seongnam	City	
———	———	Uijeongbu	City	
———	———	Anyang	City	
———	———	Bucheon	City	
———	———	Gwangmyeong	City	
———	———	Pyeongtaek	City	
———	———	Dongducheon	City	
———	———	Ansan	City	
———	———	Goyang	City	
———	———	Gwacheon	City	
———	———	Guri	City	
———	———	Namyangju	City	
———	———	Osan	City	
———	———	Siheung	City	
———	———	Gunpo	City	
———	———	Uiwang	City	
———	———	Hanam	City	
———	———	Yongin	City	
———	———	Paju	City	
———	———	Icheon	City	
———	———	Anseong	City	

Province		County		
Name	Classification	Name	Classification	Alternative Name
———	———	Gimpo	City	
———	———	Hwaseong	City	
———	———	Gwangju	City	
———	———	Yangju	City	
———	———	Pocheon	City	
———	———	Yeoju	County	
———	———	Yeoncheon	County	
———	———	Gapyeong	County	
———	———	Yangpyeong	County	
Gangwon (ROK)	Province	n/a	n/a	
———	———	Chuncheon	City	
———	———	Wonju	City	
———	———	Gangneung	City	
———	———	Donghae	City	
———	———	Taebaek	City	
———	———	Sokcho	City	
———	———	Samcheok	City	
———	———	Hongcheon	County	
———	———	Hoengseong	County	
———	———	Yeongwol	County	
———	———	Pyeongchang	County	
———	———	Jeongseon	County	
———	———	Cheorwon	County	
———	———	Hwacheon	County	
———	———	Yanggu	County	
———	———	Inje	County	
———	———	Goseong	County	Ganseong
———	———	Yangyang	County	
North Chungcheong	Province	n/a	n/a	
———	———	Cheongju	City	

Province		County		
Name	Classification	Name	Classification	Alternative Name
———	———	Chungju	City	
———	———	Jecheon	City	
———	———	Cheongwon	County	
———	———	Boeun	County	
———	———	Okcheon	County	
———	———	Yeongdong	County	
———	———	Jincheon	County	
———	———	Goesan	County	
———	———	Eumseong	County	
———	———	Danyang	County	
———	———	Jeungpyeong	County	
———	———	n/a	n/a	
———	———	Cheonan	City	
———	———	Gongju	City	
———	———	Boryeong	City	
———	———	Asan	City	
———	———	Seosan	City	
———	———	Nonsan	City	
———	———	Gyeryong	City	
———	———	Geumsan	County	
———	———	Yeongi	County	
———	———	Buyeo	County	
———	———	Seocheon	County	
———	———	Cheongyang	County	
———	———	Hongseong	County	
———	———	Yesan	County	
———	———	Taean	County	
———	———	Dangjin	County	
North Jeolla	Province	n/a	n/a	
———	———	Jeonju	City	
———	———	Gunsan	City	
———	———	Iksan	City	
———	———	Jeongeup	City	
———	———	Namwon	City	

Province		County		
Name	Classification	Name	Classification	Alternative Name
———	———	Gimje	City	
———	———	Wanju	County	
———	———	Jinan	County	
———	———	Muju	County	
———	———	Jangsu	County	
———	———	Imsil	County	
———	———	Sunchang	County	
———	———	Gochang	County	
———	———	Buan	County	
South Jeolla	Province	n/a	n/a	
———	———	Mokpo	City	
———	———	Yeosu	City	
———	———	Suncheon	City	
———	———	Naju	City	
———	———	Gwangyang	City	
———	———	Damyang	County	
———	———	Gokseong	County	
———	———	Gurye	County	
———	———	Goheung	County	
———	———	Boseong	County	
———	———	Hwasun	County	
———	———	Jangheung	County	
———	———	Gangjin	County	
———	———	Haenam	County	
———	———	Yeongam	County	
———	———	Muan	County	
———	———	Hampyeong	County	
———	———	Yeonggwang	County	
———	———	Jangseong	County	
———	———	Wando	County	
———	———	Jindo	County	
———	———	Sinan	County	
North Gyeongsang	Province	n/a	n/a	

Province		County		
Name	Classification	Name	Classification	Alternative Name
———	———	Pohang	City	
———	———	Gyeongju	City	
———	———	Gimcheon	City	
———	———	Andong	City	
———	———	Gumi	City	
———	———	Yeongju	City	
———	———	Yeongcheon	City	
———	———	Sangju	City	
———	———	Mungyeong	City	
———	———	Gyeongsan	City	
———	———	Gunwi	County	
———	———	Uiseong	County	
———	———	Cheongsong	County	
———	———	Yeongyang	County	
———	———	Yeongdeok	County	
———	———	Cheongdo	County	Hwayang
———	———	Goryeong	County	
———	———	Seongju	County	
———	———	Chilgok	County	Waegwon
———	———	Yecheon	County	
———	———	Bonghwa	County	
———	———	Uljin	County	
———	———	Ulleung	County	
South Gyeongsang	Province	n/a	n/a	
———	———	Jinju	City	
———	———	Tongyeong	City	
———	———	Sacheon	City	
———	———	Gimhae	City	
———	———	Miryang	City	
———	———	Geoje	City	
———	———	Yangsan	City	
———	———	Changwon	City	
———	———	Masanhappo	City	

Province		County		
Name	Classification	Name	Classification	Alternative Name
———	———	Masanhoewon	City	
———	———	Jinhae	County	
———	———	Uiryeong	County	
———	———	Haman	County	Gaya
———	———	Changnyeong	County	
———	———	Goseong	County	
———	———	Namhae	County	
———	———	Hadong	County	
———	———	Sancheong	County	
———	———	Hamyang	County	
———	———	Geochang	County	
———	———	Hapcheon	County	
Jeju	Province (Island)	n/a	n/a	
———	———	Jeju	City	
———	———	Seogwipo	City	
Yanggang	Province	n/a	n/a	
———	———	Hyesan	City	
———	———	Samsu	County	
———	———	Gimjeongsuk	County	
———	———	Gimhyeongjik	County	
———	———	Gimhyeonggwon	County	
———	———	Bocheon	County	
———	———	Samjiyeon	County	
———	———	Daehongdan	County	
———	———	Unheung	County	
———	———	Baegam	County	
———	———	Gabsan	County	
———	———	Pungseo	County	
North Hamgyong	Province	n/a	n/a	
———	———	Naseon	County	
———	———	Gimchaek	City	
———	———	Hoeryeong	City	
———	———	Cheongjin	County	

Province		County		
Name	Classification	Name	Classification	Alternative Name
———	———	Gilju	County	
———	———	Hwadae	County	
———	———	Myeongcheon	County	
———	———	Myeonggan	County	Hwaseong
———	———	Eorang	County	
———	———	Gyeongseong	County	
———	———	Yeonsa	County	
———	———	Musan	County	
———	———	Buryeong	County	
———	———	Onseong	County	
———	———	Gyeongwon	County	Eundeok
———	———	Gyongheung	County	Saebyeol
South Hamgyong	Province	n/a	n/a	
———	———	Sinpo	City	
———	———	Dancheon	City	
———	———	Hamheung	City	
———	———	Hamju	County	
———	———	Yeonggwang	County	
———	———	Sinheung	County	
———	———	Bujeon	County	
———	———	Jangjin	County	
———	———	Jeongpyeong	County	
———	———	Geumya	County	
———	———	Yodeok	County	
———	———	Gowon	County	
———	———	Nakwon	County	
———	———	Hongwon	County	
———	———	Bukcheong	County	
———	———	Deokseong	County	
———	———	Iwon	County	
———	———	Heocheon	County	
———	———	Sudong	County	
———	———	Geumho	District	

Province		County		
Name	Classification	Name	Classification	Alternative Name
Gangwon (DPRK)	Province	n/a	n/a	
———	———	Wonsan	City	
———	———	Muncheon	City	
———	———	Anbyeon	County	
———	———	Gosan	County	
———	———	Tongcheon	County	
———	———	Goseong	County	
———	———	Geumgang	County	
———	———	Changdo	County	
———	———	Gimhwa	County	
———	———	Hoeyang	County	
———	———	Sepo	County	
———	———	Pyeonggang	County	
———	———	Cheonwon	County	
———	———	Icheon	County	
———	———	Pangyo	County	
———	———	Beopdong	County	
———	———	Cheonnae	County	
Jagang	Province	n/a	n/a	
———	———	Ganggye	City	
———	———	Manpo	City	
———	———	Huicheon	City	
———	———	Nangnim	County	
———	———	Jeoncheon	County	
———	———	Seonggan	County	
———	———	Janggang	County	
———	———	Hwapyeong	County	
———	———	Jungggang	County	
———	———	Jaseong	County	
———	———	Sijung	County	
———	———	Wiwon	County	

Province		County		
Name	Classification	Name	Classification	Alternative Name
———	———	Chosan	County	
———	———	Usi	County	
———	———	Gopung	County	
———	———	Songwon	County	
———	———	Dongsin	County	
———	———	Yongnim	County	
North Pyeongan	Province	n/a	n/a	
———	———	Sinuiju	City	
———	———	Jeongju	City	
———	———	Guseong	City	
———	———	Byeokdong	County	
———	———	Pihyeon	County	
———	———	Yongcheon	County	
———	———	Yeomju	County	
———	———	Cheolsan	County	
———	———	Dongnim	County	
———	———	Seoncheon	County	
———	———	Gwanksan	County	
———	———	Unjeon	County	
———	———	Bakcheon	County	
———	———	Yeongbyeon	County	
———	———	Gujang	County	
———	———	Hyangsan	County	
———	———	Unsan	County	
———	———	Taecheon	County	
———	———	Cheonma	County	
———	———	Uiju	County	
———	———	Sakju	County	
———	———	Daegwan	County	
———	———	Changseong	County	
———	———	Dongchang	County	
———	———	Sindo	County	

Province		County		
Name	Classification	Name	Classification	Alternative Name
South Pyeongan	Province	n/a	n/a	
———	———	Pyeongseong	City	
———	———	Nampo	City	
———	———	Anju	City	
———	———	Gaecheon	City	
———	———	Suncheon	City	
———	———	Deokcheon	City	
———	———	Daedong	County	
———	———	Jeongsan	County	
———	———	Oncheon	County	
———	———	Yonggang	County	
———	———	Daean	District	
———	———	Gangseo	District	
———	———	Cheollima	District	
———	———	Pyeongwon	County	
———	———	Sukcheon	County	
———	———	Mundeok	County	
———	———	Seongcheon	County	
———	———	Sinyang	County	
———	———	Yangdeok	County	
———	———	Eunsan	County	
———	———	Bukchang	City	
———	———	Maengsan	County	
———	———	Hoechang	County	
———	———	Yeongwon	County	
———	———	Daeheung	County	
North Hwanghae	Province	n/a	n/a	
———	———	Sariwon	City	
———	———	Seongnim	City	
———	———	Gaesung	City	
———	———	Jangpung	County	
———	———	Hwangju	County	

Province		County		
Name	Classification	Name	Classification	Alternative Name
———	———	Yeontan	County	
———	———	Bongsan	County	
———	———	Eunpa	County	
———	———	Insan	County	
———	———	Seoheung	County	
———	———	Suan	County	
———	———	Yeonsan	County	
———	———	Sinpyeong	County	
———	———	Goksan	County	
———	———	Singye	County	
———	———	Pyeongsan	County	
———	———	Geumcheon	County	
———	———	Tosan	County	
South Hwanghae	Province	n/a	n/a	
———	———	Haeju	City	
———	———	Gangnyeong	County	
———	———	Ongjin	County	
———	———	Taetan	County	
———	———	Jangyeon	County	
———	———	Samcheon	County	
———	———	Songhwa	County	
———	———	Eunryul	County	
———	———	Euncheon	County	
———	———	Anak	County	
———	———	Sincheon	County	
———	———	Jaeryeong	County	
———	———	Sinwon	County	
———	———	Bongcheon	County	
———	———	Baecheon	County	
———	———	Yeonan	County	
———	———	Cheongdan	County	
———	———	Yongyeon	County	
———	———	Gwail	County	

Province		County		
Name	Classification	Name	Classification	Alternative Name
———	———	Byeokseong	County	
Pyeongyang	Special Administrative City	n/a	n/a	
———	———	Pyeongyang	n/a	
———	———	Gangnam	County	
———	———	Junghwa	County	
———	———	Sangwon	County	
———	———	Gangdong	County	

Notes: Administrative divisions are listed in the official order given in the respective censuses.
All provinces and countries were transcribed from Korean into English according to the RR system.

저자소개 : Daniel J. Schwekendiek

저자는 한국의 사회-경제사와 생물학적 인구통계사를 주제로 독일 튀빙겐대학에서 경제학 박사학위를 받았다. 저자는 옥스퍼드대학, 서울대학교, UC Berkeley에서 연구하였었고, 현재 성균관대학교 동아시아학술원 교수로 재직 중이다.

저자의 논문들은 *Economics and Human Biology*, *Economic History Review*, *Journal of Biosocial Science*, *Social Science and Medicine*, *Population and Development Review* 같은 해당 분야의 국제 저명학술지에 게재되었다. 이 "남한 지표 자료집"은 저자의 다섯 번째 책이다.

남한 지표 자료집:
인구, 사회, 경제활동 통계지도 가격 30,000원

2014년 3월 5일 1판 1쇄

저 자 Daniel J. Schwekendiek
발행인 임 삼 규
발행처 **지 문 당**
주 소 413-756 경기도 파주시 광인사길 85(본사)
110-360 서울시 종로구 돈화문로 82(서울사무소)
등 록 1997. 12. 30. 제406-2003-000038호
영업부 (02)743-3192~3 팩스(02)742-4657
전자우편 sale@jimoon.co.kr
편집부 (02)743-3096 팩스(02)743-0227
전자우편 edit@jimoon.co.kr
홈페이지 www.jimoon.co.kr

ISBN 978-89-6297-161-3